FIGURINES IN HELLENISTIC BABYLONIA

In this volume, Stephanie Langin-Hooper investigates the impact of Greek art on the miniature figure sculpture produced in Babylonia after the conquests of Alexander the Great. Figurines in Hellenistic Babylonia were used as agents of social change, by visually expressing and negotiating cultural differences. The scaled-down quality of figurines encouraged both visual and tactile engagement, enabling them to effectively work as non-threatening instruments of cultural blending. Reconstructing the embodied experience of miniaturization in detailed case studies, Langin-Hooper illuminates the dynamic process of combining Greek and Babylonian sculpture forms, social customs, and viewing habits into new, hybrid works of art. Her innovative focus on figurines as instruments of both personal encounter and global cultural shifts has important implications for the study of tiny objects in art history, anthropology, classics, and other disciplines.

Stephanie M. Langin-Hooper is Assistant Professor and Karl Kilinksi II Endowed Chair in Hellenic Visual Culture in the Department of Art History, Southern Methodist University. Coeditor of *The Tiny and the Fragmented: Miniature, Broken, and Otherwise Incomplete Objects in the Ancient World* (2018), she served as lead curator for the exhibition "Life in Miniature: Identity and Display at Ancient Seleucia-on-the-Tigris" at the Kelsey Museum of Archaeology, University of Michigan.

FIGURINES IN HELLENISTIC BABYLONIA

MINIATURIZATION AND CULTURAL HYBRIDITY

STEPHANIE M. LANGIN-HOOPER

Southern Methodist University

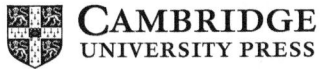

CAMBRIDGE
UNIVERSITY PRESS

University Printing House, Cambridge CB2 8BS, United Kingdom

One Liberty Plaza, 20th Floor, New York, NY 10006, USA

477 Williamstown Road, Port Melbourne, VIC 3207, Australia

314–321, 3rd Floor, Plot 3, Splendor Forum, Jasola District Centre,
New Delhi – 110025, India

79 Anson Road, #06–04/06, Singapore 079906

Cambridge University Press is part of the University of Cambridge.

It furthers the University's mission by disseminating knowledge in the pursuit of education, learning, and research at the highest international levels of excellence.

www.cambridge.org
Information on this title: www.cambridge.org/9781108488143
DOI: 10.1017/9781108769020

© Cambridge University Press 2020

This publication is in copyright. Subject to statutory exception and to the provisions of relevant collective licensing agreements, no reproduction of any part may take place without the written permission of Cambridge University Press.

First published 2020

A catalogue record for this publication is available from the British Library.

ISBN 978-1-108-48814-3 Hardback

Cambridge University Press has no responsibility for the persistence or accuracy of URLs for external or third-party internet websites referred to in this publication and does not guarantee that any content on such websites is, or will remain, accurate or appropriate.

*For my children, Myer Edward Stanton and Jeremiah Charles Stanton.
I love you forever.*

CONTENTS

Acknowledgments	*page* ix
Author's Note	xii
INTRODUCTION	1
1 A QUESTION OF INTIMACY: MINIATURIZATION AND FIGURINES	13
A Miniaturization Approach	14
Establishing the "Miniaturization Affect" of Figurines	24
"Miniaturization Affect" of Figurines, Concluded	50
2 FASCINATION WITH THE TINY: INTERACTING WITH FIGURINES	52
Playing with Fear: Horse Riders and Soldiers	53
The Gaze and the Caress: Sexualized Relationships with Figurines	65
Theatricality: "Performing" in Miniature	82
Conclusion	98
3 THREE'S A CROWD: SPECTATORSHIP OF FIGURINES	100
Meet the Baby: Woman and Child Figurines	101
Like Lovers Do: Heterosexual Couples	117
Collaboration for an Audience: Musician Pairings	132
Conclusion	143
4 IMAGES OF THE SELF: IDENTIFYING WITH FIGURINES	147
Diversity and the Male Body	148
Cohesiveness and the Female Body	166
Experimentation and the Child's Body	185
Conclusion	201

5 THE GLOBAL AND THE LOCAL: MAKING CULTURAL
  AND SOCIAL CHOICES WITH FIGURINES   203
  The "Global": Deity Figurines Engaged with the Hellenistic *Koine*   204
  At the Boundaries of the (Social) World: Figurines of Otherness   219
  Hybridity within the Local   236

CONCLUSION: LIFE IN MINIATURE   247

Notes   249
Bibliography   281
Index   313

ACKNOWLEDGMENTS

This project has been my scholarly passion for nearly half of my life. I first began researching cross-cultural interaction in the figurines of the Hellenistic Near East at the age of 20, when I traveled to the Hermitage Museum in St. Petersburg, Russia and the British Museum in London to gather data for my senior thesis at the University of Pennsylvania. Nearly every professor, student, curator, archivist, and colleague I have encountered in my career since has contributed to my thinking on this topic – and, thus, deserves thanks in this book. Despite the regrettable certainty that omissions will be made, I particularly wish to thank the following list of scholars: Frederik Hiebert, my senior thesis advisor at the University of Pennsylvania; St. John Simpson of the British Museum, who introduced me to the Babylonian figurines; Chris Gosden, Andrew Sherratt, and Roger Moorey who advised me during my MPhil at the University of Oxford; R.R.R. Smith and Chris Hallett, for instructing me on Hellenistic sculpture; and Marian Feldman, my PhD dissertation supervisor at the University of California Berkeley, who gave me excellent training on both art and theory, and who transformed me into an art historian of the Ancient Near East. I have been able to approach Hellenistic Babylonia from both the material culture and the texts due to the warm welcome I received into the field of cuneiform studies by many Assyriologists, including Steve Tinney, Jeremy Black, Stephanie Dalley, Fran Reynolds, Laurie Pearce, Niek Veldhuis, and Chessie Rochberg. Finally, I wish to thank my colleagues at Bowling Green State University (where I was an Assistant Professor of Ancient Art History, 2011–2014), and Southern Methodist University (my current institution); they have been tremendously supportive of my work, and I am continually grateful for their collegiality and feedback.

The research contained in this book took place at several different museums, all of which I wish to thank: the British Museum, Field Museum Chicago, Kelsey Museum of Archaeology at the University of Michigan, Musée du Louvre, Museum of Fine Arts Boston, Oriental Institute at the University of Chicago, Semitic Museum at Harvard University, and the University of Pennsylvania Museum of Anthropology and Archaeology. My research approach was particularly transformed during the process of co-curating an exhibition at the Kelsey Museum of Archaeology; entitled "Life in Miniature: Identity and Display at Ancient Seleucia-on-the-Tigris," the exhibit was open to the public from December 20, 2013, to April 27, 2014. My sincere thanks go to everyone who worked on that exhibition, particularly Kelsey Museum staff Sharon Herbert (my co-curator), Margaret Cool Root, Dawn Johnson, Scott Meier, Michelle Fontenot, and Sebastián Encina, as well as the student interns and digital arts specialists from Bowling Green State University (Thomas Huang, Kevin Kately, Julie Knechtges, Cathie Moore, Colleen Murphy, Jess Pfundstein, Mariah Postlewait, and Haining Yu).

Many people generously assisted with my research and/or gave me feedback on this manuscript at various stages. I particularly wish to thank: Doug Bailey, Megan Cifarelli, Henry Colburn, Jay Crisostomo, Elizabeth Eager, Sebastián Encina, Adi Erlich, Marian Feldman, Amy Freund, Amy Gansell, Sharon Herbert, Adam Herring, Adam Jasienski, Lissette Jimenez, Rosemary Joyce, Danielle Joyner, Ed Keall, Julia Krul, Jillianne Laceste, Jeffrey Lerner, Becky Martin, Brian Molanphy, Kiersten Neumann, Laurie Pearce, Lisa Pon, Margaret Cool Root, Holly Shaffer, Jonathan Stökl, Allison Thomason, Jaimee Uhlenbrock, Ron Wallenfels, and Zachary Wallmark. Roberta Menegazzi deserves special mention for her extraordinarily generous willingness to share ideas, research, and photographs. I also wish to thank the anonymous "Peer reviewer A," who provided detailed and thoughtful feedback which was very useful as I edited the manuscript. All errors remain, of course, my own. Some of the case studies and discussion in this book have been adapted from my previous publications; see particularly my articles and/or chapters in *Critical Approaches to Ancient Near Eastern Art* (2013), *World Archaeology* (2015), *IRAQ* (2016), *Studying Gender in the Ancient Near East* (2018), and *The Tiny and the Fragmented: Miniature, Broken, or Otherwise Incomplete Objects in the Ancient World* (2018). Funding for the photography, image permissions, and color printing subvention was generously provided by the Meadows School of the Arts at Southern Methodist University and a Sam Taylor Fellowship, General Board of Higher Education and Ministry, United Methodist Church. I particularly wish to thank Adam Herring and Sam Holland for their continuous support (both financial and otherwise) of this endeavor.

My family has been immensely encouraging and helpful throughout the process of researching and writing this book. My husband, David Stanton, has been my constant supporter and champion, moving across the country multiple times for my career, cheerfully accommodating my travel for research and conferences, keeping things running at home, discussing the details of my scholarship, and motivating and encouraging me every step of the way. Dave, you have my sincerest gratitude and deepest love. My parents, Ann and Jerry Langin-Hooper, were the first to believe in me. They have helped me think through many of the ideas in this book, and my father has edited many of the images. I also owe my parents a great debt for their willingness to care for my children for extended periods of time, which has greatly facilitated my ability to keep focus on my scholarship. My parents-in-law, Nancy and Chuck Stanton, have also taken many babysitting trips in service of my research, and I am very grateful for their help and support. Finally, I wish to thank my children, Myer Edward Stanton and Jeremiah Charles Stanton, who have shared their early childhoods with this book. It is no exaggeration to say that the book has grown with them. They have opened my life to new realms of the human experience, making me more empathetic and appreciative of the humanity of the ancient people who used figurines. Their imaginative engagements with the miniature objects that surround them have often spurred my own thinking. Myer and Remy, you have not only made me a mother, you have also made me a better scholar. It is to you, therefore, that I dedicate this book.

AUTHOR'S NOTE

Note that the figurines pictured in this book are not reproduced to life-size scale, nor are they shown at a consistent scale relative to one another. Rather, the figurines that are more extensively discussed in the text are usually shown larger so that small details can be more easily observed. For information on the size of each figurine, please see the measurements provided in each figure caption.

INTRODUCTION

THIS BOOK INVESTIGATES THE ROLE OF ANTHROPOMORPHIC FIGURINES AS agents of cross–cultural identity production and social negotiation in Hellenistic Babylonia. Babylonia, in the southern region of the modern-day country of Iraq (see Map), was conquered by Alexander the Great in 330 BCE. This event began the so-called Hellenistic period, a time marked by widespread migrations of Macedonian and Greek peoples (often referred to together as "Greeks") into the already ancient and culturally diverse cities of the Ancient Near Eastern region. Babylonians, other Mesopotamians, Persians, West Semitic peoples, and, eventually, Parthians also participated in these communities. Both material culture and textual records from Hellenistic Babylonia reveal a complex society defined and pervaded by cross-cultural interaction. The end date of the Hellenistic period is less fixed. The earliest date could be given as the Parthian conquest of the Seleucid kingdom in 141 BCE; yet most of the material culture, particularly the figurines, offers little evidence of a cultural or social dividing line at this date. Rather, the figurine tradition, including figurine forms and motifs (even those of Greek origin), forms an unbroken continuum well into the Parthian period. For this reason, most scholars study the Babylonian figurines of the Seleucid and Parthian periods together as one corpus, and I follow this choice. Thus, I will use the term "Hellenistic" throughout this volume to include both the Seleucid (c. 330–141 BCE) and Parthian periods (c. 141 BCE–224 CE).

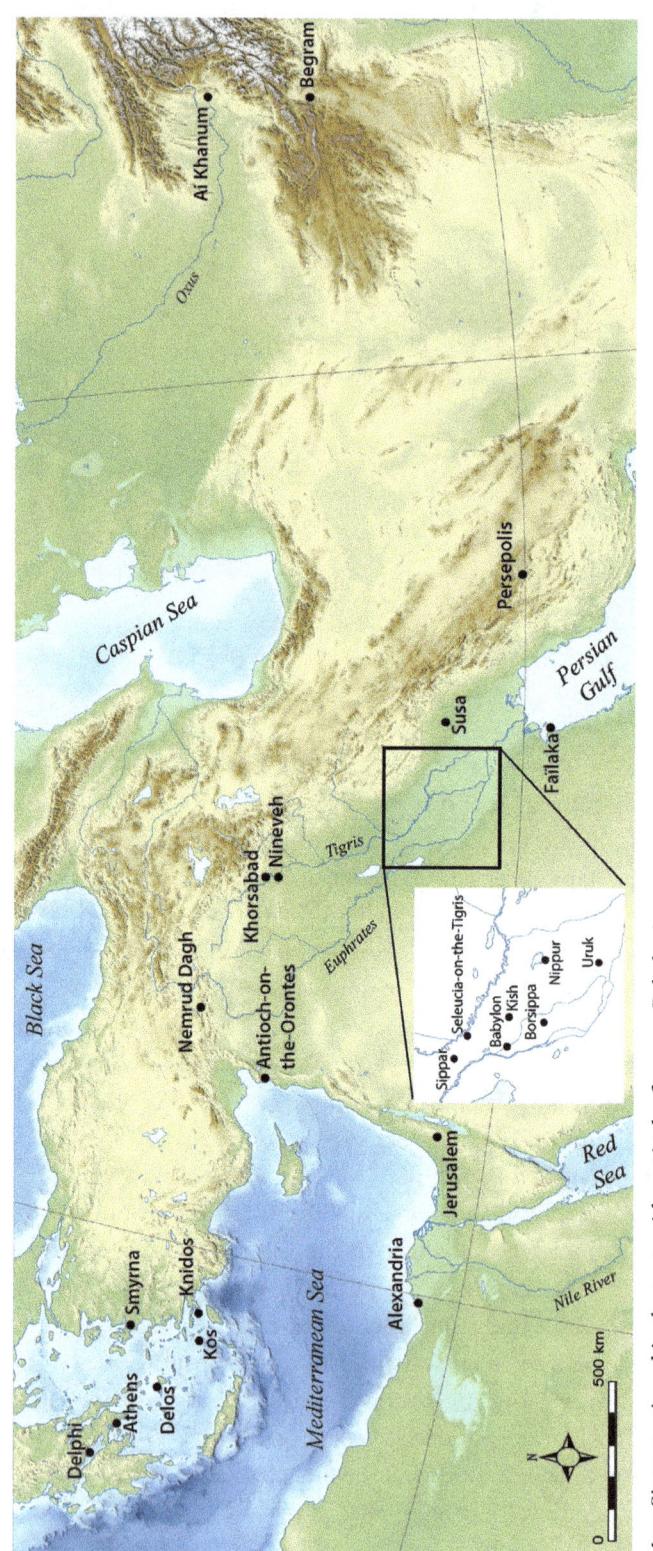

Map: Sites mentioned in the text, with particular focus on Babylonia. Cartographer: Svetlana Matskevich.

Among the vast evidence for cross-cultural interaction in Hellenistic Babylonia, the figurines are particularly noteworthy. Miniature objects – primarily anthropomorphic figurines, as well as small-scale replicas of animals, buildings, and other "full-size" objects (such as ceramic vessels) – are among the most common forms of visual culture surviving in the archaeological record of Hellenistic Babylonia. Four major centers of figurine production and use are known archaeologically from Hellenistic Babylonia: Babylon, Seleucia-on-the-Tigris, Uruk, and Nippur, with significantly smaller corpora known from Borsippa, Kish, and Sippar.[1] Each of these cities had its own distinctive social environment and material culture during this era, and substantial local variation in its use of figurine motifs, styles, and forms.

When comparing the major Hellenistic Babylonian sites strictly based on the number of figurines found, it appears that the traditions at Babylon and Seleucia-on-the-Tigris were the most robust. However, comparing the size of the assemblages is not entirely valid. The overall corpus of Hellenistic Babylonian figurines is enormous in size, with nearly 11,000 figurines excavated at Seleucia-on-the-Tigris alone. The precise number of figurines surviving in museum collections or catalogue publications can vary greatly with the duration of the excavation project at the site, the excavators' interest in figurines (or in the later periods of ancient Mesopotamian history generally),[2] or other modern circumstances of discovery, preservation, and curation.[3] These modern conditions impact the degree to which quantitative data about the Hellenistic Babylonian figurine corpus can be assembled or trusted; thus, throughout this volume, I am fairly tentative in giving concrete numbers of figurines that were made in a particular motif, style, and so forth. From those figurines that are recorded, we can nevertheless make some distinctions between the major Hellenistic Babylonian cities.

Babylon, the historic seat of power in the region and the first capital city of the Seleucid kingdom, was home to both an established local community as well as an influx of Greek immigrants.[4] Traditional structures were repaired or rebuilt, sometimes with slight modifications, but in other cases preserving the original architecture and functions of buildings such as the major Babylonian temples.[5] Many Greek institutions were not introduced overnight, but rather built gradually. For instance, the earliest textual evidence for a gymnasion at Babylon dates to 109 BCE,[6] decades after the Parthian conquest, and physical evidence for a building that might have served as a gymnasion is even later in date.[7] The building of Greek structures and the practice of Greek traditions could be blended with local Babylonian traditions, and be changed over time, as is seen in the connection between the Greek theater and local temple cult at Babylon, where the activities and performances that took place in those architectural spaces were often culturally hybrid.[8]

Seleucia-on-the-Tigris replaced Babylon as the Seleucid capital at its founding in 312 BCE, and subsequently became home to a substantial immigrant population from the Aegean and eastern Mediterranean.[9] Initially presumed to have been built on a Greek plan, further excavation revealed the incorporation of Assyrian and Babylonian principles of city design.[10] Many expected institutions of a major Greco-Macedonian metropolis have yet to be discovered archaeologically, and may never have existed or may have been built later or in a different form than anticipated by archaeologists.[11] For instance, the evidence for the gymnasion at Seleucia-on-the-Tigris is comprised of a stamp of unbaked clay referencing the civic office of gymnasiarch, which dates to 72/1 BCE – and, thus, is later than the already late evidence for the Babylon gymnasion.[12] Instead of robust evidence for the mainstay institutions of Greek civic life, a level of ambiguity and cultural fluidity can be found. For instance, when Tell 'Umar, a mound now believed to be the Greek theater,[13] was first excavated, its physical mass and structure was interpreted as a Seleucid-era ziggurat – demonstrating an ambiguity between the architecture and purposes of Babylonian and Greek performance and ritual spaces,[14] which might have been cultivated and intentional on the part of the Seleucid builders and their desires to appeal to a diverse populace.

Perhaps not surprisingly, the new Greek foundation of Seleucia-on-the-Tigris seems to have hosted the greatest variety of figurine motifs, including many connected with the Greek world (such as the athletes discussed in Chapter 4) that are not found in other cities. Figurines from Seleucia-on-the-Tigris also demonstrate the most consistent use of the double-mold technique, a technology of Greek origin.[15] Babylon follows Seleucia-on-the-Tigris in terms of figurine variety and use of the double mold; again, a perhaps not unsurprising situation given the attention paid to Babylon early in the Hellenistic period, including by Alexander the Great (who died there), and the Greek buildings constructed in the city. However, the figurine corpora of both Seleucia-on-the-Tigris and Babylon also demonstrate ample use of Babylonian figurine techniques, such as the single mold, and Babylonian motifs. Indeed, many of the figurines from both sites were insistently hybrid, showing blendings between figurine forms, motifs, styles, and techniques to create unique variants that can be assigned to no singular cultural origin; see, for instance, the female figurines discussed in Chapter 4. Babylon's figurine corpus also differs from that of Seleucia-on-the-Tigris – not only in its less extensive use of uncommon Greek motifs, but also for its increased use of other motifs, including those that were culturally hybrid, such as the female figurines with finished-off arms discussed in Chapter 2.

Uruk was also the site of substantial occupation as well as massive, predominantly Babylonian-focused, building programs in the Hellenistic period. Four Hellenistic period temple complexes built for the practice of Babylonian religious activity (the Bit Resh, Irigal, E-anna, and Bit Akitu) have been found, as well as two ziggurats (for the god Anu at the Bit Resh and for the goddess Ishtar at the E-anna).[16] While some of these structures have pre-Hellenistic precursors, some were new and all of them experienced significant building activity during the Hellenistic period.[17] The figurine corpus at Uruk reveals similar interests in Babylonian motifs and beliefs operating at miniature scale. However, a substantial number of Greek motifs were also present in the Uruk figurines – an appearance which is not, in fact, at odds with most of the other surviving evidence about the city. The new Babylonian temples were built with the support and financial assistance of the Seleucid kings, and numerous textual records also attest the existence of a palace, although whether this was a royal palace or for use by the local governors is unknown.[18] Two burial mounds of elite local rulers, possibly two of Uruk's powerful governors, were discovered in the Frehat En-Nufegi Tumuli outside of Uruk; these tumuli were made of the same mudbrick as the Bit Resh but contained culturally diverse grave goods, including two gold wreaths, furniture legs, amphora, and iron strigils.[19]

Uruk is additionally known for its substantial archive of cuneiform tablets recording economic transactions. From these documents are attested the continued survival of Babylonian customs of monetary exchange, inheritance, ownership, as well as the already-ancient and largely outmoded form of documentation itself (writing in Akkadian cuneiform on clay tablets). However, this archive also preserves evidence of Greek-named individuals marrying into elite Babylonian families, and the subsequent births of multicultural descendants whose names reflected their complex heritage.[20] Stamp seals and signet rings, most often preserved as impressions on those tablets, feature a wide variety of Greek, Babylonian, and hybrid forms and motifs; this multiculturalism is also seen in the seals impressed on the ring bullae used to encircle parchment or papyrus documents at Seleucia-on-the-Tigris.[21] Ceramic vessels known from Uruk, as well as Seleucia-on-the-Tigris and Babylon, indicate the blending of Greek and Babylonian foodways and the creation of hybrid cuisines.[22]

Unlike the other three major figurine-producing cities, Nippur hosted few building projects, and indeed had relatively little occupation, during the Seleucid period.[23] It rose to prominence again during the Parthian period. Occupation during that period is attested primarily through temple architecture, the construction of a large military fortress, as well as immense numbers of graves, which were dug down into the earlier stratigraphic levels of the site.[24] These Parthian funerary deposits usually included coffins, some of which could be quite elaborate and feature figural decoration.[25] However, relatively few grave goods were deposited and, in general, less is known about the material culture of Hellenistic Nippur than the other three sites. Noteworthy for the purposes of this volume, however, is how the surviving figurines from Nippur often attest to the continued popularity and engagement with Hellenistic figurine motifs, forms, and ideas well into the mid- to late-Parthian period. Overall, this evidence from the four major figurine-producing centers of Hellenistic Babylonia demonstrates the individualized local character and trajectory of each community, as well as a general trend of shifting, complex engagement between Babylonian (and, generally, Near Eastern) cultural norms and long-established practices with the newly introduced ideas arriving from the wider Hellenistic world.

Indeed, despite their local flavor, the figurine traditions in all of these cities can be characterized by their use of both Babylonian (or, more broadly, Mesopotamian) and Hellenistic *koine*[26] (largely inspired by Greek tradition) figurine forms, motifs, styles, and technologies of production. The communities of Hellenistic Babylonia expressed their connection to the rest of the Hellenistic world in part through their adoption and use of Hellenistic *koine* figurine motifs and styles. True imports of figurines were exceptionally rare[27]; the vast majority of the figurines found in Hellenistic Babylonia were made in the region and, in the case of terracotta figurines, from local clays. Molds used in the manufacture of terracotta figurines might have traveled more widely and may explain how specific figurine motifs were shared over long distances.[28] Prior to the Hellenistic period, Babylonian figurines had generally been made in the single mold, a technique in which moist clay was pressed into a one-sided mold (usually made of baked clay or plaster), resulting in a solid figurine that was modeled only on the front side. This technique, combined with Mesopotamian artistic conventions, produced figurines characterized by their frontality and direct engagement with the viewer. The Greek invention of the double mold, a technique which produced two-sided hollow figurines that were modeled in the round, was adopted in Babylonia in the Hellenistic period, expanding the possibilities for figurine production.[29]

In addition to these different techniques of manufacture, Babylonian and Hellenistic ideas about figurines also offered diverse – and not always compatible – options for figurine motifs. When the motifs and styles of the Hellenistic *koine* arrived in Babylonia, their acceptance and adoption was not assured. As was also the case elsewhere in the Hellenistic world,[30] the individual communities of Hellenistic Babylonia did not adopt the *koine* figurine repertoire wholesale, but selectively engaged with those forms and motifs that they found appealing – and, in so doing, often adapted them to further reflect local ideas and preferences. Negotiation also centered around the identities of depicted figures (including not just different gods but also different ideas for what kinds of mortal bodies should be shown), the acceptability of different bodily poses, clothing styles and the appropriateness of nudity, and so forth. These varying possibilities, and how the people of Hellenistic Babylonia negotiated this plethora of options in the creation and use of their figurines, will be explored throughout this book.

What unites the figurine corpora of Hellenistic Babylonia is that the rich cultural heritage of Babylonia and the Hellenistic world was utilized as a vast resource, from which could be drawn the raw material and inspiration for new forms and ideas. With extremely rare exceptions, neither the Hellenistic nor Babylonian figurine traditions were kept as culturally isolated practices, but rather were blended together in a variety of ways. Hybrid forms, motifs, and styles are common throughout the Hellenistic Babylonian figurine corpus; indicating, as I have argued previously, sustained information exchange between craftspeople, as well as consumer demand for multicultural imagery.[31] The communities of Hellenistic Babylonia thus became home to an immense quantity and variety of miniature objects – indeed, extreme diversity of figurine form, motif, and technique is especially characteristic of Hellenistic Babylonia, a fact that other scholars have also remarked upon.[32] This nearly unparalleled depth and variation of the Hellenistic Babylonian figurines make this corpus a particularly productive subject through which to study the substantial social changes of the Hellenistic period.

This book is a material culture study, with strong roots in both anthropology (particularly theories of miniaturization and human engagement, as well as the reconstruction of embodied subjectivities) and art history (with focus on iconography, formal properties, and visual engagement). Evidence of archaeological context, beyond the broad contextual information of city/site of discovery, is not taken heavily into account. The reason for this is, simply, that contextual information for these figurines is often problematic. Many were unearthed in the early twentieth century, when archaeological context was not well documented. Small finds from the late periods of Mesopotamian history, a category that includes Hellenistic-era figurines, were not particularly valued or well recorded. Due to their presence in some of the last levels of occupation prior to site abandonment, many were surface finds. Even when meticulous archaeological investigation took place, as in the recent Italian excavations at Seleucia-on-the-Tigris, difficulties with determining context or precise chronology were still common. Primary among those difficulties is that most figurines seem not to have been considered particularly valuable or sacred by their ancient users, and so could be disposed of in domestic refuse or reused (often as temper material inside of mudbricks; as an example, see Figure 4.18) – thus the final deposition context of a figurine is often not where it was originally used as a figural object. Other scholars have made valiant attempts to grapple with these archaeological issues; for instance, Roberta Menegazzi's 2014 catalogue of the Seleucia-on-the-Tigris figurines deftly explores these complexities and offers many valuable interpretations. Rather than repeat her work, or attempt to reconstruct archaeological context at other cities where the evidence is partial or lacking, I have taken a different approach in this volume. Archaeological context, and the information on figurine "function" (e.g., grave offering, votive, and toy) which that context is presumed to provide, undoubtedly has the potential to offer much in the way of understanding ancient figurines. But, I contend, the objects themselves can also be used directly as informants on their social worlds. The visual, formal, and tactile properties of figurines are not simply facts to be catalogued, but are, in themselves, a kind of evidence for how the figurines operated on and within the communities that used them. I access and interpret that evidence through the lens of "miniaturization theory," an object-centered, affect-based approach particularly utilized in the field of anthropology.

Overlaying a study of miniaturization and object affect onto an already stated aim of exploring cultural interaction and hybridity might seem, at first glance, like an excess of analytical implements, an overflowing toolbox. And, indeed, these two intersecting frameworks of the book do both shape the narrative. But rather than creating a tension by pulling in separate directions, I find it to be a productive union. Understanding hybridity and issues of cross-cultural interaction – particularly how Hellenistic Babylonian people interacted with one another and shaped their society – is the goal of the volume. Miniaturization theory is the tool used to get at hybridity, to reveal those cross-cultural interactions in ways more complex than iconographic study alone can provide.

These dual lenses work particularly well in concert because the issues with which they are concerned – cross-cultural interaction and the use of tiny things – were intrinsically linked. Intensive use of miniature objects, especially when accompanied by significant variety and diversity within a particular figurine corpus, has been correlated with widespread social change and the identity negotiations that would result. Chris Gosden attributes the diversity of small-scale objects in Roman Britain (first century BCE through first century CE, in particular) with a fluidity and renegotiation of social relationships resulting from cultural interaction.[33] Similarly, Julia Assante correlated the rapid expansion of Old Babylonian terracotta plaque types with the social changes, such as community strife and the distancing of people from access to their gods, that resulted from the fall of the Ur III state and the migrations of the Amorites, beginning c. 2000 BCE.[34] In contrast, times when social identities were coalescing around rigid ideals, usually in order to form stable homogenous communities in opposition to external forces, are marked by a similar homogeneity in the miniature objects. Ian Wilson argues that Judean Pillar Figurines of the eighth to seventh centuries BCE helped solidify a singular Judean identity in opposition to the impending threat of the Neo-Assyrians.[35]

Similar pressures toward unified group identity in the Neo-Babylonian heartland (c. sixth century BCE) may also have been expressed (and reinforced) through the standardization of the terracotta figurine tradition.[36] I have previously argued,[37] and will continue to argue in this volume, that the remarkable diversity of figurines in Hellenistic Babylonia indicates a society in flux, where identities were being renegotiated under the pressure of shifting community norms. Such miniatures functioned both as "models *of* and models *for*"[38] reality, "by shaping themselves to it and by shaping it to themselves."[39]

My desire to utilize miniaturization theory as a methodology to better access and understand cross-cultural hybridity also emerges, at least in part, from my frustration with the label of "hybridity" itself. Certainly it is preferable to scholarship's now-outdated concept of "Hellenization," the belief that Greek traditions spread over the world in the wake of Alexander's conquests, and penetrated local customs to a greater or lesser degree depending on the force of the conquerors, the receptiveness (or power) of the conquered, and the centrality (versus peripherality) of the locale to Greco-Macedonian imperial ambitions.[40] In the past few decades, many scholars have endeavored to dismantle such simplistic models of human interaction, using post-colonial theory as one of their primary tools. "Hybrid" and "hybridity" are now the terminologies most en vogue in discussions of cultural encounter in the Hellenistic world,[41] and such terms are used throughout this volume. However, many valid critiques of the notion of hybridity have also been raised[42]: it implies uniformity, it is too reductive, it reinforces the perceived naturalness of typological categories; it reifies cultural groups into isolated and bounded entities that are imagined to interact in a simplistic, recipe-like fashion, as if Greeks and Babylonians (or their figurines) were added to a bowl and stirred. Perhaps most problematic is that "hybridity" is regularly applied as a descriptive label that too often ends the discussion rather than beginning it.

I am not so bold, or so naïve, as to claim that I have completely avoided all of these traps in this book. Yet, although I use the term "hybrid" throughout the volume, I also endeavor to point out the contingent and negotiated nature of hybridity as it emerged in the figurines of Hellenistic Babylonia. There is more that can be said than simply labeling a figurine, or an entire figurine corpus, as "hybrid" and then moving on. How that hybridity was created can also be probed, investigating what particular elements of previous cultural traditions were drawn upon and how they were selectively combined in creating an individual figurine, or a group of figurines engaged with one motif, or a group of figurines from a particular community.[43] I believe that those individual choices about how to create hybridity, and what that hybridity looked like, have the potential to be deeply revealing of the social negotiations and identity constructions that underlay the ancient users' desire to own and use these objects.⁴⁴ In other words, I wish to probe beyond the "what" and the "how" to get to the "why."

To that end, I also consider what these figurines *don't* look like – what elements of previous cultural traditions were abandoned or minimized – as a reflection of individual agency and community motivations.⁴⁵ Looks alone can also be deceiving: something that might appear to belong to one culture could also have expressed core values or ideals of another. For instance, although the Greek double mold was widely used in Hellenistic Babylonia, it frequently was not deployed to take advantage of the plastic, three-dimensional possibilities of double molding⁴⁶ – thus the resulting double-molded figurines often reflected Babylonian conceptions of the body rather than Hellenistic ones.⁴⁷ All of these things are hybrid.

On the other hand, I find "hybridity" less useful in describing whole cities and communities, and their object traditions, when it is applied in terms that look for greater or lesser numbers of, or intensities of, "the hybrid." "Hybridity" was not a blanket that spread, more or less, over the Hellenistic world, covering cities like Babylon more thickly than it covered Uruk. Rather, "hybridity," for me, describes the willingness of the members of these communities to engage in a process of cross-cultural negotiation and the material expressions of that process, however complex and varied. Whether or not those objects look obviously hybrid *to us* at first glance – i.e. clearly show visual evidence of the blending of two or more cultural traditions of style, motif, and form – should not be the sole, or even the primary, criteria for determining how the objects participated in or reflected cultural interaction. How hybridity manifested in physical form as a figurine depended on a great many variables, from the concerns of that specific community to the particular motif of that individual figurine.

Discussion of how this process worked in the Hellenistic Babylonian figurines will unfold over the following five chapters. Chapter 1 presents the complexities of miniaturization theory and my intervention within that anthropological and art historical discourse. Fundamental to this intervention is the notion that, although Hellenistic Babylonian figurines were objects of simultaneous visual and tactile consumption, they nevertheless did not allow their users to completely see or touch. User desire for sensory engagements necessitated spatial proximity with the object; yet, rather than invite the user completely into a private miniature world, figurines made continual reference to the real-scale world through tangible marks of manufacture, the placement of clothing and pose to restrict human touch to socially acceptable limits, and other similar strategies. I dub this paradox of access an "intimacy illusion" and argue that this previously unrecognized concept is what allowed figurines to function so effectively. The "intimacy" enabled people to trust and engage with figurines, while the "illusion" of private encounter allowed the social world to inconspicuously penetrate the personal sphere.

This "private sociality" of figurines is explored through Chapter 2, revealing how the user's ability to manipulate the miniature bodies of particularly interactive figurines (such as soldiers with interchangeable weapons, or nude female figures with movable arms) impacted perceptions of real-life experiences (such as warfare or sex). The power of the figurine corpus to reshape social life is the topic of Chapter 3, which examines figurines of mothers with children, couples, and musician groups. The visual portrayal and tactile accessibility of these miniaturized "relationships," as well as the absence of other social relationships in the figurine corpus, established expectations and limits on acceptable social structures. The subtitles of these two chapters emphasize the particular kinds of engagement with figurines – "interacting with" (Chapter 2) and "spectatorship of" (Chapter 3) – that are revealed throughout those case studies. Both chapters demonstrate how figurine users became locked into a performative dialogue with miniature objects that, more or less, allowed the user to participate and to watch. Through these mechanisms of object engagement and object agency, the broader social implications of these figurines were brought into the private sphere in ways that were particular to the individual motifs and ideas with which each figurine was involved.

Chapter 4 shifts focus to look outward, discussing how figurines could be used as active agents to intervene in social life. Interpreting figurines as potential images of the self, which could be identified with, this chapter posits a recursive process in which figurines educated their users on socially acceptable norms of self-presentation – yet, figurines could also be used to reshape that social landscape with new bodies and senses of existence based on the preferences of their users. Distinctions of gender and age are particular focal points of this chapter's attention on identity construction and display. Issues of Greek and Babylonian identity also come more prominently to the fore than in the previous two chapters, as many of the figurines in Chapter 4, in their roles as reflections of selfhood, also provide evidence for experimental, cross-cultural negotiations between the values and customs of Greeks and Babylonians. Yet the material features of these objects also suggest that hybrid identity formations differed along gender, age, and class lines, with some sectors of society (especially youthful and female groups) more engaged in cross-cultural interaction than others.

This uneven nature of hybridity and multiculturalism is explored on a regional and international scale in Chapter 5. Situating Babylonia and its miniature objects within the wider Hellenistic *koine* reveals both the firmly local nature of this figurine tradition, as well as its connections to a rapidly globalizing Greek world. Constructs of the "global" and the "local" both come under critique, their naturalness as categories and boundaries called into question. Figurines of *koine* gods and goddesses, supposedly indicative of widely shared international concerns and beliefs, are shown to have often reflected local preferences and negotiations rather than only imported mores. The "local," too, is shown to have been more complex than is usually assumed. Substantial variation between the figurine corpora of the different Hellenistic Babylonian cities suggests the existence of more than one kind of "local" in the region. A case study of reclining female figurines *not* discovered at Nippur will reveal how the choices made within those communities and expressed in their figurine preferences — choices which are often read as greater or lesser degrees of cross-cultural engagement — sometimes reflected more than simple interest or disinterest in the Hellenistic *koine*. Figurines of "othered" bodies are also analyzed in this chapter in order to show that difference in Hellenistic Babylonia was conceived of in multiple ways, not just cultural or geographical — and that, in the end, the figurines reflect a society that was generally endeavoring to integrate and smooth over differences, rather than to highlight and ostracize based upon them.

Overall, this volume illuminates the tremendous variety of ways that Hellenistic Babylonian figurines were used in response to cross-cultural interaction. Figurines were an expressive tool kit, assisting their users in adapting to new social norms and articulating a vast range of social identities. Figurines were also proxies for the broader social contract, conveying community messages into private spaces, reshaping society even as they embodied it. The myriad possibilities offered by figurines is what gives them the power to inform upon the social landscape of Hellenistic Babylonia. Miniaturization, in the end, is like hybridity: it is not just one thing, for just as there were different kinds of "hybrid," there were different kinds of "miniatures," with a range of affects, engagements, and social possibilities. In that slippery multivalence, figurines paralleled the rich and varied texture of social life itself.

CHAPTER ONE

A QUESTION OF INTIMACY: MINIATURIZATION AND FIGURINES

... the smallest, which, to my Sight, were almost invisible; but Nature hath adapted the Eyes of the Lilliputians to all Objects proper for their View ... I have been much pleased with observing a Cook pulling a Lark, which was not so large as a common Fly; and a young Girl threading an invisible Needle with invisible Silk.

(Swift, *Gulliver's Travels*, published 1726)

Of all of *Gulliver's Travels*, it was his "voyage" to the miniaturized land of the Lilliputians that most thoroughly captured the imagination of Swift's readership and has entered our broader cultural lexicon. Fascination at the idea of a miniaturized world is a common human trait; indeed, some of the oldest artworks on earth are Paleolithic figurines, which depict the human body at handheld scale. The *Venus of Willendorf* appears conceptually little different from the refrigerator magnets, Christmas ornaments, and wedding cake figurines with which we "people" our world today – a Lilliput of our own making. The allure of the tiny seems simple: miniature things are intriguing. Their small details encourage close looking and handling. Their nonthreatening physical presence puts the user at ease. As simulacra, miniatures inspire wonder that everyday things could be translated to a different scale, to exist in a parallel tiny world that is at once both familiar and alien. When placed in proximity to our own, larger bodies, miniature things provide us with the chance to feel big, powerful, and in control, while simultaneously satisfying instinctual urges to nurture and care for the smaller and more helpless humans among us.

What is less comprehensible is why, as Swift astutely notes, we are paradoxically "much pleased" with our own inability to see the tiny details of miniature objects. Why would material culture that operates at the borders of our visual perception – and even sometimes escapes those limits, and thus our notice – be so enchanting? It is here that this volume makes its intervention into the field of miniaturization and figurine studies.

The affects of miniaturization have been complexly theorized, particularly within the field of anthropology. Emerging from this scholarship on miniaturization is an overall sense that the range of interactions that miniatures inspire and elicit from their human users can be characterized, primarily, as a shared experience of "intimacy." This volume seeks to challenge that assumption, and problematize our tendency to equate the miniature with the intimate. Rather, I argue that even when miniatures are the objects of simultaneous visual and tactile consumption, sensory probing and spatial proximity do not always yield complete understanding. Indeed, I propose that while all miniatures appear intimate, this is largely an illusion: most, if not all, miniatures fail to follow through on their offers of intimate engagements.

This proposal leads to a more nuanced accounting of how miniaturization "works" and, indeed, an acknowledgment that miniaturization works differently in different miniature objects. The illusion of intimacy can be cultivated in innumerable ways, with a wide variety of limitations placed between the user and his or her full comprehension and control over the miniature object. These limitations are, in fact, a crucial part of our fascination with tiny things; as Swift noted, we are intrigued by what we cannot truly see, cannot completely access, and cannot fully know.

A MINIATURIZATION APPROACH

The intrinsic appeal and fascination of a miniaturized human body – to which archaeologists and museum curators (and their audiences) have intuitively responded, often devoting more attention to figurines than other artifacts found in comparable or greater quantities (such as potsherds) – was not explicitly analyzed until relatively recently.[1] This analysis, termed "miniaturization theory," has its roots in the 1984 work of cultural and literary criticism by Susan Stewart, *On Longing: Narratives of the Miniature, the Gigantic, the Souvenir, the Collection*. Stewart was one of the first to articulate how "the tiny" inspires wonder and amazement, enticing audiences into sensual engagement while simultaneously freezing and abstracting both space and time. While Stewart ultimately views the miniature as a metaphor for the interiority of the self, others – particularly the archaeologists Rosemary Joyce and Douglass Bailey – have pioneered more concrete material culture applications for this type of analysis.[2] In their approaches, miniature objects are seen as inducing physical proximity, emotional connection, and intimacy with their users, who have "a sense of being drawn into another world."[3] An invitation to tactile interaction is a critical component of this dialogue, as it encourages the user's hand to bridge the otherwise disorienting and discordant scalar difference between the figurine and "real life," smoothing the user's imagined entry into (and participation within) the miniaturized landscape and inducing a "dreamy reverie of contemplation, gaze, touch, and desire."[4]

This methodology of studying figurines is broadly based on a phenomenological notion of the lived body, in which the subjective experience of the figurine's human user is foregrounded and analyzed.[5] Miniaturization theory is also in dialogue with studies of materiality and thing theory[6]; all of these schools of thought share an emphasis on understanding the physical properties of an object and the ability of those properties to exert influence over their human users – influence that may or, crucially, may not have been intended by the object's creator. Indeed, miniaturization theory hinges upon paying specific attention to agency and the balance of power in moments of encounter between the human body (especially as experienced through the senses of vision and touch) and the figurine as a material object. These adjacent theoretical fields play an often unacknowledged role in shaping the basic understanding of the human-object encounter utilized by miniaturization theory.[7] Upon this framework, scholars of miniaturization theory overlay their more specific concerns with scale and the agentive possibilities afforded by the nature of figurines as reduced-scale simulacra of human bodies.

The crucial role of tactile interaction and bodily proximity in the experience of miniaturization explains why many figurines in the ancient world (including those of Hellenistic Babylonia) conform easily – in size, shape, texture, and durability – to the human hand's ability to touch and grasp. Through these accommodations to a user's body, figurines inspire a kind of enchantment – "that strange combination of delight and disturbance"[8] – with the idea that a small-scale world could be so easily accessible.[9] When coupled with the obvious physical dominance of the user, this open receptiveness of miniatures seduces users with the opportunity to feel enlarged and empowered.[10] A miniature's "small scale invites an intimacy, control and democratization of experience"[11]; thus, regardless of his or her status in society, the user can rule and control what Bachelard referred to as a daydream of a life within a life.[12] This alluring combination of wonderment and accessibility is crucial to the social function of miniatures. By seeming so available and endearingly familiar, figurines can present alternate versions of social reality that engage with, but do not precisely reflect, the social milieu in which they circulate – and yet be accepted as "real."

Within the world of the miniature, complex lived identities can become simplified and essentialized. One of the most enduring figurine motifs in Mesopotamia presents an adult woman holding an infant child – a representation of motherhood so reductive in content and unified across time that it has been interpreted by scholars as embodying the abstract concepts of fertility and procreation themselves.[13] Concentrated focus on the mother-infant relationship was possible in figurine form, whereas the biographies and life circumstances of real Mesopotamian women who happened to be mothers would undoubtedly have encompassed identities and social relationships beyond the maternal. Bodies can also become idealized in miniature form – few women, for instance, could live up to the graceful perfection of a Tanagra figurine[14] – or be reduced to unattractive parody, as presented in the exaggerated ugliness of Hellenistic *koine* "grotesque" figurines.[15] Transitory life stages (such as pregnancy), actions (such as horse riding or athletic exercise), or events (such as ritual dedication) are permanently frozen and theatricalized through miniaturization. What living bodies can only achieve as temporary states become eternal and perfect in the world of the figurine.

The accessibility and enchantment of these objects induce their users to accept objectified social distortions as participants, role models, and influential agents of change within the real-life social world.[16] The intimacy of miniatures – often discussed as a fixed, intrinsic quality of smallness[17] – was agentive, capable of extending human social intimacy beyond that of lived experience, inculcating their users into intimate experiences with bodies and faces they had never seen in life: "proximity to the intimate portrait … could forge powerful connections of memory, imagination and meaning."[18] This intimacy of the miniature can also provide the illusion of travel through both space and time: "In fact, you need never have ventured outside the boundaries of civilization to be instantly transported and held spellbound there by these carefully rendered creatures [animal figurines]. Each day in my office, a mere glance at the windowsill becomes a way of traveling in place."[19] This power is agentive; as Rosemary Joyce argues, "rather than treat figurines strictly as 'representations' of a reality on which they have no influence, or even as models for/models of experience … I want to approach them as *instruments* of experience."[20] I have previously used the term "fascination" to describe this "mutual intimacy of miniature and user, in which each is attracted towards, and exercises power over, the other in a mutually entangled interaction."[21]

The overlap of vision, touch, and emotional experience would not have been unfamiliar to a Hellenistic Babylonian audience – indeed, such interdependencies might have been more at home within their mental landscape than within our own. Classical Greeks believed that the sense of vision worked by means of extramission, a process "akin to touch" wherein physical contact was made with the seen object.[22] While this type of contact was thought to be less direct than actual touch, it was considered contact nonetheless. Mesopotamian texts similarly indicate a significant overlap between their concepts of "seeing" and "experiencing," with the ideal object arousing allure, joy, and delight.[23] This emotional component of the Mesopotamian visual-tactile experience was also shared with Greek culture.[24] Such encounters were not necessarily positive; for instance, the late fifth-century BCE Greek rhetorician Gorgias explored how the act of viewing violent objects could change one's emotional state or social reality to one of fear and despair.[25]

Theoretical approaches to miniaturization add nuance to the traditional ways in which miniatures are studied, rather than replacing them.[26] Contextual and formal analysis, and resulting assessments of figurine function (i.e., miniature object as votive dedication, children's toy, fertility aid, or household decoration), still provide valuable information about ancient social practices and beliefs.[27] Yet, as informative as such reconstructions of figurine function are, it is nevertheless important to note that they are also limited and proximal, often obscuring the inherent plurality of a figurine's "purpose" which could change throughout its use-life.[28] As posited by Carolyn Nakamura and Lynn Meskell, this relational quality of meaning, which can never be fixed, "is precisely what constitutes the figurine as a *process* rather than simply a thing."[29] Miniaturization theory gives scholars a toolkit for deconstructing prima facie assumptions about the usefulness of figurines[30] – assumptions that only seem like self-evident explanations because of the ways in which miniatures seduce and enchant even the scholars who analyze them, convincing us that their presence and practicality is obvious and natural. Focusing on figurines as culturally situated practices rather than static bearers of singular meanings, miniaturization theory reveals the mechanisms by which figurines operated so convincingly that their use spans almost every human society at almost every point in history.

Of course, there can also be practical reasons for making things small. Yet these more quotidian rationalizations for miniaturization – cost reduction, resource conservation, or cramped display space – should not substitute as full explanations for the use of miniature objects. The existence of other solutions to such problems refute the reasoning that miniaturization was purely, or even primarily, a matter of expediency. Other strategies for coping with limited resources (besides miniaturization) include objects that were produced locally when expensive imports were inaccessible or unaffordable (as may, for instance, have been the case with Etruscan-made red-figure ceramic replacing Attic ware on the Etruscan market in the mid-fifth century BCE[31]), the bricolage repurposing and recycling of luxury objects from other eras and places (seen, for instance, in the eastern Mediterranean after the fall of the Neo-Assyrian empire[32]), and the manufacture of objects in less expensive media (such as the Athenian ceramic imitations of gold, silver, and other metallic luxury vessels, including rhyta, from Achaemenid Persia[33]).

Miniatures could also be deployed alongside larger-scale objects, suggesting that space was not always at issue; for instance, life-size votives of body parts were dedicated in Greek temples alongside miniature anatomical votives and other figurines.[34]

Thus, suggestions that miniaturization was only employed as a coping mechanism when larger-scale objects were impractical or unaffordable vastly underestimate ancient resourcefulness – in addition to underestimating the materially transformative affect of miniaturization, which seems to have been deemed an inappropriate strategy for reducing the resource burden of some kinds of objects. Examples of luxury miniatures, or miniatures deployed in elite resource-rich contexts, similarly problematize any straightforward equivalency between miniaturization and thrift. Therefore I, following on the work of Bailey, Joyce, and others, have previously posited an approach in which "miniaturization 'does' something more than just save space and resources: it creates intimate interactions and physical closeness (with feelings of pleasure and power that accompany such proximities) in ways that life-size or larger objects simply cannot."[35]

Intimacy Illusions

Yet, even as I build my analysis of Hellenistic Babylonian figurines upon this understanding that miniatures create fundamentally unique kinds of object engagement, I also wish to register a word of caution. This model of miniaturization theory – the idea that miniatures are intimate, tactile, and personal – is a line of interpretation upon which I have based much of my previous work, and which I still believe to have explanatory value. However, I also suggest that this understanding of miniaturization needs to be refined. In so doing, I return to the question that opened this chapter: why, like Gulliver, would we be particularly enchanted by miniatures that operate at the borders of our visual perception, with details that even sometimes escape those limits, and thus our notice? The answer that current miniaturization theory would offer is that visual difficulties encourage tactile handling,[36] which in turn increases the intimacy of the object. Indeed, the quality of miniaturization itself suggests touch-based analysis as an ideal entry point to this corpus of material: shrinking an object's scale compresses and obscures visual details, necessitating tactile contact in order to see clearly, while also making tactile interactions more accessible due to the ease with which a miniature can be grasped, lifted, and held. This is the premise of Grootenboer's concept of the "looking-touching of treasuring a miniature,"[37] a co-sensory experience which endears the little object to its user, who is enticed into cradling the tiny figure within his or her personal space.

While I do not question this chain of interaction – indeed, this understanding of figurine use is at the core of this volume's analysis – I wonder what happens in the next moment, after the user has taken the figurine into his or her hand, brought it near to his or her face, rubbed its contours with his or her thumb. In that moment of extreme physical closeness, there still remains much about the miniature that *cannot* be touched or felt, just as it cannot be seen. Touching the face of a figurine does not suddenly discover eyes when eyes are not depicted, nor does it suddenly provide access to bodies swathed under layers of garments. Many of the figurines discussed in this volume depict bodies whose details elude either touch or sight, or which omit some details altogether.

Current scholarly approaches to miniaturization do not usually consider such moments or their affective potential.[38] The close connection of miniatures to the human body is usually theorized only in positive terms, considering how such object encounters open up new realms of experience and possibility. The capacity of miniatures to bring human bodies, including the bodies and faces of family members, friends, or deities, into the hand of the beholder is undoubtedly one of the reasons why miniature objects have been so beloved throughout history.[39] But that potential does not mean that such objects are entirely open to human bodily interventions. Rarely discussed are the ways these objects can also close off and deny experience, sometimes resisting the user's bodily presence almost completely.

I propose that miniatures are not, in fact, always intimate. Rather, miniatures often *seem* intimate, enticing their users with the promise of personal interaction, but – once lured in – the user is sometimes constrained in his or her ability to touch, to see, and to engage. What other figurine scholars have interpreted as complete intimacy, I read as only the semblance of intimacy – a first step of personal engagement that is often not rewarded. Yet such failures of touch to completely supplement vision and facilitate the comprehensive knowability of the miniature object do not result in the discarding of miniatures and the abandonment of the object genre. To the contrary – as Swift so astutely noted, people are intrigued by the idea that there are some miniatures which we simply cannot fully access, cannot fully see. At first glance, this proposition seems absurd. Such objects would seem to fool us, the users, offering us the tantalizing prospect of full intimacy (and the entire spectrum of feelings that intimacy entails: familiarity, tenderness, affection, seclusion, sensuality), only to ultimately deny us access. Indeed, the wound goes deeper: this rebuffing of intimacy on the part of the object comes in spite of the fuller intimacy offered by the user, who has brought the object into his or her personal space, and opened access to his or her living eyes, hands, and skin. It is the user who offers true intimacy, not the object.

So why do we remain fascinated with the tiny? For (at least) three reasons. First, I suggest that we are enchanted by tiny things that operate at the borders of our sensory perception because it is through our inability to perceive that we are reassured that we are not, in fact, small and insignificant ourselves. Quite the opposite – we are too big to fully be intimate with the miniature world, thus too big to suffer the consequences of being miniscule and overpowered. We may therefore find ourselves relieved that we are "too big to fail" in the way that tiny objects can be discarded or brushed aside. As will be revealed in the next section of this chapter, several trends in the Hellenistic Babylonian figurines suggest that they were carefully crafted to deny certain kinds of in-depth intimacy in order to more firmly ground the user in the life-size real world. Stops were deliberately placed on the user's sensory apprehension and exploration of the figurines, with details left obscured, inaccessible, or even omitted. These are Swift's "invisible needles" threaded with "invisible silk." I suggest that it was through teasing glimpses of intimacy offered, and then denied, that the user was ultimately left more confident that he or she was big and powerful, a being of consequence.

The second reason why humans remain fascinated by tiny objects despite the often illusory nature of the intimacy they offer is, I argue, precisely because of that unpredictability. The invitation to intimacy issued by miniatures, and the user engagement that they entice, is only sometimes rewarded. Some figurines deny intimacy almost entirely, swathing the miniature body with layers of depicted draperies or omitting so many details as to make identifying the figure's age, gender, or other characteristics almost impossible. These figurines constrained interaction as much as – or even more than – they enabled it. Other figurines, such as the nude figurine pictured in Figure 1.1, reveal considerably more – not everything, for the user is never allowed full access to and control over the figurines of the Hellenistic Babylonian corpus, but still more can be seen, touched, and apprehended in this figurine than in others. I propose that this tenuousness and unpredictability of the intimacy miniatures can offer is part of these objects' appeal. The fact that sometimes we simply cannot see and cannot engage fully makes the figurines that *do* allow more visual and tactile access all the more appealing, for in achieving that level of intimacy we feel that we have accomplished something. The excitement of discovering miniature details, gateways to miniature realms, is heightened and intensified when access is not automatic. Similar feelings can be elicited by figurines that otherwise constrain access, such as the clothed figurine shown in Figure 1.2. Despite the thick folds of fabric depicted across this body, the swell of the figure's breasts can nevertheless be detected by the user's finger. Such small avenues of accessibility allowed the user to experience the intoxicating sense of being granted entry into an otherwise unknowable realm. The perception that luck plays a part – in addition to skill and effort on the part of the user – creates a

A MINIATURIZATION APPROACH   21

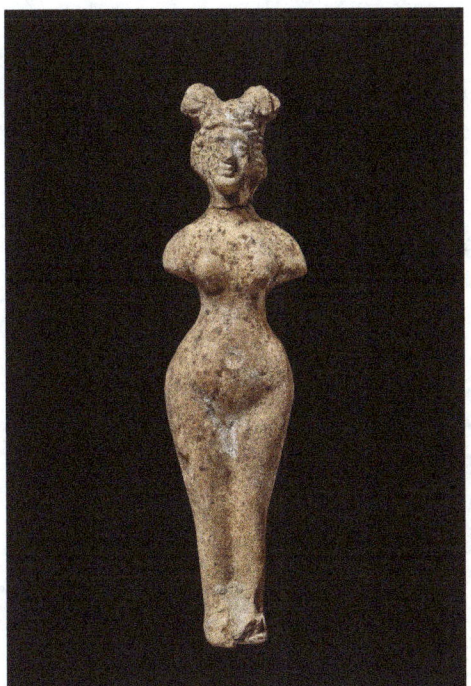

1.1. Figurine of nude female with finished-off arms (for attachment of separately modeled arms), terracotta, Babylon. Height: 15.5 cm. British Museum (BM 81–4–28–945)
Photograph © The Trustees of the British Museum.

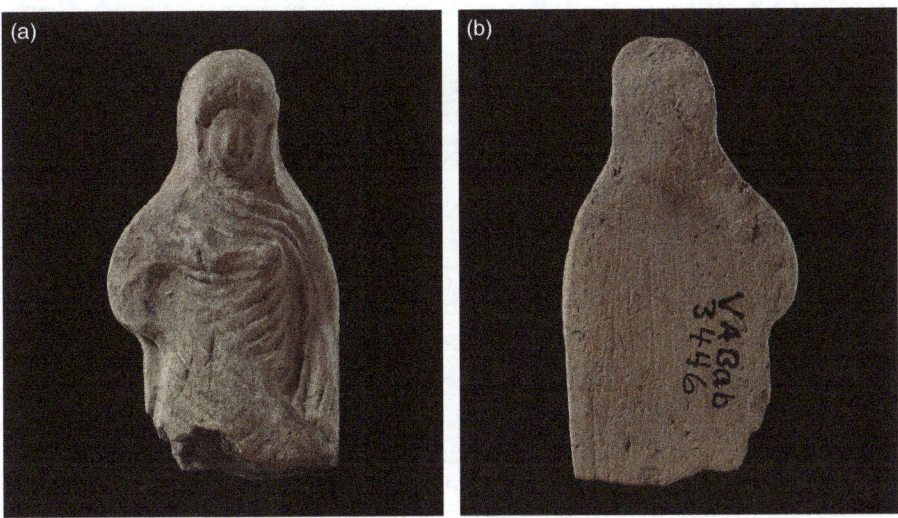

1.2 a and b. Front and back of clothed female figurine, terracotta, Babylon. Height: 7.6 cm. Vorderasiatisches Museum Berlin (VA Bab 3446)
Photographs © Staatliche Museen zu Berlin-Vorderasiatisches Museum, Foto: Olaf M. Teßmer.

"thrill of the chase" that similarly drives the nearly bankrupt gambler to return to the game. That the odds might be stacked against him or her, just as the intimacy offered by a figurine is largely a mirage, seems only to intensify the pleasure of playing. Such mindsets might have been very much at home in Hellenistic Babylonia: *tyche* – chance, fortune, or luck – was an "obsession"[40] throughout the Hellenistic world and was often personified as a goddess.[41]

The third reason why we are enchanted by tiny things whose details elude both sight and touch is that such objects give us room to think. As articulated by Douglass Bailey, the lack of certain details on figurines, created through the necessary abstraction and compression of information required when depicting life-size bodies at miniature scale, are enticing because they allow the user's imagination to fill in the gaps.[42] What the miniature does not specify, the user's preference and fantasy can supply, mentally molding the miniature to fit the user's ideal of figurine identity and function. Carl Knappett, drawing upon the work of Andy Clark, frames this abstraction and compression of detail in terms of its benefits to human reasoning and perception: miniature objects are cognitive scaffolding, "surrogate situations through which we can think more effectively about the real world."[43] The suppression of detail on the miniature object – what Clark calls "selective concretization" – improves the human user's concentration on the essential characteristics of the object, and thus his or her ability to grasp the abstract relationships and situations to which the figurine refers.[44] In short, the lack of detail prevents distraction, focuses attention, and gives the user breathing room to think without becoming overwhelmed.

This persuasive analysis informs my own work; for instance, I use the concept of imagination overlaid upon abstraction to interpret the experimental nature of figurine gender in Chapter 5. Yet, where Bailey presents this concept as entangled with intimacy – and, in some cases, fundamental in creating intimacy between user and figurine[45] – I see it as only providing the illusion of intimacy. Indeed, in using the miniature as a cognitive stepping-stone or a canvas onto which the imagination can paint what it wishes – constrained only by the basic outlines that the miniature provides – the user primarily gains intimacy with himself or herself, coming face-to-face with his or her own priorities, assumptions, and desires. The miniature, as both an object and a figure, almost fades from view, a vessel to be filled rather than a mystery to be explored. The search for details no longer matters, Swift's needles and silk are not so much invisible as make-believe. And yet, because the outlines of that fantasy are constrained by the figurine's form, we delude ourselves into believing that it is the object, not ourselves, that has determined all of what we see. We remain enchanted with the miniature because we believe that everything we imagine – the essence of our fantasies and our core beliefs about social ideals – is completely contained within the figurine. We tell ourselves that we are not inventing anything, we are only supplying the details that were intended all along. That figurines allow us – indeed, encourage us – to construct this fiction ensures that we remain charmed and captivated by our perception that the miniature world reflects all of our life priorities back to us.

Recognizing that the intimacy miniatures offer is largely an illusion is fundamental to deciphering how Hellenistic Babylonian figurines operated as regulatory social actors. By allowing only particular kinds of access, by rewarding some user explorations and yet frustrating or denying other attempts to look and to touch, figurines shaped user expectations – and even user ideals and mores – about what kinds of bodies were acceptable to see and feel, and where and how such bodies could be explored, all while grounding the user firmly in the real-world relevance, and consequences, of such actions.

This shaping of user expectations and experience was a social process, with the figurine working as both tool and active agent. Hellenistic Babylonian terracotta figurines, in particular, were mass produced through a workshop system and sold in the open marketplace.[46] Their forms almost certainly responded to, and reflected, community-wide norms and preferences for figurine production, with the desires of the individual figurine user only operating within a range of predetermined options – and, in a secondary sense, determining future trends of figurine creation by contributing to supply and demand. The decisions about which figurine forms should be more open to tactile access than others, or the selections of which specific details to omit and thus leave to the users' imaginations, must therefore be seen as a community-wide mechanism.

Indeed, I propose that the intimacy illusions of figurines should themselves be interpreted as a phenomenon that prioritized the needs of the community over the preferences of the individual. It was society that benefitted most from reminding the figurine user that the figurine object was a simulacrum, an operational member of the broader real-world community rather than a miniature world unto itself. Similarly, it was society that benefitted from intoxicating figurine users with the "thrill of the chase" for figurine intimacy, luring users with the possibility of access that was rarely, if ever, completely rewarded. Omitting certain details from figurines, and thus allowing users to imagine that their figurines faithfully and completely represented the content of their fantasies also kept users engaged, turning to figurines to see what they wanted to see. These strategies of faux intimacy kept users enchanted with and invested in miniature objects, which allowed these figurines to also work as clever disguises for the conveyance of broader social messages. Here I return to the idea that it is really the figurine user who offers true intimacy, not the figurine itself. In giving oneself over to enchantment and initiating bodily proximity to figurines, vulnerability ensues: the user opened himself or herself up to influence from the more elusive figurine – and thus, to the social norms and community preferences that dictated that figurine's form.

It is this understanding of miniatures, and the intimacy illusions that they offered, that I use as a theoretical and methodological framework for my interpretation of Hellenistic Babylonian figurines and the broader social environment in which they operated. But this is just the starting point. The specific mechanisms of user enchantment, the degree to which each figurine offered intimacy and knowability, and the social messages that each figurine carried (and shaped), varied with the specific details of each object. The field of miniaturization theory has undoubtedly brought us far in understanding the unexpected power of tiny things, yet I urge that there is still more work to be done in refining the theory and accounting for the fact that there are different kinds of sensory engagements, different levels of proffered intimacy, and, in fact, different kinds of miniatures.

ESTABLISHING THE "MINIATURIZATION AFFECT" OF FIGURINES

I propose that two qualities of a figurine particularly affected whether or not the user was likely to experience that object as somewhat "intimate." The first concerns the receptivity of the object itself: whether its materials and form responded pleasingly (and in what particular ways) to human touch. The second concerns the receptivity of the image depicted by the figurine, and to what degree that human form was accessible to the user.

Substance and Tactility

Despite the fact that material or medium, such as stone or clay, is a primary way in which miniatures are classified by archaeologists and divided within scholarly publications, there is very little interrogation as to what this means for how miniatures were experienced.[47] This lacuna exists despite the considerable discussion of the effects of these materials in large-scale sculpture.[48] Figurines, being smaller than sculpture, lend themselves to more extensive tactile interaction, and so considering their tactile effects and the reactions of figurine materials (clay, stone, bone, and metal) to human touch is crucial for understanding how figurines would have been experienced by their users. Each material offers different sensations of texture, temperature, and weight, which in turn impacted the engagement and affect of the object. Their surfaces differed as well, both in the physical traces of manufacture that such surfaces preserve, and in these materials' surface reactions to human touch. Through this exploration, I will argue that all these materials pinpointed human touch as the "life-giving" nexus of user-figurine interaction – but they did so differently, by accommodating human touch in very different ways, and thus participated differently within the human social world.

Terracotta Figurines Terracotta (fired, refined clay) was the medium used to create the vast majority of figurines produced in Hellenistic Babylonia. Clay had been a popular material in Mesopotamia for millennia, used for purposes as diverse as architecture and writing surfaces. Figurines had also been commonly made from clay since at least 3000 BCE.[49] This was likely due, at least in part, to the relative abundance of this material in southern Mesopotamia, which is resource-poor in other sculptural materials such as stone and metal. The relatively simple tools necessary for sourcing and processing raw clay, as well as the material's local availability, made clay figurines affordable – as is evidenced by the ubiquity of these objects in urban domestic spaces.[50] Indeed, from the large numbers of broken terracotta figurines found in domestic refuse or used as binding agents in making mud bricks, it is clear that clay miniatures seem to have been somewhat "consumable" – to be used up, discarded when broken (or no longer appealing), and replaced.[51] This commodification and replaceable nature of Hellenistic Babylonian figurines was integral to the ways in which they functioned as changeable and adaptable agents of social life.

Beyond the practical realities of limited resources and cost-effectiveness, clay was also appealing as a material for the creation of figurines because of its visceral connection to the human body.[52] In both Greek and Babylonian mythology, clay was the generative substance of divinely modeled human life.[53] That process was echoed and evoked by the ceramic craftsperson[54] (perhaps called a "coroplast"[55]) who similarly created "human" bodies (albeit miniature ones) in his or her workshop.[56] During the modeling process, the raw clay of the miniature-in-progress bears similar tactile qualities to human flesh and skin: responding to the heat of the craftsperson's hands, supple in consistency and springing back to the original shape when a light touch is applied.[57] Yet perhaps the most important connection of clay to the human body is its ability to be shaped directly by human hands, without the need for tools. Unmediated by the prostheses of technology, the relationship between artisan and clay material is direct and personal.

The plasticity of raw clay would not have been accessible to most users of terracotta figurines, who usually encountered these objects after their conversion to hard fired clay. While the tactile experience of soft unfired clay was likely familiar to most people in Hellenistic Babylonia, the material transformation of firing a figurine was radical and permanent, distancing the object from its primordial moment of facture. This disassociation of artistic process from final product could, in theory, have been desired by the figurine's users. Mesopotamian cult statues were enlivened, in part, through a series of incantations in which the artists who created them denied their agency in the process – going so far as to declare "I did not make it" while their hands were ritually cut.[58] While figurines were not receptacles for the divine on par with cult statues, their artistic function was similar: both cult statues and figurines were designed to create the illusion of access to another world. It would stand to reason that such an illusory effect would be more efficacious if reminders of the mundane, real-scale world – and the object's manufacture within it – were obscured or effaced in the object's materiality.[59]

Yet noticeable traces of manufacture are very common among the terracotta figurines of Hellenistic Babylonia. In many cases, little effort seems to have been expended to erase tool impressions, mold marks, and the fingerprints and fingernail indentations of the craftsperson. For instance, the head of a female figurine from Seleucia-on-the-Tigris, seen in Figure 1.3, bears the deep looping lines of a fingerprint on its left side – and no attempt seems to have been made to correct this defect. The ridged indentations of a fingerprint can also be seen on the shoulder of a figurine from Babylon depicting a reclining female figure, as viewed from the top (Figure 5.19b). The raised line of the mold join (where the front and back halves of the double-molded figurine were sealed together) on this figurine can also be clearly seen, especially where the join was smoothed flat – but not disguised – along the side of the head and top of the thigh. Similar leveling of the mold join can be seen in the side view of a figurine from Babylon usually identified as a representation of Apollo (Figure 5.9b). In this case, the act

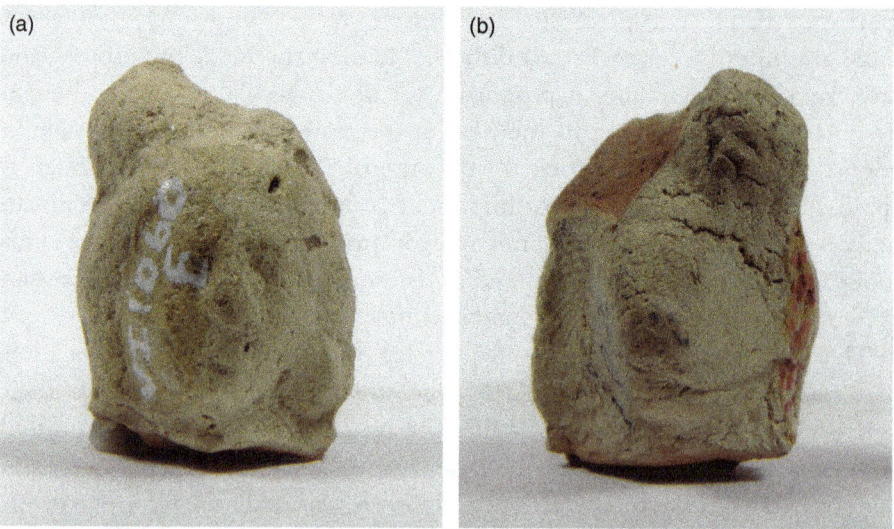

1.3a and b. Front and back of head of a female figurine, terracotta, Seleucia-on-the-Tigris. Height: approx. 2 cm. Kelsey Museum of Archaeology, University of Michigan, Ann Arbor (KM 15531)
Photographs courtesy of Roberta Menegazzi and the Kelsey Museum of Archaeology.

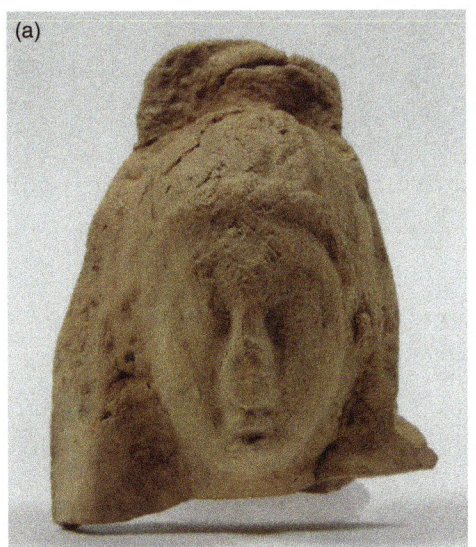 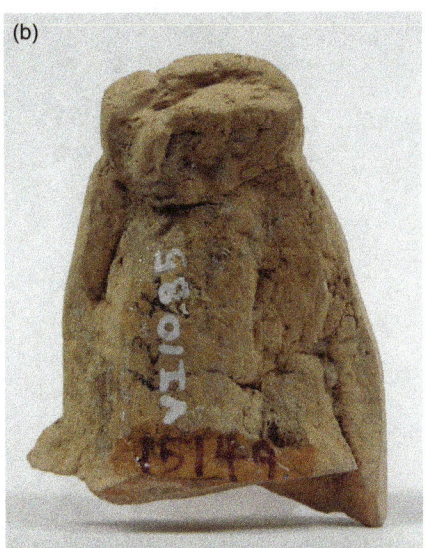

1.4a and b. Front and back of head of a female figurine, terracotta, Seleucia-on-the-Tigris. Height: approx. 2 cm. Kelsey Museum of Archaeology, University of Michigan, Ann Arbor (KM 15149)
Photographs courtesy of Roberta Menegazzi and the Kelsey Museum of Archaeology.

of smoothing the join, presumably with a blade tool, scraped flat the edges of the stringed instrument carried by the figure and the garment along his leg – both of which should have had the more rounded contours of the rest of the figurine.

Reminders of the malleable state of the clay material prior to firing are also common. Surfaces, especially on the backs and bottoms of figurines, were often rough, and small raised balls or flakes of clay were frequently not trimmed off.[60] For example, in the back view of a head of a female figurine from Seleucia-on-the-Tigris (Figure 1.4b), the rough texture of the raw clay is still clearly visible. Although presenting a somewhat smoother surface than the previous example, the back view of another head of a female figurine from Seleucia-on-the-Tigris (Figure 1.5b), bears traces of fingerprint or fabric impressions at the lower left, and of a clay flake (which adhered to the surface prior to firing) at lower right.

When compared with contemporaneous figurines from across the Hellenistic world – especially those from Hellenistic Greece – the incidence of "unfinished" elements among the Babylonian figurines is marked.[61] Such discordant traces of manufacture have earned the Hellenistic Babylonian craftspeople the reputation among modern scholars for being careless, incompetent, or untrained.[62] Yet, I would suggest that these traces of manufacture and material are more meaningful than simply as indexes of the Hellenistic Babylonian artisans' lack of skill and attention to detail. The interior of a double-molded figurine, such as that seen in Figure 3.10 – a surface which would never have been seen by a user, as it would have been hidden by the

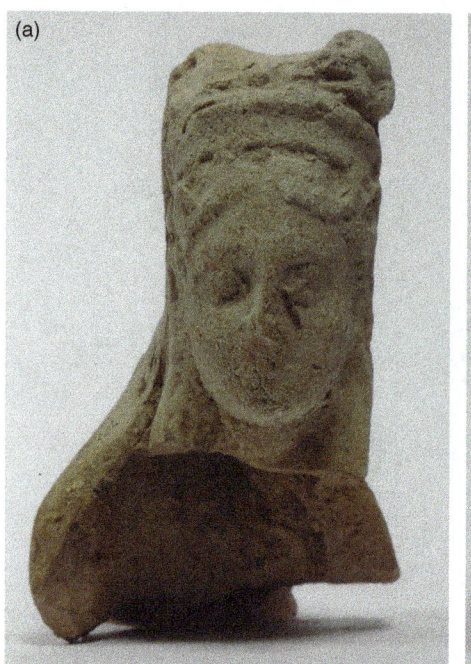 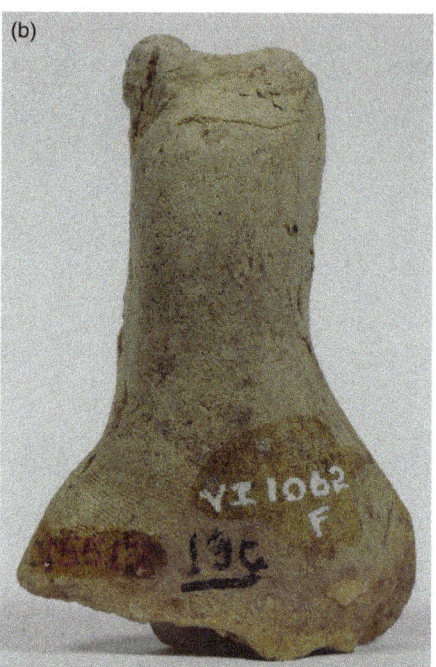

1.5a and b. Front and back of head of a female figurine, terracotta, Seleucia-on-the-Tigris. Height: approx. 4 cm. Kelsey Museum of Archaeology, University of Michigan, Ann Arbor (KM 15517)
Photographs courtesy of Roberta Menegazzi and the Kelsey Museum of Archaeology.

other half of the double-molded figurine – reveals far more fingerprints than are seen on the figurine exteriors discussed above. Clearly *most* of the fingerprints and other marks on the figurines were erased and smoothed over. It is possible that artisan carelessness is still to blame for those marks that remained; another potential explanation is that any marks would have been covered by the white ground (probably gypsum) or pigments that were commonly applied as a surface treatment to finished figurines.[63] However, as Roberta Menegazzi has remarked, Hellenistic Babylonian figurines were usually not painted across their entire surface areas and, even in the areas where they were painted, such pigmentation layers were very thin and somewhat translucent, allowing "the underlying colour of the clay to show through."[64] Additionally, as Erin Darby has discussed with reference to Judean Pillar Figurines, whitewash and paint on fired clay figurines does not last long, especially when the figurine is routinely handled, indicating that the figurines must have been considered functional even when only their clay exteriors remained as surfaces.[65] The precision with which only a few (and often only one or two) fingerprints were left behind on Hellenistic Babylonian terracotta figurines, usually positioned on less immediately visible surfaces (such as the side or back of the figurine), also suggests a more complicated explanation. A limitation on fingerprints implies that they were not appealing en masse, but the lack of total effacement or disguise suggests that they were not unappealing either – at least in limited quantities and with nonobvious placement.

Other traces of manufacturing process left on figurines also seem to demand a more nuanced explanation than simple carelessness. Hellenistic Babylonian terracotta figurine double molds were frequently made so that the two sides joined together unevenly, or created a figurine noticeably thicker than would be proportional for the depth of a real human body.[66] For instance, a side view of a figurine from Nippur depicting a female figure with an elaborate double-knobbed headdress (Figure 4.15b), reveals a raised ridge of clay where the two halves of the mold were poorly joined (although some attempt was made at smoothing the join, especially along the legs). Even if the two halves of this figurine had been joined accurately and the seam disguised, the depth of the figurine would have been much greater than would be convincing for a female body of the narrow frontal width as seen in Figure 4.15a. Although the application of white ground and paint might potentially have disguised the surface imperfections, no amount of such additions would alter this structural reality. The ineptitude of an individual artist is difficult to accept as a complete explanation here, as the "flaw" of figurine thickness resides not in slapdash figurine creation but rather in the original mold design. Additionally, this added thickness is shared across many mold designs, but not all of them. The knowledge of how to mold a more mimetic body, the knowledge of how to wipe away fingerprints – such techniques existed within the craft communities of Hellenistic Babylonia, but were not always utilized. Why not?

In order to answer this question, I suggest inverting the focus, from producer to consumer, to interrogate what might have been added to the experience of the miniature through these traces of facture. This approach, of starting with the user's experience of the miniature and working backward to figurine production and broader social engagement, will be utilized throughout this volume as a way of accessing the participation of miniatures in Hellenistic Babylonian social worlds, and the ways both the objects and the society shifted and interacted through time. In this case, focusing on the user's experience of the miniature indicates that something about the explicit marks of figurine manufacture was appealing to many Hellenistic Babylonian users – or at least not so unappealing or noticeable as to discourage users from engaging with objects that bore them.

I argue that this acceptability of manufacture marks is due, at least in part, to the role that mold lines, fingerprints, and smoothed edges played as evidentiary indexes of the creation of the miniature object by larger-scale human hands.[67] Miniatures are appealing to human users because they both are, and yet are not, tiny simulacra of the life-size world. The opportunity of entering into a miniature world is a fascinating one, yet it also provokes a crisis of scale, in which the user can feel that it is his or her body that is too large. Miniatures often counteract this effect through their abstraction – by necessity of their smaller scale and shrunken surfaces, miniatures lack the complex detail of a full-scale being or object.[68] Such absences and lacunae provide reassurance to the user that he or she exists within the "real world" and it is the miniature scale of the object that is unreal. Indexes of human facture amplify this sense of relief by providing immediate visual and tactile evidence that terracotta figurines, despite being made from clay, were not divinely formed in the way that many Hellenistic Babylonians would have believed that their ancestors had been. Clay miniatures were instead instantly recognizable as the products of the human world, created by human hands – and thus controlled by them. Reminding the user of the human-made origin of figurines – indeed, giving him or her the opportunity to place his or her finger in the exact spot as the fingerprint of the creator – transferred to the user a god-like sense of control and power over the created object. The ability to cause such illusions of omnipotence was a major appeal of miniature objects, particularly in fraught times of social instability and change.

Beyond granting personal feelings of empowerment, marks of human facture and their reminder of the dual scale – both miniature and real – at which figurines operated also helped to socialize terracotta figurines. However seemingly intimate the interaction between a person and his or her figurine, the craftsperson remained subtly but persistently present through indications of manufacture. These mark the figurine as a social object, which has been touched before by other hands, and will likely be touched again in the future.[69] Noticeable mold marks also signaled the mass-produced quality of the figurine, indicating that multiples of near-identical terracotta miniatures were made, owned, and touched by other people. Thus, even if interactions between user and figurine were personal and unwitnessed, the user was nevertheless reminded that the parameters of his or her experience were shared by other members of the community. Such interactions were thus governed by social norms, mores, and expectations in behavior – conventions either to be conformed to or flouted, but unlikely to be ignored, as the figurine's very materiality was a constant reminder of the social pressure of what "other people" were (imagined to be) doing with their belongings.

This socialization of figurines via mold marks, fingerprints, and other traces of facture amplified these objects' affect in the social world, granting them the authority and ability to operate within and upon real-scale, human society. Figurine "skin" (as an approximation of biology) was transformed to figurine "surface," an artificial space on which social messages could be inscribed.[70] In their visibility, such marks of manufacture became both technical apparatus and ornament – defining and delimiting the object simultaneously as a cultural product and cultural sign.[71] Whether knowingly or not, the viewers of such marks were thus primed to read the object as a bearer of social meaning rather than simply corporeal mimesis. The specific ways in which figurines exercised that agency to shape the social environments of Hellenistic Babylonia will be explored in detail throughout this volume. What is important – indeed, foundational – here is that figurines were able to exercise that agency in part because they were designed to be obvious products of the human world, rather than apart from it. That the physical reminders of their human manufacture and social presence were not considered unappealing (or lazy, sloppy, or gauche) by their owners and users indicates that the Hellenistic Babylonian people were comfortable, and perhaps even eager, to share their social world with these miniature clay participants.

Stone and Metal Figurines Stone (usually alabaster) and metal (usually bronze) miniatures in Hellenistic Babylonia differed from their more common clay counterparts in several important ways. Both materials had intrinsic value in resource-poor Mesopotamia,[72] and thus miniatures made in either material represented an investment of more than just skill and time on the part of the craftsperson. They were undoubtedly more expensive than clay figurines and their materials could be reused should a particular figurine become unappealing. Thus they are more rarely found in the archaeological record. Both materials take fine detail relatively well, allowing for the creation of delicate objects in smaller scale (some of them are exceptionally tiny; in the range of 2–5 cm) than what molded terracotta usually achieved.[73] Both materials are also stronger and more durable than clay, adding to their value. This combination of expense, delicacy, durability, and tiny size made stone and metal ideal materials for the creation of wearable miniatures (such as seal rings and jewelry); and, indeed, securing the miniature to a user's body might have helped ease fears of the potential loss of such a valuable, yet easily misplaced, object.[74] Freestanding miniatures in both stone and metal also existed, and it is to their sensory affects that I now turn specific attention.

One of the most alluring tactile qualities of both stone and metal miniatures was their texture: the surfaces of both can be polished to opulent smoothness.[75] Although clay figurines in Hellenistic Babylonia were often coated with layers of gypsum and pigment, they were only rarely glazed and thus would generally not have matched the surface glossiness of stone or metal.[76] This quality of stone and metal miniatures could attract the user's touch and caress with the promise of pleasurable, silky sensations. Even if the user did not actually reach out to grasp the object, the anticipation of tactile gratification was conjured by the surface sheen and luster of metal and stone, as visually apprehended.[77] Vision and touch thus operated in tandem to evoke an experience – or even an experiential imaginary – of sensory delight.

This pleasurable quality of stone and metal miniatures, whether experienced or simply conjectured, focused user attention on the moment in which he or she engaged the object, emphasizing the immediacy of touch (or the visually inspired imagination of touch[78]) and its sensual reward. The user's touch was also privileged by the fact that stone and metal do not have the malleable qualities of unfired clay, and thus miniatures in these materials did not bear the same marks of the craftsperson's hands.[79] Users of stone and metal figurines were not linked back in the production chain to the creators and previous handlers of the object; rather, their engagement with the object had the sense of being fresh and unmediated. However, once touched, both stone and metal reacted to the user's hand in more dynamic ways than relatively inert fired clay. Although generally cold upon initial handling, stone and metal miniatures respond to the body heat transmitted by their user's skin, gradually warming to an equivalent temperature.[80] The illusion of a figurine "brought to life" by human skin contact could be perceived by others if the miniature, and the residual body heat it contained, were touched soon afterward by another person.[81] In the urgency and presentness of this interaction, and the short-lived nature of its effect, we find something that seems to more closely approach true intimacy.

The intimate effects of these materials suggest that it was likely no accident that figurines in stone or metal followed different trends of form and motif from clay figurines. Hellenistic Babylonian stone and metal figurines represent a more limited iconographic corpus than their terracotta counterparts, with more emphasis on female forms – especially nude, sensual female (or, in some cases, hermaphroditic) forms that seem designed to be caressed.[82] For instance, in Figure 1.6 we see a reclining, nude female figure, with supple curvatures of breast, waist, and thigh that the carving of the stone have made accessible and available. Similarly sensuous bodies were made in clay; for instance, in Figure 1.7, a mostly nude female reclines in a posture and style comparable to that depicted in the alabaster example. Yet, despite the similarities between these examples, the stone figurine more convincingly succeeds at creating an intimate encounter between the user and the reclining female. Despite the heavy coats of plaster and paint on the terracotta example, the surface texture of the stone figurine would have exceeded it in silky smoothness and glossy reflectivity. The delicate details possible in stone carving allow for seductive access to the spaces between the arm and the body; in contrast, the right arm and body of the clay figurine are modeled as one. Additionally, the temperature of the stone figurine would warm when in prolonged contact with human touch.[83] All of these features would have granted the user of the stone figurine a greater feeling of intimacy and sensory engagement with a nude – and perhaps erotic – female body. Whether this sense of intimacy was pleasurable or off-putting likely depended on the context of use. For instance, bronze – such as was used to

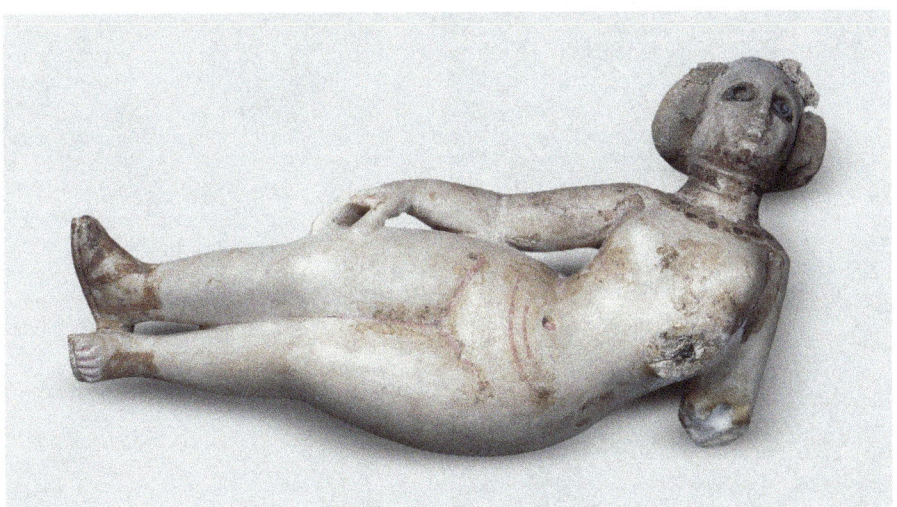

1.6. Reclining female figurine with attachment for separately modeled left arm, alabaster, Seleucia-on-the-Tigris. Baghdad (B 17805)
Photograph courtesy of Roberta Menegazzi.

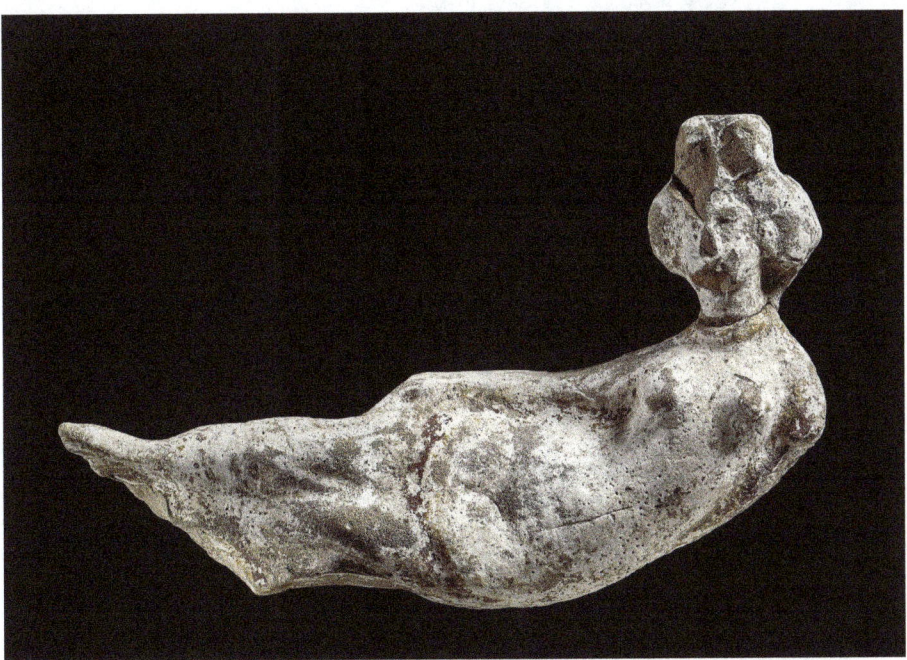

1.7. Reclining female figurine with attachment for separately modeled left arm, terracotta, Babylon. Length 18 cm. British Museum (BM 68-6-2-6)
Photograph © The Trustees of the British Museum.

depict similarly erotic female bodies like that seen in Figure 1.8 – can become sticky or emit an odor when someone touches it for a prolonged period of time. If another user were to touch the figurine soon afterward, these effects could

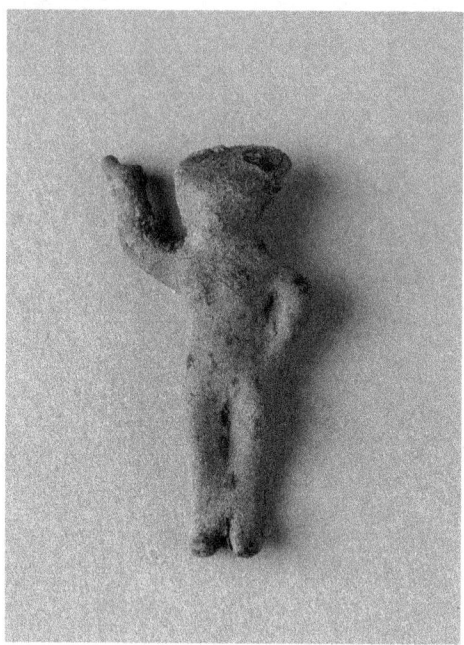

1.8. Female figurine with one arm raised, bronze, Seleucia-on-the-Tigris. Height 3.8 cm. Kelsey Museum of Archaeology, University of Michigan, Ann Arbor (TM 1931.541/KM 2018.01.0584)
Photograph courtesy of the Kelsey Museum of Archaeology.

either enhance intimacy or elicit disgust, depending on the user's connection to the person who initiated tactile contact.[84] This personal, and perhaps highly charged,[85] effect of stone and metal figurine use may further explain why many figurines in these materials are depicted nude, with both the subject matter and the material affects suggesting relatively private object-user engagements.

Yet, links to the broader social world were also created. The weightiness of stone and metal miniatures – which considerably surpasses the heft of their clay counterparts[86] – gives a sense of importance and permanence to the ephemera of intimacy. Heaviness in the user's palm implies that interactions with the object are similarly "heavy," potentially with real-world implications and consequences, not simply daydreams or fantasies. The broader social – and indeed, international – world was implicated in the fact that neither alabaster nor the metals needed to make bronze were available locally in southern Mesopotamia; both needed to be sourced and traded over great distances. As a human-made metallic alloy, bronze further links to social production chains.[87] Connections of history and culture, as well as across the divisions of scale that separate statues from figurines, were made through these materials, since both metal and stone were used in monumental sculpture in both Babylonian and Greek tradition.

Such connections do not contradict the choice of erotic subject matter for stone and metal figurines; indeed, the Knidian Aphrodite seen in Figure 4.12 (as a life-size sculpture that was both erotic and stone) famously elicited sexual attraction and even tactile contact from its admirers.[88] Although no Hellenistic Babylonian figurines attempt to model the Knidia, the well-known links in the Hellenistic *koine* tradition between stone or metal statuary and erotic intimacy would pull the user of such miniatures back into the social world.

In comparing these figurines with their terracotta parallels, we are thus confronted by the paradox of objects that were made both more deeply intimate, and yet also more outward-looking and global in connection, by virtue of their stone or metal materials. The sensory immediacy of experiencing such a figurine was tempered by its constant visual and material reminders of other scales, other places, and other times – informing the user that the wider world had a role to play in the interaction between person and object, no matter how private that encounter might seem. Intimacy is elusive, and perhaps even completely illusionary.

Bone Figurines Like stone and metal miniatures, figurines made of bone were also less common than their clay counterparts. When found in secure archaeological contexts, most date to the Parthian period.[89] While most of the Hellenistic Babylonian figurine corpus appears not to have undergone a major transformation with the Parthian conquest of Seleucia-on-the-Tigris in 141 BCE, the bone figurines may represent an exception to this. Two distinct stylistic traditions are evident in the bone figurines of Parthian-era Babylonia: the so-called schematic figurines, which represent abstract bodies (see Figure 1.9), and the naturalistic figurines, which more mimetically approximate the human form (see Figure 1.10, as well as Figure 2.10). The latter group of objects engages with, and reflects, ways in which the human body – especially the nude, frontally posed female body – was represented in other materials (clay, stone, and metal) in the broader Hellenistic Babylonian figurine corpus. The abstract figurines seem set apart from this tradition, and may represent something uniquely Parthian; as such, this group of figurines will not be analyzed in this volume, beyond some limited observations here.

Both groupings of bone figurines (schematic and naturalistic) were carved from the leg bones of a small animal,[90] and the physical traces of that origin were usually still visible on the finished object. When viewed from the top or bottom, the holes of the interior bone cavities can often be seen; when viewed from the side, many figurines curve slightly to follow the natural arc of the bone (see Figure 2.10b). Visible striations and the interior cancellous tissue of the bone are observable in many examples.[91] Thus, sections of bone that bore traces of their natural origins seem not to have been disqualified from use as sculptural material.[92] The natural shape of the bone also imposed limits on the figurine forms that were sculpturally possible. Elongated, frontal bodily poses,

36   A QUESTION OF INTIMACY: MINIATURIZATION AND FIGURINES

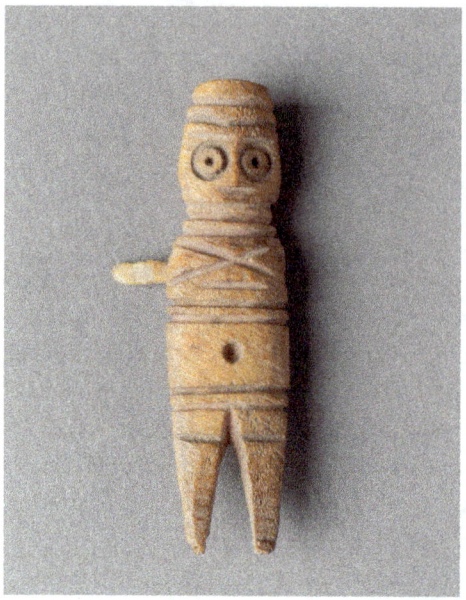

1.9. Abstract figurine with added arm, bone, Seleucia-on-the-Tigris. Height 5.8 cm. Kelsey Museum of Archaeology, University of Michigan, Ann Arbor (KM 16197)
Photograph courtesy of the Kelsey Museum of Archaeology.

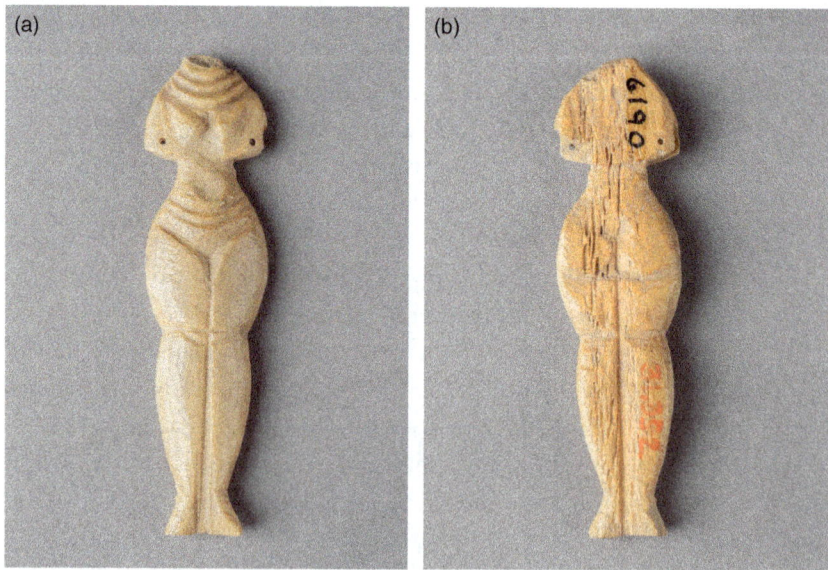

1.10a and b. Front and back of female figurine with attachments for separately modeled arms, bone, Seleucia-on-the-Tigris. Height: approx. 8.5 cm. Kelsey Museum of Archaeology, University of Michigan, Ann Arbor (TM 1931.352/KM 2018.01.0402)
Photographs courtesy of the Kelsey Museum of Archaeology.

with legs together were generally preferred. Arms were either sculpted to appear tightly pressed against the sides of the figurine's body, or the arms were separately fashioned. As seen in Figure 1.9, schematic figurines could have small "toothpick" arms inserted in a transverse hole through their bodies approximately at shoulder height; such holes might also have been used for figurine suspension, perhaps as jewelry or other body ornamentation. Naturalistic figurines also sometimes featured attachments for added arms, as seen in examples where arm stumps were severed mid-humerus with a pierced hole for the jointing of a separately carved naturalistic arm (see Figure 1.10). Such naturalistic arm joints have much in common with clay and stone figurines depicting female figures with separately added arms (see discussion in Chapter 2), yet the constraints of bone were also operational here, in that the separately added arms are straight, rather than bent in a position of offering or carrying, as seen in some stone and clay examples.

These accommodations to the bone material emphasized the relic-like quality of such figurines as the bodily remains of a living being – indeed, visibly and noticeably evidencing that origin. Conflicts of scale are thus particularly vivid in miniatures made from bone. As the corporeal remnant of an animal, bone miniatures are both a visual representation of a living being at miniature scale and also an indexical referent to the body of a life-size living being. The use of bone to create figurines with separately added arms was particularly intense, invoking a double fragmentation: the once-living animal body was violently broken in order to create a more life-like appearance of movement in the fragmented body of a jointed figurine.

That the organic origins and material aspect of the bone was often highlighted and used on Hellenistic Babylonian figurines, rather than effaced or disguised, indicates that the interplay between nature and culture involved in using a piece of a real animal body to create a represented human body that was then touched by a real human body was a crucial aspect to these figurines' functionality. Through it, bone figurines evoked (and indeed, explicitly referenced) the paradox of miniaturization: that both the life-size and miniature scales exist simultaneously, and the gap between them must be bridged during human interaction with figurines. Tactile interaction on the part of the user is thus explicitly called for by these figurines' very materiality. That human hands were responsible for not only touching the finished object, but also producing the sculpted form and (likely) killing the animal from which the material was violently extracted, evokes a sense of deep knowledge and power over the complete life cycle of the object[93] – and, by extension, over the miniature world and its life-size corollary.

This sense of knowledge, power, and control could have been further intensified by the ways in which bone material responds to tactile contact. Bone, like stone and metal, has sensuous, alluring material properties[94]: it can

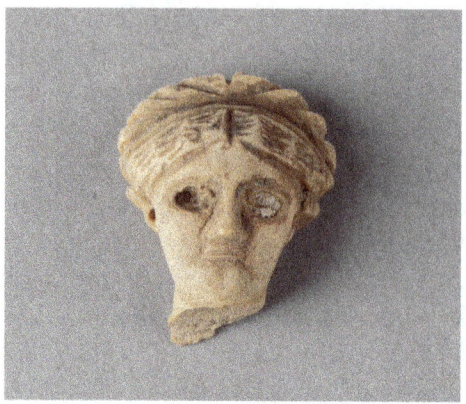

1.11. Head of female figurine with inlaid eyes, bone, Seleucia-on-the-Tigris. Height 2.9 cm. Kelsey Museum of Archaeology, University of Michigan, Ann Arbor (TM 1931.476/KM 2018.01.0521)
Photograph courtesy of the Kelsey Museum of Archaeology.

be polished to shimmering smoothness, take a high level of detail, and can be inlaid with other materials (see, for instance, the inlaid eyes of the head of a bone figurine in Figure 1.11).[95] But bone differs significantly from stone and metal in its reaction to oils in human skin: organic bone begins to discolor and form a second "skin" over its carved surface.[96] This change supplemented the origins of the miniature body – which came from an animal's interior – with an exterior that was now a product of the human world twice over: first through sculpting and second through this surface reaction. That the figurine became more and more a part of the human world with each successive instance of tactile contact points to the invasiveness of that encounter in transforming a figurine's fundamental identity. Yet there were also social implications of that intimate touch, for it was the definition and place of the object in society – now reaffirmed as a participant more human than animal, more reactive than passive – that was at stake. Unlike with metal or stone figurines, bone miniatures permanently transformed in response to tactile engagement with users, preserving in time the physical closeness of human touch and allowing it potentially to be witnessed by others long after the initial encounter. Thus, regardless of how intimate the interaction was between user and object, the ramifications of that contact extended outward into the broader social world.

Objects vs. Representations: "Skin" Contact with Figures and Figurines

In establishing the miniaturization affect of figurines, I have thus far concentrated on how different figurine materials could react to human touch – specifically human hands and human skin – during the events of their manufacture and use. The substance of which the object was made and the surface of that object were the two principal features that determined the material interaction between miniature and user. However, those materials and surfaces are not unique to figurines. Many of the observations about object affect presented in the previous section would apply to other kinds of objects — including nonfigural objects like tools or bowls — although the sensory experiences created by substances and surfaces undoubtedly took on particular significance when associated with miniaturized human bodies.

This section continues with an exploration of the miniaturization affect of figurines by focusing on the moments of user-object interaction from the perspective of figurine "skin" rather than figurine "surface." In so doing, I am drawing careful distinction between the whole miniature as an *object*, which was made of clay or other material and had a corresponding surface, and the depicted figure as a *representation*, which could be presented as wearing clothes or other ornamentation and whose bodily surface might be imagined as equivalent to living human skin. This distinction is critical for a discussion of intimacy. While the miniature as an object is always accessible to and controllable by its user, and thus can be compelled into bodily proximity, the represented figure depicted in miniature can limit or even prevent such interactions. Conversely, when the represented figure presents the illusion that the user is experiencing real skin-to-skin contact with another, albeit much smaller, human body, the imagined closeness that is created has the potential to be much more intensive and meaningful than a skin-to-surface encounter with a nonfigurative vessel or tool.

This discussion of figurine "skin" will engage with three particular features of figurine design — clothing, pose, and method of manufacture — which share responsibility for the level of visual and tactile access that the figurine's user had to the skin and body of a miniature representation. Clothing could obscure the body or it could tantalizingly encourage tactile interaction with the suggestion of imminent disrobing. The figure's pose constrained where and how the user could see and touch, allowing access or limiting it with the bend of an elbow or the placement of a hand. Figurine manufacture determined what parts of the figure existed at all: single mold use resulted in figurines with flat and unmodeled backsides,[97] while double mold use could create more naturalistic bodily features for a figurine's back — although this capability was not always employed.

Although the figurines of Hellenistic Babylonia certainly fall along a spectrum of openness to user vision and accessibility to user touch, none occupy the extremes of either completely excluding the user, nor — and this is crucial — completely welcoming user intervention, permitting all possible user intrusions or manipulations. Rather, all Hellenistic Babylonian figurines occupied a middle ground between completely excluding the user and submitting fully to his or her desires. Such delicate balances of inviting and rejecting the user could result in regulated, carefully curated intimacy, which was often more illusory than real. Perhaps most importantly, the discussion in this section establishes that agency should be granted to the figurines themselves, through recognizing their role in creating the conditions of their own use. In broadly acknowledging that figurines were capable of placing limits on user power and directing the course of user-figurine interactions, I here begin the more detailed process of identifying the social norms and pressures that were at least partly responsible for the particular affects of Hellenistic Babylonian figurines – a project that will continue throughout this volume.

Fully Clothed Figurines The extent of allowable sight and touch of figurine "skin" varied among Hellenistic Babylonian figurines. Many were depicted fully clothed, rendering most of the miniature figure's "skin" permanently off-limits and inaccessible, since it does not exist as a separate surface beneath the clothes that were modeled as one with the body. For instance, the body of the female figure seen in Figure 1.2 can only be accessed in a few limited ways. The only uncovered skin is that of the face; the rest of the body is covered with thick drapery. Indeed, the deep grooves indicating drapery folds are the most eye-catching visual features of the piece, presenting a study in clothing that obscures and envelopes, rather than showcases, the body that is imagined to be present beneath the garments. While this overwhelming, graceless, and somewhat clunky depiction of clothing might be the result of poor craftsmanship, a worn-out mold,[98] or the limitations of terracotta as a medium, its visual and tactile effect could also cause the viewer to question whether a human body even existed beneath the clothes. Certainly, reconstructing corporeal wholeness and visualizing the precise form that such a body would take requires a certain amount of imaginative effort here, distancing the user from the figurine.

Direct sensory contact is possible, but only in limited ways. The figure's round breasts, positioned high on her chest as a likely indicator of youthfulness,[99] swell slightly beneath her wrapped mantle, allowing their contours to be felt by the user's touch – yet, not fully accessed, and certainly not seen in their revealed nudity. Concave depressions between the body and arm indicate a waist, but do not admit more than superficial access by the user's fingers. The flatness of the figurine, and its side contours that only roughly approximate the human form, add to the object's impenetrability. The model for this female form was Hellenistic statuary as well as other figurines, such as those of the Tanagra tradition. It participates in a Hellenistic *koine* ideal of beauty, and yet is completely inaccessible and untouchable. She cannot be undressed, her body cannot be revealed. Overpowering – even breaking – the *object* is certainly possible, but this would do nothing to disempower the depicted figure, violence against whom would yield only dull clay fragments and dust while her modesty would remain intact.

ESTABLISHING THE "MINIATURIZATION AFFECT" 41

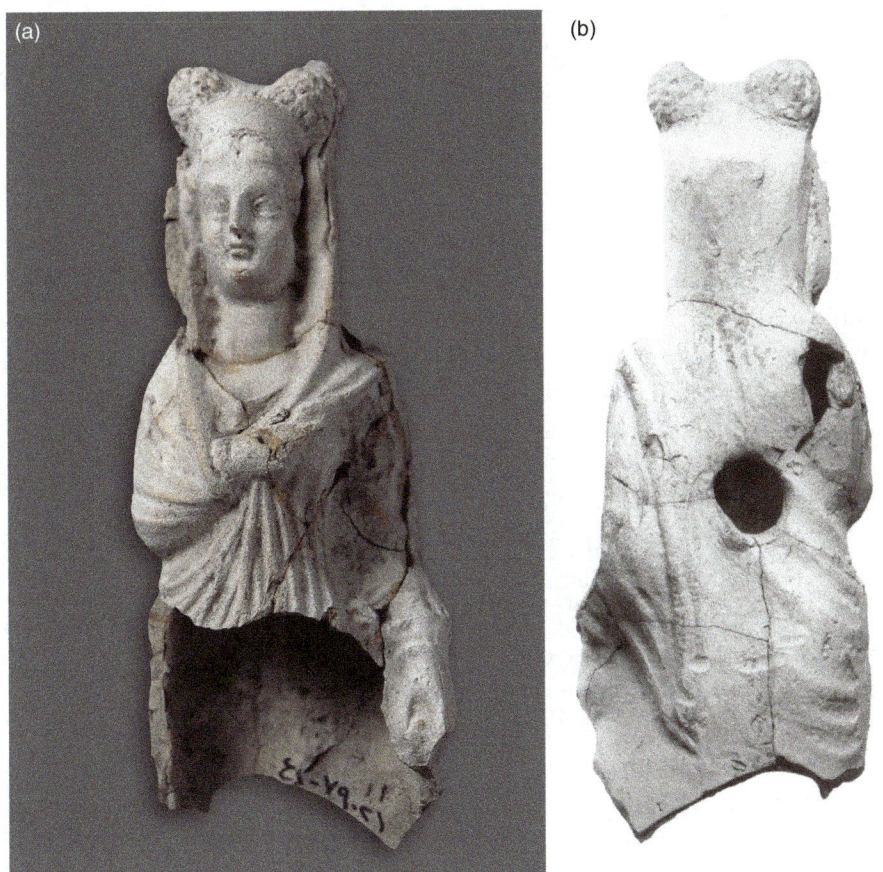

1.12a and b. Front and back of standing female figurine, terracotta, Seleucia-on-the-Tigris. Height 15.7 cm. Turin Excavations at Seleucia (S11,111)
Photographs courtesy of Roberta Menegazzi.

The single-mold manufacturing technique in which this figurine was made also contributed to its inaccessibility. The use of a single mold rendered a figurine that was only modeled on the front; the back was usually smoothed flat, as seen in Figure 1.2b, or made slightly convex. This technique resulted in a solid, durable object that could endure repeated tactile handling and use. However, that functionality of the object came at a cost to the mimetic qualities of the figure, which is only illusionistically representational on the front half of its body. There are no clothes on the back of the figurine to prevent tactile access and no skin underneath them to be imagined – rather, there is only clay surface, only manufactured object. Yet, even when the double mold was used to create fully clothed figurines, tactile access to the body did not automatically follow. As can be seen in Figure 1.12, the modeled back of some figurines follow only the contours of the human form. The few details multiply the amount of clothing shown, rather than revealing the body beneath them.

Indeed, even the head is obscured from the back, covered by a veil that descends from the elaborate double-knobbed hairstyle. The double-molded back thus grants the opportunity for greater sensory appreciation of the depicted fabric, with its many contours and folds, but not greater access to the body or "skin" of the figure herself.

These examples show how clothing can be used to divert intimacy. Close engagement with the figure's body is denied, with curiosity and attention redirected to clothing, draperies, veils, and fabrics.[100] From the standpoint of established miniaturization theory, in which bodily intimacy with the human figure is thought to be paramount, such figurines would seem to be frustratingly aloof. Yet, their broad popularity in Hellenistic Babylonia indicates that these objects fulfilled a social need. As discussed by Megan Cifarelli, the work of "signaling" done by dress increases in intensity during "times of social, political, or cultural change"[101]; such observations may be applicable to Hellenistic Babylonia. Clothed figurines best approximated the daily public appearances of people living in Hellenistic Babylonia – and, as such, came the closest to engaging with human members of society on a peer-to-peer basis. The attention to clothing in the figurines may replicate similar attention paid to the styles of garments and personal adornment on living bodies – informing the figurine user both of the limits of acceptable social norms and the more frivolous rules of fashion trends.[102] As with the department store mannequins of today, the body beneath may not really have been the point.[103] Intimacy with it may not have been desired – or, if it was desired, the figurine's impenetrable surface and lack of skin access strongly signaled that such fascinations were frowned upon. In art, as in life, not all bodies are available to be viewed and touched.

Partially Clothed Figurines Partially clothed figurines, despite their tantalizing glimpses of sensuous corporeality, also retained fixed limits on the skin-to-skin access they provided. The bodies of both the male and female figures depicted in the figurine seen in Figure 1.13 are naked above the hips, providing both visual and tactile access to their faces, arms, and torsos. The curvature of their waists, the indentations of their navels, the smooth arcs of their necks and jawlines as the two faces lean toward one another to share a kiss – all of this can be experienced by the user in multisensory delight. True intimacy seems possible here, as the user is granted access to an intensely private moment between lovers caught in the act of embrace.

Yet, much about these bodies cannot be accessed by the figurine's interlocutor. Despite being depicted in the nude, the female figure's breasts are unelaborated (without nipples) and are markedly different in size (possibly as a result of poor modeling or molding technique) – formal features which together disrupt the illusion of mimesis. As can be seen in Figure 1.13b, the back of the figurine is lacking in illusionistic detail, despite the fact that it was made in a double mold that would have allowed for naturalistic modeling. Instead, it follows only the vaguest contours of the two human figures – thus rendering invisible and inviolable half of their turned heads and faces (the woman's right side and the man's left side), their (presumably) intertwined arms, their naked backs, and all other features a user would expect to see when viewing this pair in the round. While the back of the figurine can certainly be touched – indeed the thick walls of the mold-made figurine and the wide base created by the cavernous use of double molding make this figurine particularly durable, stable, and thus able to withstand manual use – the complete lack of details prevents the user from even imaging that he or she was touching the real skin of the couple's naked backs and buttocks. The *figurine* as an object can be seen and touched, but are the *people* or the *bodies* truly on offer here for visual and tactile consumption?

The depiction and placement of the clothing similarly renders ambiguous the user's dominance over the figurine. The tightness of the folds around the legs means that these limbs – particularly the woman's entire legs and feet, as well as the man's lower legs – can be seen, and their contours caressed. The tautness of the fabric in revealing the couple's lower bodies also allows the amorous pose of the woman seated across the man's lap, with her legs draped across his thighs and her pubic region in close proximity to his, to be clearly intelligible and revealed to the user. As Greek sculpture of the Classical era exploited to an expert degree,[104] depictions of carefully positioned clingy fabric can show almost as much as they hide. This figurine owes much to that tradition and the coy eroticism created by such sculptures.

In addition to offering a revealing transparency, the clothing also seems in imminent danger of baring the bodies directly. Placed well below the waist, skirting even slightly below the hip bones of both the male and female figures, the draperies this couple wear are on the verge of exposing the genitalia of both figures. At any moment, the fabric might slip and the pubic regions of the couple will be laid bare. This is the allure of the striptease, drawing user interest and heightening the erotic tension of the scene. As with the semi-transparent drapery clinging to the legs, this effect of imminent disrobing was also fully explored and exploited in Greek statuary, in which clinging, filmy draperies on the verge of flying apart, falling open, or slipping off had been depicted since the Classical period, and became even more popular in the Hellenistic period.[105] Yet unlike with many standing statues of the Hellenistic *koine* tradition, whose garments draped loosely around the lower hips often seem to be held on by only the slightest tension,[106] the clothes depicted on this figurine do not seem quite so ready to slip off of their own accord – if the figures were to remain seated and still. And yet, the user can delightfully and imaginatively anticipate that neither the male nor female figure shown here intends to sit quietly. Their intertwined bodies and passionate kiss indicate

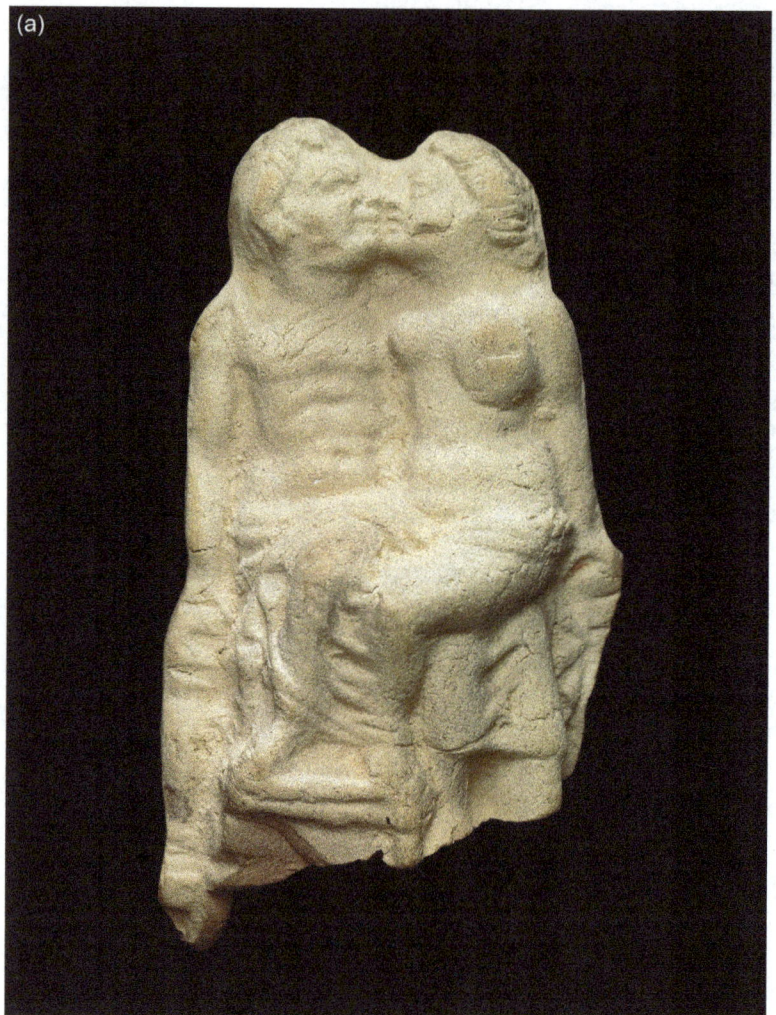

1.13a and b. Front and back of couple figurine, terracotta, Babylon. Height 11 cm. British Museum (BM Sp. III 21+ = 91789)
Photographs © The Trustees of the British Museum.

that the couple's further movement and amorous intent will surely cause their garments to be discarded, whether by accident or design. That such a disrobing might be only moments away builds a sense of pleasurable anticipation.

And yet it is an anticipation that goes unfulfilled. The man and woman shown here will not, in fact, move. Their garments will remain stubbornly in place. The user's pleasure remains entirely in the realms of fantasy and unrequited desire. A pleasure, nonetheless, but one with fixed limits. There is nothing that the user can do, should he or she want to see the fulfillment of the erotic promise of this figurine – the figurine, not the

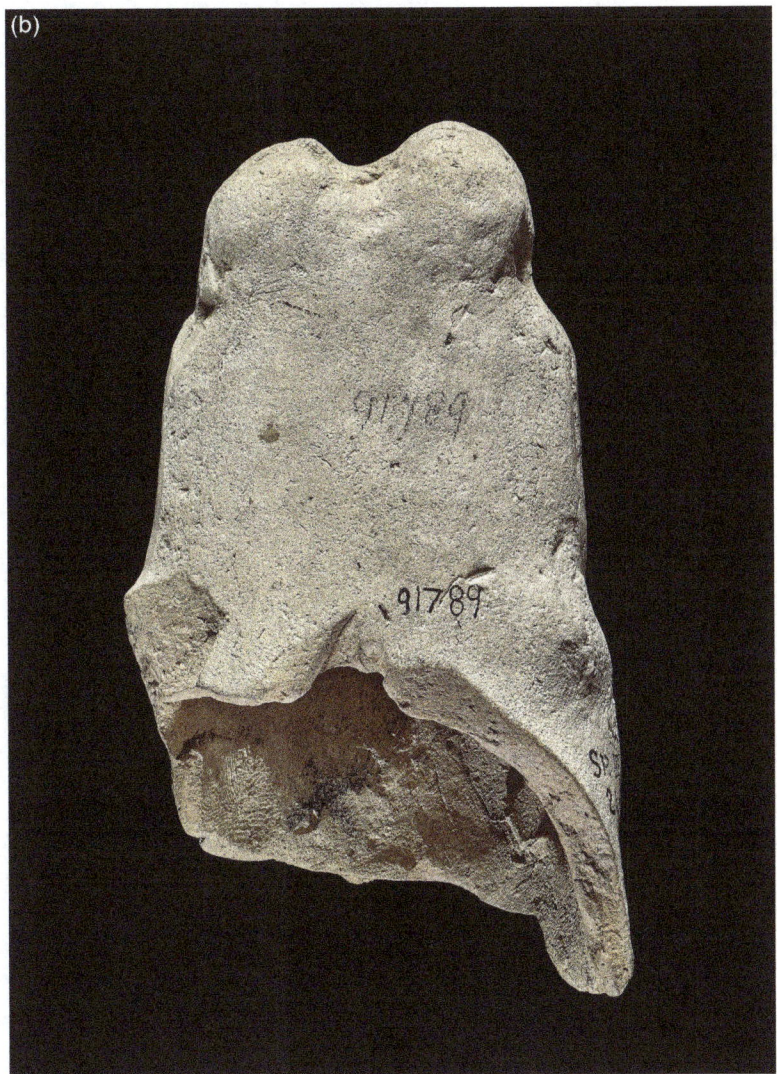

1.13a and b. (cont.)

user, is in control of the situation. Partially clothed figurines are permanently "dressed" – or, rather, "non-undressable" – their clothes cannot be removed, regardless of how flimsy they appear or how tantalizingly they seem ready to slip off the body. Unlike real, living bodies, such figurines persist in their liminal state, regardless of the user's desires and in mockery of the user's greater physical presence and strength. As with the clothed figurines, attempts to overpower the couple depicted in Figure 1.13 and force the consummation of the erotic promise offered by their clothing and pose would lead only to damage of the object and destruction of the fantasy, not to its fulfillment.

Both clothed and partially clothed miniature bodies thus provided a kind of physical closeness that regulated intimacy as much as they supplied it. Tactile interaction that can never truly touch – this frustration of enforced limits on user's actions was an available tool that could be used (and *was* used) to construct ideas of acceptable versus unacceptable access to specific types of bodies and people. These were socially prescribed through the kinds of figurines that were suitable for workshop production and public sale in Hellenistic Babylonia, and reinforced by the widespread use and acceptance of such images by those who acquired the figurines.

Nude Figurines Nude figurines also contributed to such constructs of socially regulated intimacy, though in ways somewhat different from their clothed and partially clothed counterparts. At first glance, nude figurines seem very intimate. They present a bare, unclothed human body to the sight and touch of the figurine user. No drapery or clothing obstructs the most personal gazes and caresses, the illusion of human skin touching figurine "skin." The user could feel in full control over a body that is literally laid bare to his or her whims and desires. That many of these figurines, such as that seen in Figure 1.14, are depicted with anatomical accuracy, heightens the sense of complete access to the body parts of another person. This particular figurine was also created in a double mold with the backside fully modeled, thus the nude body presented can be fully viewed and handled in the round – appreciated and ogled from all sides, touched in many places. The possibilities of bodily access with nude figurines are seen even more clearly in Figure 1.15, where the detailed genitalia of this figurine particularly signaled a kind of rare body-to-body interaction that took place outside the common social realm, or at least within a specific, restricted social sphere, such as the bedroom, brothel, or gymnasion.[107] Such spaces and their activities were explicitly referenced in some nude figurines, such as those depicting male athletes. Nude figurines might even have been used in such spaces – particularly in private rooms of the domestic spaces in which they are routinely found – perhaps enjoyed and caressed largely in secret and providing a similar kind of intimacy that a visual or tactile encounter with a living, nude person would offer.

Yet what appears convincingly to be true intimacy with a miniature body laid bare to the whims of the larger user, unable to protect itself from being handled and viewed in its most private places, was still mediated by and framed within the context of what society deemed appropriate. Such restrictions can be seen even in the bodily poses of such nude figurines, which always prevent access in some ways. For instance, the female figurines seen in Figures 1.14, 1.15, and 4.9 display their breasts to the user yet also limit tactile contact with them. In each figurine, the breasts are partially covered by the figure's hands, which cannot be removed

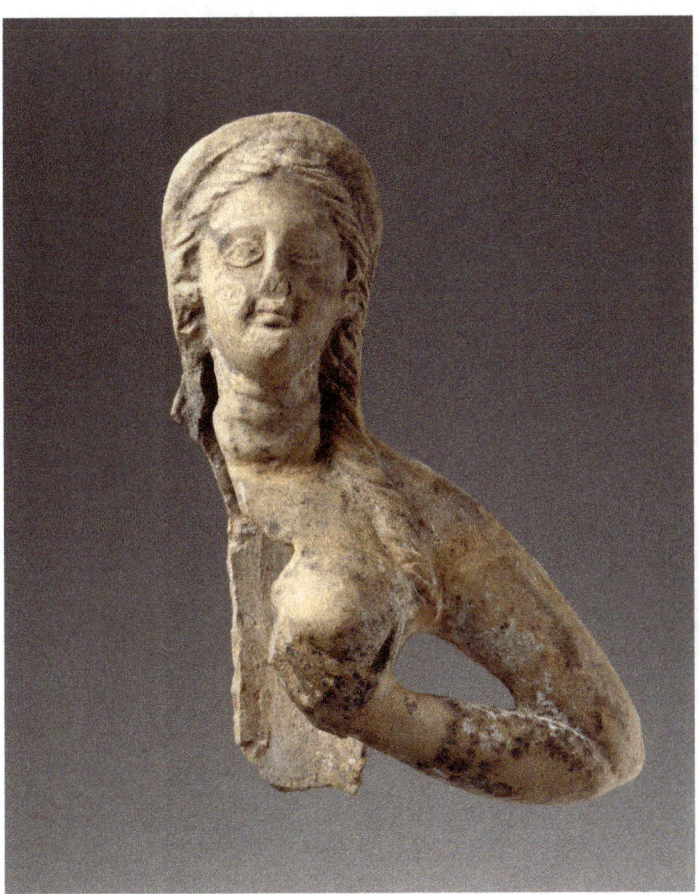

1.14. Nude female figurine, supporting breasts, terracotta, likely from Babylon. Height 14.8 cm. Musée du Louvre (AO 1496a)
Photograph courtesy of Art Resource and the Musée du Louvre.

without breaking the object – and, even if they were, there is no "skin" beneath the hands to be touched.[108] Frequently inaccessible are the spaces between the upper and lower arms, bent as they are against the body; the figurine in Figure 1.14 is a rare exception to this. While the pubic triangle and labia are clearly delineated, the space between the legs is firmly closed, as is any potential access to the actual procreative region of the body. The female figure seen in Figure 1.15 touches her labia – a seemingly erotic gesture that is extremely uncommon in the Hellenistic Babylonian figurine corpus. Yet, even as she might have provocatively encouraged a user's sexual interest, actual access was denied – both the tight closure of the legs and even the placement of the hand, which cannot be moved, prevented both visual and tactile exploration of her genital region.

The archaeological contexts and formal construction of some nude figurines also suggest that their use might have been broader and more public than the

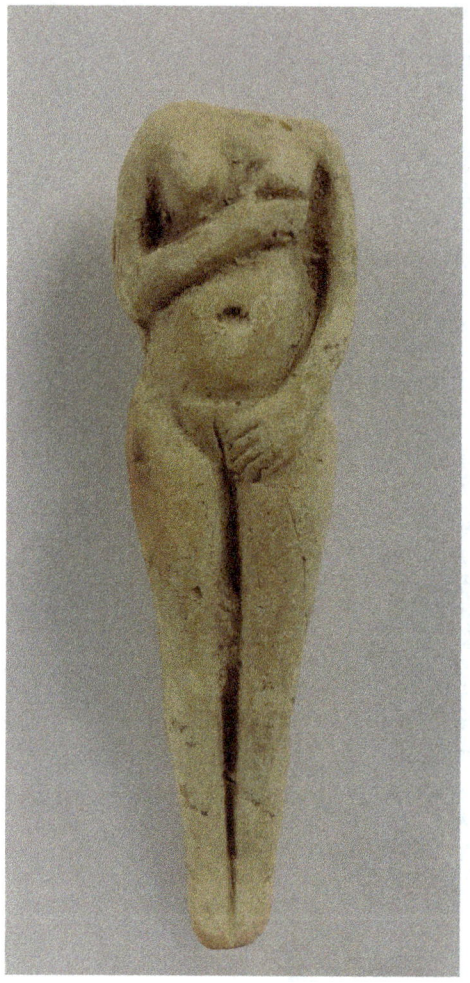

1.15. Standing nude female figurine, supporting breast and touching labia, terracotta, Seleucia-on-the-Tigris. Height 11.4 cm. Kelsey Museum of Archaeology, University of Michigan, Ann Arbor (KM 16059)
Photograph courtesy of the Kelsey Museum of Archaeology.

restricted spaces in which living people in Hellenistic Babylonia were allowed to be naked. For instance, at Seleucia-on-the-Tigris, nude female figurines were excavated not just from houses and workshop areas, but also from the area of the Seleucid Heroon and a temple near Tell 'Umar.[109] Such contexts indicate that at least some nude figurines would have been seen, and likely been used, in public. From the perspective of figurine construction, the base platform of the nude figurine seen in Figure 4.8, which was modeled as one with the figure and on which the figure's feet stand, indicates that this figurine was primarily intended for display, rather than more intimate use as an erotic tactile object.

A more public, display-oriented use for these nude figurines is unsurprising given both the Babylonian and Greek precedents for depicting naked bodies. Nude female figurines had been created and used in Babylonia for millennia prior to the Hellenistic period; some of the earliest examples of Mesopotamian figurines are very similar in form, pose, and nudity to the Hellenistic Babylonian figurines just discussed, with a strongly frontal posture, direct forward gaze, hands supporting the breasts, elaborated genitalia, and legs held tightly together.[110] Male nudity was more problematic in Mesopotamian art, as will be discussed in Chapter 4. Although stylistically different, Greek tradition also embraced the depiction of the nude body. Male nudity was the more common focus of Greek sculpture, with female nudes (albeit lacking in elaborated genitalia[111]) becoming more popular in the late Classical and Hellenistic periods.[112] Members of both cultures were likely familiar and comfortable with sculpted nude bodies circulating in more public contexts than those in which living human nudity would have been appropriate.

In this way, nude figurines in Hellenistic Babylonia were deeply social and agentive. Like their pre-Hellenistic Babylonian and Greek precedents, they portrayed to users what contemporary society thought about naked bodies, how men and women might look under their clothes, and the parameters of ideal body types. The nude figurines thus accomplished the work of social communication about ideals and norms that actual people were not able to fully accomplish themselves. Rather than directly comparing one's own naked body with the bodies of peers – which may or may not have been viewable at all (depending on the rules for gymnasia participation and other social customs), and certainly not viewable from all angles, in all postures, and in all contexts – figurines substituted as more easily accessible representations of nude bodies. In the fact that they were created and sold socially, subject to the pressures of community norms and marketplace economy, figurines could also be trusted as commonly accepted ideals of what nude bodies looked like. Indeed, they were perhaps more authentic in their generalization than a living nude person would have been, whose body would have been shaped by individual idiosyncrasies of genetics, diet, health, and personal habits, rather than forced to conform (as only representations and images can) to a more rigid, socially agreed-upon ideal.[113] In their accessibility and perfection, figurines were a particularly effective form of citational precedent – visual quotations of personhood, which could be "cited" by living members of Hellenistic Babylonian society in the ways that they carried their bodies, moved, gestured, arranged their hair, participated in intimate activities, attended to hygiene, and so forth.[114] The figurine does not show what people looked like, but rather what people might aspire to.

Nude figurines thus had perhaps the most powerful social role of all, in that they showed the nudity that people themselves (usually) could not, and revealed ideas (and, in some cases, ideals) that living bodies could never fully reflect. It is because of this that I prefer to use the term "nude" more often than "naked," "undressed," or "bare" when describing these figurines. "Nude" has a sense of sociality to it, as a juxtaposition to clothes and a possibility of operating in the same arena as clothed bodies. The nudity of these figurines is constructed rather than natural, since modeled terracotta bodies do not have an organic state of undress, no "birthday suit" as a primordial state. Their nudity was deliberate, a choice made within a context of clothed options, and often more painstaking to create in miniature form than clothed versions of the same body type. The naturalness of the nude figure as an organic, authentic body was an illusion, in much the same way that the intimacy it offered was carefully constructed.

"MINIATURIZATION AFFECT" OF FIGURINES, CONCLUDED

Miniature objects were capable of offering different kinds of access and of demonstrating differing levels of receptivity to vision and touch. While all miniatures as *objects* were subject to the whims and desires of their larger, more powerful users, touching the surface of the object (the figurine) was not necessarily the same thing as touching the surface of the depicted figure, the representation (the miniature human body). Figurines that made it impossible for the miniature body to be touched could rebuff intimacy in a way more concrete and final than even a real man or woman is capable of — living people can always be undressed, by force if necessary. In this way, figurines had intensely powerful social agency: serving as surrogates for boundaries, enforcing inviolable limits on unwanted touches, and providing cues about the social rules of proper conduct.

This is why I argue that figurines only *seem* to provide intimacy to their users. Moments of seeming intimacy with miniatures — whether intimacy mostly satisfied, intimacy initiated but ultimately denied, or intimacy almost completely prevented — were all constrained by the object. In turn, that object was manufactured in — and in response to the pressures and expectations of — the broader social world of the craftsperson's shop, the marketplace economy, and community norms. This entanglement of miniatures and broader social life is a benefit to our understanding of figurines, as it helps alleviate concerns about how and when figurines were used — and if people were observed in their use or could engage with miniatures privately – as a precondition for knowing whether or not that use of miniatures was "social." All use of objects that were produced and purchased outside the home is, to some degree, social. That some of these miniature objects might have been specifically designed for seemingly intimate use made society's intrusion into the personal space of the home, body, and psyche all the more penetrating. Such seemingly intimate miniatures thus have the potential to be deeply revealing of their broader social imaginary. That is the project of this volume.

CHAPTER TWO

FASCINATION WITH THE TINY: INTERACTING WITH FIGURINES

Among all the figurines discussed in this book, interactive figurines – such as those with movable pieces, openly tactile bodies, or other features that invited user participation – would seem to have been particularly intimate. Such figurines encouraged close looking and touching for long periods of time, luring the user into another, miniature world. The ability of a user to "act" in miniature, using the figurine body as a collaborator and prosthesis, created the illusion that this tiny, fascinating world was real – real movement, real interactions, and real events were possible there. The figurines discussed in this chapter invited and encouraged scalar displacement, almost to the point that the human user's real-scale, and real-life, identity would seem to slip away, being temporarily forgotten as he or she became "lost" in the fantasy of tiny play.

Yet even though the fascinations created by interactive figurines were largely personal encounters, they were also inherently social. Indeed, it was through their reference to larger-scale society that figurines held much of their power to captivate and to comfort. A user's ability to manipulate the miniature bodies of particularly interactive figurines impacted his or her perceptions of real-life experiences, granting potent feelings of empowerment over the outside world. Destabilizing social events, such as war, were made to feel manageable and controllable through interactive soldier and cavalry figurines – figurines with such a compelling affect and appeal that they were used not only within domestic spaces, but also accompanied the bodies of both children and adults into their graves. Sexually desirable bodies, almost exclusively representing adult women, could be made to pose and gesture in ways appealing to their owners. The thrill of theatrical performance could be shared by making a puppet-like figurine's legs dance, and by providing the voice for the open mouth of a terracotta mask.

But through the act of manipulating the bodies of these figurines, their owners also performed, and conformed to, the social roles and expectations represented. Desires for fame, power, and sexual gratification could thus be both privately indulged and socially limited. The range of available figurines, and the implicit understanding that other members of the community were also using the same selection of objects, suggested the most socially appropriate avenues for Hellenistic Babylonian individuals to direct such impulses. Thus, although seemingly intimate, figurines that encouraged private and prolonged use were a powerful conduit for the issues of broader society to trespass and impose themselves in the most personal of spaces.

PLAYING WITH FEAR: HORSE RIDERS AND SOLDIERS

The unassuming and nonthreatening size of figurines is crucial to their ability to fascinate. Their diminutive scale suggests that they can be completely overwhelmed and dominated by their user, whose body feels enlarged and empowered in comparison.[1] While authority over tiny objects is seductive regardless of the subject matter depicted, it is particularly alluring when figurines represent animal, human, or supernatural beings that are usually more powerful – physically, cosmically, politically, or socially – than the human user. Such miniatures make the stressful realities of life in the full-size real world more manageable by shrinking intimidating forces to tiny, controllable proportions.[2] Horse riders, who were often depicted as soldiers, were among the most popular terracotta figurines in Hellenistic Babylonia,[3] and are an informative example of such power dynamics with miniature objects.

Abstraction and Play

Many horse rider figurines, such as the example seen in Figure 2.1, were modeled partially or entirely by hand. Facial features could be given crisp form by the use of a mold stamp, and paint could add details of the horse trappings and other features.[4] In general, however, surface embellishment and anatomical detailing do not seem to have been primary concerns. In some cases, the bodies of the horses and riders blend together, with the rider's legs fusing to the forelegs of the mount, even to the point of disappearing altogether. Much might have been added in paint, but as most of these figurines currently appear, the sex of either the rider or horse is often not indicated, clothes are generally

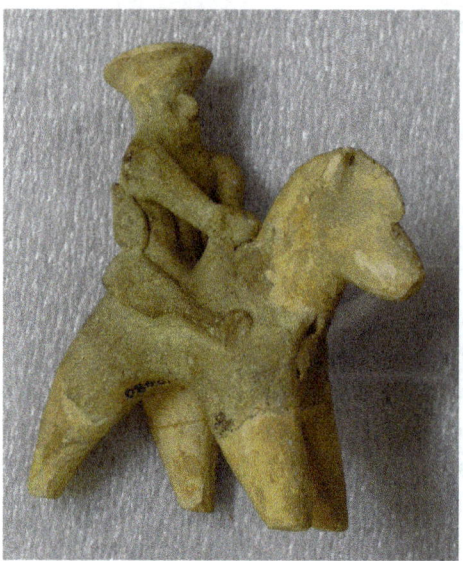

2.1. Handmade horse and rider figurine, terracotta, Nippur. Height: 12.5 cm. University of Pennsylvania Museum of Archaeology and Anthropology (B 15480)
Photograph by author, printed courtesy of the University of Pennsylvania Museum.

assumed to exist but are not explicitly depicted, and further indications of weaponry, saddle, skin color, hair color, and other details may have been left completely to the user's imagination. Even if every handmade horse rider was lavishly painted, modeled details of anatomy, such as the joints of the horse's legs or the tapering of fetlocks to powerful hooves, would necessarily remain absent.

Such abstractions and omissions of information – a feature shared, to greater or lesser extent, by all miniatures[5] – would have encouraged the user to supply the missing details from his or her imagination. It would also have focused attention on the specific information that such figurines *did* provide. The basics of horse, rider, and the activity of horse riding are certainly specified; beyond this, the physical durability of the object and the flexible identification of the figure present themselves. When all four horse legs are preserved, most horse-rider figurines easily stand alone. The width of the horse body and the sturdiness of the unelaborated human torso make secure grasping points for the user's hand. While not indestructible, these figurines are remarkably robust for such a complex composition in terracotta. Tactility, movement, and play all seem to have been the focus here.

The seemingly obvious explanation for these features is that such horse riders were designed to be children's toys[6] – as, indeed, they might have been. Yet, such an explanation is not an end to the analysis, but rather a beginning. As scholarship on the archaeology of childhood has explored, objects dismissed as "toys" can reveal a great deal about the society in which children are encouraged to use them.[7] First of all, children *are* members of society with the power to influence and change their environment[8] – in many cases, exerting that influence through their play and experimentation with toys.[9] In the ancient world particularly, children were also more present and visible in a larger range of social situations than they are today.[10] Playing in the street, completing chores in their parents' shop, participating in public festivals, or training in apprenticeships and schools – all of these situations integrated children and their belongings into the wider social world.[11]

Toys themselves also have broader social lives beyond just interacting with their child owners.[12] Adults create toys, adults supply toys to children, and adults demonstrate the proper mechanical functioning and imaginative potential of different kinds of toys. Adults can spend their own time with toys, sometimes even when the child is not physically present, in order to fix toys when broken, locate toys when lost, and clean up toys if they are left on the floor. Crucially, adults also play with children, suggesting through example and explicit instruction that certain kinds of play are appropriate and other kinds are inappropriate (including play based on the age, gender, class, and status of the child). This is not to over-sentimentalize childhood in the ancient world, which was likely experienced through much different conceptual parameters than what most modern, Western children would recognize.[13] Moments of play might have been fleeting, interspersed between the performance of more practical tasks and work, and with less consistent oversight and intervention than many modern children receive. The acknowledgment that childhood and adulthood were likely less separated as unique states of existence in the ancient world than they are today is a strong argument for considering toys as consequential to Hellenistic Babylonian society as a whole.

The connection that toys provide between adults and children can be powerfully seen in Figure 2.2, a handmade rider figurine from Nippur. While the horse is now missing, the figure's arms (since broken at the elbows) arch out and down, probably to grasp a horse. The right leg flares out at an extreme angle before bending downward, probably to fit easily on a horse's back. The rider's hips are asymmetrical, with the left hip much higher than the right. While visually incongruous, the result of this anatomical distortion is that the figurine can be effortlessly held – my right thumb and forefinger easily fit the figurine around the waist from the back. To be precise: the indentation for the forefinger fits my hand perfectly, while my thumb is slightly too big. The hands that made this object, squishing the clay of the rider's waist to create a permanent handhold, must have been of a similar size as mine. While this is obviously an unscientific measurement, the size of human hands varies greatly with age[14] – thus this was certainly not the work of a young child. Did a parent craft this as a plaything for his or her son or daughter? Did a teenager make this for a sibling – or, perhaps for himself or herself? It is unlikely we will ever know

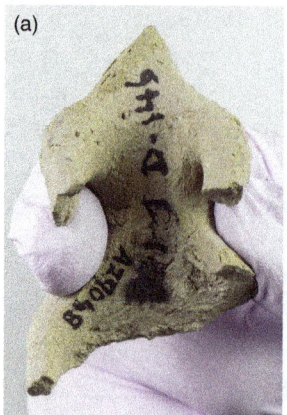 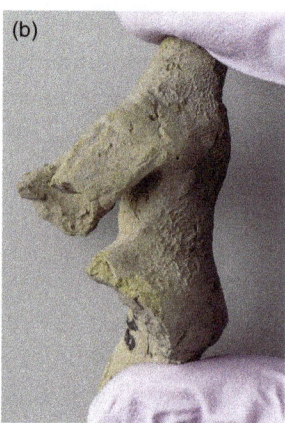

2.2a and b. Front and side of handmade horse and rider figurine, terracotta, Nippur. Locus TA Foundation II between 6 and 9 (likely Neo-Babylonian or Achaemenid period). Height: 5.2 cm. Oriental Institute (OI A29048)
Photographs courtesy of the Oriental Institute of the University of Chicago.

for certain; indeed, even this object's identification as a toy is conjectural. If anything, the material evidence of the object itself locates it in the world of adults – who may, perhaps, have shared it with children.

The archaeological context for this figurine provides some additional evidence: it was excavated at Nippur, in Locus TA Foundation II between rooms 6 and 9. TA II was a Neo-Babylonian or Achaemenid house[15]; thus, this figurine likely predates the Hellenistic period, and was used in a domestic space. Yet, despite dating earlier in time than the focus of this book, this rider figurine is strikingly similar to many handmade horse riders found in every major corpus of Hellenistic Babylonian figurines: Babylon, Seleucia-on-the-Tigris, Uruk, and Nippur.[16] Specific details could vary; some, such as the figurine from Babylon pictured in Figure 2.3, have long beards and peaked headgear (possibly a version of the Phrygian or Scythian cap, or the later Parthian *kolah* or tiara[17]) that may reference Parthian riders. Others, such as the figurine from Nippur pictured in Figure 2.1, have a flat-topped hat that was more closely connected with the Hellenistic world; possible identifications for this hat include the *petasos*, a broad-brimmed Greek sun hat,[18] or the *kausia*,[19] a flat, rounded hat associated in the Hellenistic period with Alexander and his Macedonian successors, generals, and military.[20] Still other horse rider figurines retain the vagueness and abstraction seen in Figure 5.15, with their failure to specify sex or culture opening the possibilities to the user's imagination. Overall, the ubiquity of these durable horse riders, which can easily be grasped and galloped across a table or floor of a home, point to their enduring intersection with issues and identities that retained their importance from Achaemenid through Parthian times.

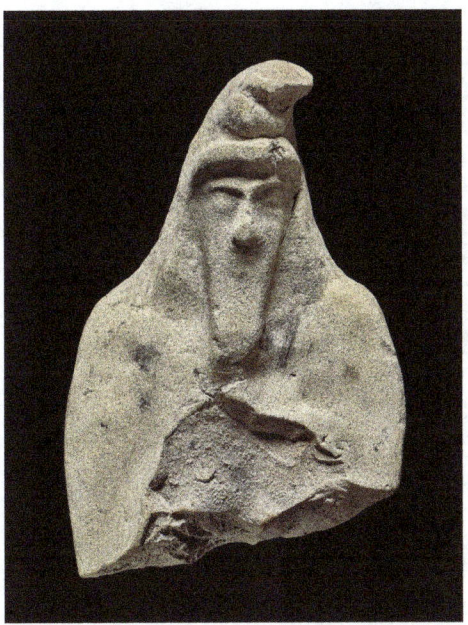

2.3. Male figurine, likely a rider modeled with the horse (now broken), terracotta, Babylon. Height: 8.5 cm. British Museum (BM 81-3-24-349)
Photograph © The Trustees of the British Museum.

Mounting the Horse, Arming the Soldier

This robust tradition was supplemented in the Hellenistic period by mold-made figurines of horse riders, which were functionally similar to the hand-made horse riders but with an added level of surface detail. Among these were an even more interactive version of horse rider figurine, wherein the riders were molded separately from their horses (see Figure 2.4). The idea of "horse" and "rider" as two separate terracotta entities was not, in itself, new. Indeed, handmade one-piece figurines show evidence that their horses and riders were also made separately; indentation marks on fragmentary examples indicate that the two pieces were attached while the clay was in a soft, but semi-dry, state. The two-piece molded versions thus do not differ in their initial conceptualization of horse and rider as distinct figures, but rather in their impermanent jointure of the two.

Yet, despite their existence as distinct objects, the construction of these molded riders demands unification with their mounts. In particular, their widely spread legs look out of proportion when the figurine is viewed alone, encouraging the placement of the figurine on the back of a terracotta horse, as seen in Figure 2.5. When united with their horses, the riders' exaggerated stance becomes visually congruous and the overly long legs serve a practical function of balance, preventing the rider from easily slipping off. This

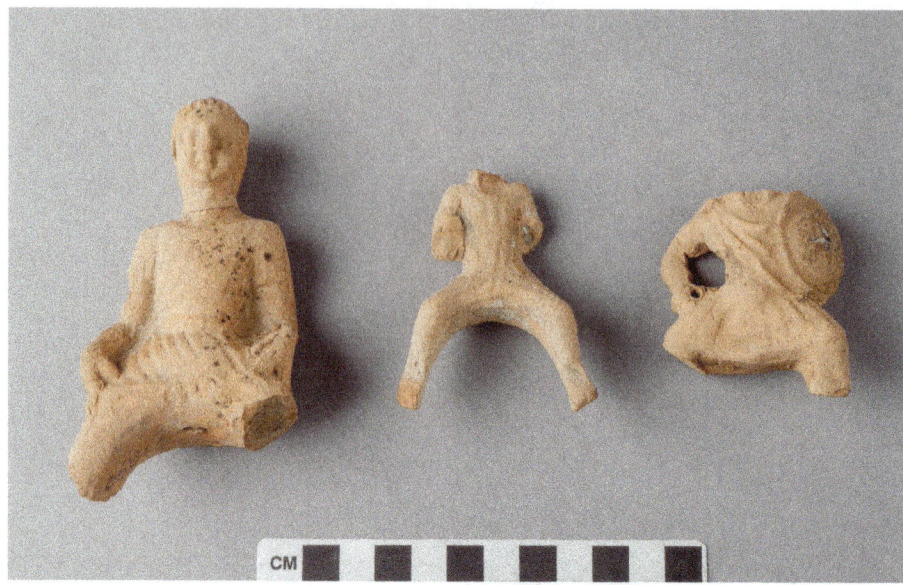

2.4. Three male horse rider figurines, terracotta, Seleucia-on-the-Tigris. Kelsey Museum of Archaeology, University of Michigan, Ann Arbor (from left to right: KM 14053+16116; KM 14017; KM 14496). Height of Figurine KM 14053+16116: 11.6 cm. Height of Figurine KM 14017: 7.3 cm. Height of Figurine KM 14496: 6.6 cm.
Photograph courtesy of the Kelsey Museum of Archaeology.

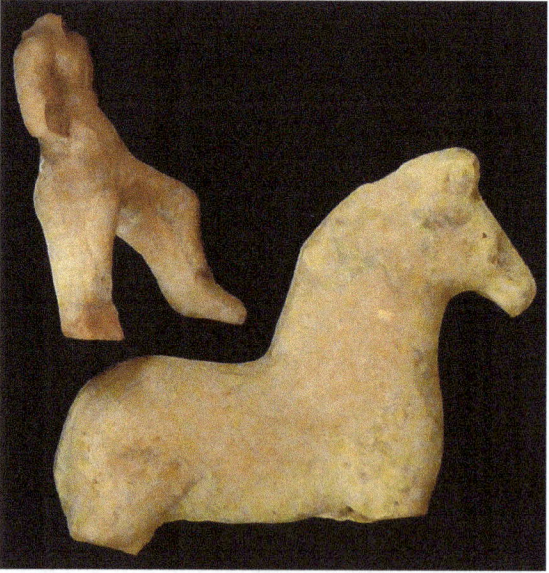

2.5. Horse and rider figurines, posed as if in use, terracotta, Seleucia-on-the-Tigris. Kelsey Museum of Archaeology, University of Michigan, Ann Arbor (Rider: KM 14017 and Horse: TM 1929.98/KM 2018.01.0030) Height of KM 14017: 7.3 cm. Height of TM 1929.98/KM 2018.01.0030: 8.5 cm.
Photograph by author, printed courtesy of the Kelsey Museum of Archaeology.

functionality was clearly intrinsic to the purpose of these figurines, as the long, thin legs are otherwise impractical to create in a mold and are particularly susceptible to breakage. Pinched waists on several riders make easy grasping points for the human hand, facilitating the user's encounter.

The interactivity evident with the mold-made horse and rider pairs parallels the play of horse riding encouraged by the one-piece handmade figurines, but with added specificity that directs user attention to a particular activity. To wit, it was not the "riding" that was made most interactive in the two-piece figures, but the "mounting." Indeed, it is much easier to playact the *riding* of a horse with a figurine wherein the horse and rider have been fused, the two operating as if with one mind and one body in imitation of all great equestrianship. That the horse and rider seen in Figure 2.1 cannot be separated also meant that – except in cases of extreme damage to the figurine – neither component would be lost, leaving behind a functionless half as a disappointing index of that loss, marking play that could not be realized and fun that would not be had. The two-piece molded figurines risk that loss for the sake of an increased interactivity that, ironically, makes them more difficult to use. Balancing the rider on the horse while at play is challenging; even if the two pieces were semi-permanently affixed using plaster (traces of which are occasionally preserved on the backs of the horses[21]), the join spot would nevertheless be more fragile than with the handmodeled figurines. Some degree of delicacy would be needed when using these figurines to playact a gallop – which calls into question both who used them, and what they were used for.

While toys do not necessarily need to be robust in order to be successfully used by children, both the fragile construction of these horse riders and their archaeological contexts indicate their use by adults as well. For instance, horse rider figurines have been occasionally found in the graves of both adults and children.[22] In particular, the figurine seen on the right in Figure 2.4 was found between two graves buried beneath the floor of a residential space at Seleucia-on-the-Tigris (Room 97, Section B, Block G6). Each grave housed the remains of a male adolescent or young man. The skeleton in Grave No. 202 is described as a "youth" based on the lack of wisdom teeth; however, the considerable length of the femur (43 cm) would indicate full adult height. The skeleton in Grave No. 203 was estimated to be 15 years old, and measures 30 cm at the femur.[23] In this funerary association with young adults, it is possible that the figurine was understood as a toy, deposited as a sentimental reminder of their recent childhoods. Yet, it seems equally, perhaps even more, probable that a miniature horse rider might have represented the current or intended occupation of the deceased young men,[24] or the worship of a mounted deity, such as one of the Dioscuri. Note that funerary contexts for terracotta figurines of any type are very rare in Hellenistic Babylonia; like other figurines, horse riders were generally discovered in domestic or refuse contexts. This indicates that, as with other figurines, horse riders were responding to widespread needs throughout broad segments of the Hellenistic Babylonian population.

The types of interactivity that the two-piece horse rider figurines encouraged may offer some clue as to what those needs might have been. In addition to inspiring the user to enact the "mounting" of a horse rather than "riding" it, other kinds of interactivity were sometimes encouraged. For instance, the rider discussed in the previous paragraph, discovered between the graves of two young men, was depicted wearing a skirted tunic and the *chlamys* of a Greek horseman,[25] gripping a round shield, and holding his right fist close to his thigh. That right fist was pierced through with a hole to allow the insertion of another object, now missing. The figurine's martial costume and shield suggest a weapon as the obvious choice to fill that hole, the emptiness of which is vividly incomplete and calls out for user assistance. In attending to that demand for interaction, the user seems to have been left with considerable agency. Whether to supply the rider with a weapon or to leave his hand empty was only the first possible choice – and perhaps not even a binary one at that, as other, nonviolent objects could presumably have been inserted should the user wish to divert from the thematic design of the object. If a weapon was indeed chosen, that selection would open up the possibility of several additional choices. What kind of weapon? A spear? A sword? What type or design should be followed in creating that weapon, and from what materials (wood, terracotta, metal) should it be made? Is one weapon sufficient, or should multiple weapons be fashioned, in order to exchange them during play? These, and likely myriad other, questions were presented by that small empty hole. In this way, the hole functioned similarly to abstraction in the handmade horse rider figurines, where the lack of information encouraged user engagement and compelled the user to exert imaginative – or, in this case, practical – effort to fill the gaps. Agency for the user comes at the price of mental and physical exertion.

In the case of this mounted warrior, that price was not only the human labor required to acquire or fashion a weapon and the materials used to make it, but also a certain submission to the figurine's idea of what constituted the "important" aspects of horse riding. The real time, effort, and resources expended on filling the hole in the rider's fist elevated that emptiness to prominence over the other details of the figurine and the other potential actions in which it could be engaged. Specifically, the hole in the hand focused user attention on the act of "arming," rather than the act of "fighting." Indeed, the figurine's receptiveness to moments of "arming" do not add tremendous functionality to the object as a "fighting" figure; a more secure socket, with a more permanent attachment for an added weapon, would have been more effective if miniature combat was desired.

Soldier, General, King

The distinction between the preparations for battle versus fighting itself can also be seen in figurines of soldiers. Many soldier figurines are depicted in static frontal poses that do not indicate that the figure is fighting or in battle. For instance, the figurine seen in Figure 2.6 does not appear to be moving at all, but simply standing at attention and displaying his weapon and/or shield. This soldier was made in a single mold with an unmodeled backside, further indicating a frontal display. The double mold could also be used to create such standing warriors; in either case, the base of the figurine was often flared in order for the figure to stand alone. The materiality and design of these figurines would have directed playacting to moments of battle preparation – standing at attention, marching, and troops in review – rather than the melee of combat. That is if, indeed, such interactivity was intended at all – many of the soldier figurines do not overtly suggest manual engagement and play as the user's

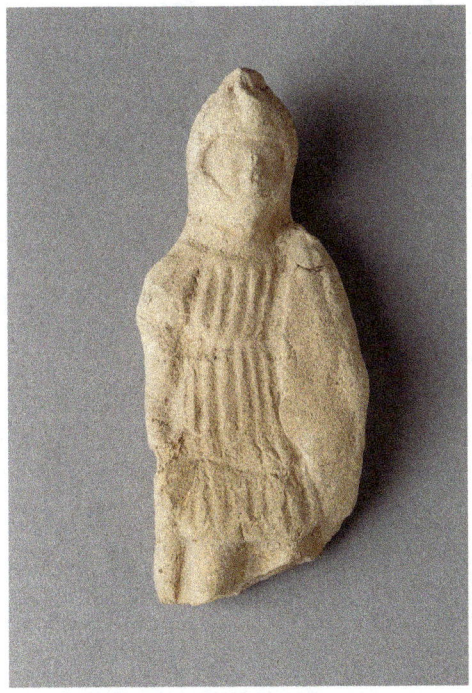

2.6. Soldier figurine, terracotta, Seleucia-on-the-Tigris. Height: 11.7 cm. Kelsey Museum of Archaeology, University of Michigan, Ann Arbor (KM 15711)
Photograph courtesy of the Kelsey Museum of Archaeology.

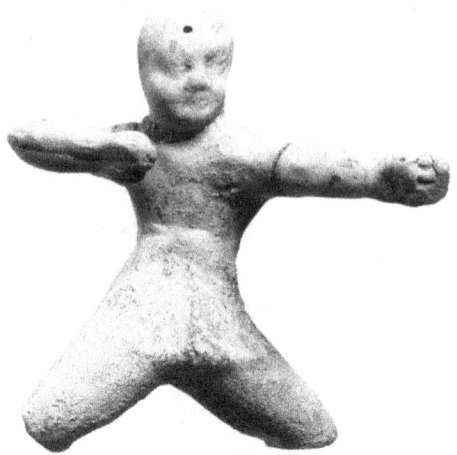

2.7. Archer figurine, terracotta, Seleucia-on-the-Tigris. Height: 7 cm. Turin Excavations at Seleucia (S11,223)
Photograph courtesy of Roberta Menegazzi.

primary mode of access, and assumptions should not be made based simply on their martial motif.

A few archer figurines – perhaps six known examples from Seleucia-on-the-Tigris – do seem more interactive and depict the body in a more energetic pose. For instance, the figurine seen in Figure 2.7 depicts the warrior or hunter in an active stance, with the left arm extended to grasp the bow and the right arm drawing the bowstring taut before shooting. The legs are widely splayed, adding to the sense of drama and vigorous action. Although a bow and arrow would need to be added separately or imagined by the user, the figurine nevertheless focused user attention on the act of fighting or hunting through its undeniably aggressive pose. This figure is clearly *using* the weapon, not just *receiving* it, and thus the emphasis in this figurine runs counter to the general trend in both the soldier and mold-made horse rider figurines to focus attention on the preparations for battle rather than their fruition. This divergence from the trend may account for the relative lack of popularity of these fighting figurines. The archer figurines from Seleucia-on-the-Tigris were all part of the same mold series and were all excavated from a deposit associated with a public/commercial area of the city, and possibly a specific figurine workshop.[26] The relative lack of such figurines in contexts indicating their purchase and use at Seleucia-on-the-Tigris, as well as their absence at other Hellenistic Babylonian cities, may point to a corresponding lack of user interest in the kinds of interactivity that they demanded.

While particular variations on the horse rider or soldier motif (such as the archers) may have been somewhat unsuccessful, in general such figurines were among the most popular in Hellenistic Babylonia.[27] They continued

Achaemenid and earlier traditions of horse rider figurine use in the region,[28] and are attested in Hellenistic levels in all of the major Babylonian cities. In seeking an explanation for this widespread appeal of horse rider and soldier figurines, I return to the power that miniatures grant people, by virtue of our larger scale, to be masters over their tiny worlds. Engaging with a figurine's interactive features, the user could pretend to be a soldier – or perhaps, empowered by his or her authoritatively superior size, the user could pretend to be the commander who directs soldiers on the battlefield. In this more grandiose role, the user could choose whether to put the miniature soldier on the horse (and thus send him into battle) or to leave the horse in his stable – power usually possessed only by kings and generals. Many of the figurines leave open the possibility of whether they were to be used in a simulation of war at all. The empty hole in the rider's hand could be supplied with something other than a weapon. The rider could be moved from a battle-ready steed to an alternate mount; indeed, figurines of boys riding sheep, as well as sheep figurines that could accommodate separately made riders,[29] opened the possibility that the user could make a less violent, perhaps even humorous, choice. Mundane as they might seem, such choices paralleled – and, to some degree, mimed – perhaps one of the gravest and most consequential choices a Hellenistic king could make: should we go to war? Actual Seleucid and Parthian kings answered this question in the affirmative on a regular basis: a fact that the residents of the Hellenistic Babylonian cities were no doubt familiar with, and because of which they may have routinely suffered.[30] The focus that many of these figurines placed on the moments of mounting and arming, rather than fighting, suggests that this commanding control over the miniature and the prospect of high-ranking decision-making – along with the opportunity to perhaps make a different choice than was made by the real-life king – was particularly alluring.

The handmade horse rider figurines, with their accommodations to the user's hand and sturdy construction, similarly offered the potential for control through seemingly low-stakes play.[31] Unlike real soldiers in the heat of battle, who do not always precisely follow the intentions or commands of their leaders, the handmade horse riders offered their stability and dependability in submission to the user. The permanent fixture of rider to horse, to the extent that their bodies were often melded together as one, promised that the cavalryman would not be unhorsed nor abandon his post. Taking physical control over this maximally compliant little soldier and his steed miniaturized the battle – as well as any dangerous enemies – making such conflicts and threats seem smaller and more understandable. By bringing the battle "to life" in the tactile immediacy of the miniature horse rider, the historical reality of any particular war was erased; instead, the potential was opened for new narratives to be played out within the "presentness" of miniature scale.[32] Positive outcomes could be imagined, achieved by the "perfect" soldiers who completely followed the commands of the user-*cum*-king.[33] Any fear associated with war was twice displaced: once by promoting the user from commoner to commander, and again by promoting the user to almost god-like scale over miniature armies that had become literal playthings. This illusion of power over the wars that commonly afflicted Hellenistic Babylonia might have been especially seductive, and could explain these figurines' popularity.

A Diverse Army

In spite of the political and militaristic tensions which these figurines expose, the miniature horse riders do not provide evidence of strain between cultural groups. For instance, the figurine seen in Figure 2.4 (right) appears culturally hybrid, with a round shield and tunic derived from Near Eastern tradition, but wearing a Greek *chlamys*. It was also made using a Greek double-mold manufacturing technique and detailed modeling style.[34] Other mixtures of military garments, armaments, and styles were common throughout the Hellenistic Babylonian horse rider figurine corpus, and these combinations were not strongly correlated with any particular cultural group.[35] Even the so-called Parthian riders, with their distinctive peaked caps and long beards, can be difficult to categorize in terms of ethnicity. As seen in Figure 2.3, their garments are mostly unelaborated, leaving the user to imaginatively supply the missing details with whatever particular costume he or she desired. Additionally, their supposedly specific "Parthian" features cannot be easily distinguished from Achaemenid horse rider figurines – providing a visual continuity across time, space, and culture that also points to a lack of defined ethnic specificity. The horse rider figurines thus seem to have encouraged feelings of empowerment that were not particularly connected with cultural identities.

The lack of cultural specificity among the horse rider figurines likely mirrored the ethnic and cultural diversity of the members of the real-world Seleucid army (including the cavalry), which drew upon the military recruitment strategies established by the Achaemenid Persians and utilized the available manpower of the entire Seleucid empire.[36] This is in striking contrast with modern scholarships' "invention" of Seleucid disquiet with the employment of Mesopotamian, Persian, and other Near Eastern soldiers in their armies.[37] This relationship between multicultural militaristic figurines and cultural heterogeneity within the armed forces may have been paralleled in Ptolemaic Egypt, where the military was similarly diverse.[38] Cavalry forces were a major component of the Parthian army[39] and some of the horse rider figurines may reflect that reality; however, social ideas of warfare in the Parthian era would also have encompassed local and mercenary forces, which were often relied upon (including in Mesopotamia) in the ethnically diverse Parthian Empire.[40]

In reflecting that multicultural reality, even to the point of depicting individual riders in culturally hybrid or indistinct dress, the horse rider figurines suggest that Hellenistic Babylonians were familiar and comfortable with an ethnically heterogeneous military – or, at least, they were supposed to be. Such figurines allowed the desire for martial power and security from the destabilizing effects of war to be privately indulged, but they also placed a social limitation on that fantasy. The range of available figurines, and the knowledge that other people were also buying and using them, reinforced the idea that it was not socially acceptable to attribute victory and military prowess only to one particular ethnic or cultural group. Interactivity and play made the message more personal, compelling the user to not only observe but also reenact and participate in that vision of a culturally diverse army. This agency on the part of the object could easily have gone unnoticed – indeed, because the miniature horse riders evoked primal emotions and grandiose aspirations, they likely left the user intoxicated with his or her own sense of power rather than cognizant of being acted upon. Thus, the combination of intimacy and engagement seductively offered by interactive horse rider figurines can be understood both as a vehicle for the creation of a private refuge and yet, at the same time, as a subtle (perhaps even insidious) tool for the dissemination of the broader social contract.

THE GAZE AND THE CARESS: SEXUALIZED RELATIONSHIPS WITH FIGURINES

To further explore how figurines enforced social norms by dictating private experience, I turn now to one of the most private experiences of all: sexual attraction and arousal. The analysis of miniature sexed bodies as inspiring feelings, as well as outcomes, of sexual arousal, intimacy, intercourse, and fertility, is routine (and, indeed, somewhat overplayed[41]) within the field of figurine studies. As will be further discussed in Chapter 4, not all female figurines – indeed, not even all nude female figurines – in Hellenistic Babylonia lend themselves to such an analysis. What distinguishes the figurines discussed in this section from other female figurines is the ways in which they encouraged interactions from their users. Exaggeration of sexual anatomy was portrayed in ways that were accessible to both sight and touch. In many cases, the arms of the figurines were jointed and impermanently attached, encouraging the user to manipulate and pose them. These specific kinds of interactivity suggest that these figurines created a very particular kind of human-object engagement, and were deployed for a very particular purpose.

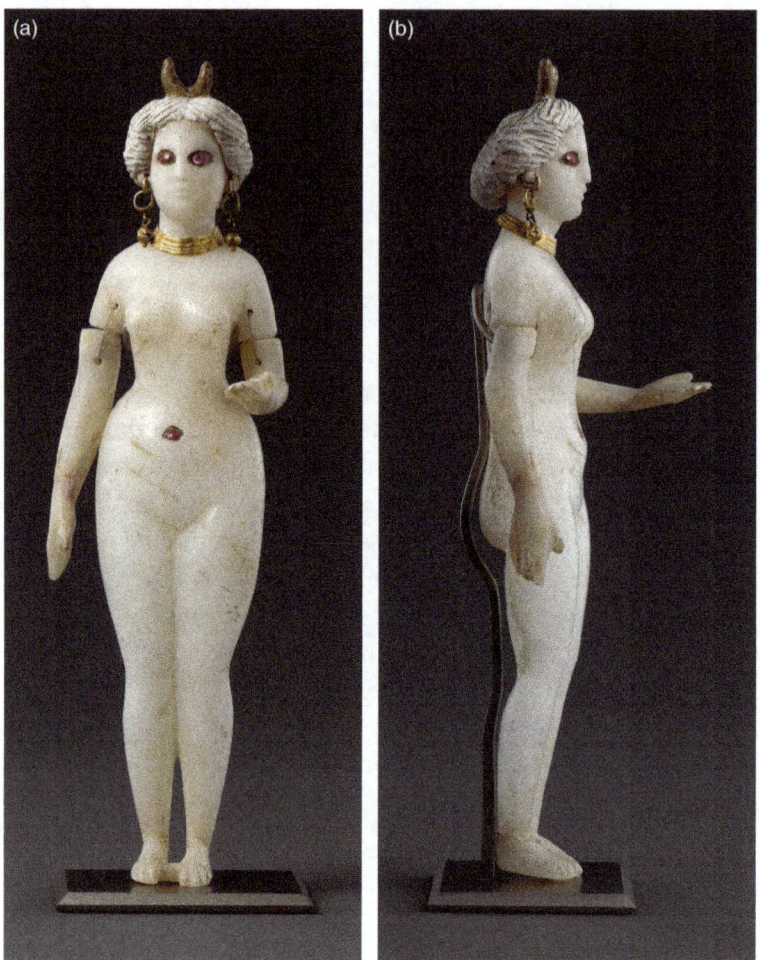

2.8a, b, and c. Front, side and back of nude standing female figurine with articulated arms, alabaster with gold incrustations and rubies, Babylon. Height: 25 cm. Musée du Louvre (AO 20127) Photographs courtesy of Art Resource and the Musée du Louvre.

Movable Arms

As seen in the alabaster figurine from Babylon pictured in Figure 2.8, most female figurines with movable arms stand with a directly frontal posture and gaze. In this instance, the figure's stucco hair is softly swept back in a rolled chignon, on top of which a crescent symbol is displayed. Her oval face has delicate features that contrast with the large eyes inlaid with bright red rubies. These gemstones endowed the object not only with greater value and exoticism (the rubies likely came from Myanmar via sea trade[42]), but also a penetrating gaze. The black bitumen that adheres the rubies to the alabaster appears as an encircling ring around each gemstone, outlining the eye in the fashion of kohl cosmetics and calling further attention to the intensity of her stare. Exaggeration is a theme of the figure's head adornment: the gold earrings that hang from her ears are extremely large for

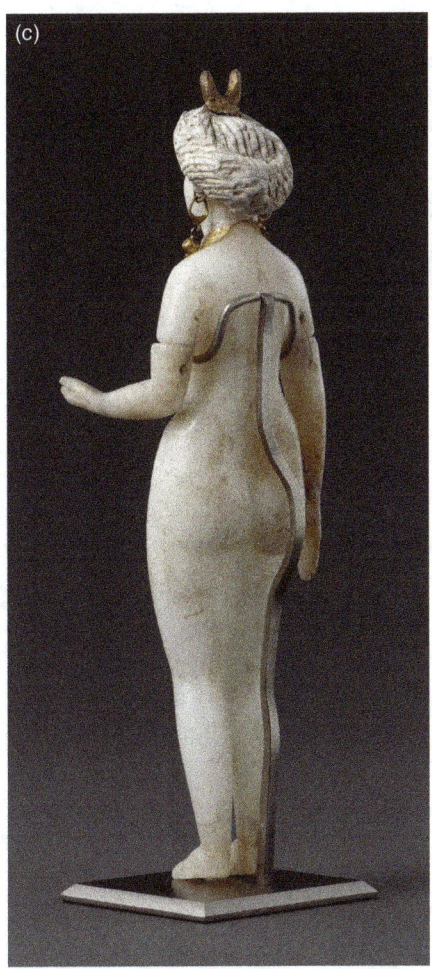

2.8a, b, and c. (cont.)

the figurine's scale, and several bands of a gold necklace tightly encircle a neck that is scarcely narrower than her waist. The use of large size and composite materials were distinctively Mesopotamian sculptural strategies to attract user attention, convey a sense of importance, and even embody divine radiance.[43]

Yet, despite their colorful and exotic luxury, the adornment of the head and neck were not this figurine's only eye-catching qualities. Slim shoulders curve down to upper arms that are severed and pierced with holes. Threads of gold wire originally looped through these holes to connect the body with movable lower arms.[44] The figure's right arm is held to her side, with the open hand parallel to the body; the figure's left arm is bent at the elbow, with the forearm held out in front of the figure, hand open with palm upward. The torso of the figure displays small, firm breasts and a narrow waist accentuated by a large navel inlaid with another ruby gemstone.[45] The ample hips curve down to rounded thighs, with only slight indications of a crease delineating a pubic region. The thighs are tightly pressed together until the knees, where the legs separate. Slender calves taper down to tiny feet. Despite their delicacy, these legs and feet were sculpted as one piece with the body. Thus, by contrast, the separately made and movable arms were marked as a particularly noticeable focal point – and a locus of interactive encounter.

Similar figurines with separately made arms were also made in bone and terracotta. The method of joining the arms varied: either a pierced hole or smooth, flat arm stumps (see Figure 1.1) to which a lower arm could be attached via semi-permanent or temporary adhesive, such as wax.[46] Although they can rarely be reunited with their original figurine body, examples of separately modeled arms do survive; most of these depict the arm bent at a ninety-degree angle at the elbow (see Figure 2.11).[47] When attached, such arms would extend outward in front of the figure. If attached loosely enough with a flexible material, these separately modeled arms could also swivel from side to side, rotating the extended lower arm from a frontal to a lateral position, perpendicular to the plane of the body, or be posed at any point in between these two extremes. This range of movement is not extensive and, even in its limitation, it may not have been possible with every figurine. The arms of the alabaster figurine can be so tightly tied to the body as to prevent much movement; the "finished off" stumps could allow more permanent adhesive attachment if desired.[48] Nevertheless, such jointed appearances give the visual impression of potential movement – and thus an invitation to tactile interaction, if only to test the limits of what the figurine might allow.

Jointed arm terracotta figurines were by no means the most popular way to depict a naked female figure in Hellenistic Babylonia; figurines modeled as one piece, with the arms either by the sides or supporting the breasts, significantly outnumber the jointed-arm terracottas.[49] Yet a few peculiarities of this corpus suggest that it merits special attention. First, examples of these terracotta figurines were found not just at Seleucia-on-the-Tigris, where figurine forms heavily influenced by Greek culture were commonly used, but also at Babylon, Uruk, and possibly Sippar.[50] Indeed, they seem to have been most popular at Babylon, relatively speaking – despite the significantly smaller overall figurine corpus from that site, there are almost as many jointed-arm standing female figurines from Babylon as from Seleucia-on-the-Tigris.[51] These contexts suggest that, despite the seeming Greekness of their softly modeled bodies, these figurines might have had a particularly Mesopotamian appeal.

The construction and ornamentation of these figurines is also noteworthy. Most were considerably less ornate than the alabaster figurine seen in Figure 2.8, which has accents in gold and precious stones; as with all Hellenistic Babylonian figurines, terracotta was the dominant medium. The terracotta versions could be painted; some heavily so, as can be seen in Figure 2.9. Vivid paint colors over the white base coat mimic the appearance of more costly statuary made of composite materials; the painted pink navel imitates a ruby, while the orange bands across the ankles simulate gold jewelry. Real composite materials, albeit less expensive than gold and gems,

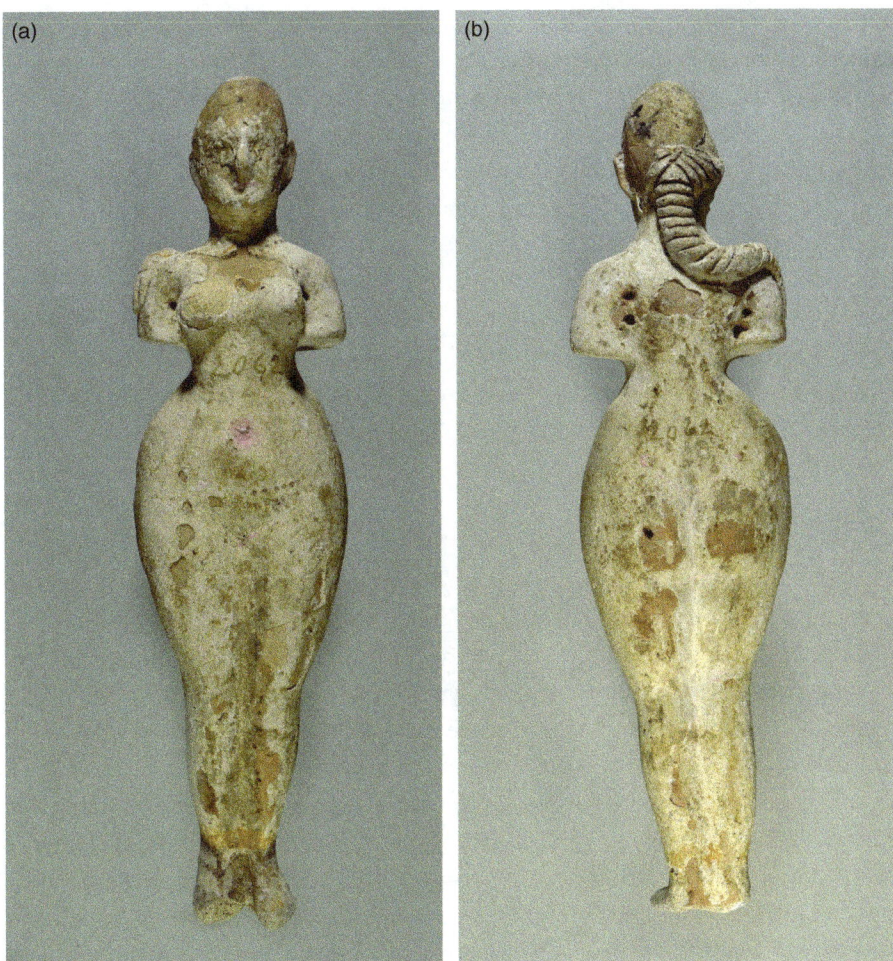

2.9a and b. Front and back of nude standing female figurine with attachments for separately modeled arms, terracotta, likely Babylon. Height: 26.5 cm. Harvard Semitic Museum (1899.2.684) Photographs courtesy of the Semitic Museum, Harvard University.

were also added to these terracotta figurines. The thick braid of the terracotta figurine (particularly visible in Figure 2.9b) would have been easily recognizable as different from the rest of the figurine's modeling, even before the coiffure began to peel away from the head. The deep grooved style of the braid, and its obviously composite nature, are starkly distinct from most female hairstyles in Hellenistic Babylonian terracotta figurines. It instead recalls the added plaster hair of the alabaster figurine. While the separately modeled arms were perhaps the most noticeable, and certainly the most interactive, of these figurines' added features, they were not the only ones.

Additionally significant is the use of bone to create figurines with jointed arms. Most figurine motifs were rarely, if ever, carved in bone; the corpus of naturalistic bone figurines from Seleucia-on-the-Tigris catalogued by Wilhelmina Van Ingen can be divided into just four motifs: naked female supporting her breasts, naked female with added arms, reclining female, and standing/squatting boy (possibly hermaphrodite).[52] The bone figurines could also be given a composite appearance; see, for instance, the inlaid eyes in the bone figurine pictured in Figure 1.11. Their arms, however, differed: as seen in Figure 2.10, the separately added lower arms of bone figurines were carved in straightened positions. This positioning of bone arms might have been due to the constraints of the raw material, which more easily yields long, thin sections than the more volumetric pieces required to carve a bent lower arm. Yet however practical the choice, the effect was significant: straight bone arms had a different range of motion than the bent stone or terracotta arms, being raised up and down at the sides rather than swiveling across the body. These bone figurines were predominantly excavated in Parthian contexts, and may represent a specifically Parthian variation on the purposes for which these figurines were intended.

A Votive Function?

What those purposes were is not fully known. Some of these figurines may represent deities; the horned headdress, gold jewelry, and precious gem accents of the alabaster figurine suggest the representation of a goddess, such as Ishtar, Nanaya, Astarte, Aphrodite, or some syncretized combination thereof.[53] The terracotta examples might have represented similar deities in a more economic fashion – or they may have been designed to represent mortal bodies in votive poses that echoed, and thus honored, their divine patronesses. Surviving lower arms in terracotta suggest this votive function, as their hands are usually designed to hold something (see the range of terracotta arms in Figure 2.11). Specific objects could be supplied, such as fruit or bowls that were modeled as one with the hand. In other cases, the preferred item would need to be supplied separately – attached by being hung through a hole in the clay fist or balanced in an open palm. Miniature terracotta platters heaped with clay fruit and other foods suggest possibilities for what such hands might have carried,[54] although the user could undoubtedly have chosen from a wider range of possibilities – or manufactured his or her own options. But the idea of carrying *something* was suggested by most of these poses. The broader figurine repertoire echoed this message: poses of holding or carrying also appear in a group of figurines that depict a clothed female figure with permanently affixed arms that have bent elbows and forearms outstretched to carry a tray.[55] Such trays or platters might have supported offerings, and thus all of these figurines may have fulfilled a votive function, regardless of whether or not their arms could move. The user of a figurine with movable arms might have prized such impermanency for the arms' ability to be lifelike and interactive, giving greater enchantment and potency to the votive offering,[56] or for their ability to be interchanged (from a hand holding a bowl to a hand holding a fruit, for instance) as the occasion, season, or festival demanded. This flexibility would have enabled owners to adjust their figurines as needed, just as the people themselves would have conformed their own bodily practices to the particular demands of different events. In creating this

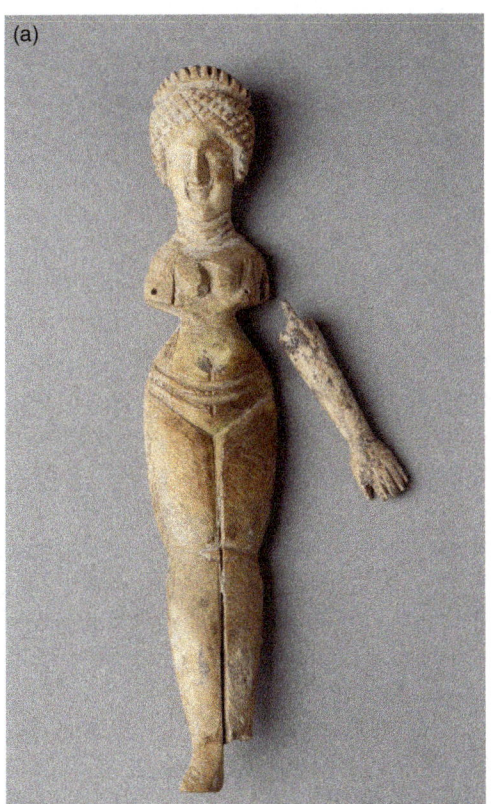
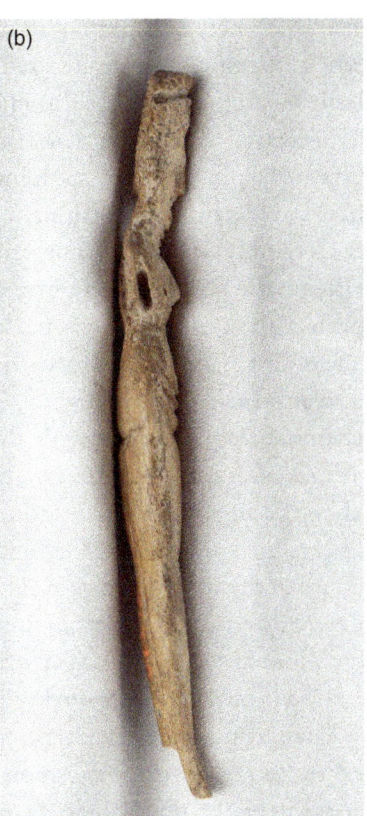

2.10a and b. Front and side of nude standing female figurine with attachments for separately modeled arms, and one separately modeled arm (not necessarily part of the same figurine in antiquity), bone, Seleucia-on-the-Tigris. Height of female figure: 13.7 cm. Kelsey Museum of Archaeology, University of Michigan, Ann Arbor (body: TM 1931.340/KM 2018.01.0390 and arm: TM 1931.477/KM 2018.01.0522)
Photographs courtesy of the Kelsey Museum of Archaeology.

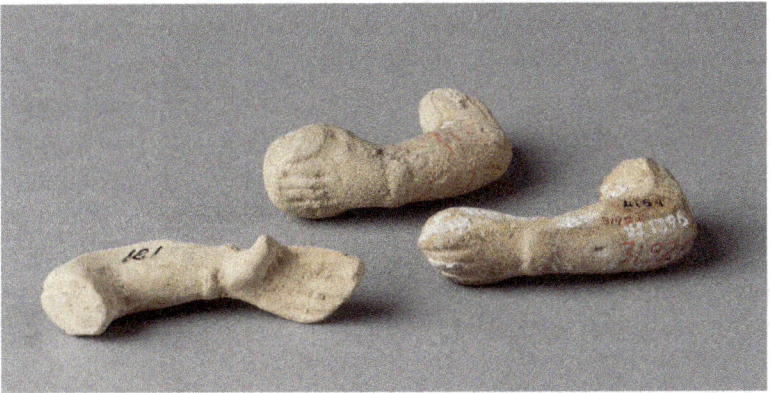

2.11. Selection of arms, separately made to be added to figurines, terracotta, Seleucia-on-the-Tigris. Kelsey Museum of Archaeology, University of Michigan, Ann Arbor (left to right: KM 14945, KM 16066, and KM 31925)
Photograph courtesy of the Kelsey Museum of Archaeology.

equivalence between the bodies of the figurines and their owners, the lifelike aspect of the moving arms fostered a close connection between person and object – both as substitutes for one another, and as performative collaborators.

This votive interpretation for the jointed-arm figurines is alluring in its offer to satisfactorily pin down the meanings of one figurine type within a figurine corpus where easily definable meanings are elusive. However, there are problems with this seemingly open-and-shut case. These votive interpretations are based primarily on the poses of the figurines, rather than on a complete accounting of the figurines' materiality or a discussion of their archaeological contexts. To address context first: large-scale votive deposits of figurines in temples, as have been found at several sites in Classical Greece and Magna Graecia,[57] are not found in Hellenistic Babylonia. As with almost all figurines from Hellenistic Babylonia, figurines with movable arms were primarily excavated from domestic contexts, such as the small household rooms of Block B at Seleucia-on-the-Tigris,[58] and there are many possibilities for figurine use within such domestic spaces. Largely because of their posture and arm position, Wilhelmina Van Ingen proposed that these figures were used within domestic shrines – however even the existence of such shrines, not to mention the placement of jointed-arm figurines within them, has not been confirmed archaeologically.[59]

Alabaster and bone examples are sometimes found in tombs, particularly of the Parthian era.[60] As the deposition of figurines in funerary contexts was a rare practice in Hellenistic Babylonia (including in the Parthian era),[61] the use of these particular figurines in tombs seems especially meaningful, and may provide contextual evidence for the notion that such figurines had a role in connecting their user to the divine. The particular burial of one such bone figurine on the breast of a deceased person[62] suggests that such miniatures also had a particularly potent connection with the human body, perhaps even as a representation of the deceased[63] – an association that may have preceded death and internment. However, the leap from this evidence to "votive" is a substantial one.

To turn now to a more complete accounting of these figurines' materiality and affect as miniatures: beyond their possible role as votives, the interactivity of these figurines, and the bodily proximity that such interactivity requires, seems to have been a major part of their appeal. Despite their greater fragility, female figurines with separately added arms far outnumber their counterparts with permanent outstretched arms, of which only a few exist.[64] While most Hellenistic Babylonian figurines are somewhat fragile, these naked standing female figurines were remarkably so. The terracotta examples were made in double molds, and thus are hollow, with exceptionally shell-thin clay walls (much thinner than the average Hellenistic Babylonian double-molded figurine); see, for instance, the delicacy of the break in the front of the figurine pictured in Figure 2.12. The stone and bone examples were often carved to an extreme slenderness at the gracefully pinched waist, neck, and ankles. These features would require any user to be cautious and gentle in handling the object.

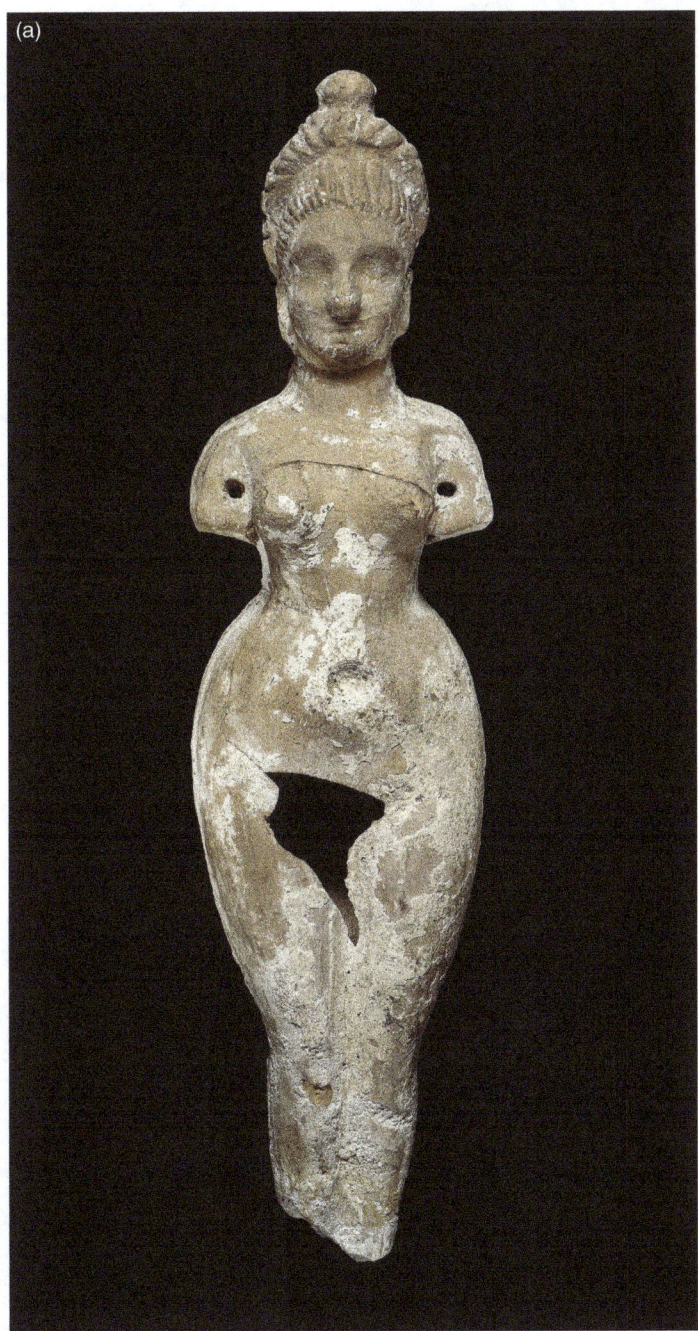

2.12a, b, and c. Front, side, and back of nude standing female figurine with attachments for separately modeled arms, terracotta, Babylon or Sippar. Height: 23 cm. British Museum (BM 81-7-1-3368 = 121212)
Photographs © The Trustees of the British Museum.

74 FASCINATION WITH THE TINY: INTERACTING WITH FIGURINES

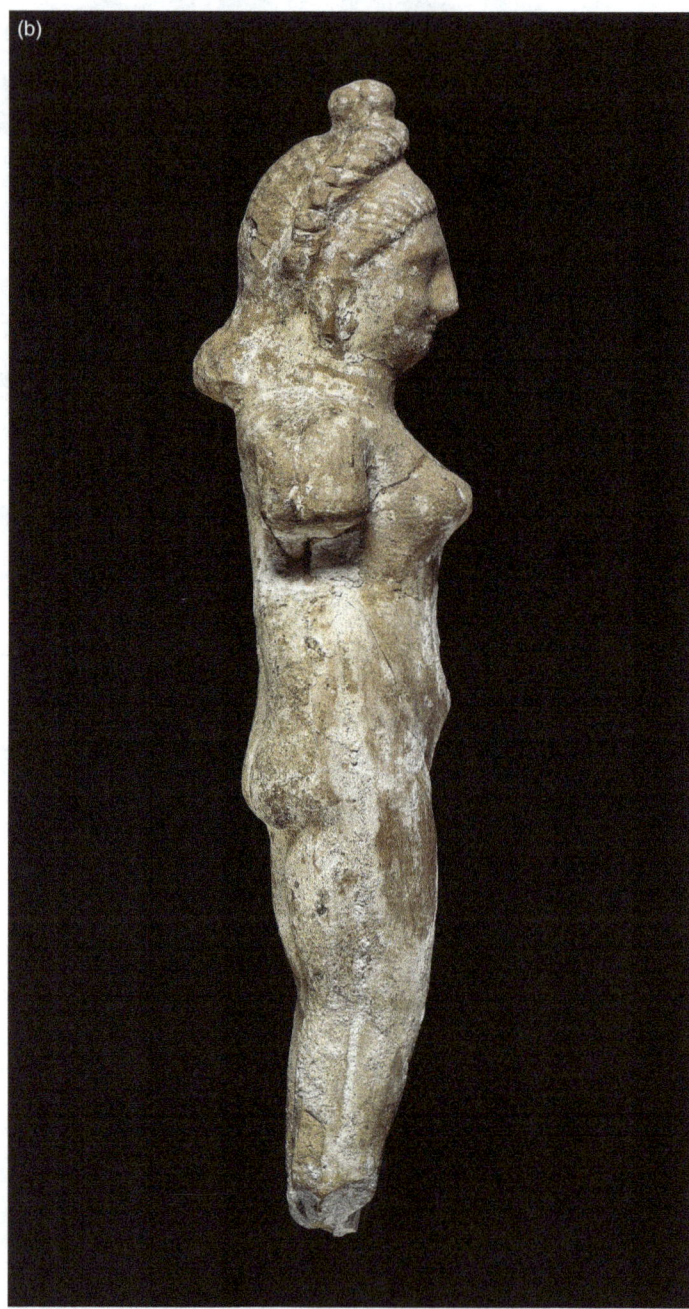

2.12a, b, and c. (cont.)

Additionally, the techniques involved in manufacturing the delicate limbs as separate pieces, and rigging the joint apparatus that connected them with the figurine body, would have been complicated and labor intensive. The holes and pin attachments, especially on bone figurines, are minute and precise. The

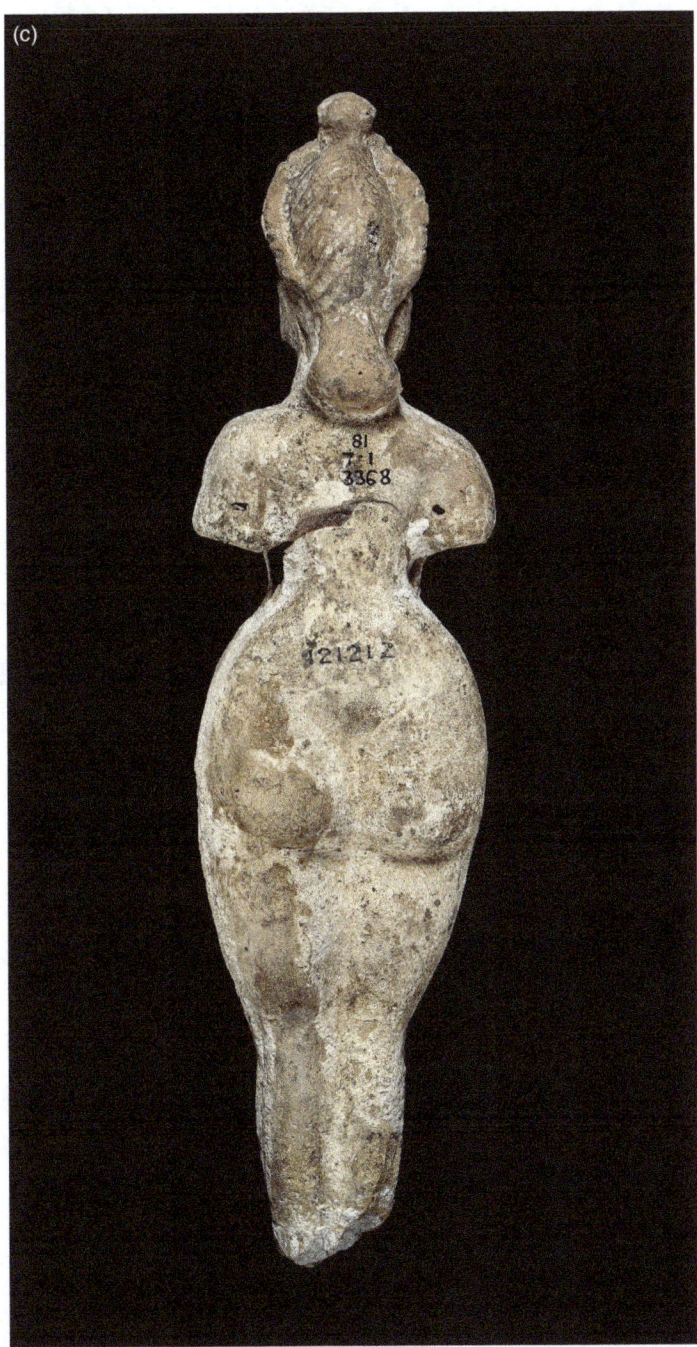

2.12a, b, and c. (cont.)

materials used to attach the arms, such as the gold wire originally joining the arms of the alabaster figurine pictured in Figure 2.8, would necessarily have been pliable and thus susceptible to fraying and breakage. Such arm joints would have been far less durable than a permanent clay or plaster join, and could have been easily damaged. If a votive function was the exclusive purpose of the bent arms, then the more durable examples with permanent arms – rather than the delicate added arms – would seem the more logical choice. Additionally, a votive explanation does not easily account for the jointed figurines, especially those made of bone, in which the arms can only be positioned to rest at the figure's side or be held laterally outward at a ninety-degree angle. Such poses do not suggest offering-bearers or a votive function; neither does the palm-downward position of the hands on these figurines, which is not a natural posture of carrying. Instead, establishing interactivity between figurine and owner seems to have been the primary function of these movable arms.

Fragility and Sexuality

In seeking an alternate explanation for these figurines' focus on creating delightful interactivity, it seems worthwhile to describe with more precision what kinds of interactions were solicited by these figurine bodies. Naked female forms were not uncommon in the figurine repertoire of Hellenistic Babylonia, nor in earlier periods of Babylonian figurine production. Additionally, female bodies without arms, or with attachments for adding arms, could be found in figurine assemblages in Classical Greece and elsewhere in the Hellenistic world.[65] However, the specific group of Hellenistic Babylonian figurines with jointed arms stand out as more exaggerated and hyper-sexualized than their Greek and Babylonian precedents or their Hellenistic contemporaries. Many have extremely narrow waists and wide hips that are seemingly out of proportion, such as is seen in Figure 2.8c. The figurine in Figure 2.12 also demonstrates this body type, along with exceptionally enlarged buttocks. Despite the lack of naturalism to these bodily proportions, the contours of the waist flow smoothly into the spreading hips and ample thighs, with a softness that invites caress – indeed, the narrowness of the waist fits easily into the grasp of a user's thumb and forefinger. This invitation to touch may also explain the disproportionately common use of alabaster, other stones, and bone to manufacture these figurines – each of these materials would have lent a silky smoothness to the figurine, further encouraging lingering caresses. Sexual details are legible by both sight and touch: the bellies of such figurines are full and protrude slightly (especially visible in Figure 2.08b), with disproportionately large, rounded navels and creases indicating a pubic region. Breasts are high and full, denoting a youthful physique. Sexuality and eroticism are evoked through these exaggerated displays of the distinctive features of the female body at the peak of its reproductive potential.

Extensive tactile engagement, in particular, seems to have been not only encouraged, but also required, by several aspects of these figurines' construction. Most Hellenistic Babylonian figurines can stand alone – reinforcing visual, not tactile consumption, as the primary mode of user interaction. In contrast, these female figurines with separately added arms cannot stand on their own. The lack of base and the compactness of the little feet and ankles make it clear at first glance that such figures cannot stand and, indeed, give the impression of a helpless person who would barely be capable of walking.[66] Even if propped up with supports (as can be seen in the photograph on the cover of this book), these figurines will only balance precariously and topple easily – a particularly dangerous experiment, given their breakability. It would have been difficult, if not impossible, to display these figurines vertically without human aid or external support apparatus, making their usefulness as votive offering-bearers somewhat suspect. While these figurines could have been lain horizontally on a flat surface, the visual features of many of these figurines do not indicate that this was likely either; most have very detailed, modeled backsides – a feature uncommon in the Hellenistic Babylonian figurine tradition, as even clay figurines made in double molds were often relatively undecorated on the back. This careful, and uncommon, elaboration indicates that these figurines were particularly interesting, both visually and tactilely, from both sides and all angles.

All of these qualities – the figurines' fragility, lack of stability, and sculptural detailing – demand that they be held in the hand. This enforced tactility, which was required if one wished to look closely or otherwise engage with the object, recruited the user (wittingly or not) into physical interaction with the miniature. As such, the seeming helplessness of these figurines – which relied on their human interlocutors to move their arms, hold them upright, and protect their fragile bodies – was actually quite powerful. These figurines demanded a commitment to tactile participation that was extensively interactive, yet was constrained by the material and physical limitations prescribed by the especially sensitive object.

This understanding of these figurines' interactivity requires a reexamination of their supposedly votive pose. Not particularly functional as a surrogate for a (presumably absent) person, these figurines seem more likely to have recruited their owners into collaborative performances that were taking place in the moment and, at least partially, in the world of miniature scale. Perhaps these were performances of piety before a deity, or perhaps they had a different intent entirely. The figurine's arms outstretched within the presence of the human owner – indeed, while within his or her personal space – call into question the intended recipient of this supplication. Was it a deity who was implored through the gesture? Or was the human owner the intended audience for the outstretched arms?

This potentially adulatory, even adoring, dynamic between miniature and user was reinforced by design features that not only made these figurines hypersexual but also largely incapable of warding off sexual advances. The slightly parted legs seen in some alabaster and bone examples give a thrill of bodily access – one which was very uncommon in the Hellenistic Babylonian figurine corpus, as the carved separation of the legs renders each of them more fragile than they would have been together. Many of these figurines' heads are tipped slightly upward, as if acknowledging – and seeking attention from – the larger-scale user to whose grasp and control they submit. The alabaster figurine's piercing ruby gaze is one of the most elaborate examples of this seeming desire for eye contact. The bodies of these figurines also encouraged user intervention; they are almost completely open to touch and access, as their arms and hands could not be positioned in such a way that they covered the breasts or genitals to shield the body from the user's gaze or caress.[67] Even if the user *wanted* these figurines to "cover up," the objects' materiality makes it impossible – indeed the arms cannot be twisted even in approximation of the pseudo-modesty of the *Aphrodite pudica* motif that was en vogue across the Hellenistic world (see, for instance, the Knidian Aphrodite in Figure 4.12).[68] Stark nudity is the only option with these figurines, and the fact that their arms can actually move makes that nudity seem less exploitative and more willingly submissive. The arms exist and move in order to serve, not to deny (or even coquettishly feign to deny) the user any access or pleasure.

Broken Bodies and Hyperreality

It seems beyond question that such interactions, and the figurines that produced them, were intensely intimate. Indeed, if any figurines were to challenge a major theoretical tenet of this book – that Hellenistic Babylonian miniatures only *seem* intimate as a strategy of encouraging human enchantment and engagement – these would be the figurines to topple my hypothesis. Yet I would argue that these nude females with movable arms prove just the opposite. For there is nothing more pseudo-intimate than the close physical interactions that these figurines require, demanding constant attention and specific caresses that are nevertheless completely removed from real human intimacy. The ruby eyes of the alabaster figurine are unnatural in both their overly large size and blood red color; their gaze is both arresting and unsettling. While the figurine's face is sculpted to appear placid, beautiful, and whole, it is difficult to look at her without experiencing the vague, disconcerting notion that a real human face with eyes so swollen and crimson had undergone significant trauma. Similarly, moving the arm of one of these figurines is nothing like moving the arm of a living person, as the figurine arms swivel at a non-anatomical joint. The holes pierced through the mid-humerus to facilitate arm attachment would have been both intriguing and jarring. Lured in by the seductiveness of the nude female, the user might eagerly explore and test the joints in order to intuit their functional purpose for the object, yet also be forced to reconcile his or her playful fascination with the visual appearance of foreign and painful intrusions on a human body.

The tension between curiosity and awareness of trauma would have been especially potent in these miniatures whose materiality insists that they be held in the hand, and thus placed in close proximity to the user's body. Such figurines offer a particularly intense experience that encompasses both "sanctuary (fantasy) and prison (the boundaries or limits of otherness, the inaccessibility of what cannot be lived experience)."[69] "Prison" is perhaps not too hyperbolic of a word to use here. Like the separately made riders discussed in the previous section of this chapter, whose widely spread legs or open holes in the hand call out for attention, so too do the movable arms of these nude female figurines demand actions from their user.[70] Should the user decline to participate and choose instead to imagine that the figurine could move her own arms, the terror of autonomous animation is invoked: "for such movement would only cause the obliteration of the subject – the inhuman spectacle of a dream no longer in need of a dreamer."[71] Yet, should the user acquiesce and acknowledge his or her greater agency by moving the figurine, the prison remains. By directing their request for assistance and movement toward horrifically unnatural joins and what appear to be painful actions, the nude female figurines force the user in a single instant to play the role of both adored god and feared torturer.

This effect reached a climax if the arms were removed, either intentionally or accidentally. The potential for such removals to be effected without destroying the figurine as an object could be seen as the extreme submission of these figurines to a user's desires: should he or she decide that the moving arms were an impediment, the user could easily render the tiny female figure an amputee. Indeed, a rare version of this figurine body type has arm stumps that were intentionally left as triangular stubs coming out from the shoulder.[72] With no obvious way of attaching arms, the hyper-sexualized bodies of these figurines were left completely at the whim of the user. Yet, such unmitigated helplessness seems not to have been generally popular. The clear preference across the corpus for figurines with added arms suggests that it was not just the gratification of the user, but also the figurine's implied complicity in (and perhaps even enjoyment of) that gratification, that was particularly alluring.[73]

This combination of sensuality and power, of dominance over a fragile, vulnerable, and yet hyper-erotic figure, is the stuff of sexual fantasy.[74] Indeed, Greek fantasies in particular fetishized abstracted body parts and "bodies in pieces," similar to the broken and reconstructed bodies of these jointed-arm figurines.[75] A more straightforward and self-possessed female sexuality is celebrated in many Mesopotamian texts (especially odes to Ishtar),[76] but similar ideas of a stripped, powerless, but also alluring female body can be found (such as in "The Descent of Ishtar to the Netherworld").[77]

Yet the possibility of arm removal also granted power to the figurine itself. Were the arms to be taken off, these figurines would allow the user to literally dismember a miniature body and touch the "inside" surfaces of the shoulder stump and severed arm – rendering the arm more completely visible and knowable than either a normal figurine arm or a living human arm. Through the expanded specter of intelligibility that they offered, these miniature and fragmentary arms operated in an intensified state of hyperreality, seeming to "over exist" or be more real than the real thing.[78] The hyperreality of these fragmented arms removed the sexuality of the figurine encounter from real life, highlighting the artificiality of the experience even as it intensified the illusion of intimate knowledge of a naked female body. The figurines' superhuman ability to emerge more "whole" from fracture – not just overcoming both pain and trauma, but actually gaining an additional, functional arm joint at mid-humerus, rather than losing the arm entirely as a living amputee would – further enhanced the uncanniness, and power, of otherwise seemingly helpless naked female figures.

The Boundaries of Attraction

The hyperreality, hyper-sexuality, and hyper-wholeness of these figurines all presented a user experience that was unique among the figurines of Hellenistic Babylonia. The distinctiveness of this group of figurines suggests that their affect and appearance was experimental, yet also curated and negotiated. Multicultural appeal – and, perhaps more crucially, nonoffence – to both Greeks and Babylonians was the likely goal. The alabaster figurine seen in Figure 2.8 is a particularly stunning example of such cultural hybridity, combining the techniques and effects of Mesopotamian composite statuary with rounded Greek bodily forms.[79] Yet all the figurines with separately added arms participated in this multicultural dialogue to some degree. The exaggeration of hip to waist ratio has parallels in the pre-Hellenistic figurine tradition of Mesopotamia, as does the strongly frontal posture and the depiction of female nudity. The influence of Greek tradition is strikingly evident in the rounded modeling of the face, depiction of elaborate hairstyles, and the use of the double mold for the terracotta examples (a technology which needed to be expertly wielded to successfully create such thin-walled, delicate figurines). As already mentioned, figurines with finished-off arm stumps were also used elsewhere in the Hellenistic world; additionally, the concept of an attached-arm figurine made using pierced holes through the arms as the mechanism for their attachment had roots in Greek tradition, although employed differently there.[80]

But perhaps more telling than the Greek and Babylonian contributions to these figurines' appearances are the concessions that seem to have been made to avoid offending either group. Mesopotamian views on nudity were generally privileged, as depictions of the naked female form were far more acceptable in Babylonia than Greece.[81] Traces of paint on alabaster examples suggest that the nipples, pubic hair, and the separation of the labia could be depicted in vivid, lifelike color, indicating their importance in a manner that aligned with Mesopotamian cultural norms.[82] Yet the female genitalia were not elaborated in three-dimensional sculptured form, but rather left smooth in possible accordance with Greek artistic conventions.[83]

Additional negotiations between cultural mores may be seen in the limitation of this corpus to adult female figures. The bodies of male children and teenagers – which were considered highly erotic in Greek culture (in the tradition of *ephebophilia*), and which are depicted in sexualized ways in a few Hellenistic Babylonian figurines (as will be discussed in Chapter 4)[84] – are *not* shown with movable arms or other interactive features. This difference may reflect a consideration of Mesopotamian views on sexuality, which did not usually advocate male-male attraction.[85] With these concessions, limits on what constituted acceptable sexual attraction and sexualized viewing were imposed.

Thus I suggest that these figurines presented not just the use of tactile, desirable bodies as a means to encourage arousal, but also (and perhaps more powerfully) as a means to regulate and control it. Although experimental in form and playful in use, the limited scope of iconography and motifs among this group of miniatures imposed restrictions on sexuality. One body type – and one body type alone – was made enchanting and seductive, presented in miniaturized form where it could be touched and controlled. The difference between this body type and the bodies of most female figures with which it was contemporary may have served to set these figures apart from everyday life and mortal identities – including making a distinction between the vision of sexual attraction presented here and how sexual attraction operated in reality, where neither arousal nor its consequences could be so tightly monitored. As in modern mainstream pornography, certain fantasies were celebrated and indulged in these figurines to a degree not possible in real life – but within the strictures of externally imposed perspectives on what those fantasies should be.[86] In highlighting bodies that were considered appropriate receptacles for desire, and offering tantalizing opportunities to "play with" such desires, these figurines prescribed the boundaries of attraction – boundaries that conformed to a common ground of social acceptability in both Greek and Babylonian cultures.

THEATRICALITY: "PERFORMING" IN MINIATURE

All of the figurines discussed in this chapter encouraged their users to interact, and thus to "perform" actions, in miniature. Seemingly intimate as such encounters were, they were also inherently theatrical. To imagine one's body entering the small-scale world of the miniature is an act of dramatic play, to which the outside world is a constant referent and audience – for, without the real-scale world, the efficacy of the miniature disappears.[87] The more frequently and enthusiastically a user touches a miniature, and the closer the user keeps the miniature to his or her person, the greater the possibility that, at some point, he or she will be observed "in the act" by others. The realization that other members of society were buying and using similar, commercially produced figurines would also grant social implications to this personal drama, no matter how secluded its enactment.

This dualism of privacy and theatricality in figurines can be most vividly seen in interactive figurines that directly depicted or otherwise linked to real-world performances. Such figurines seem intimate in their invitation for the user to engage in close tactile encounter and manipulate their body parts. But they also overtly reference the stage, and thus the audience – vaulting the encounter between user and figurine into the public arena. In some cases, this public audience was merely implied, and thus was largely imaginary. In other instances, these figurines were used in public, possibly within social contexts or during events where real-life performances were also taking place. Such moments of parallel theater elided the differences of scale, with the figurine paradoxically serving as catalyst – not to draw the user into the world of the miniature, but rather to facilitate the user's engagement in the drama and spectacle of the life-sized world.

Puppets

Terracotta "puppets" with movable legs are one group of interactive performer figurines that fit within this framework of overt theatricality. An example of such a figurine can be seen in Figure 2.13, which depicts a male performer holding a musical instrument. The style and form of the figurine are culturally hybrid: the pointed beard derives from Mesopotamian or Parthian tradition and the wreath worn on the head is Greek, while the non-specific costume and schematized lute instrument are (perhaps intentionally) vague in cultural origin.[88] His tunic flares below the hips, with a thick hemline marking the end of his "body." Other examples of such puppet figurines have wide bell-shaped bodies that even more clearly denote the divide between garment-clad torso and the thin, dangling legs beneath.[89] Underneath that garment, the figurine was made hollow for the insertion of two strings to hold his separately

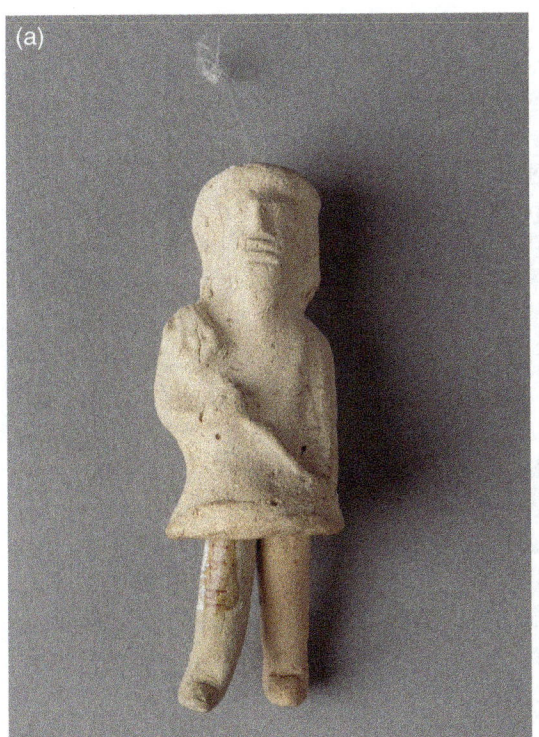 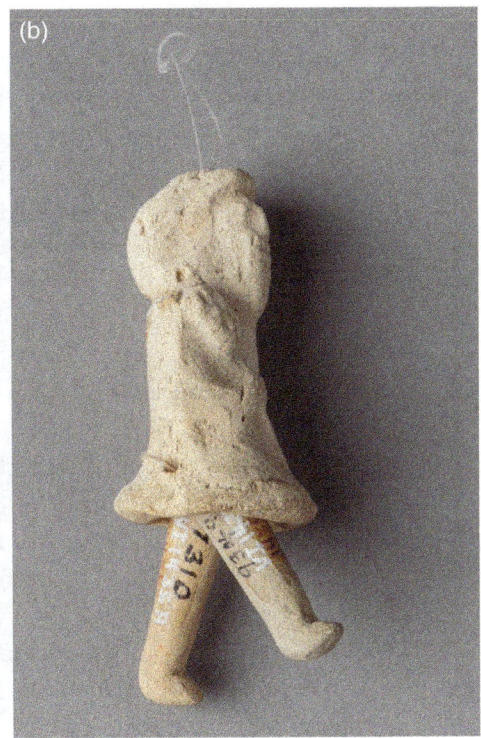

2.13a and b. Front and side of puppet-like figurine, terracotta, Seleucia-on-the-Tigris. Height: 8.2 cm. Kelsey Museum of Archaeology, University of Michigan, Ann Arbor (Body: KM 15632; leg: KM 14397; leg: KM 14476; modern assembly)
Photographs courtesy of the Kelsey Museum of Archaeology.

made legs. One string secured the legs at the appropriate height and was tied through holes in the back of the tunic (see side view in Figure 2.13). The other string was threaded down through a hole in the top of the head, and then looped or tied around the first string; it was this string that could be pulled to cause the legs to bounce and twitch in imitation of dancing.

This complicated internal rigging requires both user's hands for precise operation of the puppet-like features. Pulling on the head string alone causes a jerking motion of the legs, or – if pulled too quickly – no separate movement at all. It is only by holding the body of the figurine with one hand and pulling the head string with the other hand that the user can give controlled movement to the figurine's legs. The necessity of two-handed manipulation means that the user must hold and touch the terracotta, not just the string. This close physical connection draws the user into collaborating with the figure's "performance." It is human touch that gives life – perhaps the most intimate of all acts – to the figurine's legs, and enables their theatricality. Enchanted by the idea that careful touch could enliven the dancer, the user would perhaps be inspired to add to the performance by helping the figurine to speak, sing, or do other human-like activities. The instrument held by the figure, and the deep horizontal lines indicating a widely open mouth, might have given creative stimulus to the user by specifying the sorts of performances that the tiny figure was meant to reenact.[90]

Real-world performances would likely have also offered inspiration to the users of such figurines. Dancing puppet figurines almost certainly imitated real-life Hellenistic entertainers, such as traveling musicians and "troupes of professional actors."[91] Theaters were one of the most popular exports of Greek culture into the Near East, and there is archaeological evidence for the building of large Greek theaters at Babylon and Seleucia-on-the-Tigris.[92] The users of the puppet figurines may have seen real-life performances on one of these stages. Such spectacles would surely have been entertaining, but would also have provided audiences with the opportunity of connecting with the wider world beyond their immediate communities.[93] With the entrance of the first actor onto the stage, a Babylonian audience could be transported to Delphi, Athens, or Alexandria – or even further afield, to the realms of myth and the gods. There is no reason to believe that only Greek dramas would have been performed on such stages; actors, musicians, and dancers from other regions, perhaps even beyond the borders of the Hellenistic world, might also have entertained Babylonian audiences.[94] Attending the theater was thus about more than simple enjoyment; the experience also allowed an audience member to become temporary owner and master of vast realms, all while showing off his or her sophistication in knowing that such experiences were worth the time and money to acquire.[95] Hellenistic performances were particularly designed to appeal to this "theatrical mentality" of the spectator, who expected to be dazzled and transported.[96]

The real-world theater made this possible within the Babylonian communities; the figurine version encapsulated this experience and made it possible within the Babylonian home, held in the Babylonian hand.[97] Popular festivals were also the occasions for dancing and musical performances, and these too may have been referenced by the puppet figurines.[98] Such festivals, accompanied by music and dancing, had a long history in both Greece and Babylonia; indeed, the connections between festivals in these two cultural traditions were actively promoted by Seleucid kings in order to solidify their reigns.[99] It is thus likely that some types of musical and dancing performances would have been seen by many people in Hellenistic Babylonia, and would have been connected with aspects of the multiple cultures that made up their society. The actions of the little puppet figurines were likely a common touchstone, and a positive one that embodied the delights of festivals and theaters: pleasant sights and sounds, an atmosphere of celebration and leisure.

In addition to evoking such pleasurable moments of festival-going and theater attendance, the puppet figurines, by means of their invitation to interactivity, also offered the chance of participation. No longer relegated to a passive seat in the audience or membership in the throng, the user was promised the opportunity to star in the production and bask in the adulation of the crowds. By pulling the strings and collaborating with the figurine to create a performance, the user of this miniature object could pretend that – like a real-life performer – he or she was also on a real stage receiving applause. The vagueness of many of these figurines' details, such as clothing and faces, could allow for a broad range of people to self-identify with the little performer and envision that they too were in the spotlight.[100] Targeting desires for acclamation and fame, such figurines provided a conduit for fanciful indulgence in the grandiose. Indeed, even Hellenistic kings sometimes appeared on stage dressed as actors[101]; thus, these figurines allowed their users to play with the idea of assuming identities that were not just famous but also powerful and regal.

Yet the actual "performance" with a figurine took place in the low-stakes world of the tiny, where everything is enchanting and it seems that nothing really matters. Stage fright, butterflies in the stomach, and other manifestations of the anxiety most people feel when faced with a staring crowd could – the figurine promised – be overcome by physically miniaturizing the stage and consigning the audience to an implied, but invisible, abstraction. They were, in fact, the perfect audience – assumed to be adoring and applauding, and physically incapable (by virtue of their nonexistence) of indicating otherwise. Puppet figurines could thus be particularly enchanting because they offered their owners the upper hand, granting them control over the stage to act as they wished with society as the silent audience, forced to watch without comment. As audiences in the ancient world were known for being potentially volatile, even violent, this ensured docility would be especially appealing.[102] Fame without critique is alluring indeed.

However, should critique indeed come – whether from a passerby who happened to observe the user's interaction with the dancing puppet, or from another, possibly even imagined, source – the pose and form of such puppets suggest that they, not their users, should be the target of any disapproval. The arms of Hellenistic Babylonian puppet figurines were not movable, but rather were molded as one piece with the figurine's torso. These arms were fixed in one of three general positions: playing a stringed instrument, hands clasped high above the head (possibly holding an instrument like hand cymbals, or simply whirling), or hands "clapping" while held out in front of the face.[103] These postures all clearly indicate dancing or musical performance, and allow very little room for alternate interpretations of the actions depicted. A user of such a puppet thus had few choices in how to use the object – it was a performance or nothing. Even the more interactive legs offer few options for movement: they do not have knee or ankle joints, and so their range of motion is confined to a simple back-and-forth or up-and-down. Elegance and grace cannot be easily supplied here; rather, user-assisted leg motion provides a more rudimentary "action" that is functional primarily in its vivid suggestion that the depicted activities of the upper body – activities over which the user has no direct control – have similarly come to life. This denial of agency to the user seems strange if viewed from the perspective that miniatures are designed to create intimacy. Why would such a figurine offer the tantalizing prospect of making decisions over another human body, allowing the user to become a literal puppet master to which the tiny object must submit – only to ultimately deny almost all choices over that figurine's movements? Indeed, it was the figurine that exercised much of the agency in this encounter: it was the figurine that forced the user to conform, to use his or her fingers to perform the prescribed actions that the figurine's pose and construction made possible, and thus it was the user's body that was manipulated.

But perhaps this was the point. The specificity of the puppet and the lack of choice it offered its user also meant that any critique of the performance, any audience distaste or mockery, was directed onto the object itself. The user was not to blame for any poor performances that might result.[104] A Hellenistic Babylonian user might have chosen this object and willingly engaged with it for this very reason. The prospect of intimacy with objects can be alluring, but distance can be attractive as well if it means that risk can be redirected away from oneself. The puppet figurine can thus be understood as a site of experimentation through play, where daring "performances" could be staged without the user's identity, ego, and personhood being inextricably implicated in the process.[105]

The occasional portrayal of so-called grotesque body types in puppet figurines also supports the idea that enforced distance and deliberate nonintimacy were appealing for the puppets' users. While most puppet figurines portray a slim male figure, a few examples have bodily features generally considered less ideal, such as dwarfism, baldness, facial contortion, and corpulence.[106] For instance, the figurine seen in Figure 2.14 displays a satyr-like male figure with snub nose, contracted brow, stocky proportions, and balding head. Those physical features alone would likely mark this body as an appropriate target for mockery (although see Chapter 5 for a broader discussion of the "grotesque" in Hellenistic Babylonia), and for viewers aware of Hellenistic theater, connect this figurine with characters from New Comedy.[107]

Any potential laughter would be intensified by the figurine's functionality as a puppet. Although the figurine is broken at the waist, the characteristic hole in the top of the head identifies it as a puppet, and the right arm wrapped tightly against the body identifies it as an orator or performer. Many Hellenistic Babylonian figurines, particularly of women, have poses modeled after an Athenian orator type, best seen in Late Classical portraits of Aeschines and Sophocles.[108] But irony is clearly intended here, for this pose within its original

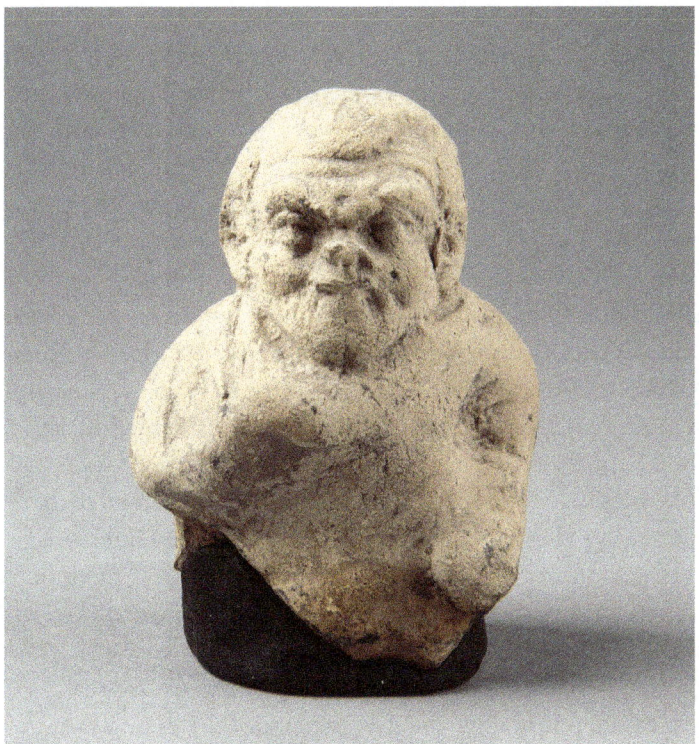

2.14. Puppet-like figurine (fragmented, supported by modern base), terracotta, Seleucia-on-the-Tigris. Height: 9.7 cm. Kelsey Museum of Archaeology, University of Michigan, Ann Arbor (TM 1930.148/KM 2018.01.0101)
Photograph courtesy of the Kelsey Museum of Archaeology.

Athenian context indicated the physical self-restraint considered ideal in a public orator, who should convince his audience through words alone – and yet this figurine's legs are designed to twitch and kick.

There may have been a theatrical aspect to the pose as well; Aeschines was a stage actor before his rise to civic life, while Sophocles was a playwright.[109] However, the serious use of this pose in so many Hellenistic Babylonian figurines suggests that such intricacies might not have been well known so far from Athens. From the Hellenistic Babylonian perspective, the exaggerated ugliness and dwarfism of the figure, along with the jerky dancing movements of his puppet legs, would have directly contradicted the staid self-control of the draped matrons (discussed in Chapter 4). Thus the user's actions in operating the puppet would have served primarily to make the little figure an object of further laughter and scorn.

It seems unlikely that most users would wish to self-identify with such a comic figure and, indeed, such portrayals of "otherness" might have been appealing precisely because the user and the figurine would not be easily confused for one another. Rather than becoming a performer, the user could remain more comfortable and empowered in the role of stage director and slave master – forcing an "other," marginalized body to dance, while remaining at an emotional distance.[110] Fear of the other could, the figurine suggested, be conquered through a laughter that implied both superiority and mastery.

Beyond encouraging play and jests, the light-heartedness and lack of intimacy characteristic of the puppet figurines may also have been appealing because of the deeper levels of social negotiation that these features encouraged. As Roberta Menegazzi has astutely commented upon, most of the puppet figurines depict male bodies, which is a striking contrast with the rest of the Hellenistic Babylonian corpus that focuses primarily on depictions of women and children.[111] As acting was an exclusively male profession in Classical Greece, it does not seem odd at first glance that the figurines depicting actors and performers should be male as well. However, while on stage, Greek actors used masks and costumes to transform themselves into characters of both genders and almost all ages – thus, "female" bodies were seen on Greek stages. In emphasizing the masculinity of the actors, the Hellenistic Babylonian figurines have, in effect, "unmasked" the performers, pushing them into (or at least closer to) the real social world and their real identities within it. The social implications of the figurines could thus also be understood as "real."

Additionally, most of the puppet figurines were portrayed wearing nonspecific costume that appears vaguely like a Parthian tunic; when found in secure contexts at Seleucia-on-the-Tigris, almost all of them come from early and mid-Parthian era levels of the site.[112] Yet, in their association with the theater and, in some cases, specific connection to the Greek New Comedy, the figurines also overtly reference Hellenistic *koine* cultural tradition and its acceptance within Babylonian cities. In short, many of these puppets show a perhaps Parthian-attired man giving a Greek performance in a Babylonian space – a very specific combination of cultural features that points to a particular kind of social negotiation. Although some of these puppets may have been children's toys,[113] and many are found in domestic spaces,[114] others were discovered in more public contexts that similarly indicate a level of high-stakes cultural interplay.

For instance, the bearded lute-playing dancer seen in Figure 2.13, along with other figurines, was found in the area of Room 19[115] of a monumental building that was likely a Seleucid Heroon,[116] dedicated to the Seleucid kings at Seleucia-on-the-Tigris.[117] Room 19 adjoins at least one room (Room 4), and possibly a second room (Room 18), with exterior doorways into the temple.[118] Additionally, much of Room 4 was paved with baked brick,[119] indicating some level of public access.[120] Because of the overtly political as well as religious associations of the Seleucid Heroon, this quasi-public space was likely to have not only shared the Hellenistic Babylonian "focus on visibility, spectacle and assembly" in cultic practice,[121] but also to have been an especially dynamic arena for cultural negotiation.[122] The figurine seen in Figure 2.13 might have functioned in both. It dates to a critical cultural moment in the history of Seleucia-on-the-Tigris:[123] Level II, which in the Seleucid Heroon likely dates to the period after the revolt of 39–43 CE, when the people of Seleucia-on-the-Tigris waged (and lost) a "bitter struggle" with the Parthians for autonomous status, on the basis of their Greek descent.[124] Use and repair of the Heroon continued during the Parthian period.

In the aftermath of Greek-Parthian tensions, the continued use of (at least partially) Greek material culture in a newly Parthian space speaks to both conflict and mediated engagement. The presence of a culturally hybrid figurine that could move and which imitated a performer clearly referenced prior, successful social negotiations between Greeks and Babylonians regarding theaters and festivals, and thus provided a path forward in reconciliatory social negotiations between cultural groups. The vaguely Parthian costuming of some of these figurines may have invited Parthians to see themselves represented within such discussions, encouraging them to join in the "performance" of Seleucian identity, along terms already established by Greeks and Babylonians.

However, the particular popularity of these figurines in the Parthian period, and the othering and distancing they encouraged, may also point to some level of cultural conflict. For Greeks and Babylonians nostalgic for Seleucid rule, it may have been pleasurable to make a Parthian "dance" at their whim, if only in miniature. A more generous interpretation would be that the distancing of these dancing Parthian figures allowed the extant Hellenistic Babylonian community some measure of remove from the Parthian reality, to play with it and become accustomed to it as a means of gradually accepting it. As I will argue in Chapter 4, similar tricks of enforced distance between athlete figurines and their users were also used to slowly introduce Greek customs such as gymnasion use into the Babylonian community. The pseudo-intimacy of miniatures – alluring and seemingly personal, but ultimately exclusionary – allowed such figurines to function as social tools.

Masks and Babies

Other Hellenistic Babylonian miniatures that recruited their users into supplying performances include miniatures with cut open mouths, which "interacted" by implying the production of sound. Miniature terracotta versions of theatrical masks, such as that seen in Figure 2.15, often have mouths that were delicately cut open after the clay was molded, with considerable care expended to create a realistic appearance of sound-making capacity. The large protruding eyes and contorted facial features of this mask would also have been attention-grabbing, and may have associated this miniature with Greek theater masks.[125] When used in Hellenistic Babylonia, such masks overtly referenced the same

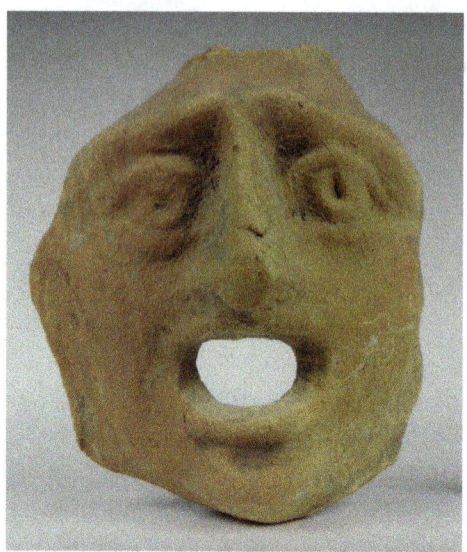

2.15. Miniature theatrical mask, terracotta, Seleucia-on-the-Tigris. Height: 9.8 cm. Kelsey Museum of Archaeology, University of Michigan, Ann Arbor (TM 1930.146 /KM 2018.01.0099)
Photograph courtesy of Roberta Menegazzi and the Kelsey Museum of Archaeology.

kinds of performances and public spectacles with which the puppet figurines were entangled, although with a more obviously Greek inflection. They also similarly granted their user the ability to experiment with performance and bask in the idea of fame, while simultaneously distancing himself or herself from potential criticism via the conceit of miniaturism.

How that distancing worked, however, was different in the masks than in the puppets. Almost all Hellenistic Babylonian terracotta masks can be classed as "miniatures" because they are smaller than the human face; some, like the example seen in Figure 2.16, are markedly so.[126] Also noticeable on this mask are the pierced holes at the top, common to many examples and presumably used for suspension. Some Babylonian versions, such as the mask seen in Figure 2.16, also have holes pierced through their eyes; others, even more rarely, have holes in both the eyes and the mouth as would be necessary if worn in a theatrical production.[127] However, many Hellenistic Babylonian miniature masks have no holes at all, and so look more like faces than true masks — it is their facial features and lack of a back to the head, rather than their functionality, that distinguishes them. Too small for a person to wear, often blinding and/or muting for anyone who made the attempt, and not appropriately pierced for a string to tie around the back of a person's head, such masks clearly indicate that they were to be displayed and looked at rather than function as wearable objects.

Yet, other aspects of these masks' materiality stubbornly refused to conform to the role of inert and lifeless thing, to be hung on the wall and occasionally

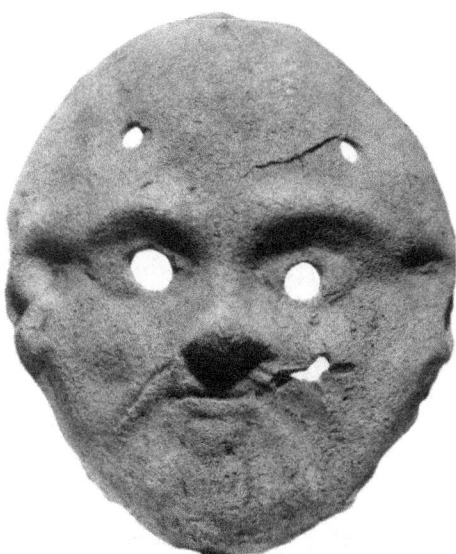

2.16. Miniature theatrical mask, terracotta, Seleucia-on-the-Tigris. Height: 12.6 cm. Turin Excavations at Seleucia (S4690)
Photograph courtesy of Roberta Menegazzi.

glanced at. Many miniature masks, such as the one pictured in Figure 2.15, retained the convex shape of a real mask, curved in perfect accommodation of the human face and visually evoking the tactile idea of a mask-as-worn – creating a remote haptic perception of what it would have been like to perform the wearing of the mask.[128] The asymmetry of the features, with the crooked nose that is off-center to the figure's left and the mouth that gapes open more widely on the figure's right, fits the ideal of Classical Greek mask-making, wherein the "asymmetry creates the illusion that the faces are mobile [and, thus, are performing on stage] rather than frozen in time."[129] Bodily proximity, or the imagined experience thereof, was also encouraged by the examples that had cut-out eyes and mouths, or the animated facial expressions of those which did not. These features perhaps inspired the user to peer closer or even speak in response to the open, though voiceless, lips.[130] Such performances were simultaneously personal and theatrical – although not fully operational in either capacity, as the small size of such masks did not allow either complete intimacy as a face-covering or complete functionality as an actor's costume. Rather, the scalar difference between living face and miniature mask reinforced the divide between user and object. Even if the user held the mask in his or her hand, the object would seem to *belong* to someone else, to fit another face – or even to take on a life of its own.[131]

Lifelike qualities were also characteristic of a group of Hellenistic Babylonian figurines depicting babies or young children which, like the masks, also featured cut-out mouths. As I have noted elsewhere,[132] the similarity between

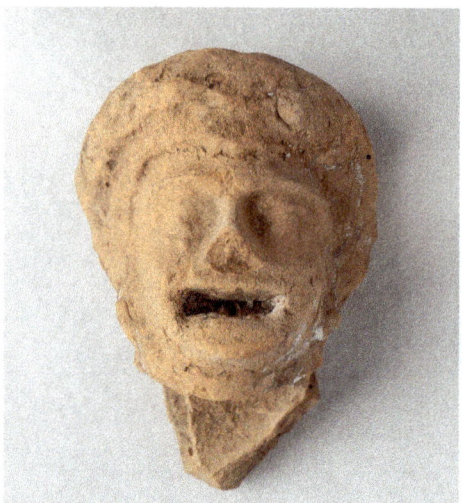

2.17. Head of a child figurine, terracotta, Seleucia-on-the-Tigris. Height: 8.8 cm. Kelsey Museum of Archaeology, University of Michigan, Ann Arbor (KM 14556)
Photograph courtesy of the Kelsey Museum of Archaeology.

these two groups of figurines – which would seem to belie traditional typological categories – may point to a shared functionality. Carving a mouth into the clay after molding added an additional step to the production process and cut marks still visible on some figurine interiors (such as on the inside of the neck of the baby figurine seen in Figure 2.17) provide evidence of the repeated small incisions necessary to precisely cut a small hole in a round or rectangular shape. In light of the obvious care given to incising these mouths, it seems to have been important that such figurines look lifelike in their sound-making capacity.

Apotropaism and other ritual functions would be the obvious explanation for this need for realness, especially given the display function of the terracotta masks. The use of terrifying faces, including masks, to ward off evil had a long history in both the Mediterranean and Mesopotamia.[133] Making such faces seem more "alive" added to their magical potency. From the Babylonian perspective, the specific act of cutting open the mouth might have contributed additional functionality. Rituals of "mouth-opening" (*pit pî*) and "mouth-washing" (*mīs pî*) were a crucial part of the process of enlivening some statues, such as cult images or other statues associated with deities.[134] Tablets containing the incantations of the *mīs pî* ritual from second century BCE Uruk attest to the continued knowledge and practice of mouth-opening ceremonies in Hellenistic Babylonia.[135] In these rituals of animation, physical actions were taken to open and wash the statue's mouth – actions which might have been procedurally and somatically (if not ritually) similar to the process of cutting open the mouths of infant figurines and miniature masks. This is not to say that such rituals were necessarily being performed on terracotta figurines or that these figurines directly represented ritual actions. However, the cut-open mouths of these objects would have visually resonated with such practices, and perhaps encouraged their users to believe that the miniature masks and baby figurines were also somewhat "alive" and magically operational.

Yet, however efficacious, what such lifelike features did *not* do was encourage the user to enter too deeply in performative collaboration with the object. Despite their shared use of a real, lifelike hole from which sound could (be imagined to) emanate, the masks and infant figurines imply the production of very different noises. Theatrical dialogue parallels adult human speech, albeit in a more formalized and prescribed version; thus the masks would indicate that shared performance with an adult user was possible. Yet, the smallness of the masks and their display function limits that possibility. On the other hand, the infant figurines exist in three-dimensional space, to be cuddled and caressed in presumably intimate ways. But their open-but-silent mouths insist upon the production of a noise that no user could fully approximate; even the cries of a child old enough to play with and carry such a figurine (if such a toy-like use was, in fact, allowed) differ markedly from the distinctive cry of a newborn. In the absence of plausible sound production, the infant figurines remained quiet – unable to close their mouths, and thus marking by their silent yowls an artificiality and remove from reality.

Both the masks and the infant figurines inspired and encouraged a performance that, by design, would always be inadequate and never be complete. That lack of perfect performative mimesis meant that the user, no matter how interested in the object, was never quite allowed to fully inhabit the role, becoming truly an "actor" or truly a "parent." Instead of encouraging their users to enter fully into the realm of the miniature, such objects redirected attention to the real-scale social world, where such actions and roles could be fully realized and, thus, where any such aspirations should be exercised.

This is not to say that these figurines could have no role in social negotiation and change. For instance, the mask pictured in Figure 2.15 was found beneath Level IV of the Heroon at Seleucia-on-the-Tigris.[136] As Level IV dates to c. 290–143 BCE, the mask's context prior to Level IV places its manufacture, use, and deposition within the earliest years of the city. This miniature mask, displayed and used in a public space[137] (although possibly one that dates prior to the Heroon construction), referenced performances – perhaps of the Seleucid royal "hero" commemorated in the Heroon, or a character from Greek tragedy. In viewing – and maybe even imagining oneself taking on – such roles, a more general performance of Greek cultural identity new to the region was also enacted and, thus, familiarized. However, because both the masks and the infant figurines emphasized the artificiality and inadequacy of the real-life performances they inspired, the social negotiations in which they were engaged were also kept at a comfortable distance.

Rather than being frustrated at the tiny dimensions of this Greek theater mask, users might be pleasantly content with the reassurance that, no matter how hard they tried to cover their faces, the object could not completely obscure their true identities. The real face remained visible, despite the user's tentative engagement (real or imagined) with an alternate persona.

The appeal of such a "low-impact" experimentation with cross-cultural negotiation may also explain why, out of all the many figurine motifs in Hellenistic Babylonia, cut-open mouths were only used to induce interactivity with figurines depicting masks or babies. Both actors and infants produce sounds, sometimes shockingly loud ones, to which audiences and parents are, by the very nature of their roles, supposed to hear and respond. Yet "hearing" is not the same as "listening" or "comprehending." The sounds made by babies and actors share a certain level of inconsequentiality: they "speak," but not always rationally; they demand attention, but only sometimes is it clear how and when to respond. Unpracticed actors inhabiting ill-written characters give botched and garbled performances, colicky babies refuse to be soothed – both uttering nonsocial sounds into a social world, the liminal speech of beings that are not quite fully human.[138] Social negotiation in such spaces, using such marginal bodies, could be figuratively "loud" in its voiceless shouting while simultaneously remaining at a comfortable remove from the identities of the people who engaged with them. As I proposed earlier in this chapter with reference to the puppet figurines, it is quite possible that people often did not *want* intimacy with miniatures – even those miniatures with which they were inspired to directly interact. By emphasizing the artificiality of such interactive engagements with the miniature world, the masks and infant figurines both pointed to the social world as the real space of intimacy and, simultaneously, made the real cross-cultural negotiations happening in that social space seem less threatening.

Rattles

Figural rattles, the final group of interactive figurines discussed in this chapter, might not be consistently classified as "figurines" at all. Like figurines, these figural rattles were made in molds and depict the human form in miniature, yet they were experienced aurally as well as (and perhaps even in preference to) visually. The Hellenistic Babylonian figural rattles generally depict the face and upper bust of a child. The rattle is finished off by a flat bottom at approximately the child's waist. Double molding does not seem to have been used to provide details to the backside of the figure, but only to allow for an internal hollow space, within which small objects were placed that create a tinkling sound when the rattle is shaken. Details were provided on the fronts of such rattles: the child was generally shown wearing a three-peaked hat, earrings, and a band

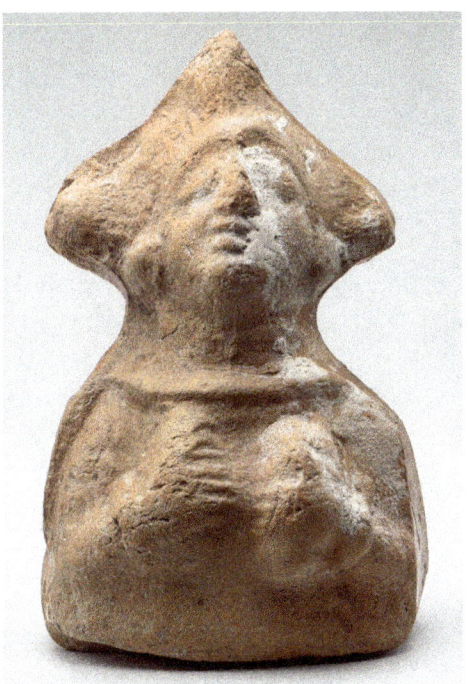

2.18. Rattle in the form of a human figure (head and upper torso, likely of a child), terracotta, unknown provenance (likely Babylon). Height: 8.4 cm. Musée du Louvre (AO 24674) Photograph courtesy of Art Resource and the Musée du Louvre.

necklace. The child's face looks directly forward or slightly upward, with the hands clasped tightly to the chest. In some cases, the child is holding an object in his or her hands: for instance, the rattle seen in Figure 2.18 depicts the child holding two oblong objects, one of which appears to have the head of a bird; other examples, such as that seen in Figure 2.19, hold a round, flat disk that resembles a tambour-style frame drum. However, in most cases, the surface of the figurine is too vague to be able to determine the identity of the held object or even if any objects were being held by the child. Indeed, some of these figures cannot have been holding objects of any volume under their hands, and may simply have been clasping their hands across their chests.[139]

The arm postures of these rattle children, along with their action of holding objects, closely connect the figural rattles to Hellenistic Babylonian figurines of women and children, which often hold their hands to their chests. More detailed exploration of what this posture might have meant in figurines of children and women can be found in Chapter 4. For the purposes of this discussion, it is most crucial to note that the rattles engaged with the larger corpus of figurines in a few, select ways that echoed ideas of power and the divine. Not all child figurines wear three-pointed headdresses; however, all of the rattles do. This headdress has been linked with the child-god Harpocrates,

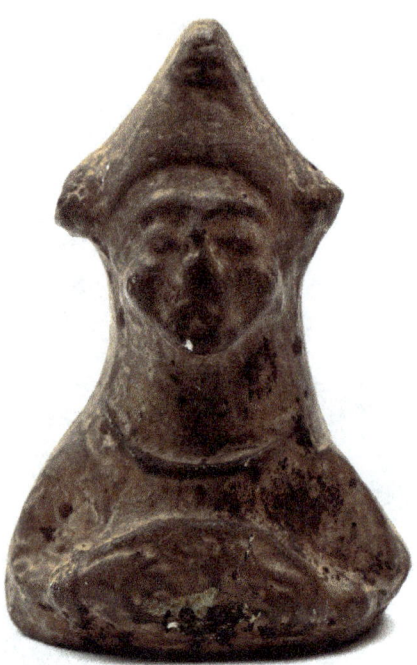

2.19. Rattle in the form of a human figure (head and upper torso, likely of a child), terracotta, Nippur. Height: 9.3 cm. Modern cast. University of Pennsylvania Museum of Archaeology and Anthropology (B 1954)
Photograph courtesy of the University of Pennsylvania Museum.

and may point to a ritual function for these rattles in evoking Harpocrates's healing power.[140] The objects held by the children depicted in rattles may too have had a ritual function. In particular, depictions of the tambour-style frame drum, when combined with the rattle's function as an actual musical instrument, doubly invoked the idea of sound production – both in miniature and real-scale worlds. It may have been particularly meaningful that both instruments (the actual rattle and the depicted frame drum) were percussion instruments, which generally had close connections to ritual practices in both the Greek and Babylonian traditions – thus the double reference to musical instruments may have pointed to a precise magical efficacy.[141] Beyond the specifics of what objects were held, it is additionally noteworthy that not all child or female figurines hold their arms to their chests, but all of the rattles do – either to hold an object or simply to assume this pose. The pose of women holding one or both arms to the chest, particularly to support the breasts, had a long history in Mesopotamia[142] and, through their similarity, the rattles evoked the visual power of that traditional motif. The interactivity that the rattles encouraged might have amplified that power, bringing it from the static world of inanimate figurines to the enlivened and ritually efficacious world of magic through the inducement to shaking and the production of sound.

Yet, not every aspect of the rattles conveyed a greater force and impact than is seen in the figurines. Unlike the figurines which can stand alone with their entire bodies depicted, the rattles represent an abbreviated version of the body that is finished-off at the waist. Arms are included, but the lower torsos and legs are always absent. This severing of bodies and omission of limbs echoes aspects of the sexualized female figurines with added arms, as well as the puppet figurines, discussed earlier in this chapter. Of all of these, the rattles have the most abbreviated bodies, with the possibility of adding limbs and rectifying the loss of bodily wholeness completely denied by the sealed and flattened "base" of the rattle. Even identifying these figurines' intended life-stage and sex – child (usually male child in the Hellenistic Babylonian corpus) or adult woman – can be difficult considering that these figurines have no corporeal space for genitalia or reproductive anatomy.[143] They are both hobbled and castrated, half-bodies entirely dependent on their human users for movement and care.

This lameness and impotence, which is in sharp contrast with the implied power of the figures' poses and garments, may be explained by further exploring their theatricality. As with the puppets, masks, and infant figurines, the rattles are engaged with issues of performance. However, they differ from these other miniatures in two crucial aspects. First, they do not *reference* performances enacted in other places and times. Instead, the performances with which the rattles were involved existed primarily in the actual moment of user-object interaction. Rather than serving as a fantasy refuge into which the user could submit and escape, even temporarily pretending to take on another, on-stage identity, the rattles demanded that the user become a performer in the here-and-now.

The second crucial difference between rattles and other theatrical figurines builds upon the first distinction, in that the rattles do not fully allow their users the option of whether or not to participate in that here-and-now performance. Unlike the puppets which could be held without their legs being operated, or the masks and babies which did not need to be raised to the face or supplied with voices, the rattles made a noise the moment that the user touched them. The cascading of the small objects inside the rattle cannot be stopped; if the rattle is disturbed, a high-pitched tinkling sound is produced. Indeed, this sound can occur even if human agency is not involved: a bump of the table, the shaking of a passing ox-cart, an accidental brush by the tail of a dog – any of these could cause the rattle to make a noise. This distinguished the rattles from many other real-world musical instruments, such as lyres or double-pipes, which could be handled or carried without that action resulting in the production of sound. The ease with which sound is produced within these rattles, and the relative helplessness of the human interlocutor to control when sounds were made, make the rattles seem almost alive or sentient. This aspect of the rattles might have made them particularly appealing both as ritual objects and as children's toys – or both, as rattles could have had an apotropaic function in protecting infants who shook them.[144] Indeed, in many ways the rattles paralleled the behavior of children – both the children that they might have depicted and the children that might have used them – in that children are also unpredictably noisy.[145]

In that lifelike quality, the rattles would perhaps have a claim on being the most intimate of all the figurines discussed in this book, offering their users the closest chance of truly gaining entry into "life in miniature." Yet, the sharp curtailing of the figure's body in these rattles prevented any illusion that the miniature person was truly alive. Unlike the prospect and contemplation of trauma induced by the female figurines with movable arms, the radical truncation of the rattle bodies goes beyond horror and pain into the realm of the obviously fictional. Intimacy with a real person was not possible in the rattles because, the object suggests, a "person" was never really here. This obvious artificiality may have been comforting to the Hellenistic Babylonian users – or the parents of potential child users – reassuring them that the figurines will not, in fact, come to life, and any magic activated by their poses and noises could be contained. Not only do the bodies of these figural rattles clearly indicate that they could not "walk away," but their finished-off torsos also provide conveniently flat bases that give the rattles vertical stability and allow them to be displayed – and, perhaps more importantly, stored – on a flat surface. The user was thus offered some respite from the intense prospect of intimacy with a "living" sound-producing figure through the possibility that its potential might be contained to moments of use, when the remainder of the figure's body may have been imagined. The rest of the time, the user could easily and reassuringly slip back to reality, where the rattle's body only had an artificial half-existence and the rattling could be (mostly) silenced by resting the object on a shelf.

CONCLUSION

Interactive figurines offer the greatest range of possibilities for the life-size human user to enter into the small-scale miniature world. Actively recruiting not just sight but also touch and hearing, these figurines lure us into close physical proximity and emotional engagement. Play with new and unfamiliar identities is made possible, with the user given opportunities for experimentation and expression. Larger-than-life forces and situations, such as battlefield combat and theatrical performance, were made manageable and accessible. Yet, as was seen throughout this chapter, such prospects came with a price. Opening oneself up to closeness with the figurine world also meant opening oneself up to "influence in miniature" – influences that were shaped by the larger social world in which such figurines were manufactured, sold, and considered acceptable. Interactivity with a commercially produced figurine always entails interaction with the social world. The illusion of intimacy smoothed the path and lowered personal defenses, allowing social norms, ideals, and limitations to intrude on the user's most private moments, personal spaces, and desires. By encouraging closeness and interaction, the interactive figurines were among the most constricting of miniatures, regulating as much as they provided the opportunity for expression.

Socially useful as it was, impediments were also placed on that user-object closeness. The interactive figurines discussed throughout this chapter were activated primarily by touch and enlivened through real movement. Yet, "dancing" or "horse riding" in miniature is distinctly different from reality. Unlike their figurine counterparts, living horse riders do not mount their horses by flying in from above, and living theatrical performers are not animated by means of a string through their heads. The apparatus needed to make such figurines functional also distanced the miniature from the real action depicted – imperiling (or at least making more oblique) the user's self-identification with the object. Users were inspired to see themselves as performing *with* the miniature dancer or *controlling* the horse rider, not necessarily *being* either one. Thus, these most intimate of miniatures were also, in many ways, the most artificial. Some of this was perhaps by necessity, in order to make the figurines movable. Yet, at least some of this artificiality was by design. The arms of sexualized female figurines could have been jointed to move in more lifelike ways. The rattle figurines could have been given whole bodies and the masks could have been made the size of a real human face. Instead, these were terracotta fictions – and obviously so. They called the user to interact and play, but as a collaborator with – and, insistently, an outsider from – the miniature world, rather than a full participant within it.

In contrast to the artificiality of the miniature-user relationship created by the interactive figurines, there were some Hellenistic Babylonian figurines that depicted more natural, lifelike interpersonal engagements. These "group figurines," which depicted two bodies interacting at miniature scale within the same figurine object, are the subject of Chapter 3. Yet neither they nor any of the rest of the figurines discussed in this book will reach quite the intensity of intimacy illusions that were made possible by the interactive figurines discussed in this chapter. Even with these most engaging of objects, Hellenistic Babylonian users had to content themselves with "fascination" rather than true intimacy.

CHAPTER THREE

THREE'S A CROWD: SPECTATORSHIP
OF FIGURINES

IN THIS CHAPTER, FOCUS SHIFTS FROM FIGURINES THAT WERE designed to interact with the user, as discussed in Chapter 2, to figurines that were designed to show interactions or relationships between figures within an individual figurine. These "group figurines" all depict two human bodies together on a single object, permanently fused into an inseparable relationship and unable to be parted from one another – except by using a level of force that would destroy the figurine. The figures depicted in these group figurines *belong* together. Of course, the group figurines were not the only possible assemblages of miniature bodies that could be displayed or used together in Hellenistic Babylonia. Figurines depicting just one human form, which constitute the vast majority of the figurine corpus, could be gathered and utilized together in any number of different combinations – and, indeed, likely were, as archaeological evidence indicates that figurines were often found in multiples within single rooms of domestic dwellings.[1] Yet what differentiates those figurine assemblages from the group figurines is that those choices were impermanent, could be changed, and responded to the desires of the individual user. With the group figurines, the Hellenistic Babylonian user had the choice of whether or not to purchase the figurine or, once purchased, whether or not to keep the object in his or her possession. But this was largely a binary choice: acceptance of a predetermined association between miniature human bodies or not. The user did not have a choice in which human bodies were brought together in a permanent relationship, how that relationship was displayed, the relative poses and interactions of the bodies, and so forth.

This lack of choice and agency on the part of the individual consumer is particularly important given that the range of options for Hellenistic Babylonian group figurines was quite limited. Three main categories of group figurines existed: adult women with children (usually infants), heterosexual couples, and musician pairs. This is not to say that all of the relationships shown in the group figurines were presented in the same way, with the same level of interaction between the miniature bodies or offering the same level of interaction to the human user. Indeed, one of the main focal points of this chapter's discussion will be the degree to which the poses, body language, gestures, and physical construction of these objects either welcomed the user or enforced a certain degree of distance. For instance, the features of some figurines, such as the mothers with children, suggest that spectatorship is welcome. Others, particularly the heterosexual couples, imply that the user is an interloper, that "three's a crowd." Yet despite this range of receptiveness to the user's gaze, almost every group figurine demonstrates an awareness of the user's presence. It is rare to encounter a Hellenistic Babylonian group figurine made to appear as if the participants in the miniature interaction were completely unaware of being observed. Thus one of the primary unifying aspects of this corpus is a sense of performance before an audience – and spectatorship on the part of the user. This is strikingly different from the more overtly interactive figurines discussed in Chapter 2, which lured their users into co-performances. This chapter therefore moves even further from the prospect of true intimacy being created between user and figurine. Many of the figurines in this chapter will offer views onto intimate moments – but the user is usually relegated to a third-party audience role, rather than clearly invited into the encounter.

MEET THE BABY: WOMAN AND CHILD FIGURINES

It is perhaps not surprising that one of the few types of relationships depicted in Hellenistic Babylonian figurines was that between an adult woman and a child, usually an infant. The connection between an infant and an adult, often female, caregiver is the first relationship that most people experience in their lives. It is also one of the most important, as the perpetuation of human society – indeed, the survival of the human species, given the unparalleled helplessness of our offspring – is dependent on such acts of nurture and protection.

Perhaps because of the primal nature of this relationship, depictions of an adult woman with a child have a long history in the figurine traditions of the ancient world. In Mesopotamia, figurines of women with children were already common by the third millennium BCE.[2] Hellenistic Babylonian figurines depicting women with children more immediately followed upon the intense popularity of the nursing mother motif in the Neo-Babylonian era.[3] In their form and style, they were also in close dialogue with other woman and child *kourotrophos* (child carrying) figurines of the Hellenistic *koine*, particularly figurines from Israel,[4] Ptolemaic Egypt,[5] and the Greek cities of southern Italy.[6] However, it is notable that the motif of the mother-and-child, particularly the nursing mother, is almost completely absent in pre-Hellenistic Greek art.[7] As has been argued by Adi Erlich,[8] the figurines of the "Hellenistic *koine*" and the figurines of "Greece" should not be considered commensurate traditions, and *kourotrophos* figurines are a prime example of this divergence. In utilizing this motif, the people of Hellenistic Babylonia demonstrated their deep local roots in Mesopotamia, as well as their connections with the wider Hellenistic world, but averred sharply from Greek tradition in so doing.

It is possible that users of woman-and-child Hellenistic Babylonian figurines engaged with these objects, at least in part, because of a desire to participate in these deep temporal and geographic connections. The subject matter itself, an awareness of the motif's existence in long-standing traditions, and perhaps also a sentimentalized recollection of one's own childhood or motherhood experiences, may have combined to endow such figurines with a sense of timelessness. The human life cycle is perpetual: babies are born every day, and have been for millennia. Figurines, such as that pictured in Figure 3.1, offer a window onto that eternal process of new life created, birthed, and nurtured. Woman-and-child figurines also provide a more literal timelessness, giving their users the opportunity to freeze an otherwise transitory stage of human development. Real infancy slips by in a matter of months; squirmy toddlers quickly age out of being carried in the manner that the woman in Figure 3.1 supports the baby, cradled across her lap and tucked into the crook of her elbow. Alternately, and tragically common in the ancient world, babies die, even despite the best efforts of their caregivers. The moment depicted in the woman-and-child figurines is an enormously important and ever-present part of human life, but also a temporary and fragile one. The power that such figurines offered to reduce the liminality of this relationship may help account for their widespread appeal. Connection of these figurines with depictions of goddesses, and, in some cases, the direct inclusion of divine attributes, may have given supernatural potency to the figurine's implied ability to make permanent – and thus protect – this most essential, vulnerable, and (crucially) transitory of human relationships.

Audience Admiration

A desire for permanency in the adult-child relationship may explain why many of these figurines were modeled with stable bases that facilitate easy upright

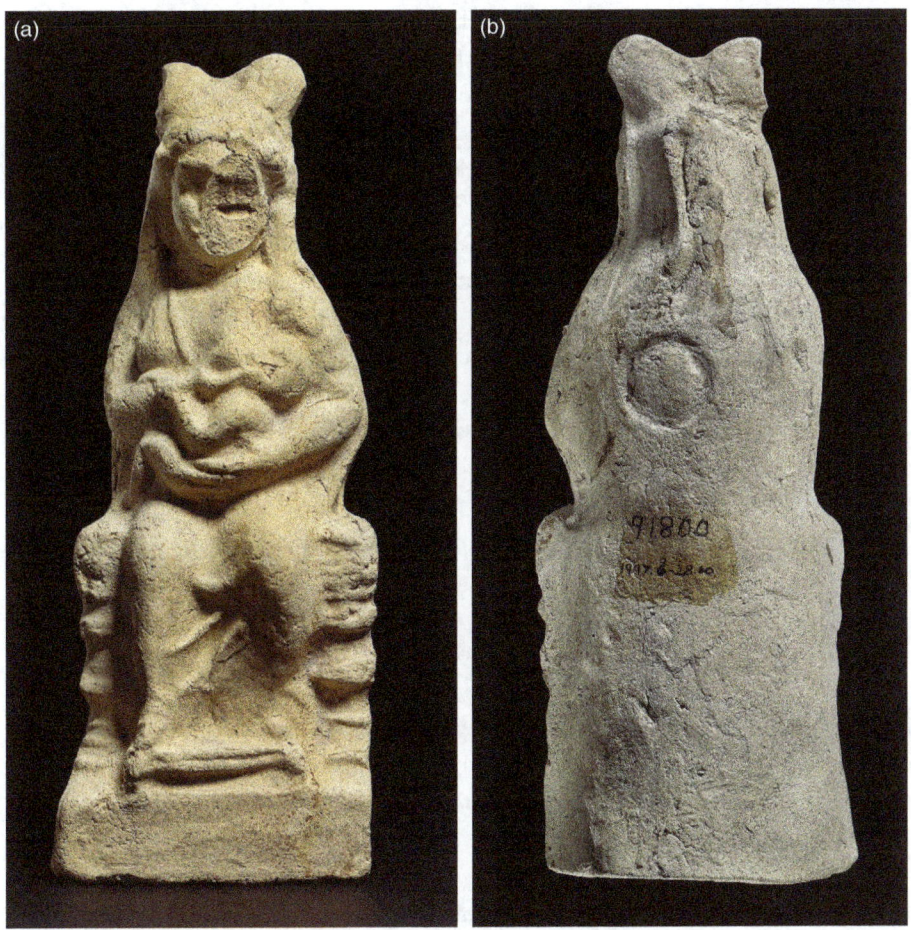

3.1a and b. Front and back of woman and child figurine, terracotta, Babylon. Height: 15.5 cm. British Museum (BM 91800)
Photographs © The Trustees of the British Museum.

display. Some figurines, like that seen in Figure 3.1, depict the woman seated on a throne or chair. Conical bases or couch bases were other options for granting vertical stability to figurines depicting seated women with children. Standing women holding children could be shown on a plinth or thick flared base. The ability of most of these figurines to stand alone, without human aid, distanced them from a potential user. Unlike the majority of the figurines discussed in Chapter 2, these woman-and-child figurines do not need tactile contact to "come alive" – in fact, they do not ask for tactile contact at all. The babies in particular are very difficult to touch, as their bodies are often more implied than fully modeled in three dimensions. The women's bodies are more accessible, although their heavy drapery and unmodeled backsides (even when double molds are used, as in the case of the figurine in Figure 3.1) do not reward tactile exploration. Bulky when single molded and thick-walled when double molded, the technical construction of these figurines also favors the sturdy and powerful rather than the pleasantly tactile and portable.

A lack of vent holes on double-molded examples of this figurine motif similarly reinforces this impression of solid stability. The back of the figurine in Figure 3.1 features the impression of a 1.6-cm-diameter guide for a vent hole, intended to be pierced through to allow hot air to escape the figurine during firing and thus prevent the figurine from exploding. However, the vent hole was never cut out. Refusing to cut the vent hole granted a greater sense of wholeness and solidity to the figurine despite the technical risk. Such autonomous strength was not only distancing; it was also timeless, locating the women and children outside of the realm of normal concerns and quotidian worries – such as whether or not a figurine might break during firing. Similarly, the chairs and plinths frequently used as bases for these figurines raise the women and children off the ground, placing them at a remove from human hands and, indeed, from the human world. These women and children seem to occupy an alternate space, which parallels and facilitates the perception that they also occupy an alternate time, a temporal plane in which babies neither age nor die. These babies are literally "out of reach" of mortal woes, instead existing forever in a mother's protective embrace.

Desires for an artificial, timeless permanency may also explain why most Hellenistic Babylonian woman-and-child figurines rarely depict the connection between the two figures as one of shared intimacy. Although the woman and child are almost always engaged in close physical interaction – usually with the woman holding or even nursing the child – the woman is consistently shown gazing outward. Smaller infants are generally positioned laterally and thus their gaze would be directed toward the woman – if they were, in fact, meant to appear awake and with eyes open, a level of detail which is often not provided on the figurines. However, some infants do look out; see, for instance, the swaddled baby in the figurine pictured in Figure 3.2. Older children, such as the toddler carried on the woman's hip as seen in Figure 3.3, almost always stare outward.[9] In figurines ostensibly meant to celebrate a nurturing bond, this lack of visual connection between the adult and child tempers any emotional intimacy.

It also belies the substantial responsibility and labor-intensive nature of parenting. We are not shown a woman who toils and feels drained by continual physical and emotional demands; rather, the figurines fix the woman's attention elsewhere. Her head is raised, her gaze directed away rather than down at the child, her right hand guiding her breast to the infant's mouth as if by habit. Visual interaction with the nurturing adult and the face-to-face attention so crucial to infant development is denied. What has distracted this woman? In all likelihood, we have – the viewers and users of the figurine. And yet rather than making us feel like outsiders and interlopers, the woman's frontal posture, erect

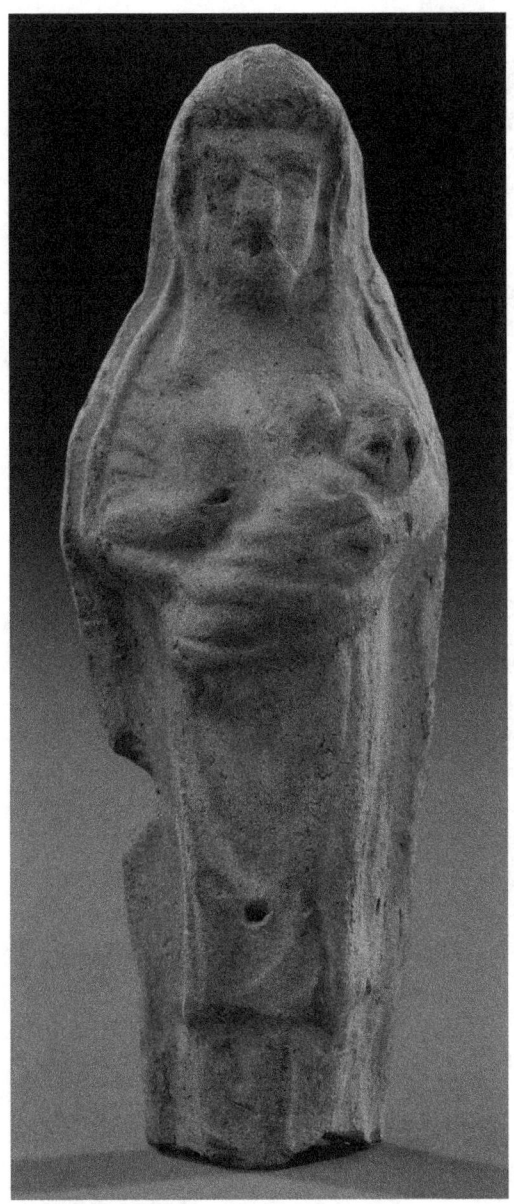

3.2. Woman and child figurine, terracotta, Babylon. Height: 9.4 cm. Vorderasiatisches Museum Berlin (VA Bab 989)
Photograph © Staatliche Museen zu Berlin-Vorderasiatisches Museum, Foto: Olaf M. Teßmer.

torso, and forward gaze seem to welcome us – or, at the very least, imply that we are expected witnesses. The plinths and chairs that elevate these women above the mortal plane also structure the figures in a frontal-facing manner, exposing the entire scene to easy legibility from a single vantage point. Indeed, without the viewer's presence, the pose makes little sense. This is a posture of

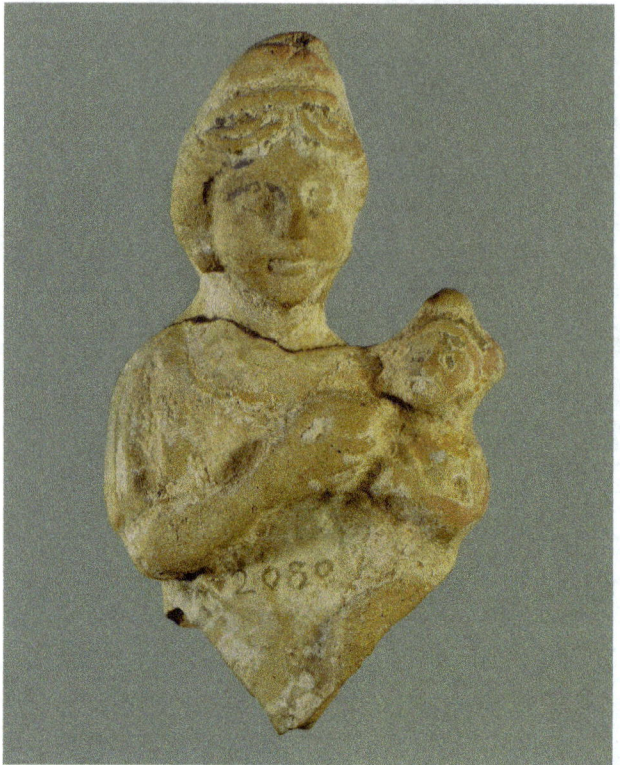

3.3. Woman and child figurine, terracotta, likely Babylon. Height: 10.5 cm. Harvard Semitic Museum (1899.2.702)
Photograph courtesy of the Semitic Museum, Harvard University.

interaction with the outside world, a pose of being watched. It displays the relationship between woman and child, frozen in time despite the usually transitory nature of this life stage, for the leisured appreciation and pleasure of a spectator. To riff on the title of this chapter: in this case, three is definitely not a crowd.

The projected image made available to that spectator is one of exceptional maternal competence and leisured bliss. The distracted breastfeeding of the female figure in Figure 3.1 projects the easy accomplishment of a process that, while natural, is surprisingly difficult to master.[10] Especially with an infant so young, effortless breastfeeding is uncommon, as both baby and mother must learn the technique – sometimes without success.[11] The figurine woman's ability to nurse her infant while engaging with an audience exudes a proficiency and confidence that real women often only aspire to. Yet, she is not truly "multitasking" either, in the way that mothers of infants who are established, secure breastfeeders can go about performing daily household responsibilities.[12] Indeed, the women depicted in these figurines seem immune to the whole host of chores and challenges that even mothers who breastfeed easily must deal with – of which inconsolable crying, sleepless nights, and soiled diapers are only the most routine, and by no means an exhaustive list. These figurines have thus frozen and made timeless not only a temporary life-stage, but also a truly fleeting moment of calm serenity within those brief newborn months. Often placed literally on a pedestal, this mother is both symbol and impossible standard, her openness to spectatorship implying that this perfect maternal ideal should be witnessed, understood, and emulated. She looks to us in order to await our applause – or, at least, our admiring reverence.

An Iconography of Service

This lactation and nursing competency was crucial to child survival in the ancient world, but – due to high maternal mortality during childbirth, the difficulty some women experience with nursing, or simple convenience – this nurturing act was not always provided by the biological mother. Scholars often refer to these figurines as "mothers," however the assumption that the woman depicted was always interpreted by ancient viewers as the child's mother should not be uncritically accepted. Wet nurses could be hired to breastfeed children in ancient Mesopotamia,[13] as is documented in law 194 of Hammurabi's law code; note that the wording of the law clearly indicates that the child's biological mother was still alive while the wet nurse's services were being utilized.[14] Contracts for employing wet nurses have been found in Hellenistic and Roman Egypt.[15] In Greece, women often nursed their own children, but wet nurses were not uncommonly used by women for whom breastfeeding was difficult, or in elite households.[16] In such cases, wet nurses were hired or one of the household slaves was required to perform the task.[17] The bond that developed between a wet nurse and the child she suckled is described in both Greek and Mesopotamian sources as an affectionate and loving one. Greek vases depict aging wet nurses openly mourning the deaths of adults they cared for as children[18]; reciprocally, loving grave epigrams were dedicated to deceased nurses by the children they had reared.[19] Several Mesopotamian documents reveal that royal children often referred to their wet nurses by affectionate names, such as "mother," and adult princesses would sometimes take their wet nurses with them when they married.[20] The bond and closeness between woman and child that can be observed in the Hellenistic Babylonian figurines therefore does not necessarily preclude the identification of "nurse."

Similarly, the age and dress of the terracotta figures may not firmly clarify the woman's identity. Most of the woman-and-child figurines from Hellenistic Babylonia show the female figure with a slender, firm body type and elaborate, often Greek-style drapery. Such indicators of youth and wealth may make it more plausible that these women were meant to be seen as the mother of the child. In contrast, nurses in the Hellenistic *koine* figurine repertoire were shown as older women with sagging breasts, likely connected to the "Old Nurse" character type of the New Comedy.[21] However, Greek vase painting and stelae often depicted younger women as slaves engaged in childcare,[22] and it can be difficult to distinguish "nurses" from "mothers" in Greek representations of private life.[23] Regarding the elaborately pleated drapery, Mesopotamian records indicate that wet nurses were given allowances of clothing and, in some cases, very expensive gifts.[24] Further muddling any close reading of the figurines for marks of "mother" versus "nurse" is the possibility that these objects may more strongly reflect Hellenistic Babylonian negotiations regarding female bodies generally (as will be discussed in Chapter 4), rather than a specific identity distinction. Overall, it seems possible that at least some of these figurines were interpreted by an ancient user as depicting a nurse and child, rather than a mother and child.

Additionally complicating the identification of the adult female figure was the practice of forcing or hiring slave women to conceive offspring for families in which the wife was experiencing infertility. This custom is extensively referenced in the Hebrew Bible[25] and was a part of Mesopotamian social norms as well. In one of the earliest documented cases, an Old Assyrian marriage contract stipulates that if the new wife does not bear a child, she will provide her husband with a slave for that purpose.[26] Similar evidence in Old Babylonia indicates that infertile wives could create legitimate children for their husbands through slave-surrogates; such children were not legally considered the child of the slave woman, and might have been taken by the wife immediately after birth.[27] Slave women who bore their master's children were sometimes accorded status of "second wife" to the husband, but they were still slaves in relationship to the first wife and could be sold either directly after childbirth or later on if they committed a transgression or offended their mistress.[28] These women are often referred to in contemporary scholarship as "surrogates"; while this term does not capture the lack of female consent, as well as the sexual and emotional violence, that likely accompanied many of these arrangements, it does reflect the reality of a woman pregnant with what was (socially and legally, if not biologically) someone else's child. Whether or not these women were actually involved in the raising of their offspring, especially at the infancy and nursing stage, or if they were expected to immediately relinquish the baby, is not always known, and may have varied according to region and time period. Additionally there is evidence that more equitable surrogacy practices were also possible in Babylonia, in which a second wife could be adopted as a "sister" of the first wife, the two then sharing their marital and parental duties as equals.[29]

The contractual and legally regulated practices of surrogacy (hired or enforced pregnancy and infant relinquishment) and wet-nursing has important implications for the kinds of relationships that these "woman-and-child" figurines depicted.

They not only portrayed a physical and emotional bond between two people, but also potentially revealed a network of social and economic connections. Even if the figurine's user interpreted the image as a mother and child in the traditional sense, the commodification of nursing and childbearing located these acts of mothering conceptually, if not also physically, in the public sphere. It is likely that the act of nursing a baby routinely took place in front of spectators, such as other members of the family or even, when a nurse was employed, in the third-party presence of the mother herself.[30] Wet nurses were sometimes contracted to nurse the child in his or her parents' house, while in other cases the woman took the child back to her own home.[31] Thus the act of nursing could bring the child into not just the care of a single non-relative nurse, but also larger social circles beyond his or her biological family at a very young age – creating relationships that, in some cases, could last a lifetime.[32] The pose of the figurine anticipates this diverse spectatorship. Indeed, it implies that the woman should not only accept, but actively receive and welcome the intrusion of spectators – viewers who may have been less interested in *her*, and more interested in the services she could provide, seeing her body primarily as a means toward a desirable end.[33]

While there are many idealizing aspects to this imagery, as discussed above and as will be returned to below, it seems worthwhile to dwell a moment on the ways in which this particular pose of infant display and rapt attention directed toward the audience casts the woman in an admired light specifically because of these services that she was performing for society. The figurine is imbued with this sense of service even if the woman is identified as both the biological and social mother of the child. The particular motif of the enthroned mother has strong parallels in representations of the goddess Isis suckling the god Horus (also known as Harpocrates in the Hellenistic period) – imagery that was widely popular throughout the Mediterranean in the Hellenistic period – as well as in the later Virgin Mary and Christ imagery that was derived from it.[34] Venerated as sacred, these women were nevertheless celebrated primarily for what they could provide – and, particularly, for whom they could provide it. The Virgin is celebrated because she bears Christ; the suckling incarnation of Isis is a support for Horus, god of kingship.[35] Mortal women could share in this imagery as well; indeed, one of the earliest known examples of the motif is seen in an Old Kingdom calcite figurine (Dynasty 6, c. 2278 BCE) depicting the Egyptian Queen Ankh-nes-merira holding her son, the child-pharaoh Pepi II, across her lap in celebration of her care for him as both mother and regent.[36] While these women may have been enthroned, it was primarily so that their bodies could serve as even more luxurious, living thrones for their children.[37] As with all thrones, wooden or otherwise, their role thus became one of public presentation, displaying the enthroned child to the admiring gaze of spectators, for the benefit of society at large.[38]

Hellenistic Babylonian figurines may directly depict such goddesses; for instance, the figurine in Figure 3.1 could potentially be identified as Isis with Harpocrates or Cybele with Attis, although this figurine lacks a crown or other unambiguous goddess attributes.[39] However, such figurines may also have been plausibly identified as mortal women; the vast majority of such figurines, including the example seen in Figure 3.2, have no attributes or other indications of royal or divine status.[40] When this maternal "iconography of service" was transferred out of any specific focus on powerful or celestial women, and applied to the depiction of perhaps more ordinary mothers and nurses, it elevated and idealized. An equivalency between mortal and divine, royal and commoner was drawn – offering the promise that the lowliest woman, perhaps even a slave, could achieve perfection through her devotion to a child. However, it also made these women's roles as human thrones – useful primarily as social conduits for the supported child – more likely to overwhelm their personal identities. Indeed, if ideal mothers – women enthroned and crowned like goddesses or queens, women who presumably had the power to ensure their own privacy – appeared eager to respond to intrusive and curious audiences, a mere mortal would hardly have cause to reject such glances and (potential) admiration. Instead, the women become almost literal stepping-stones for introducing the child to community connections and the broader social world that the child would soon inhabit on his or her own terms. The posing of the figurines may reflect this progression, with the increasingly older children taking on outward-looking poses, reflective of and under the protection of the women who hold them, but with attention focused elsewhere (as seen in Figure 3.3).[41]

This is not to say that the images of maternal competence these female figures presented would have been regarded as any less ideal for their service-oriented role. Indeed, the female figure was shown taking on even more responsibility, serving both as a perfect caregiver for the child as well as the social conduit for the relationship of that child to a wider audience, including his or her family as well as the broader community. The figurine shown in Figure 3.2 demonstrates how both facets of idealization could be packaged for the viewer's easy understanding and internalization: the woman holds her right breast while the infant looks out toward the viewer, indicating that he or she has finished nursing and yet surplus milk remains. This bounty is offered to the viewer, as advertisement, if not for literal consumption. Her body's ideal – even superlative – ability is available to serve not just the child, but everyone, just as the child too is nurtured primarily in service of peopling the community and facilitating future social connections.

Models, Not Mirrors: Holding the Child on the Left

The intertwining of idealization with service also inflected the specific depiction of how the child was supported by the woman. In Hellenistic

Babylonian figurines, there seems to have been only one correct way to carry a baby: on the left side of the woman's body. If the child was held on a seated woman's lap, it was depicted with its head on the woman's left side and, sometimes, nursing from the left breast. Infants and older children could be shown balanced on the woman's left hip or standing at the woman's left side and (usually) holding her hand. The rare exceptions to this left-side trend were figurines that were overtly supernatural, depicting a goddess with a winged child (likely Aphrodite with Eros) either at her right side or flying over her right shoulder (see Figure 5.2, as well as discussion in Chapter 5). This left-side preference for mortal (or, at least, not overtly divine) mothers is observable in older Mesopotamian figurines as well. Some of the earliest examples of the woman-and-child motif depict the baby's head on the left side.[42] Closer in date to the Hellenistic era, the Neo-Babylonian woman-and-child figurines also exhibit exclusive preference for positioning the child on the mother's left side.[43] Invocations, or simply continuations, of this tradition may explain the similar depictions of infants held on the left side within the Hellenistic Babylonian figurine corpus.

This pose was potentially meaningful within Mesopotamian constructs of how power and gender were mapped along the vertical axis of the body. Most Mesopotamian stelae and other monuments present the right side of the king's body to the direct sight of the viewer. Irene Winter has theorized that this focus on depicting the king's right side stemmed, at least in part, from the importance of the perfectly formed right arm as a visual metaphor of the king's power and authority.[44] By fully presenting the king's right side for the viewer's inspection, there could be no question of hidden defects or deformities in the king's physical or political power. It is possible that similar concerns were at play in the depiction of women and children in figurines: by placing the child on the woman's left side, the woman's right side was fully exposed to view. While the women depicted in these figurines were clearly not kings, power and strength could reasonably have been considered a part of their role as caregivers and protectors of children. Indeed, when this iconography was used to portray powerful women, such as goddesses and queens, it was particularly associated with women who needed to act decisively and proactively as "single mothers" (or, conceptualized differently, as savior figures), caring and advocating for the child without the benefit of the immediate presence of the child's father (usually due to his death, or his supernatural remove to the underworld or divine realm).[45] Thus, a visibly perfect and unblemished right side – with the sense of physical power and strength that it would have conveyed to a Mesopotamian audience – might have been an important aspect of the woman-and-child motif.

However, this reasoning on the importance of an observable right side does not easily extend to depictions of the child, who is usually visible only on the left side of his or her body and is often shown nursing from the woman's left breast. In addition to echoing earlier figurine tradition, this preference for left-side nursing may be explained through the Mesopotamian association of female characteristics with the left side of the body.[46] The child is shown receiving nourishment from the more maternal and "female" of the woman's two breasts, while the more powerful right side of the woman's body was left free to be active – and, if necessary, protect the child. The necessity of protecting the child may also explain why the right side of the child's body is usually kept hidden, pressed close to the woman's flesh and thus obscured. As babies or toddlers, children cannot yet fend for themselves; with the exception of rare mythological examples (such as Herakles), their future power was understood to be yet nascent and unrealized.[47] It may thus have been especially important to protect the child's right side and right arm, which needed to remain perfectly formed into adulthood when its power could be revealed and brandished. In this way, the woman's body and the protection she offers served as a postnatal incubator, nestling and shielding the most important parts of the child's body and identity so that they could mature in safety and later emerge in fully grown potency.

In addition to these culturally specific meanings – which may or may not have been legible and meaningful to all members of Hellenistic Babylonian society – I additionally propose that the left-side positioning of the child also reflected a psychological and neurological ideal of mothering behavior. Several recent psychological studies have revealed that most people, particularly women, naturally carry babies on the left side, regardless of whether they are right- or left-handed.[48] Theories regarding this preference suggest that the posture promotes infant development, particularly social and emotional skills such as the ability to interpret facial expressions.[49] In contrast, studies suggest that children routinely held on the right side of their caregiver's body have more difficulty with such social cues.[50] Additionally, women who routinely hold their babies on the right side of their bodies are more likely to be experiencing maternal stress and depression, factors which can also create a less than ideal environment for their offspring.[51] Psychologically and neurologically, left-side placement of a child is ideal: for maternal health, for infant development, and – crucially – for enabling the child to develop successful relationships later in his or her social life.

Obviously, the Hellenistic Babylonian makers and users of woman-and-child figurines had no access to psychological research of this sort. But the consistent positioning of the child on the left side of the woman's body may reflect the craftsperson's daily observation of mothers and caregivers in action, the vast majority of whom would have naturally positioned their children in this way. It is even possible that some recognition of the negative developmental effects and/or maternal unhappiness linked with right-side placement were reflected in the figurines. The nurturing women depicted in figurines, who served as both support and conduit for the child's eventual social life, ideally positioned that child, giving him or her the best possible chance at a positive future.

Regardless of the specific reason for the child's left-side placement – or, indeed, if these figurines represent a combination of many meanings – it is crucial to note that the figurines do not literally *reflect* the lived practice of women holding their babies on the left side of the body. I have previously argued that the outward gaze of such woman-and-child figurines invited users to see themselves in the object, to identify with the essentialized image of ideal motherhood as aspirational or even as an accurate personal depiction.[52] While I remain convinced that such self-identification with figurines was encouraged by many aspects of this motif, I now suggest that it was tempered by the left-side pose. If, as the research suggests, we assume that the average living woman in Hellenistic Babylonia carried children on the left side of her body, then if she looked into a mirror, the reflection staring back at her would be inverted and show a right-side carrying posture. Such a woman approaching one of these figurines would not have had that feeling of reflection. Her gaze might have met the terracotta woman's gaze, but her child would have been completely misaligned with the terracotta baby – a noticeable disjuncture.

Men, older women, and other members of society might have looked at such figurines and seen a representation of an adored member of the family: his wife, her daughter, the family's beloved nurse. But the child-carrying woman herself would not only have seen an almost impossible ideal of competence, lactating abundance, social poise, and protection – she would also have clearly seen that "this isn't me." Rather, the experience of viewing such a figurine would have more closely resembled that of approaching another child-carrying woman, such as a sister or friend. The figurine women were thus not mirrors, but compatriots – and, due to their idealizing aspects, role models.

Social Conduits, Social Expectations

While many aspects of the woman-and-child motif discussed thus far could also have applied to life-size statuary, or even two-dimensional images, they would have been particularly intensified – or, rather, compressed and concentrated – in miniature. Making such an eager, outward-looking "mother" into a figurine positioned her as a willing participant in the twice-over commodification of her body, which was depicted as a vehicle for infant sustenance (that could be rented out or enslaved, if necessary) and also literally ownable in miniature form. She was an ideal, but an ideal that seemed happy to consent to being possessed, understood, controlled, and enjoyed.

It was not just motherhood as a skill and a practice that was being modeled in these figurines; it was also the social space allotted to mothers themselves and their relationships with their children. That social environ was one of both privilege and exposure. The paradoxical tension of motherhood and childhood as built upon private relationships and yet absolutely crucial for the existence of a "public," serving as the building blocks of societies and nations, was resolved in the Hellenistic Babylonian figurines firmly on the side of the public good. The figurines instructed that the primary value of such woman-and-child relationships was as a conduit to children joining the broader community. The woman's role was one of facilitator: literally, because maternal care ensured that children were protected and alive in order to mature to adulthood, and also socially, because the women depicted in these figurines were always shown looking outward, introducing the children to others, sending them out into the world. The figurines suggest that women who succeeded in emulating this model were worthy of thrones and crowns.

The actual relationships of living women to such ideal figurine models must have been complex and negotiated. For the Hellenistic Babylonian woman who owned such a woman-and-child figurine, the ideal of motherhood was literally at her fingertips, the figurine's open posture and expression implying a willingness to share and to teach. The miniaturization of such ideal maternal bodies made them easily accessible; despite their pedestals, such women were located physically, if not conceptually, within the human sphere. Together these features suggest a maternal ideal that could, or at least "should," be easily comprehended and emulated. The illusion of intimacy created by the properties of miniaturization had the potential to be particularly punitive here. If the human user felt that she had true intimacy – close, personal connection and deep understanding – of a figurine of ideal motherhood, and yet failed to attain such perfection in her own childrearing attempts, such "failures" may have been all the more painful.

Yet such a masochistic relationship may not have been the only way of interacting with the woman-and-child figurines. With memories tinged by sentiment and the passage of time, adult children might have been particularly likely to see their own mothers (or beloved wet nurses) in these epitomes of perfection. Older women might have similarly viewed such figurines through the blurry lens of nostalgia, remembering "the good old days" when their children were young. Some younger women may even have felt that their skills and talents as mothers did live up to the miniaturized flawlessness depicted in the figurines. For those who did not, the open "teaching" postures of the forward-facing women in the figurines – which, as I have already noted, were positioned as role models rather than reflections – may have encouraged women to seek out and accept guidance from other mothers in their communities. Indeed, while many of these figurines' idealizing aspects imposed a rigidly high standard of social *expectations* upon mothers, they also offered a clear social *conduit* for how such skills could be developed and such knowledge obtained. These figurines created a community of mothers and mothering through the act of their use, by spurring onlookers to remember their own experiences as young mothers (or as the children of young mothers) and by reminding each young mother herself that role models were available and she was not alone.

This tension between punishing idealism and caring reassurance was, I argue, at the heart of these figurines' function and appeal. Women themselves might have been collaborators and promoters of this figurine imagery and its underlying implication that motherhood was a difficult skill worthy of admiration. So too might women have derived power and prestige from the figurines' message that motherhood was primarily a social role and a public good. Women in the Hellenistic world experienced an elevation in status compared with their earlier counterparts in Classical Greece, which affected the treatment of the female body in everything from art to medicine[53]; this rise of women was partially due to the institution of royal families in the Hellenistic kingdoms, which relied on queens as successful mothers in order to continue dynastic lines and ensure political stability. The practice of royal women leveraging their positions as mothers, particularly to sons, in order to gain political power for themselves has occurred throughout history all over the world (Cleopatra VII, the last ruler of Hellenistic Egypt, being one particularly famous practitioner), but even more ordinary ancient women could raise their status in the family, and in society, by successfully bearing children.[54] Non-royal (albeit elite) women in Hellenistic Babylonia also enjoyed relative financial autonomy and social status, and these powers were often exercised in venues that emphasized the women's family ties and roles, such as wife and/or mother.[55] Thinking through how motherhood could be thus used in Hellenistic Babylonian society – promoted as a daunting task required of women for the public good *and* as a high-status role, worthy of enthronement, that enabled claims on other types of power – reveals how immediate and contemporary the figurine depictions of woman-and-child may have been.

The remarkable variety and deeply cross-cultural hybridity of the Hellenistic Babylonian figurines depicting women with children echo this sense of *au courant* vibrancy. Of all the figurines in Hellenistic Babylonia, depictions of caregiving women with children – which portrayed a primordial biological role and a very ancient figurine motif – would seem to have been most ripe for traditionalism and singular cultural focus. Copies of the highly standardized Neo-Babylonian versions of this figurine motif would have been easy to produce. But rather than rest upon tradition, the producers of the woman-and-child figurines, and presumably the members of the public who purchased them, opted to mobilize this archaic imagery and role in strikingly contemporary ways. The cross-cultural reality of Hellenistic Babylonian motherhood seems to have been particularly echoed in the figurine depictions. For instance, the soft naturalism seen in Figure 3.1, as well as the slight contrapposto posture (with the figure's left leg drawn back), indicates Hellenistic influence, and bound these Babylonian figurines together with contemporaneous images from far-flung locales such as Egypt and Italy. Yet, as already noted, the origin of the breastfeeding motif, as well as the particular pose of cradling a child in the figure's left arm and holding the infant across the body, evoked Mesopotamian figurines from the Neo-Babylonian period and earlier. The female figure's double-knobbed hairstyle, which was derived from Hellenistic Greek statues of Aphrodite with a topknot or bow of hair,[56] was enlarged and flattened here in a common Babylonian adaptation. The figurine's manufacture was similarly hybrid, combining the double-mold technique utilized primarily by Greek coroplasts with the frontal posture and unmodeled backside characteristic of Babylonian tradition. This combination of cultural features in the figurine pictured in Figure 3.1 does not follow a rigid formula; indeed, many of the other woman-and-child figurines combined cultural features in other ways. What seems most important to note is not the specifics of each combination, but rather their variety – along with the variety in the other formal features of these figurines, which could show women seated or standing, with infants or older children, with or without divine attributes, etc. This complex web of differing motifs and imagery suggests a living, vital tradition – one in which there was a broad agreed-upon sense of motherhood as an admired role and a social good, but within those parameters was a spectrum of lived identities and personhoods.

Yet, within that range of identities, the social relationship itself was depicted very narrowly. If these figurines were meant to represent family relationships, they did so in a very limited view. Many other potential relationships are missing from the figurine corpus: siblings, fathers with children, grandparents, extended family, etc. Even older mothers with their teenaged or adult children are conspicuously absent. This is a notable disjunction with the broader Hellenistic *koine* figurine corpus; the Tanagra figurines, in particular, depict older women in the company of younger women, likely their daughters, which follows on a Classical Greek figurine tradition of depicting the mother-daughter goddesses Demeter and Persephone.[57] Yet in Hellenistic Babylonia, the young woman holding an infant or toddler stands (or sits) alone, a solitary synecdoche of the entire family and the wealth of relationships it could contain.

This is certainly not to say that mother and child relationships were the only type of family relationships that existed in Hellenistic Babylonia, nor does it seem likely that this was the only kind of family bond that was valued. Figurines were not literal reflections of society; they were participants in dialogue with it. What that dialogue reveals is that woman-and-child relationships were the only family bond that was deemed worthy of celebration across Hellenistic Babylonian society as a whole. This placed an intense burden on a motif that, as I have discussed, was already heavily burdened with the weight of social expectations. It also limited the agency of the individual figurine user. If he or she wished to represent the family in figurine form, celebrating cherished bonds and happy memories, the options were severely restricted. Mental return to this primal moment and formative relationship was enforced, an eternal "back to the beginning" that implied, through its uniqueness, that similar perfection could not be replicated later in life or with other relationships. The child will grow, must grow – the world must "meet the baby," and vice versa – but no future relationship could ever be as perfect or as pure.

LIKE LOVERS DO: HETEROSEXUAL COUPLES

The only other group of Hellenistic Babylonian figurines which might plausibly have represented family relationships are those that depicted an adult male and female pair. Such figurines were often overtly sexualized, with the figures shown embracing, kissing, or with intertwined limbs indicative of a prelude to sexual intercourse. Figurines of couples and figurines of women and children might also have been linked in their functionality, possibly serving as magical aids or the physical manifestation of prayers for a fruitful marriage and the birth of healthy offspring.[58] However, caution should be exercised in assuming the link between the depictions of lovers and the depictions of mothers was too firm or obvious.[59] Figurines such as that pictured in Figure 3.4 are about intimacy and sexuality, but are not necessarily about fertility or family. Some of these figurines may indeed have been thought by their users to depict the marital relationship, but most examples are less clearly "family oriented" than simply depictions of sex and/or love.

Indeed, a striking contrast can be observed between the few figurines that seem to present a permanent and socially observed association between an adult man and woman (which will be discussed later in this chapter), and the more common depictions of an embracing and intertwined couple who often seem unaware that they are being observed. Are we, as viewers of figurines such as that seen in Figure 3.4, being allowed a clandestine peek into the private boudoir of a happily married couple? Or are we observing a less permanent union – between secret unmarried lovers, adulterous risk takers, master/mistress and slave, customer and prostitute? The figurines do not make these identities clear, nor do they even guarantee that sexual intercourse will occur. All of these couples could be interpreted as referencing sex in some way, whether sex that has already occurred in the past as a foundational act of

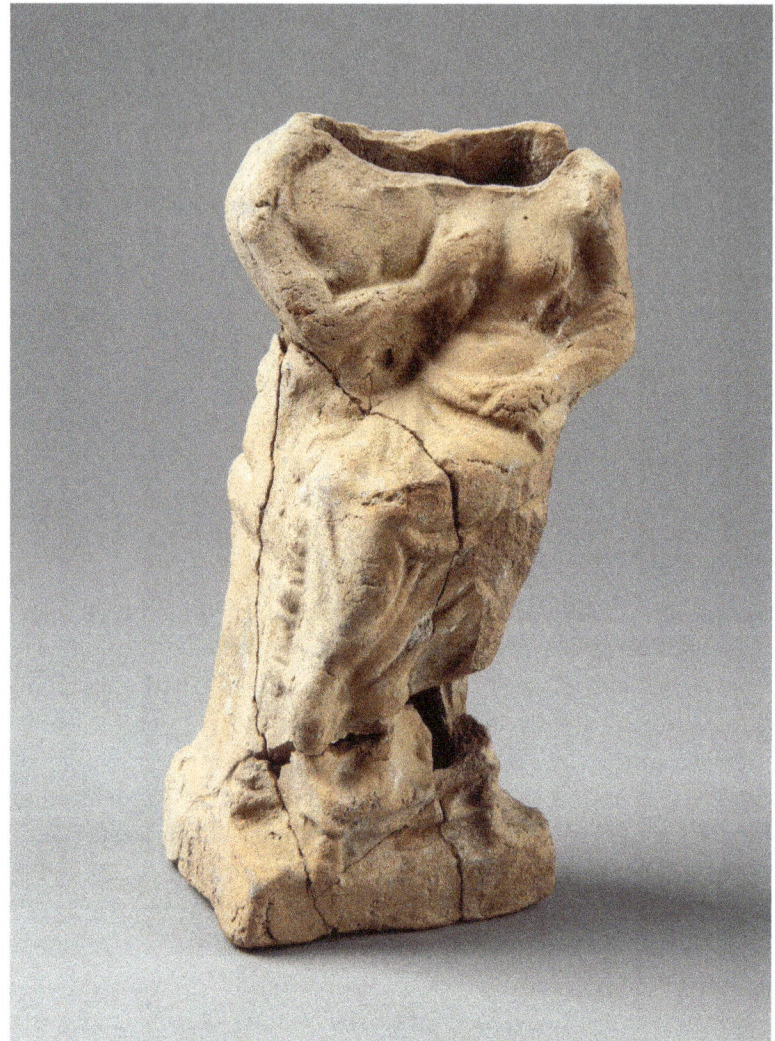

3.4. Embracing couple figurine, terracotta, Seleucia-on-the-Tigris. Height 18.3 cm. Kelsey Museum of Archaeology, University of Michigan, Ann Arbor (KM 15848) Photograph courtesy of the Kelsey Museum of Archaeology.

a marital union or sex on the brink of taking place in the future as the natural outcome of passionate embraces. But the act itself is never shown. Rather, it is left to the viewer's imagination.

Desire and Imagination

The flight of erotic fantasy inspired by such figurines would seem, at first glance, to be an intimate one. The figurine seen in Figure 3.4 offers up an intensely private moment between lovers to the user's inspection and for the user's enjoyment. A lack of clothing on the upper bodies clearly reveals youthful torsos at the peak of their sexual attractiveness. The man's hand reaches across his body to fondle the woman's breast in an overtly erotic gesture. Note particularly that it is the woman's right breast which is grasped, perhaps in a sexualized contrast with the more maternal emphasis on left breasts used for nursing infants, as discussed in the previous section of this chapter. Despite being covered with drapery, the lower bodies of the pair also exhibit sexualized features: the pose of the woman sitting in the man's lap implies genital proximity, while the tautness and sensual folds of the clothing call attention to the lithe limbs beneath. Additionally, and perhaps most importantly, the careless gathering of the fabric around the hips of each figure seems precarious and liable to slip off at any moment – particularly if the couple were to become more animate, perhaps changing positions, during the course of their amorous encounter.

Yet, as tantalizing and intriguing as such possibilities were, these figurines placed firm boundaries on the user's sight and touch – and, by extension, on the user's desire and wish-fulfillment. The figures will never move and the terracotta drapery will not, in fact, fall to the ground. The fantasy will not be consummated, and the figurine user can never access the intimacy that seems promised. The genitals of both figures are permanently invisible, as is the woman's right breast, which is obscured beneath her partner's hand and which does not exist as a separate surface, and so could not be accessed even if his arm were forcibly broken away. Such limitations were similarly imposed by the structure and manufacture of the figurines. Although the figurine seen in Figure 3.4 (as well as Figure 1.13) was made in a double mold and featured a hollow internal cavity, the back half of the mold lacked detailed modeling. The texture of the clay and an awareness of the surface of the object are the only sensory rewards to the tactile exploration of these figurines' backsides. This not only denied the user the pleasure of discovering these miniature bodies, but disrupted the ability of the miniature to function as a convincing mimetic replica of living people. Not only intimacy, but the illusionistic enchantment of the miniature itself was at stake here.

With so much at risk, and the object on the verge of being unconvincing and unsuccessful, why would such a figurine be made in this way? Here I return to the construct outlined in Chapter 1 of this volume: namely, that we are enchanted by tiny things that operate at the borders of our sensory perception because it is through our inability to perceive that we are reassured that we are not, in fact, small and insignificant ourselves. Erotic, sensual figurines, which particularly enchant the user into close sensory contact and with which the user might easily develop a sexual and emotional connection, threaten this boundary between the miniature and life-size world. Features like those seen in the amorous couples – the fixed position of the clothing, and the choice to not exploit the sculptural possibilities of the back half of the double mold (and yet use it anyway) – are stops placed on the user's sensory experience, which serve as a forceful denial of entry into the figurine world and thus reset the boundary between real life and life in miniature. The couples' bare yet invisible backsides, their not-quite-revealed genitalia – these are Swift's "invisible needles" threaded with "invisible silk."

I therefore suggest that it was through this teasing glimpse of intimacy offered, and then denied, that the user was ultimately left more secure and stable within the real-scale world of his or her social environment. This effect was not limited to a few examples; rather all known terracotta figurines showing embracing couples from Hellenistic Babylonia were either made in a single mold, or in a double mold with the back unmolded or showing only minimal details.[60] The similarity between these figurines indicates that they reflected – and aided in constructing – broader social and community conventions about how such imagery should be shown. The enticing eroticism offered by the couple's passionate embrace and revealing garments allowed the user a foray into the miniature world that was enchanting, but brief. As the other features of these amorous couple figurines denied complete access, the user was pulled back into the life-size world with abrupt reminders of the wider social environment and its limits.

Exclusion and Voyeurism

In addition to how these figurines denied user access through their physical construction and materiality, several of these figurines also discouraged user intimacy through their figural aspects. The intimate poses of the figurines, while capable of eliciting curiosity and desire, also imply through their closed body language that an additional third party is neither expected nor welcomed. In striking contrast with the woman-and-child figurines, whose open and outward postures encourage outside viewership, figurines of couples usually present a more exclusionary relationship. As the lovers' arms and legs intertwine, they create a cohesive unit, shielding each other from view and concentrating their attention solely on their partner's body and face. In the less common plaque-style examples of this motif from Seleucia-on-the-Tigris, known from just a few examples, one of the lovers even turns his or her back to the viewer.[61] This exclusion of the viewer is particularly noticeable in the positions of the lovers' faces, which kiss or lean in as if to initiate a kiss as seen in Figure 3.5, as well as Figure 1.13. Their cheeks often touch so that part of each face is completely obscured. Most crucially, the eyes of the figures lock in a shared gaze, rather than staring outward at the viewer – implying that the viewer is either being willfully ignored or perhaps that his or her presence has gone undetected by the amorous pair. In either case, the user is obviously not

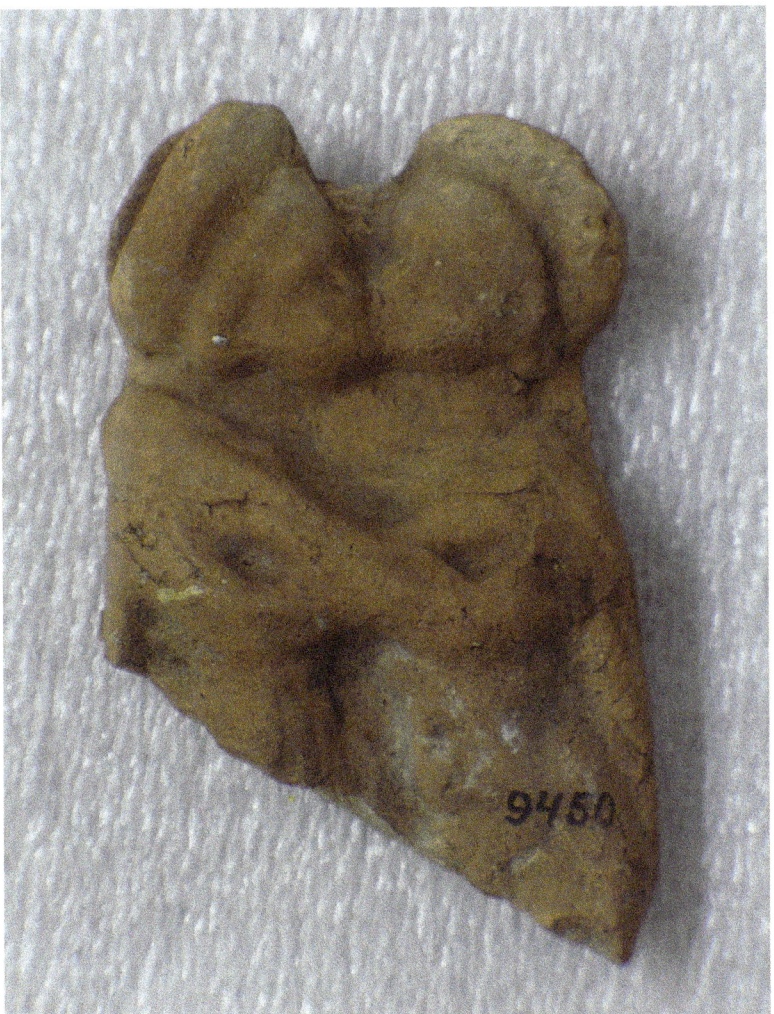

3.5. Embracing couple figurine, terracotta, Nippur. Height: 9.3 cm. University of Pennsylvania Museum of Archaeology and Anthropology (B 9450)
Photograph by author, printed courtesy of the University of Pennsylvania Museum.

invited to partake in the intimate acts and feelings depicted. Three is definitely a crowd.

While this exclusion of the user seems clear, what is less straightforward is how such exclusion might have been interpreted by the Hellenistic Babylonian users of these figurines. As seen throughout this volume, most Hellenistic Babylonian figurines depict miniature figures with an outward gaze and body posture. This usual openness to visual engagement – and even manual contact, as seen in the figurines discussed in Chapter 2 – would have created a set of expectations for the Hellenistic Babylonian user, who likely saw figurine accessibility and human-figurine interaction as commonplace.[62] Anticipation of access would have thrown into striking relief just how private the self-contained interaction was within the figurines of amorous couples. The lovers' passionate embraces and closed body postures alone made the user an interloper; the unexpected lack of access where a friendly welcome was anticipated made the user an awkward and perhaps uncomfortable voyeur.

After the initial shock of attention rebuffed had worn off, it is difficult to say whether a user would persist in feeling discomfited or rather become excited by the prospect of unobserved spying on a scene of lovemaking in progress. In a miniature milieu in which so many figurines "demanded" something of their users, the true spectatorship offered by the figurines of embracing couples may have been a welcome relief. Additional pleasure, particularly of a sexual nature, was also possible. Much has been written in art historical scholarship about the gratification of voyeurism and scopophilia; particularly the thrill that art can provide in giving safe access to otherwise taboo spectatorship onto the intimate moments of others.[63] Figurines were like any other art in this way: their closed intimacy was, of course, constructed, and despite their conceit of excluding the viewer, the entire object was intended for use and designed with the viewer in mind. The user's gaze literally "hits the side of [their] face"; yet unlike the statue in Barbara Kruger's photograph,[64] the figures in Figure 3.5 are made to seem deliberately, and perhaps deliciously, unaware of that fact – allowing the viewer's gaze to linger unchallenged.

Pleasurably erotic voyeurism over unaware subjects was also a theme of Hellenistic sculpture in the so-called Rococo style,[65] and such large-scale statues may have served as inspiration for the Hellenistic Babylonian amorous figurine couples. Sculptors in the broader Hellenistic world utilized several conceits in order to render their sexualized subjects plausibly nude (or in a state of partial undress) and plausibly unaware of being observed. These included portraying the subject asleep (as in the "Barberini Faun," as well as many sleeping Hermaphrodites and Ariadnes),[66] engaged in *symplegmata* (sexualized struggle or fighting, as seen in sculptures depicting satyrs as pursuers of Hermaphrodites or Nymphs), or participating in less overtly violent scenes of seduction and/or amorous embrace (such as Pan with a shepherd boy or Eros and Psyche; for more on the latter group, see the section below).[67] Although the original contexts and precise functions of many of these Hellenistic statue groups are unknown, they generally seem designed to be appreciated in the round by a privileged and informed audience[68] who could luxuriate in the allure of watching an erotic scene while safe in the knowledge that their gazes would be neither confronted nor returned. Drawing on this *koine* statue tradition as inspiration, the creators and users of the Hellenistic Babylonian figurines similarly explored the tantalizing appeal of intimacy acted out for the viewer's enjoyment.

Miniaturization would have further inflected and intensified this voyeuristic and probing effect by adding a tactile component – the "Caress" – to the thrill of the "Gaze," creating a multisensory paradise of exploration over the landscape of erotic (partially) nude bodies. Large-scale Hellenistic statuary could, of course, be touched and there are several stories of statues being fondled or even assaulted by amorous viewers.[69] Yet the fact that such stories were recorded suggests something illicit and shocking – and probably rare – about such manhandling of statues. Figurines, on the other hand, were of a scale to be conveniently and privately touched – indeed, completely grasped and enveloped by the user's own living body. While they excluded the user from participation in the intimate acts depicted, the figurines did offer up such intimacy as a packaged commodity, available for unchallenged ownership, viewing, and handling at leisure by a user who doubly dominated figures who were both powerlessly tiny and unaware of their subjugation.

Or were they? Closer inspection of the details of several of the amorous couple figurines suggests that this illusion of unawareness may have been more ambiguous to the Hellenistic Babylonian user than what I have described thus far. For instance, the terracotta figurine from Nippur seen in Figure 3.5 depicts sexualized intimacy between a male and female pair. Yet, upon closer inspection, many of the details of this figurine are shown in a frontal and open manner. Posed as if sharing a kiss, the lips of the two figures do not quite seem to touch; rather, the viewer is allowed to see almost the entire face of each. Although the bodies should be facing one another, the figures stand in parallel formation, opening each of their torsos to visual inspection. The awkwardness of this pose is apparent in the unnatural lengthening of each figure's arm from the elbow to the wrist, which enables the reach across their bodies to clasp their partner's shoulder. This ungainliness, and the use of anatomical distortions in order to achieve frontality and visual access, is particularly noticeable in this example – a fact that is not surprising, given that many figurines in the Nippur corpus do not fully exploit the plasticity and three-dimensional potential of terracotta as a medium. However, while the awkwardness that this figurine reveals may be particularly apparent here, it was by no means confined to Nippur.

A fresh look at the figurines seen in Figures 1.13 and 3.4 reveals that while their artistry was somewhat more fluid and their illusionistic mimesis more compelling than the Nippur example, they were similarly composed to privilege a frontality and openness that is somewhat foreign to the interpersonal activity of lovemaking – and, in some cases, is even at cross-purposes with the figures' presumed sexual intent. The torsos of the man and woman seen in Figure 1.13 are parallel to each other and frontally displayed. As a result, their necks must turn sharply in order for them to partake in a kiss that almost takes place over their shoulders. Their visible arms (her left arm, his right arm) do not reach toward the partner – and thus obscure the user's view – but remain conveniently tucked away to the sides of the composition. Similarly, rather than turning her body closer to her partner, the woman's frontal hips and foreshortened left leg make her appear in danger of sliding away from him and off his lap – a momentum opposite to that needed for successful sexual intercourse. While more entangled, the figures seen in Figure 3.4 have similarly frontal torsos and the woman's left arm is held loosely by her side, and out of the way, with her hand in her lap.

This frontality – which could be either more or less awkward, and more or less noticeable, depending on the figurine, but which seems to have been widely shared among the figurines of amorous couples – should be assessed in comparison with the other figurines of Hellenistic Babylonia. Strong frontality is a primary trait of this corpus, likely deriving from Babylonian tradition, both in terms of Mesopotamian stylistic preferences and the technical possibilities of the single mold. Despite the ways in which figurines of amorous couples break with the traditions of their corpus by excluding the viewer, a complete departure from Babylonian expectations of visual access might not have been possible, or at least not desired by most users. The amorous couple figurines can thus be seen as a point of negotiation between the pull of Babylonian tradition and the broader Hellenistic *koine* approach, such as the rapturously intertwined bodies of Eros and Psyche from Hellenistic Rococo sculpture, as seen in an example from the Capitoline in Figure 3.6. Although the hips of each figure in the sculpture twist forward to give some sense of openness to viewership, the faces and torsos of the figures are locked in mutual attention that denies user access. Eros wraps his left hand around Psyche's head, burying his fingers in her hair, while his right hand is raised to caress (and thus obscure) her face. Her arms are similarly engaged in passionate embrace, rendering her breasts invisible as their bodies meet. Even the few figurines from Hellenistic Babylonia that attempt to depict this sort of intertwining embrace show the hands lowered away from the faces, overlapping the arms so they obscure less of the torsos, and more fully twisting the waists into a frontal position.[70] No matter how convincingly the figurines seem to exclude the viewer, in the end, they were all made with concessions – some subtle, some less so – to the Hellenistic Babylonian desire to see and participate with frontal miniatures.

This "stylistic" difference between Hellenistic *koine* Rococo statuary and Hellenistic Babylonian figurines had important consequences for the affect of the figurines as objects. Openness to external vision meant that users were not quite as able to lose themselves in the miniature world, surrendering to the pleasures of scopophilia and unchallenged spectatorship in which one's own, life-size bodily presence is ignored and seems to dissolve away. As the bodies of the miniature lovers turn toward the viewer, offering access but not intimacy, they demonstrate an awareness that they are being watched by a nonparticipant in their encounter. At any moment, they might turn their heads, look out at us, and demand an explanation for our presence and our lascivious stares. The figures threaten to hold

LIKE LOVERS DO: HETEROSEXUAL COUPLES   125

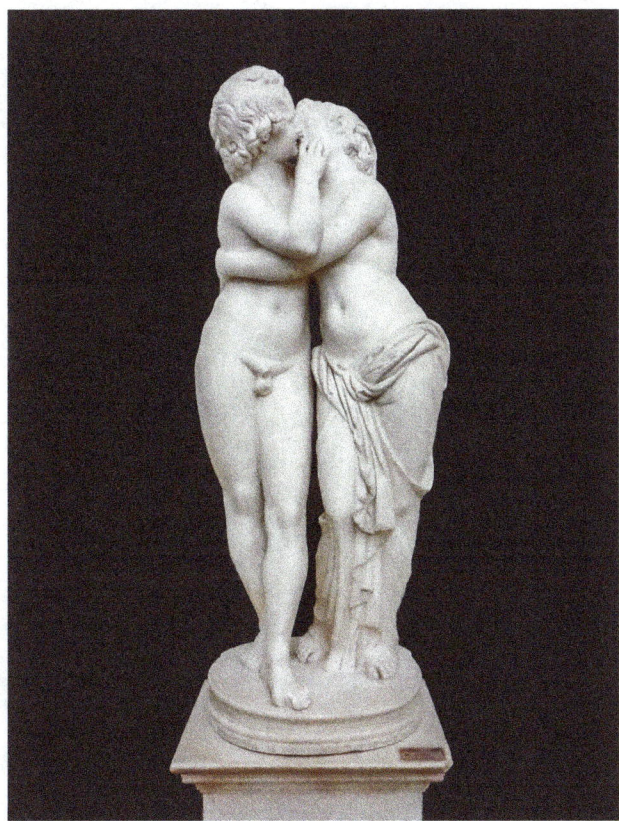

3.6. Statue of Eros and Psyche, marble, Rome. Height: 1.25 m.
Roman copy or adaptation of an original of c. 150-100 BCE. Capitoline Museum.
Photograph © 123RF.com

us accountable in a way that Hellenistic *koine* sculpture usually does not, although such statues could play on similar themes of both enticing and embarrassing the viewer with his or her erotic urges: for instance, confronting the viewer with his or her lechery and arousal through the playful peek-a-boo of male genitalia on sleeping Hermaphrodite sculptures.[71] What distinguished the Babylonian approach was its heightened sense of confrontation and its downplaying of mischievous trickery. Directness and seriousness pervade these figurines, especially when viewed against the backdrop of the treatment of similar themes in other parts of the Hellenistic world. This suggests that the relationships the figurines portrayed and the uses of such figurines in society were similarly to be taken seriously.

Mortals vs. Deities

The subtle seriousness of the amorous couples, however, is eclipsed by the modesty and earnest solemnity of the other major group of couple figurines: the fully clothed husband-and-wife pair. As seen in Figure 3.7, the man and

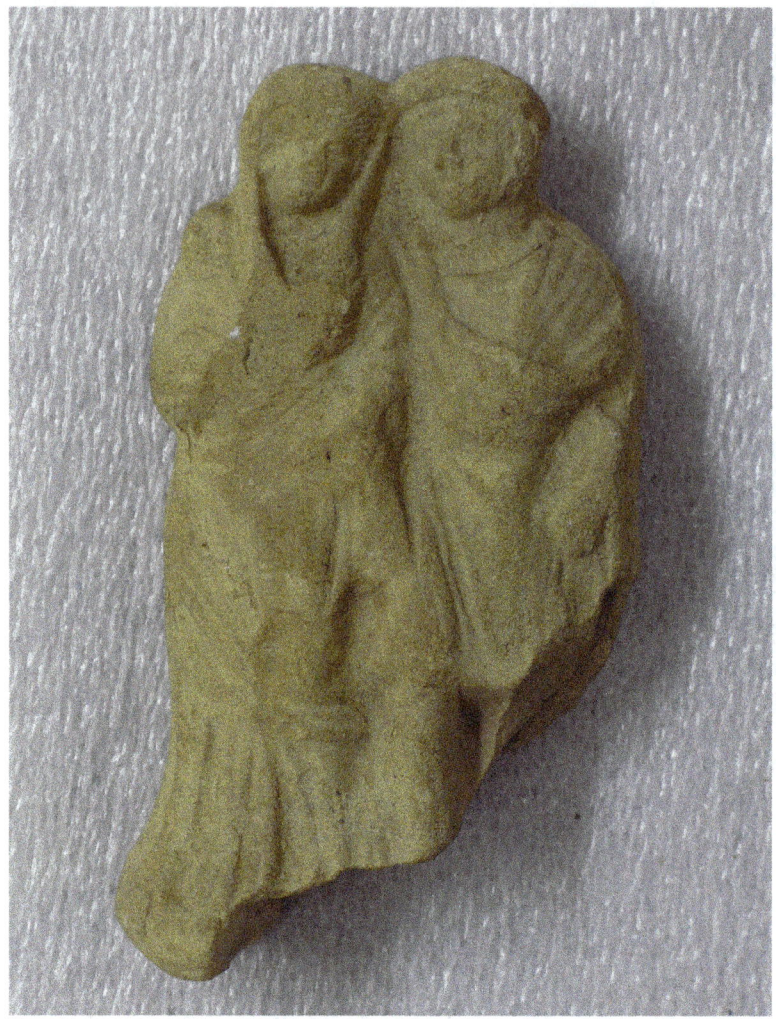

3.7. Couple figurine, terracotta, Nippur. Height: 13.5 cm. University of Pennsylvania Museum of Archaeology and Anthropology (B 9449)
Photograph by author, printed courtesy of the University of Pennsylvania Museum.

woman in such couples stand side-by-side in a frontal position, interacting almost exclusively with the viewer rather than each other. Their bodies are almost completely clothed, and they do not touch each other's skin – indeed, the woman does not touch the man at all. Their only embrace is his right arm around her shoulders, in an affectionate but not necessarily sexual gesture, while their heads incline slightly toward each other. External viewership and public engagement are the primary emphases of such figurines. Unlike the amorous couples' coy awareness of being watched, the clothed spouses were positioned to expect and invite interaction, in much the same way that the woman-and-child figurines discussed earlier in this chapter were receptive to viewership.

The clothed modesty seen in these figurines was also publicly appropriate for everyday, mortal people. The figures seen in Figure 3.7 wear carefully wrapped drapery; the woman's head is veiled and her right arm is enveloped in her garment. Similar clothing can be seen on figurines of men and women alone, which will be discussed in Chapter 4; in all cases, the garments likely suggested aspects of restrained public behavior that were considered ideal for both men and women. The woman's sharply bent and wrapped right arm, pressed close to her chest, evoked the particular pose of the Athenian orator wrapping his arm to prevent gesticulating during speeches and thus demonstrating his self-control (*sophrosyne*); the pose is best seen in Late Classical portraits of Aeschines and Sophocles.[72] Such ideas of public decorum on a more general level were associated with this pose as it spread more widely through the Hellenistic world, and similar values may have been expressed in this and other figurines.[73]

The pose itself also invites spectatorship; as argued by Jane Masséglia, the bound arm pose changes the role of the viewer from "incidental voyeur of a private scene" to "member of the audience for this public display."[74] Hellenistic *koine* statues of married couples in similar poses and garments were exhibited outdoors in civic space, or at least for community viewership (see, for instance, the statues of Kleopatra and Dioskourides from Delos[75]), and were likely a source of inspiration for the Hellenistic Babylonian figurines. In Figure 3.7, the woman's left hand gesture, which tugs at her mantle perhaps to reposition it on her body, also has an "everyday" quality to it – indeed, such sartorial adjustments were shorthand in Hellenistic art for identifying women as mortal: "goddesses, that is, would not fuss with their clothes."[76] Because of this clothed and restrained appearance, such figurines likely depict a mortal, everyday married couple[77] in Hellenistic Babylonian society – or, at least, an ideal representation thereof.

This equating of clothes with mortality, such that the modestly draped pair are interpreted as a human couple, is often juxtaposed in the scholarship with the parallel categorization of the semi-nude lovers as deities, particularly Eros and Psyche.[78] Such labels are not without merit given the close connection of these figurines with Hellenistic *koine* sculpture. Beyond similarities of pose and gesture, some of the Hellenistic Babylonian figurines explicitly evoke depictions of the Greek gods. For instance, two known figurines show a small wing on the woman's back, at shoulder level, which would be consistent with Psyche's iconography and, Psyche or not, clearly indicates a supernatural status.[79] Yet most amorous couple figurines do not have either supernatural attributes or the tightly intertwined poses traditional to Eros and Psyche depictions in Hellenistic statuary. As a result, such figurines could have been interpreted as representing human couples.

Additionally complicating the issue of mortal versus divine identification is the fact that not all of the figurines depicting couples fall neatly into two categories, either nude, amorous lovers or clothed, restrained spouses. In between these two extremes, figurines were produced that engaged with aspects of both motifs. These included figurines in which one partner was shown clothed while the other was nude, yet their bodies were posed in a side-by-side stance that suggests public engagement.[80] Similarly confounding easy interpretation are figurines in which two wreathed partners recline on a couch while facing the viewer, as seen in Figure 3.8.[81] Wreaths may suggest some degree of divine status and the sharing of a couch implies erotic intimacy. Despite the fact that their bodies were depicted only in a cursory fashion, their amorous posture suggests how the user's imagination should fill in the blanks. However, there is no reason to solely equate eroticism with Eros and Psyche, and the motif of a couple reclining on a couch had pan-Hellenistic, and earlier, associations with the funerary monuments of mortals.[82] Wreaths, reclining luxury, and banqueting cups suggest that this couple's appearance and posture was inspired by some sort of special occasion, but that does not mean they are gods; indeed, even ordinary people host parties. As with the clothed couples, the frontal gazes and body posture of the figures indicate that social interaction is expected.

Instead of dividing figurines depicting male-female couples into two groups of "mortal" and "divine," I suggest it is more productive to consider figurines of couples as representing a spectrum of options for conceptualizing interactions between men and women. At any point, by any user, it is possible that any of these figurines could have been interpreted as a divine pair – indeed, even the more staid, clothed couples could have conceivably been used to represent particularly demure deities. But the lack of clear divine attributes and poses on almost all of these figurines introduced a level of ambiguity that allowed these objects to be interpreted as representations of mortal, everyday members of the Hellenistic Babylonian communities. That lack of specificity was important, for it meant that all these figurines of couples could respond to, as well as influence, ideas and ideals of what it meant to be in a heterosexual relationship in Babylonia during the Hellenistic period. Further, the imaginative effort that the figurines required – where even sexual intercourse was implied rather than shown – recruited the user as a participant and collaborator in visualizing these figurines, and the outcome of their actions, as part of the community.

Social Roles and Cross-Cultural Interaction

As was established at the outset of this discussion, the lack of fully elaborated details and complete bodily access on figurines depicting couples imposed firm limits on users' fantasy immersion into the world of the miniature lovers. Instead each user was reminded of reality and its limits. The figurines themselves were the gatekeepers in this process, just as, I argue, the figurines were

LIKE LOVERS DO: HETEROSEXUAL COUPLES 129

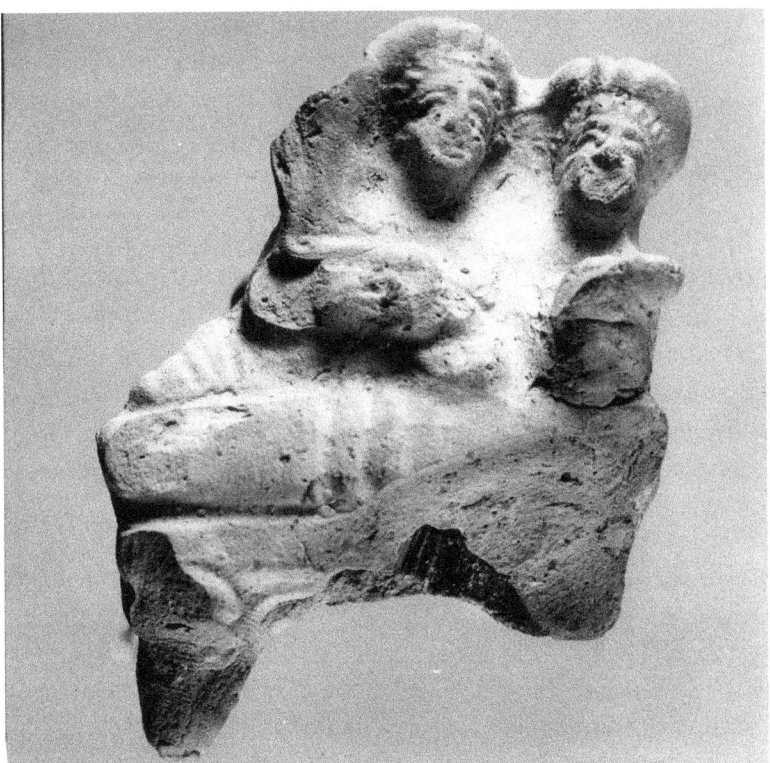

3.8. Reclining couple figurine, terracotta, Seleucia-on-the-Tigris. Height 7.7 cm. Baghdad (B6446)
Photograph originally published as Van Ingen 1939, No. 850.

regulators of real-world social ideals of heterosexual relationships through what they depicted – and, crucially, did not depict.

There are several trends in the figurine corpus that seem worth noting in this regard. First, there was a sweeping lack of options for romantic relationships outside the pairing of an adult man and an adult woman of conventional sexual anatomy and gender distinction. Homosexual lovers are not visualized within this corpus, nor are erotic encounters between adults and children of either sex. Intersex and unconventionally gendered individuals are also not shown in amorous pairings, despite their inclusion in the Hellenistic Babylonian corpus as individual figurines (see Chapter 5). Similarly, depictions of individuals with dwarfism and disabilities are not included here – a particularly noticeable lacuna, given the overt sexualization of the bodies of dwarf figurines (which was a trend common throughout the figurine traditions of the Hellenistic world[83]). Indeed, the Hellenistic Babylonian figurine corpus writ large demonstrates that many kinds of sexed and gendered bodies were possible – yet, the figurines seem to imply, only a particular subset of those bodies should act on their erotic and romantic impulses. Of course, it is entirely likely that the living residents of Hellenistic Babylonia did, in fact, engage in sexual encounters outside the limited range of possibility presented in the figurines. But they did so against a carefully curated and restricted backdrop of social expectations about what kinds of sex were proper, celebrated, and ideal.

Beyond the limitations of "adult man and woman" placed on couple figurines, careful examination indicates that an even stricter ideal of age was imposed on these bodies. Deducing the "ages" of the figures depicted in figurines is a tricky and unscientific business, yet there are a few markers that indicate general parameters. The members of the couples are usually of the same or similar heights and sizes, indicating the status of both partners as adults. When nude, their bodies are shown as sexually mature but firm, with the man possessing well-defined chest musculature while the woman has small, high breasts – all features that indicate idealized young adulthood or youth.[84] Additionally, and perhaps most revealingly, the man is always shown without a beard. Adult male beardlessness was generally a sign of emasculation in pre-Hellenistic Mesopotamian art[85]; in Classical Greek art, it generally denoted youth.[86] Beardlessness as an indicator of age is more difficult to utilize with confidence in the Hellenistic period because of its heroic associations with Alexander the Great.[87] However, a sense that it was associated with youth – particularly fashionable, clothed young men – in Hellenistic Babylonia can be deduced from a broad survey of the male figurines (see Chapter 4).

This age specificity has significant implications for our understanding of the Hellenistic Babylonian figurine couples. It would be easy – and perhaps not entirely unfounded – to remark that many people would prefer to look at erotic scenes in which the participants are youthful and attractive. Yet the many Hellenistic Babylonian figurines depicting a nude, middle-aged Herakles with full beard and rippling muscles indicate that an older male body type could also be an object of sexual allure. By giving the man a youthful and idealized appearance that was similar in age to his partner – as opposed to an older, bearded appearance – the couple figurines presented a same-age peer relationship as the ideal of sexual-romantic partnership.

Very little evidence exists regarding the relative ages of actual married couples in Hellenistic Babylonia, but there are records indicating the average age at marriage in both Classical Greece and late first-millennium BCE Babylonia. Both of these traditions give similar indications: women were considered to be marriageable at a young age (around 14–20 years old), while men married at a somewhat older age (26–32 years old).[88] If such conventions persisted, it is possible that some brides in Hellenistic Babylonia were roughly half the age of their husbands. In light of this potential reality, the youthfulness and beardlessness of the figurine couples seems almost insistent that this age *discrepancy* was not really an age *difference*, and that male-female bridal couples were considered age-peers. A similar phenomenon was also common in the art of Classical Athens, particularly in vase painting depictions of wedding celebrations: the bride is shown "matured," whereas the groom is shown "youthened," so that both appear (to modern eyes) as approximately 20 years old.[89] Hellenistic Babylonian figurines of couples, like Classical-period Athenian wedding depictions, thus show the figures as embodiments of a youthful ideal – an ideal which did not necessarily represent "reality" as we might perceive it, but which presented an ancient perspective on male-female couple identity.

The sense of equality established by the figures' ages pervades the corpus of Hellenistic Babylonian couple figurines more generally. The male figure is rarely shown as more sexually aggressive than the female and there are no hints of sexual violence or struggle. The woman and man stand or sit at equal or nearly equal heights, despite the reality of significant discrepancies between the average heights of adult men and women. Some of these features of the corpus may be explained as the products of careful negotiation between Mesopotamian and Greek value-systems. For instance, the lack of explicit sexual violence follows Mesopotamian artistic norms – and, indeed, the subject matter of a heterosexual, normatively gendered pair engaged in non-violent eroticism fits easily into long-standing Mesopotamian traditions of depicting sexual activity between men and women in miniature form.[90] In contrast, many Hellenistic *koine* statue groups, with their inclusion of specifically Greek mythological characters (such as satyrs), sleeping as a form of sexual disarmament, the coy display of hermaphroditic bodies, and overt sexual aggression, violence, and frustration, had less obvious parallels within Mesopotamian art and may thus have found a less willing audience among Babylonian consumers.

Indeed, despite the clear Greek style of many of the couple figurines, with their dynamic intertwined poses, head wreaths, and Hellenistic clothes, concessions to Babylonian figurine traditions and modes of viewing dominate the corpus. The figurine shown in Figure 3.7 is overtly Hellenistic in style, even to the fine details of the woman's thin mantle (possibly meant to "evoke the fashionable silk of Kos"[91]) wrapped tightly over a thicker tunic, a ubiquitous mode of female dress in statuary from across the Hellenistic world. Yet, the pose of a fully clothed couple standing or sitting side-by-side has a long history in Mesopotamia.[92] Additionally, the figurine itself was made in the Babylonian single-mold technique, as was the wreath-wearing figurine derived from Eros and Psyche imagery seen in Figure 3.5. Babylonian social norms may also account for the lack of adult-child and same gender amorous pairings as neither of those types of unions were generally acceptable within Mesopotamian culture. The limited range of possible romantic pairings represented in the Hellenistic Babylonian figurine corpus may have been the result of careful negotiation between Greek and Babylonian cultural norms.

However, the seeming equality of the male and female figures – men and women who stand shoulder to shoulder, embrace mutually, neither taking precedence nor control – was not mandated by either culture. It may represent a Hellenistic Babylonian understanding of marital and sexual ideals. Parallels can be found in Hellenistic Babylonian economic documents, which evidence substantial freedom and independence for women, who were able to act on their own account in major financial transactions.[93] Admittedly, the texts only document a very small, elite section of Hellenistic Babylonian society. However, the figurines, as more widely accessible objects, suggest that such independence for women and parity within marital relationships were also the norm – or, at least, an aspired-to ideal – across Hellenistic Babylonian society more generally. The range of possible romantic encounters seems to have been tightly circumscribed, both in their public presentation and in their private erotic activities. But within such relationships, the possibilities of equality, agency, and personal freedom may have been vast indeed.

COLLABORATION FOR AN AUDIENCE: MUSICIAN PAIRINGS

From scenes of family and love, I turn now to the last group of Hellenistic Babylonian figurines that depict a relationship in miniature: the musicians. Figurines depicting people playing instruments were very popular in Hellenistic Babylonia, with several hundred known examples found across each of the major sites. The majority of these portray a single figure, playing his or her instrument alone; fewer than one hundred figurines depict two musicians together. Yet the smallness of this fraction aside, the musician pairs are hugely significant – not only because a group of several dozen objects across all the Hellenistic Babylonian centers is quite sizable, but also because the musician pairs represent the only other type of relationship seen in the entire figurine corpus.

Instead of an overtly familial relationship, the bond between the two instrument players seems based on shared occupation. Thus the two figures might be imagined to have a range of possible acquaintance with one another – perhaps they are, in fact, relatives, or perhaps they are professional collaborators as part of a usual "duet" act, or perhaps they have only just recently met. This lack of specificity shifts emphasis elsewhere, onto the actions of the figures as musicians, rather than on their relationship to one another as people. Given the already limited corpus of Hellenistic Babylonian figurines depicting an association between people, it is especially striking that one of the three major groups of such objects was not really about a "relationship" at all, but rather the service that two bodies in unison could provide to an interested onlooker and audience.

Performance and Repetition

The paired musicians on Hellenistic Babylonian figurines were usually, although not always, depicted as female. Always clothed, usually in thick garments that obscure most of the body, the gender of the figures can nevertheless be identified by their breasts. The two (presumably adult) women stand side-by-side in a frontal facing position. The shoulders touch – indeed, in most cases, the sides of their bodies are pressed together and, in instances where the figurine or its mold was somewhat worn, the bodies of the two figures are fused and no separation between them is distinguishable.

Yet despite their extremely close proximity, the figures do not seem to interact with each other via eye contact, gesture, or embrace.[94] Rather, in its parallel formation and mutual frontality, the pose of the paired musician figures seems designed to be seen by an audience. In this attention outward, the Hellenistic Babylonian musician pairs are very different from Old Babylonian figurines depicting couples playing musical instruments, often while simultaneously engaged in sexual intercourse.[95] While these two corpora of figurines are sometimes compared,[96] the Old Babylonian couples were clearly shown interacting with one another, not just through their shared sexual activity, but also through the figures' positioning to gaze and gesture toward their partners. In contrast, the Hellenistic Babylonian musicians are not playing music privately for each other, but performing for an outside audience – presumably the user who, cued by the sight of two people playing instruments, would imagine the auditory component of the experience.

The clothes and body types of the two figures further add to this sense of performance. On each figurine, the two figures stand at almost precisely the same height, are often identically dressed, and have similar facial features. For instance, in the musician figurine seen in Figure 3.9, the two women are of equal height, with low headdresses (possibly wreaths, which can be seen more clearly in the figurine pictured in Figure 3.10) and oval faces framed by ridged curls. They wear identical garments, of which the thick hems of the scooped necklines stand out above their high breasts, while their arms curve underneath the breasts to grasp their instruments. Those arms are bent at almost identical angles, despite the fact that their instruments – and, presumably, the gestures and actions needed to play them – are different. The women's lower bodies are completely obscured beneath the thick pleats of their cascading drapery, of which the bottom hems are pulled back to reveal small feet in wide stances on the figurine's plinth base. In almost every respect – crucially excepting their choice of instrument – the two women are essentially identical.

This is not to say, however, that all the figurines in this corpus are identical with one another and/or were made in the same mold. Quite the opposite: while there are many points of similarity between figurines of musician pairs,

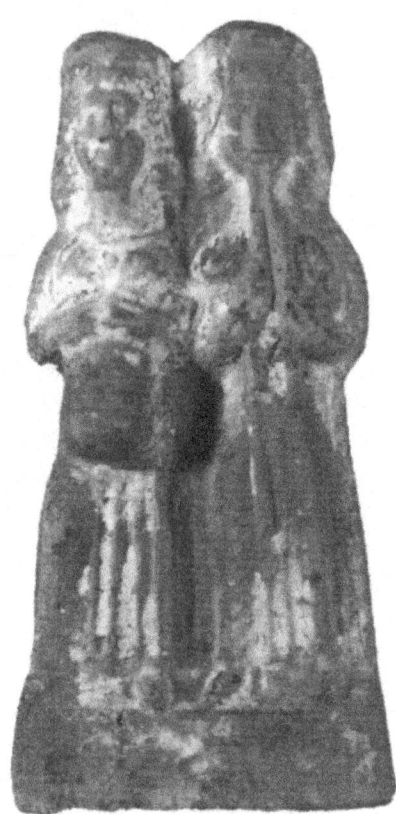

3.9. Musician pair figurine, playing double-pipe and drum, terracotta, Babylon (EH-I, grave, level 2). Height: 14 cm. Baghdad, National Museum of Iraq (IM 94897)
Photograph adapted from Karvonen-Kannas 1995, No. 327.

the small details of facial features, clothing folds, headdress decoration, and precise pose are not identical, and there is substantial variation of figurine size. Thus, rather than creating legions of identical figurines, the focus instead seems to have been on portraying the two instrument-playing women on any given figurine as doppelgangers, a matched pair, or twins. Indeed, the close pairing of the two women on almost every figurine is a striking aspect to this corpus. Some of the visual similarities between the two figures may be marks of the craftsperson's individual hand or style, yet others, such as the identical height of the two figures, were choices. Through this deliberately constructed visual parallelism between the two female musicians, the feeling of doubleness was conveyed.

This twinning of the musicians has powerful consequences for how their bodies would be seen – or, perhaps, not seen – by the user. Attention is directed away from the women as individual bodies or persons, and perhaps away from the visual entirely, to the realm of the (imagined) auditory. The women are

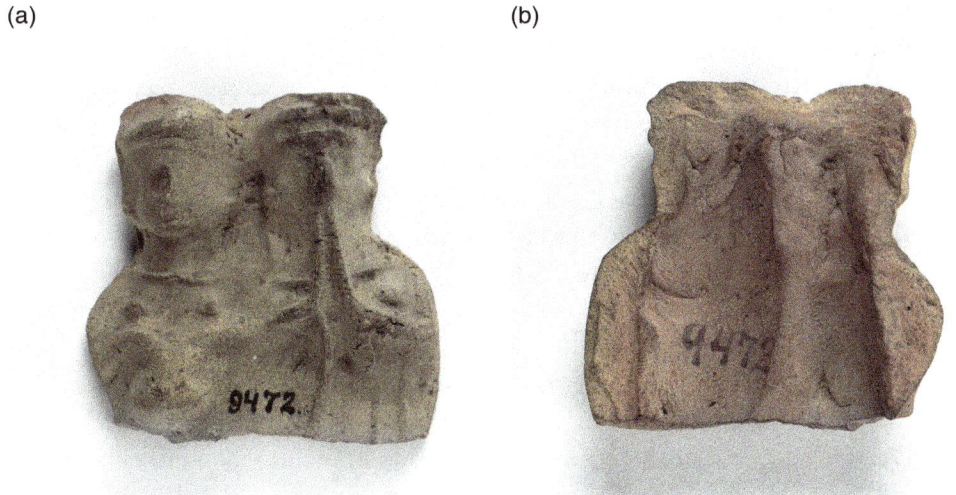

3.10a and b. Exterior and interior of front half of double-molded figurine, depicting a musician pair playing double-pipe and drum, terracotta, Nippur. Height: 5.8 cm. University of Pennsylvania Museum of Archaeology and Anthropology (B 9472)
Photographs courtesy of the University of Pennsylvania Museum.

interchangeable, exchangeable, each easily confused for the other. Their distinctiveness is not as individuals but as members of a larger unit – like a chorus of synchronized dancers, where a large measure of the beauty of the performance is that individually separate bodies have been trained to act as one.[97] Such performances rely, in part, on the illusion that no active collaboration or consultation between the performers needs to take place.[98] The conjoined bodies and lack of obvious interaction between the musician figures heightens this effect of duplication, emphasizing the non-communicative nature of their shared, almost instinctual, intent – as if they were two hands or feet of the same body, paired and moving in complementary ways via automatic and seamless reflex in order to produce music in perfect harmony.[99] Greek choruses "very often chanted and marched in unison"[100] and were particularly praised for the pleasure of such coordinated performances that made them "worth seeing and worth hearing."[101] Thus the visual, auditory, and emotional effect of such performances would likely have been familiar to many ancient spectators of these figurines.

The twin bodies of the musician figurines also created the illusion of repetition, with their overt duplication invoking an implied replication of the musical performance. It takes little imaginative effort to view the repeated figures in repeated clothing and repeated poses, and then extrapolate that their actions were repeated, and repeatable, as well. Such a sense of repetition grounds the depicted performance of music – which, in its real-life enactment, is a temporary and ephemeral phenomenon – with enduring weight. One body, one musician could easily replace another in never-ending sequence, allowing the song to go on indefinitely. This repetition would have been experienced, in a sense, by the figurine user every time he or she used, or even happened to glance at, the figurine and see the duplicated bodies, standing at eager attention in anticipation of an audience, with their fingers and lips engaged in the playing of their instruments. Neither the arms nor the bodies of these figurines move – indeed, they are very solidly modeled with the instruments and limbs tightly pressed to the torsos. As such, the musicians can never stop playing, so every time they are viewed, the (imagined) performance begins again.

The repetition of the musicians' bodies seems even more important in light of the fact that it is among their only noticeable aspects. Many of the Hellenistic Babylonian musician pair figurines were made in molds that were either worn out from use, and thus could no longer impart much surface detail, or were not well made to begin with.[102] The finished figurines themselves might also have become heavily abraded with use. The figurine seen in Figure 3.9 is one of the best preserved examples of this group; its surface detail is striking when compared with the almost schematic rendering of the human bodies in the figurine seen in Figure 3.11. Any terracotta figurine and/or its mold is susceptible to this type of wear-and-tear; what distinguishes the musician pairs is that this kind of heavy surface degradation is common and is seen in examples from all the Hellenistic Babylonian cities.[103] This suggests that such figurines were not viewed as unsuccessful or unworthy of use in the way that their worn or abraded counterparts depicting other motifs might have been. Why the difference? It might have been advantageous with these particular figurines. The musicians' identities and corporealities recede into the background, literally fading from view, often retaining only enough bodily presence to continue to stand upright, face their audience, and play their instruments. The aural thus supersedes the visual – at least, as much as is possible in an object that does not actually make noise.

In their noticeable duplication, fading of bodily details, and lack of interaction, the musician pair figurines were quite different from the couples and women with children. In general, the makers and users of the musician figurines seem not to have been concerned with depicting the relationships between two bodies as lived; rather, the figures almost seem not to have living bodies at all. Instead, their bodies exist as props to provide actions: holding and activating the instruments, repeating their performances through unspecified spans of space and time.

The Pipes and the Drum

The twinning of almost every detail on the musician pair figurines also encouraged the user to see what *was* different about the two bodies: namely

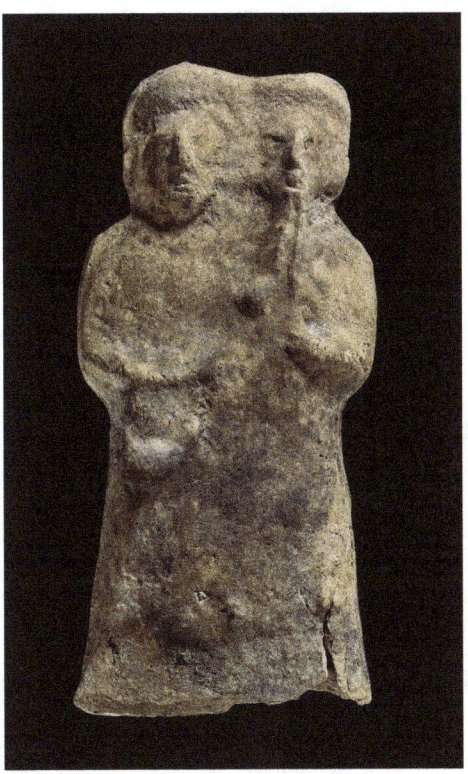

3.11. Musician pair figurine, playing double-pipe and drum, terracotta, Babylon. Height: 13 cm. British Museum (BM Sp.III 15+=91807)
Photograph © The Trustees of the British Museum.

the instruments that they held. Different instrument options were available, such as the double-piped instrument paired with a lute, or a stringed harp-like instrument paired with hand cymbals, as seen in Figure 3.12. But the combination of a double-piped wind instrument with a small drum was by far the most common,[104] and examples of musician pair figurines playing these instruments can be found at all the major Hellenistic Babylonian cities. The pipe and drum duos were also the most visually cohesive. In contrast, the two musicians seen in Figure 3.12 share neither gender nor clothing, as the right figure is female and wears a full garment that covers the body from neck to below the knees, whereas the left figure is male, and wears only a small cloth wrapped around the hips. These two musicians do share similar facial expressions and are similarly posed in a contrapposto stance with their left legs drawn back. However, these gestures toward parallelism throw into sharp relief how strongly duplicated the pipe and drum playing pairs usually appear.

Assigning specific names to these instruments – and, thus, linking them to textual descriptions of functions and purposes – is a somewhat difficult process. The figurine depictions of the wind instrument show a double set of pipes, the barrels of which join at the player's mouth but are held separately, with one end

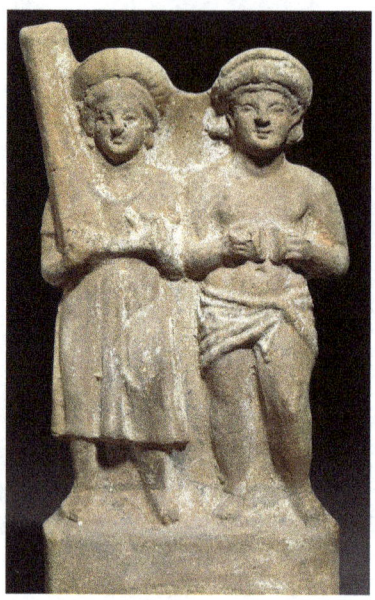

3.12. Musician pair figurine, playing stringed instrument and hand cymbals, terracotta, Babylon. Height: 16.5 cm. British Museum (BM 80-6-17-1697=91794)
Photograph © The Trustees of the British Museum.

in each hand, forming a triangular shape. The Greek name for a double-piped wind instrument is *aulos*.[105] However, there is some visual discrepancy between the Hellenistic Babylonian figurines and the traditional Greek depictions of the *aulos*.[106] Double-piped instruments also had extensive pre-Hellenistic precedents in the Ancient Near East, including in terracotta figurines of musicians.[107] The ambiguity and cross-cultural resonance of this double-piped instrument was likely a major reason for its popularity in the musician figurines of Hellenistic Babylonia. Due to its long history of use around the Mediterranean and Near East, almost any Hellenistic Babylonian figurine user could potentially have identified the instrument as an *aulos* or by another name – and thus seen it as local and familiar rather than foreign.

The types of music played on the pipes and the occasions on which the pipes were heard are similarly difficult to reconstruct. Since they have not been plausibly connected with an instrument name recorded in the Seleucid texts, it is difficult to know what particular uses, roles, and associations the pipes had for a Babylonian audience. From the Greek perspective, the *aulos* had a checkered reputation. Many Classical authors, such as Aristotle and Plutarch, discuss the *aulos* as an ignoble instrument, not conducive to virtue.[108] However, Sheramy Bundrick cautions against overreliance on the textual sources when determining the status of the *aulos* in the Greek mindset, pointing out that vase painting shows the *aulos* being played in several "respectable" contexts, such as in sacrifice scenes and weddings.[109] The *aulos* could also be utilized on occasions of lamentation,[110] and the choruses of

Greek tragedy would sing to the accompaniment of "a pair of *auloi* played together, as was normal tragic practice."[111] The *aulos* was also associated with foreigners, "others," and particularly with professional female musicians who performed in the erotically charged environment of the Greek symposion. These women were understood to be both sexually available and sexually skilled.[112] The unifying factor in these various uses of the *aulos* is that it was generally an instrument of professional performance rather than of amateur amusement and self-refinement.

A professional use for the Greek *aulos* accords nicely with the Hellenistic Babylonian figurines of musicians who seem to be performing – likely in an organized, professional performance, given their costumes and posture – before an audience. To beholders informed by Greek musical tradition, an *aulos*-like instrument would be an appropriate choice. Yet, the erotic associations of the *aulos* were scrupulously avoided in these figurines. The figures are fully clothed – indeed, so carefully and austerely clothed that the prominent high necklines and thick folds running down the legs threaten to (and, in some cases, do) completely obscure and even obliterate the body beneath. Even the figurines with few surface details, such as that seen in Figure 3.11, depict blank expanses more consonant with stretches of fabric than human anatomy. The hands of the pipe player, positioned to grasp her instrument, often cover her breasts, blocking them entirely from view. A small number of musician figurines, such as that seen in Figure 3.12, show more naked bodies and those musicians, crucially, are not double-pipe and drum playing pairs.[113] That particular duet in Hellenistic Babylonia seems to have been specifically disconnected from nudity or sexual activity.

But if the double-pipes were appealing precisely because of their connection to both Greece and Babylonia, then why go to such efforts to avoid depicting one of the primary Greek uses of the instrument? The answer may lie in its pairing with the other instrument, the small drum. Although it is difficult to deduce many details about the instrument from the figurine depictions, it is clearly a percussion instrument and it seems likely that the body of the drum was rigid with the top of the drum covered by a membrane (likely animal skin) which could be struck in order to create sound. Hovering at the woman's waist with no obvious means of support, the drum may have been secured to the musician's body by a belt.[114] Her hands are positioned above the drumhead, in a gesture more evocative of "playing" than "holding." However, as can be seen in Figure 3.9, the hands are sometimes depicted with the palms facing the woman's torso, rather than positioned downward on the surface of the drum as would be expected during playing. This somewhat awkward positioning may have been preferred since it allowed for a careful elaboration of all ten fingers of the musician which, in turn, could draw attention to her physical competency and dexterity for her musical task. In figurines that are less elaborated, such as is seen in Figure 3.11, the hands meld together with the drum in a functional symbiosis.

As with the pipes, identifying the drum by name is also difficult. Several Greek writers record the use of drums in conjunction with the *aulos* for cultic activity, specifically situations of religious frenzy.[115] Yet generally, percussion instruments were a minor part of Classical Greek musical traditions[116] and none of the major classes of Greek drums[117] can be plausibly connected with these terracotta depictions. In contrast, a great variety of percussion instruments formed a staple of Mesopotamian musical practice, including in Hellenistic Babylonia specifically. Some information about the appearance of drum types played in Seleucid Babylonia can be deduced from lexical lists and descriptions of their use; based on this information, the *šem/meze* drum or the *ub/uppu* drum seem like possible identifications.[118] Both were membranophones made with animal hide, rather than metallic idiophones (such as cymbals or sistrums), and both could be played by a solo performer rather than by a group of musicians (and thus were potentially small in size). Both instruments were primarily used for rituals of mourning. In particular, the *ub/uppu* was likely held at the chest while played in a gesture associated with lamentation: one reference to the instrument describes how a mourner "[beats] his breast like an *uppu*."[119] Another possible identification for the drum is the *alû*, which is described on a statue of Gudea as being played in concert with a flute.[120]

To be clear, such identifications are only conjectural; it is quite possible that the drums played in the figurines were not ritual in nature or did not otherwise merit naming and description in Seleucid texts. Nevertheless, based on the extant texts, we can surmise that the depiction of a drum player in musician duets would have sparked several associations for the Hellenistic Babylonian viewer. First, the drum would have localized the performance, tying it directly to Mesopotamian tradition and current Hellenistic Babylonian musical practice. Second, the standard use of small membranophone drums in Seleucid Babylonian rituals, particularly lamentation rituals, might have conjured a mournful association.[121] As the Greek *aulos* could also be utilized on occasions of lamentation, the pairing of these two instruments on the figurines may indicate a shared function in rituals of grief. Such an explanation for these figurines correlates well with some of their archaeological findspots; for instance, the figurine seen in Figure 3.9 was excavated from a grave. Hellenistic Babylonian figurines were rarely found in tombs, which makes this context especially meaningful. In circumstances of mourning and lamentation, the instruments would likely be played by professionals which, in turn, accord easily with the strongly professionalized aspects of the figurines' self-presentation.

Professional Distance vs. Amateurish Immediacy: Comparison with the Solo Musicians

These professionalized aspects of the musician pairs – their parallel pose and performance, nearly identical bodies and costumes, and anticipation of viewership – were additionally reinforced by the technical construction of the figurines themselves. The pipe and drum playing pairs were modeled in double molds,[122] some of which were cavernous in their interior spaces. The bases of the figurines were made thick and solid; as can be seen in Figure 3.9, the rim of the base often flares outward to reinforce the vertical stability that such construction provided. These figurines were clearly intended to stand alone. Their lack of intricate visual details discourages close looking and the tactile contact required to facilitate it. There are no benefits to observing a figurine like that seen in Figure 3.11, with its blank expanses of clay, up close. Together, these features not only reinforced the perception that the musicians were professionals playing for an audience, but also a sense of distance between performer and spectator. This formal, performative distance may have paralleled the events which the figurines represented. If the figurines did reference Seleucid-period associations between drums and lamentation rituals, then such somber performances may account for the statue-like stability of the figurines and their discouragement of active user handling.

This sense of professional distance is especially noticeable when the musician pairs are compared with the more numerous figurines depicting a single musician playing an instrument alone. The corpus of solo musician figurines is extensive and varied: some depict or reference gods, particularly Apollo; others are similar in pose to the musician pairs. One popular group of solo musicians hold a tambour-style frame drum over their left shoulder.[123] These figurines are especially distinctive for their manufacture: many of them were made either in the single mold or modeled by hand with mold stamped faces. In some cases, the mold-made details of the figurines were accentuated by hand after the clay was withdrawn from the mold.[124] For instance, as seen in the figurine pictured in Figure 3.13, thick indentations in the clay delineate the fingers on the hand that beats the drum – marks that could have easily been made by a stylus dragged through clay by an untrained, amateur hand. Hand-modeled figurines are exceptionally rare in the Hellenistic Babylonian corpus and, as such, their schematic, somewhat crude style is immediately noticeable. Also noticeable would have been the frequent lack of stable bases on the tambour-style drum players – without the ability to stand alone, these figurines would have needed to be held in the hand.

The musical events to which these figurines referred might also have been quite different than with the musician pairs. There is a long history of frame-drums in Mesopotamian art, including figurines[125]; many of the earlier

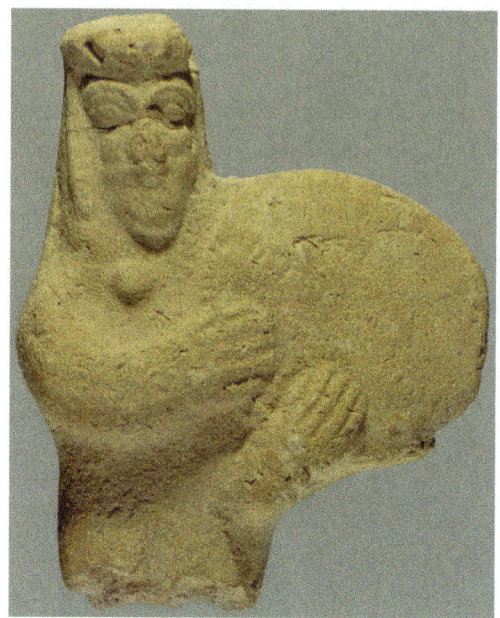

3.13. Solo musician figurine, playing tambour-style frame drum, terracotta, Nippur. Height 7.8 cm. Harvard Semitic Museum (1955.4.11)
Photograph courtesy of the Semitic Museum, Harvard University.

figurines also evoked tactile immediacy both in their manufacture and their use. The frame drum (*tympanon*[126]) was also part of the Greek musical tradition, where it was particularly associated with nymphs and devotees of Dionysos.[127] Dionysian worship was especially popular throughout the Hellenistic world,[128] and the intersection of this currently en vogue religious practice with the long-standing Mesopotamian use of this instrument may explain the popularity of these solo musicians in Hellenistic Babylonia. The tambour-style frame drum held at the left shoulder was also part of the iconography of the nature and mother goddess Cybele – a deity whose worship could similarly be associated with music, wine, and wild behavior.[129]

This is not to suggest that the figurine seen in Figure 3.13 was meant to depict Cybele; indeed, as Adi Erlich notes, unambiguous depictions of the goddess are rare outside of Hellenistic Greece, Macedonia, Asia Minor, and a few sites in Israel.[130] However, the wild, sensorial immediacy and communal engagement of festivals to popular Hellenistic gods such as Dionysos or Cybele may have combined in function and affect with the strongly tactile, unrefined quality of figurines depicting frame-drum players in the Mesopotamian tradition. In both aspects, there is a sharp distinction between the human-object engagement with the solo frame-drum players and the musician pairs. Like the figures they depict, the figurines seem to have been divided between professionally distant and amateurishly immediate, a contrast that would have been accentuated by the common use of both the musician pairs and the solo frame-drum figurines within the same Hellenistic Babylonian social environment.

Within this wide spectrum of professionalism/amateurism, enforced distance, and performance, all of the musician figurines accommodated both Greek and Babylonian traditions. Some, such as the figurine in Figure 3.12 with its depiction of wreathed heads, soft naturalistic faces, and contrapposto poses, more strongly evoke Greek style. Others, such as the solo frame-drum players, have a flatter, frontal, and more Mesopotamian aesthetic, although they play an instrument that had strong connections with the rest of the Hellenistic world. The double-pipe and drum players fall squarely in the center of this cross-cultural spectrum: the thick folds of the musicians' garments, the wreaths that encircle their heads, and the double molds in which the figurines were made all derive from Greek tradition, while the frontal and flat style of the figures (which extends even to details such as the treatment of the hair) has more in common with earlier Mesopotamian figurines. Additionally, and perhaps most crucially, the instrument combination of the double-pipe and drum, as well as the style of play,[131] fit more fully and directly within Mesopotamian tradition.

We are unlikely to ever ascertain whether such figurines depicted actual moments of musical performance in real life, where identically robed women faced a crowd while playing a pipe and drum duet. It is similarly unclear whether living musical performers, and performances, made such an effort to be culturally inclusive. Yet, it nevertheless is worthwhile to note that the figurines which referenced professional musical performances – and constructed ideals around the bodies, actions, and songs that would have been seen and heard during those moments of spectatorship – did effect a bridging between cultures that also slightly privileged, and thus made locally specific, the Babylonian roots of the performance. The figurines' insistence on the overtly public nature of that performance, taking place at a professional distance from the audience, situated this cultural negotiation within a similarly social sphere[132] – even if the figurine itself, and its never-ending, infinitely repeatable song, was enjoyed only in the private space of the user's home and imagination.

CONCLUSION

In concluding, I return to the ideas of relationships and spectatorship around which this chapter is centered. While the musician pair figurines clearly evoke a directed gaze and an audience, they are less obviously concerned with relationships. Indeed, these figurines scarcely depict an interaction between two people; to label their side-by-side pose as a "relationship" seems an exaggeration. As the Hellenistic Babylonian corpus of figurines that depicted associations or connections between people was severely limited in motif to only three primary groups – woman and child, couples, and musicians – it seems especially notable that one of these groups does not seem to depict a relationship at all.

In attempting to explain this seeming anomaly, I hesitate on its significance. On the one hand, it may simply illustrate that I have drawn a false parallel in assembling all "group" figurines into one chapter and one discussion. The perils of grouping objects according to modern norms and categories is a fraught issue that I explored at length in my doctoral thesis[133] and, while I do now utilize object categories in my work, I nevertheless continue to eschew firm typologies and to question even the groupings themselves when appropriate. This is one of those instances. Simply put, it is possible that a Hellenistic Babylonian user would have seen no natural connection between a figurine of a woman and child and a figurine of two musicians simply because two human bodies were depicted in each object.

Yet, I also believe that some useful information can be gained in comparing these figurines, even if there was not a direct connection between them. For in that miniatures of women with children, couples, and musicians were the *only* common depictions of associations between people in figurine form, these objects shaped a set of expectations about what kinds of human groupings were appropriate and "made sense." And, I argue, the fact that such groupings could include both professional and personal acquaintances highlights the overt exclusion of other types of relationships. If, for instance, the only figurine groups depicted either the bonds of motherhood or marriage, it would be easy to assume that only the most intimate and enduring of human associations were seen as worthy of representation and celebration. In contrast, the inclusion of a professional association, based on shared activity rather than obvious interpersonal intimacy, drastically expands the scope of possible "relationships-in-miniature" in Hellenistic Babylonia. This possibility throws into sharp relief the lack of figurines depicting other family relationships (fathers with sons, siblings, mothers with adult children, etc.) or other social relationships generally (friends, patrons, military units, ritual activities, etc.). These were not excluded from the corpus because they were "impossible" within the internal logic of Hellenistic Babylonian figurine use; rather, the existence of the musician pairs suggest that other figurine pairings were simply not wanted.

The limited number of "relationships in miniature" within the Hellenistic Babylonian corpus has multiple implications for how we can use these figurines to understand the social imaginary of Hellenistic Babylonia. On the one hand, they would seem to offer a limited and imperfect outlook on that social world, which must surely have been more diverse in human interaction than the figurines imply. On the other hand, the figurines may reveal a great deal about the extremely limited range of social encounters that were idealized and honored. Figurines both reflect and create the society in which they operate, imposing certain views on the consumer browsing in the shop or the visitor observing them in a friend's home – views of what ideal interpersonal relationships should look like, who participates in them, and how they should be experienced. The narrow scope of that figurine window into human interaction was all the more intense for its lack of expansiveness – figuratively placing the core relationships of family and a professional association under a social microscope. Perhaps because of this penetrative gaze, the relationships depicted in all three groups of figurines are unambiguous. There is little room for confusion about the identities of the figures involved: the lovers are clearly not of the same sex, the woman clearly has a maternal relationship (if not an actual biological bond) to the child, the standing duo are actively playing musical instruments.

Yet the figurines were not so specific as to make possible an identification with individual nameable personages, particularly gods. Instead, the presence of the second figure (the infant, the intimate partner, the musical collaborator) serves as a prop to identify, as well as simplify, the social role depicted – to make the portrayal of "mother" or "spouse" clearly recognizable and, as such, essentialized. These are figurines of "motherhood," "romance," "marriage," "performance," and so forth, not figurines of particular people. Although many are similar to divine groupings, each figurine also bears sufficient differences from unambiguous representations of gods that it is only the relationship between the figures, rather than the identities of the figures, that can be conclusively ascertained. As such, the creators of these figurines seem to have walked a very careful line: specific enough to make the relationship unambiguous, but not too specific to risk individual identification. Such meticulousness suggests that these objects were the result of painstaking dialogue between the various communities in Hellenistic Babylonia – a process which might have yielded a precise and narrow list of options for idealized interpersonal communication. Relationships that were incompatible with one groups' ideals and norms – such as, perhaps, Greek interest in homosexual relationships, which was not shared in Babylonia – seem not to have been idealized in miniature form, regardless of whatever actual relationships and behaviors were taking place in the real-scale world.

One of the most striking discrepancies between figurine relationships and real ones is that all the miniature versions of social bonds were mediated by women. Every Hellenistic Babylonian figurine that depicts two people includes a female body. These women were shown as caregivers, lovers, spouses, and co-musicians – often, though not always, to men. In the idealized world of Hellenistic Babylonian figurines, women were the social conduit, the vehicles for all the interpersonal interaction of the community and the center around which it revolved. Of course, this does not mean that men simply did not interact in Hellenistic Babylonia. Nor does it mean that women had more agency than men or were more highly regarded. Rather, it suggests that the role of female figurines was conceptualized differently than that of male figurines. This difference between gender roles in miniature will be explored in Chapter 4.

CHAPTER FOUR

IMAGES OF THE SELF: IDENTIFYING WITH FIGURINES

THE CONSTRUCTION OF THE SELF THROUGH FIGURINES IS THE FOCUS of this chapter. In order to analyze how figurines could be used as tools to create personal identity in Hellenistic Babylonia, this chapter will exclusively analyze miniatures that depict single individual figures, standing or seated alone, without interactive features such as movable limbs. I focus on the isolated figure because it allows the best window onto the possibilities for self-identifications with figurines. Absent are the distractions of playing with miniature bodies and entering their world; gone, too, are the miniature figure's relationships with other tiny "people" in that realm. Indeed, the isolated figure's participation in the world of the miniature often seems questionable – it is frequently not clear what these figures are "doing," if they are doing anything. Rather, they stand or sit and face the user, presenting themselves for both encounter and inspection – as companions or, perhaps, as mirrors of real people and real identities as lived in the wider social world of Hellenistic Babylonia.[1] As objects, these figurines also physically occupied that real world, participating in its social space by displaying, with their clothing, poses, gestures, facial expressions, adornments, and activities, visions of how people could "be" and what people could "do" in Hellenistic Babylonia.[2]

This is not to say that these figurines – indeed, any figurines – represented real personhood or real people in Hellenistic Babylonia. Resolutely miniature, these objects were also necessarily abstractions and intensifications of real identities.[3] They could be manipulated and even exist at (and beyond) the borders of human perception, fading in and out of resonance with the real-scale world. As I have argued elsewhere,[4] we cannot look at figurines and expect mimesis – these are not real people, real gender, real age differences, real social roles. They are sideways glimpses at those things through the particular prism of miniaturization. In some ways, they are lesser versions of human identities, for they can never completely represent the sum complexity of lived personhood and the variety of roles that any individual human must inhabit.

Yet in other ways, figurines are intensified versions of human identities, which could impose more rigid ideals or allow experimentations that exceeded what real humans, with all their messy complexity and embodiment, were expected to (or even able to) provide. The female body seen in Figure 4.14 has remained perfectly dressed, posed, and coiffed for millennia; the male bodies seen in Figures 4.7 and 4.8 continue to exercise (albeit without all their limbs intact) centuries after their gymnasion has fallen into ruin. Real bodies are more fragile, organic, and unmanageable, just as real people are both more and less than the perfect matron or athlete. Figurines can therefore tell us both more and less than what we would learn were we able to observe passersby on a Hellenistic Babylonian street. Figurines engaged with how people *thought* about real bodies and identities. Sometimes they show us visions of perfection to which their users aspired.[5] In other cases, we see experiments with identity or even a distance enforced between reality and those miniatures that showed new or uncomfortable identities. Not every figurine in this chapter is an "image of the self," to quote the chapter's title. But I argue that all of them tell us something about what selfhood meant in this particular place and time.

DIVERSITY AND THE MALE BODY

I begin this exploration with a discussion of the adult male form. This is not because such figurines were more numerous or more important than others – indeed, in keeping with Greek and Mesopotamian traditions, there are far fewer surviving figurines of men than of women in the Hellenistic Babylonian corpus.[6] Rather, what distinguishes the corpus of adult male figurines is its variety. The male body in miniature was depicted at a variety of ages, from infancy and childhood, to youthful vigor, to bearded maturity. The activities in which those male bodies could be engaged were equally diverse. These included several behaviors and professional endeavors already discussed elsewhere in this volume, such as the horse riders, soldiers, and performers discussed in Chapter 2 and the lovers, husbands, and musicians discussed in Chapter 3. Additional activities, such as religious offering and athletic exertion, will be discussed in this section.

This male figurine variety, in both ages and actions, may indicate a similar diversity of masculine roles within Hellenistic Babylonian society. As both echoes of and contributors to the real-world communities that they occupied, such figurines indicated that many sorts of opportunities and identities existed, available for almost any man to claim. As will be seen later in this chapter, the range of female identity options represented in the figurines was more tightly circumscribed. Overall, the world of possibility (in miniature) provided to Hellenistic Babylonian men is unsurprising. It not only accords with the greater freedoms granted to men in the ancient world generally; it also fits within the overall ethos of the Hellenistic era as a time of nearly infinite possibilities, provided that a person had luck on his side.[7]

Indeed, what seems more surprising in the Hellenistic Babylonian figurines of male bodies is that the possibilities, while wide, do not seem to have been endless. Mature bearded males were honored, but also presented in limited roles connected with statues and religious activity. More youthful, beardless men had the greatest range of identities open to them, but were not celebrated in the nude except in certain circumstances. Athletes, as one of the specific activities in which the nude male body could be shown, were given both elaborate terracotta constructions and a singular Greek cultural focus – but, at the same time, were created in such a way that their bodies ultimately appeared artificial and distant from reality. Thus, in spite of – or, rather, through – the significant diversity of the male figurine corpus, social roles for men were both suggested and constrained.

Admired from a Distance: Figurines of Mature Males

Hellenistic Babylonian figurines could portray the male body at a variety of ages. The eldest men on this continuum were those that have a thick beard and, in the case of the nude examples, a heavily muscled body. The beard had been a mark of mature masculinity and virility in both Greek and Mesopotamian cultures prior to the Hellenistic period.[8] After the life of Alexander the Great, men wore beards less frequently in imitation of the famous conqueror[9]; even Seleucus I, who took the throne of the Seleucid Empire as an older man, consistently portrayed himself as beardless in both statues and coins.[10] Beardlessness became a way for Hellenistic men, particularly kings, to distinguish themselves from the now bygone eras of the Classical Greek polis and the Achaemenid royal court.[11] This is not to say that no Hellenistic men ever wore beards. For instance, the so-called Terme Ruler statue, seen in Figure 4.1, sports a short beard.[12] This Hellenistic bronze statue depicts an unidentified ruler or prince, confidently surveying the landscape while leaning on his spear.[13] Notably, his facial hair is etched into the bronze rather than sculpted in volumetric detail; the visual effect is of a beardless man when seen at a distance, with the beard revealing itself only when the viewer is in close proximity to the statue. This play with the presence and absence of a beard

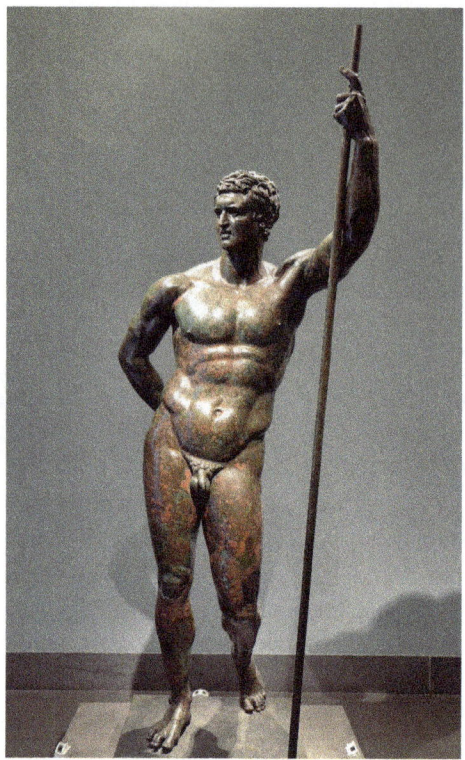

4.1. Terme Ruler (Statue of a Hellenistic ruler), bronze, Rome, second century BCE. Height: 2.37 m. Museo Nazionale Romano, Palazzo Massimo alle Terme.
Photograph courtesy of Carole Raddato, Frankfurt, Germany (Creative Commons License).

clearly demonstrates that to portray a man with a beard in the Hellenistic period was a statement, not just an age marker. Long full beards in particular linked the male body to earlier, traditional systems of power, masculinity, and authority – but at the cost of potentially making the man also seem outdated and irrelevant.

Evidence from the Hellenistic Babylonian figurines indicates that similar cultural logics were at work in this context. As has already been seen in the male figurines discussed thus far in this volume – for instance, the horse riders or the couples – the majority of Hellenistic Babylonian "men in miniature" were beardless. This was not a rigid rule; for instance, the puppet figurine seen in Figure 2.13 has a beard and some of the horse riders do as well. Yet, such beards appear relatively infrequently and suggest that a mature male appearance and facial hair were not the body type preferred by most Hellenistic Babylonian figurine owners.

There are two figurine motifs in which beards are found more consistently. The first of these two groups of male figures were rigidly similar in their dress, pose, and actions. As seen in the example in Figure 4.2, these figurines depict men wearing elaborately pleated and belted tunics. The tunics vary in length

DIVERSITY AND THE MALE BODY 151

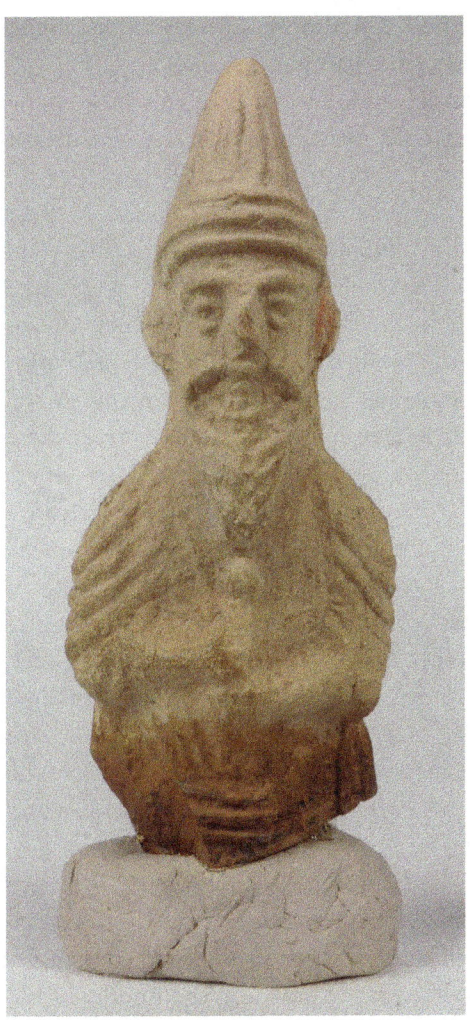

4.2. Clothed, bearded male figurine holding object (supported by modern base), terracotta, Seleucia-on-the-Tigris. Height 8.8 cm. Kelsey Museum of Archaeology, University of Michigan, Ann Arbor (TM 1929.99/KM 2018.01.0031)
Photograph courtesy of Roberta Menegazzi and the Kelsey Museum of Archaeology.

between mid-thigh and mid-calf; trousers are usually worn beneath them.[14] This style of dress is manifestly not Greek and has been linked to the Persians or Parthians.[15] Figurines with similar motifs have also been found in Central Asia, including from the later Parthian and Sassanian periods.[16] The long beards of the figures sometimes terminate in a squared-off end[17] that links them to Mesopotamian and Persian art, such as the beards of Darius and Xerxes on the so-called Treasury Relief at Persepolis. When the heads are preserved, the figures often wear a tall conical cap, which likely also linked them to the eastern-most regions of the Hellenistic world.[18] The figurines were generally made in a single mold, with flattened and unelaborated backsides, although their bases are often flared so that the figurines can stand alone.[19]

Taken together, all of these features strongly indicate a singular cultural focus on the Ancient Near East – and an avoidance of Greek cultural traits. To what degree these figurines truly engaged with just one culture is unclear, as they may represent a blending of Persian, Parthian, Mesopotamian, and other traditions. In their frontal posture, mature bearded masculinity, and arm poses these figurines echo earlier, Neo-Babylonian figurines[20]; however, their tunics and headgear are quite different. For the local Babylonians, such figurines may have seemed just as "foreign" as images of Athena and Apollo – in this case, evidence of Iranian ideas and traditions, linked to the Achaemenids but primarily following on the heels of the new Parthian invaders.[21] It is revealing that these figurines were contemporaneous with so many figurine motifs that were inspired by Greek ideas, visual logics, or technologies. The Parthian invasion did not result in a large-scale shift in the figurine repertoire; indeed, many of the Greek-influenced figurine types continued in use or even became more popular in the Parthian period.[22] Against the backdrop of such Hellenistic figurines, the distinctiveness of these bearded tunic-wearing men that were so definitively *not* engaged with Greek tradition seems striking indeed. Such isolation is mirrored in the findspots of these figurines: for instance, at Seleucia-on-the-Tigris, no figurines in this motif have been found in the major deposits of terracottas near the Archives Square, the figurines in which include many of the common motifs in the Hellenistic Babylonian corpus.[23]

What is also striking about these bearded tunic-wearing figurines is that they are nearly unified by pose. Almost every example depicts the man in the act of carrying an object. One or, usually, both arms are bent at ninety-degree angles and held tight to the body, firmly grasping a small object in the middle of the chest. The objects held can vary – some appear to be a small box, circular disk, or cup, while others are too vague to be identified by modern scholars.[24] Whether the identification of these objects would have been immediately legible to the ancient users, or left to their imaginations, is unclear. The hands of the men encircle the objects with great protectiveness and care, often almost entirely obscuring them. The frontal posture of the figures and the central positioning of the objects indicate that display and presentation to an audience was desired, but the obfuscation verging on illegibility suggests that perhaps the human owner of the figurine was not the intended, or at least the primary, viewer. Other scholars have suggested that these were votive figures or priests[25] – a compelling interpretation because of the figurines' offering pose. Starkly unlike the potentially votive female figurines discussed in Chapter 2, these male figurines do not ask for human intervention or interaction. The objects they hold, and their actions, seem distinctly *not* meant for us; we are observers, not the recipients of their gestures.

The offered objects and culturally distinct dress of these figurines may indicate the adoption of new cultural and religious practices in Babylonia, possibly during or after the Parthian conquest of 141 BCE. However, the uniqueness of the motif and the singular unwillingness to adapt it to the Hellenistic conventions popular in the region also isolated that new cultural or religious practice, relegating it to the margins of the social imaginary. The vision of mature masculinity presented in these figurines may similarly have been limited, with the old-fashioned beard imparting an air of traditional dignity that was at odds with everyday life. Religion here is presented as an activity undertaken by a small group of identically embodied and distinctly unfashionable old men, not as a widespread revolution in belief systems and gods. The Parthian tunic found more *au courant* use among figurines depicting younger men, as will be discussed in the next section of this chapter. But the beards and the offering postures seem to be linked, each localizing the figure in an otherworldly sphere – a realm which undoubtedly had religious consequence, but provided less incentive for self-identification and emulation.

The second group of bearded mature male figures have a more distinctively Hellenistic appearance, and may have represented the god Herakles, who was especially popular in the Hellenistic Near East.[26] Usually fully nude, these figures have lined foreheads, sagging shoulders, and creases around the mouth that indicate men who have reached middle age, if not more advanced years. They nevertheless are shown with well-muscled, powerful bodies, as seen in the figurine pictured in Figure 4.3, which also holds the club and lion skin that were crucial features of Herakles mythology. The head inclines downward, the body is dynamically positioned in a contrapposto pose, and the right arm is held behind the back – all features that echo the Lysippian *Weary Herakles* sculpture (see Figure 5.6). With evidence pointing toward a Herakles identification for these figurines, it might seem odd to include them here, in a discussion about more generic male figures. Herakles as a figurine motif will be addressed specifically in Chapter 5, within a broader consideration of the Hellenistic *koine* deities.

Yet it is nevertheless worthwhile to consider the influence of this version of the mature male body on broader Hellenistic Babylonian conceptions of masculinity. There is considerable variety among the figurines that share this motif, and it is possible that not all of these figurines were thought to be Herakles by their original users. The club could switch hands or be absent altogether. Some figurines are lacking the contrapposto stance; others attempt to portray that dynamic posture within the limitations of a single-molded design.[27] The abdominal musculature could be depicted with greater definition. Rare examples exhibit the limbs modeled in an openwork design that allows free space between the legs and the bend of the right arm.[28] In my previous work, I explored the implications of this diversity on the ability of

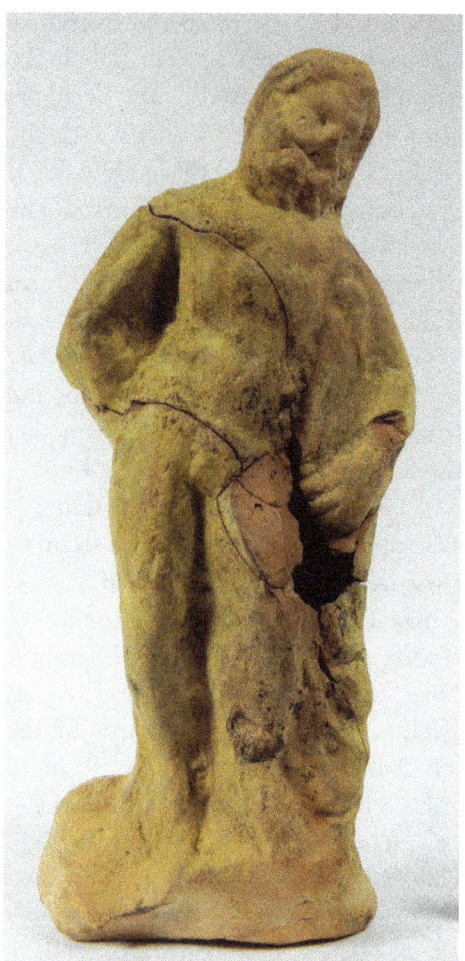

4.3. Nude, bearded male figurine, possibly Herakles, terracotta, Seleucia-on-the-Tigris. Height: 13.6 cm. Kelsey Museum of Archaeology, University of Michigan, Ann Arbor (KM 14884) Photograph courtesy of Roberta Menegazzi and the Kelsey Museum of Archaeology.

modern scholars to categorize these figurines.[29] In particular, I argued that although all of these figurines undoubtedly engaged with the broader Hellenistic conventions of depicting Herakles, these figurines cannot all be unequivocally, or exclusively, identified with that hero-god. Rather, the Hellenistic Babylonian users of these figurines were interested in experimenting with the bodily forms, poses, and styles of these dynamic lion hunters – and thus, perhaps, were interested in questioning the role of the mature, bearded male body itself.

Within this diversity of form, importance was routinely placed on the statue-like display quality of these figurines. Several of the features of these figurines were designed or manipulated for the purpose of keeping the figurine in a vertically stable position. Plinths in particular not only added to the vertical stability of figurines by creating a wide base, but also constructed a visual divide between the figurine and the surface on which it rests. The image is literally raised up and away from the mundane world, as if it were a statue to be viewed from afar rather than an active participant in its surroundings.

This viewing experience is especially relevant within a broader consideration of mature, bearded men as portrayed in figurines. Together, these examples indicate that representations of mature middle age were not incompatible with the desired, and desirable, viewing of the male body in Hellenistic Babylonia. But beyond their similarities in age and facial hair, the two groups of figurines I have discussed here – the bearded, tunic-wearing men who hold an object and the nude bearded men similar to Herakles –have little in common. Indeed, I would argue that they deliberately represented quite distinct visions of mature masculinity. Despite all the avenues by which Herakles-like figures could be appealing to a Mesopotamian audience (as will be discussed in more detail in Chapter 5), there was a certain level of cultural specificity in each of the two figurine motifs.

This is perhaps not surprising, as mature male bodies were often synonymous with power in the ancient world – bearers of tradition and enforcers of social codes.[30] What is more surprising is how the Hellenistic Babylonian figurines effectively subverted that traditional role for the mature male body even as they appeared to honor it. In both cases, the figurines present mature bearded men through a lens of admiration, but also one of isolation. The roles offered for bearded male bodies are limited in the figurines by their extreme specificity. They are relegated to a statuesque domain and pushed to the margins – honored margins, in touch with the divine, but margins nonetheless. Even the cultural specificity of these figurines is at odds with the vast majority of Hellenistic Babylonian figurines – and, thus, potentially was at odds with how most Hellenistic Babylonians saw themselves. It is difficult to imagine that most real Hellenistic Babylonian men of advanced age would find much to identify with here.

I suggest that this was precisely the point. In an era of cultural negotiation in which many mature men were going against long-standing traditions, such as by choosing to shave their facial hair, these figurines could offer a dual comfort. First, the honoring-in-miniature of the more traditional version of mature masculinity could provide reassurance that customs had not been lost and conventional values could still be respected. Someone somewhere was still upholding old-fashioned standards and morals, even if it was the priests or votaries and the hero-gods they honored. The second comfort offered by the figurines, which was very much related to the first, was the freedom they offered contemporary Hellenistic Babylonian men of every age to *not* fit the mold of traditional bearded masculinity. Not just outmoded, that version of male self-presentation now seemed almost impossible, an attribute of the gods and their devotees, not of the everyday man. Indeed, maintaining a desirable distance between oneself and the gods also seems to have been a major theme in Hellenistic Babylonian figurines of younger men, as is discussed in the next section.

Young and Beardless: Self-Identification and the Royal Image

Figurines depicting idealized beardless youths occupy the middle range of the male age spectrum seen in Hellenistic Babylonian figurines. Many of these beardless youthful bodies were shown engaged in a particular activity – for instance, the soldiers and horse riders, the husbands and lovers in the couple figurines, the male partners in musician figurines, and the athletes. This diversity of forms and activities reveals that it was the youthful beardless man that was deemed the most operational and agentive male in Hellenistic Babylonian society. Unlike his bearded elders who were relegated to a statue-like distance and limited, although honored, by their explicit connection to the divine, the young man was the man of action and social consequence in the here and now. His place on the age-range spectrum, while young, was also bracketed by the popular figurines of male children. Viewed in light of those figurines, the beardless young man is youthful, but not the most junior or most immature vision of masculinity offered by the miniature corpus. Instead, he occupies a comfortable middle ground and an apex of agency.

As many of the youthful male bodies engaged in "actions" are discussed elsewhere in this volume, I turn attention here to the figurines that present young men simply standing before the viewer, with no obvious activity or motivation other than to engage the viewer's attention. As seen in Figure 4.4, the posture is usually frontal; even in cases like this one where the figure is dressed in Greek-style clothing, the range of Greek sculptural poses, such as contrapposto, was not extensively utilized. Their heads are generally held level, with faces that gaze directly outward. This head positioning coupled with the frontal pose facilitates direct visual interaction with the user. Yet this interaction is of a very different type than that encouraged by figurines with movable components or theatrical elements, which lured the human user into the miniature world – onto the battlefield, into the bedroom, and onto the stage. Rather than creating interactions that existed primarily in the fantasy world of the miniature, these figurines of young men served as iconic referents to real identities being performed in the large-scale social world. Their lack of specific activity or attribute allowed them to become a figurative "blank slate," onto which anyone with sufficient shared characteristics (namely masculinity and beardlessness) could overwrite their own identity and personhood.[31] Almost every man in Hellenistic Babylonia could identify with such images, therefore almost every man was also constrained by them.

DIVERSITY AND THE MALE BODY 157

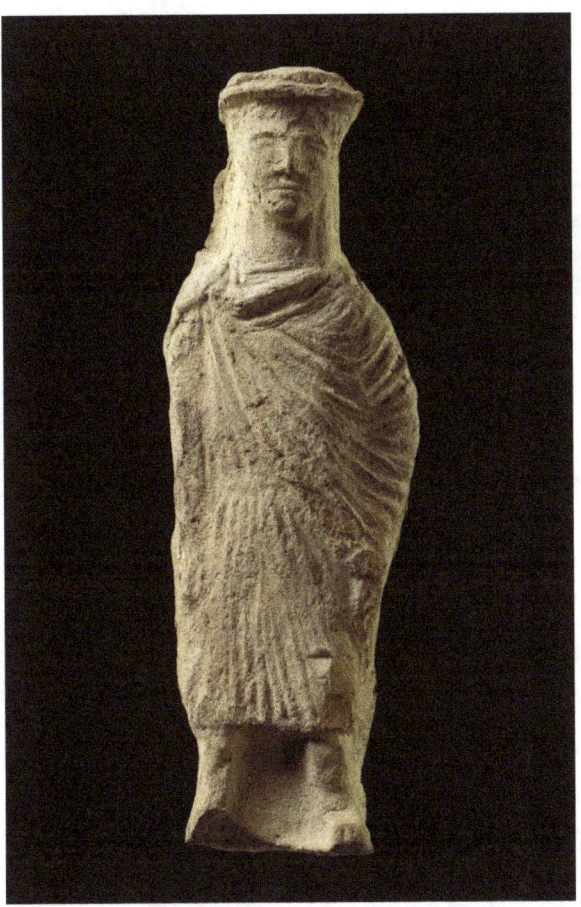

4.4. Clothed male figurine (wearing *chiton*), terracotta, Uruk. Height: 17.8 cm.
Vorderasiatisches Museum Berlin (VA 14620)
Photograph © Staatliche Museen zu Berlin-Vorderasiatisches Museum, Foto: Olaf M. Teßmer.

The features of that constraining vision of masculine identity are profoundly revealing of the priorities and ideals of Hellenistic Babylonian society. Crucially, and commensurately with many of the other figurine motifs discussed in this volume, that identity seems to have been inclusive of both Greek and Near Eastern cultural backgrounds. For instance, as seen in Figure 4.4, the youthful male figure could be dressed in Greek-style attire. This figure wears a long *chiton* covered by a mantle, in which his left arm is wrapped, while his head is covered by a flat hat, associated with the Greeks and Macedonians.[32] However, the figurine itself is not only frontally posed in accordance with Babylonian modes of viewing but was also manufactured in the Mesopotamian single mold, with a solid construction and flat, unelaborated backside. Thus the frontality and engagement of the figure were privileged over the potential for exploiting Greek technologies and sculptural styles.

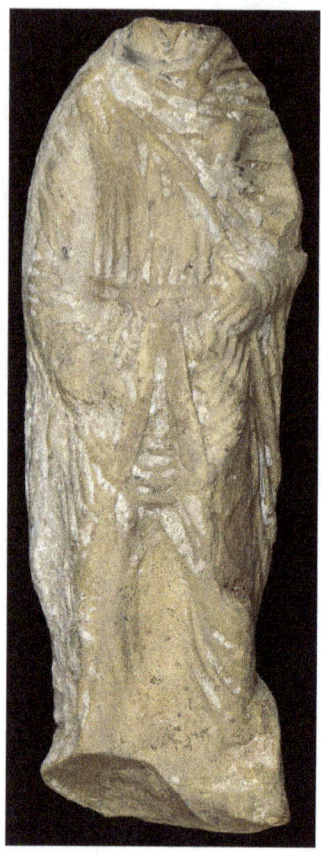

4.5. Clothed male figurine (wearing belted tunic), terracotta, Babylon. Height: 14 cm. British Museum (BM 80–11-12–1935)
Photograph © The Trustees of the British Museum.

Additionally, although the dress of this figure is Greco-Macedonian, the details of its depiction and appearance overlap significantly with other Hellenistic Babylonian figurines of young men in "Parthian" costume. For instance, as seen in Figure 4.5, the body of a young man is shown wearing a belted tunic, similar to the tunic worn by the bearded figure seen previously, in Figure 4.2. However, in place of the rigid offering posture and beard, a more ambiguous pose was created for this figure. His head is now missing, but evidence of a triangular beard as seen in Figure 4.2, which falls well past the level of the shoulders, is absent.[33] His left arm is bent with the thumb hooked over his belt in a jaunty, almost casual way, that echoes the slightly bent left arm of the Greek-attired example. Both figurines have a prominent strap or hemline that crosses the body from the figure's right shoulder to the left hip; in the case of the Parthian-attired figure, that strap reduces the vertical linearity of his tunic pleats and gives an air of complicated wrapped Greek garments. Indeed, the folds of both the Parthian tunic and Greek *chiton* are virtually indistinguishable in terracotta. I should emphasize *in terracotta* – indeed, any visual similarities we perceive between these two figures would probably not have been paralleled in real-life worn versions of these garments, in which a leather strap could be easily differentiated from a hemline, regardless of their position on the body. It was the conceit of miniaturization, where these clothes were translated in scale, detail, and medium, that allowed visual similarities to be played with and emphasized. And emphasized I believe they were – indeed, both of these figurines were modeled such that small fragments of either (a swatch of vertical pleats, for instance) could be confused for the other. In this manner, the figurines accommodated the different modes of dress among the youthful beardless men who populated the streets of Hellenistic Babylonia, while simultaneously suggesting that there were few real differences between them.

This is in striking contrast with the figurines of bearded mature men already discussed, and the comparison between the two groups reveals how figurines had the power to include or to ostracize. Both the bearded mature male and the beardless young male were given "Greek" and "Near Eastern" options for their identities in miniature. Yet the figurines imply that such a choice was less consequential for younger men than for their elders. For a young man, either mode of dress could be worn, either cultural tradition adhered to in some superficial ways, provided that the frontal, direct engagement with society and the beardless standard of the day were adhered to. Bearded mature men, on the other hand, made a significant choice in opting to either emulate Herakles or the devoted offering bearers. Or, as I have already suggested, this was really no choice at all, as bearded male figurines and the other-worldly identities they embodied were specifically packaged so as to be unrealistic and therefore impossible to use for coidentification purposes.

Yet for all the cultural fluidity that the figurines of younger men seemed to offer, they did impose a significant restriction on the male body: it must wear clothes.[34] Nude adult male bodies in Hellenistic Babylonian figurines were almost exclusively reserved for two types of situations: first, when gods, such as Herakles or Apollo, were referenced or, second, when the male figure's nudity was an integral part of the action in which he was engaged, such as the male partner in the amorous couples or the athletes. Such restrictions on adult male nudity sharply differentiate this age and gender group from the female figurines and the child figurines; as will be discussed later in this chapter, both of those groups could present the nude body in a direct way, without invoking specific divine identities or social circumstances to explain the figures' lack of clothing. Additionally, the strict limitation on the portrayal of the nude adult male body was in striking contrast with the Classical Greek and Hellenistic *koine* traditions, both of which emphasized the aesthetic appeal of the nude bodies of youthful, beardless men.[35]

Mesopotamian tradition may partially explain this aversion to the nude adult male body. Outside of rare associations with priestly purity or mythological heroes, male nudity was generally coded negatively in the Ancient Near East. In art, it was most frequently a sign of humiliation reserved for prisoners of war and dead enemies, or the emasculation of palace eunuchs (many of whom were likely slaves and/or foreign captives).[36] Within the multicultural context of Hellenistic Babylonia, it is possible that many people still had a distaste for depictions of the nude adult male body, particularly when nudity was not necessary for the man's role or the figurine's purpose. In the absence of a compelling reason for nudity, clothing was the default option – perhaps in large part because it was more acceptable across cultural lines.

Figurines of nude beardless males may also have been avoided because of the connection between youthful male bodies and the Hellenistic kings. Evidence from Seleucid coins, seals, and Roman copies of Seleucid statues clearly indicate that the kings themselves were routinely shown young and beardless.[37] In the full-size statues (none of which survive, unfortunately) it is likely that the Seleucid kings – like Alexander the Great before them and the Terme Ruler with which they were contemporary – were shown as heroic nudes.[38] Such statues not only echoed those of other Hellenistic rulers, but also the younger generation of Greek gods, such as Apollo and Dionysos, whose worship was especially popular in the Hellenistic period. Apollo was particularly special to the Seleucid kings, as the Seleucid royal family claimed Apollo as their direct ancestor.[39] As seen in Figure 4.6, Seleucid coins often immediately juxtaposed images of the Seleucid king on the coin obverse with a young Greek god, such

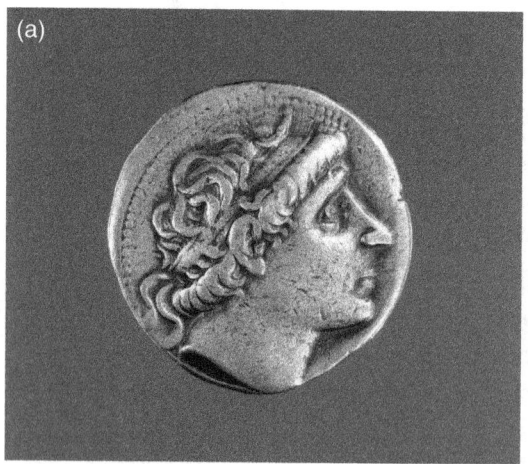
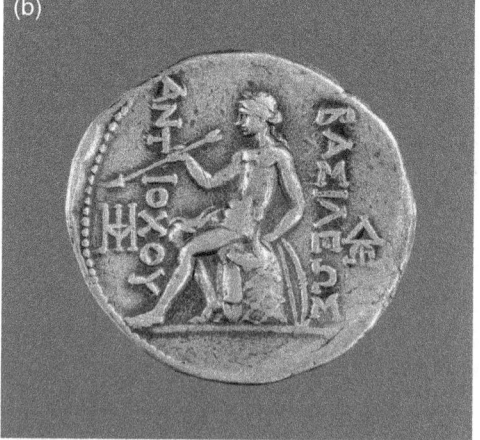

4.6a and b. Obverse and reverse of Tetradrachm with Antiochus I, silver, Seleucia-on-the-Tigris, c. 281–261 BCE. Diameter: 2.5 cm. The J. Paul Getty Museum Villa 80.NH.2.27
Photographs courtesy of The J. Paul Getty Museum, Villa Collection, Malibu, California, Gift of Chester B. Franz.

as Apollo, on the reverse.[40] The entire body of Apollo was usually shown, and thus the god could clearly be distinguished as youthful, beardless, and nude.[41] Seal impressions on tablets and bullae similarly brought Seleucid royal faces and the nude bodies of youthful gods into association, on the same object and in the same visual plane.[42] The wide distribution of such images – particularly coins – and their constant use by the populace ensured that this connection of the youthful nude male body with the Seleucid kings was well known. Indeed, their interconnection likely allowed each to substitute for the other, with the youthful male body becoming a politicized shorthand for Seleucid leadership, and the Seleucid king in particular.[43]

So why do we not see such connections in the figurines? Indeed, images of either the Seleucid king or the generic nude youthful male body are almost entirely absent from the corpus altogether. I suggest that the reason may lie in the tactility and particular kinds of intimacy illusions that figurines encouraged. Both seals and coins allowed personal handling and tactile access to their miniature images, enabling members of the public to own, touch, and caress the king's face and the nude male bodies associated with him. Yet, unlike figurines, both seals and coins are low relief images, barely three-dimensional. In a primarily flat depiction of a human body, the viewer is obligated to look at the figure from one specific perspective. Since coins were controlled by the government,[44] and royal portraits on seals were modeled on coins,[45] that specific perspective was restricted by the palace. As seen in the coin in Figure 4.6, access to most of each figure's body was denied. The user does not see and cannot touch any of the king's body besides the side of his head; more contact was permitted with the youthful nude male body, but at least half of his form was similarly off-limits. Three-dimensional figurines, on the other hand, permit much more comprehensive bodily access. Of course, this receptiveness to the user was not total nor universal, even in figurines; many of the case studies in this volume explore how user access to figurine bodies could be constrained. However, the severe restriction on viewpoints and perspectives imposed by coins and seals cannot be achieved in a three-dimensional figurine. Any figurine, regardless of the positioning of its body or the vagueness of its anatomical details, can be grasped in the hand, seen from all angles, overwhelmingly possessed and owned.

Such tactile handling of figurines also routinely took place in private spaces, such as within the home, where official oversight and control were unlikely to intervene. Coins and seals could also be handled in private domestic spaces, but those were not their primary purposes. Rather, coins and seals became fully actualized as objects through their public use: coins as instruments of monetary exchange, seals as signatory devices to commercial transactions. Government oversight did extend to those sectors, especially through the collecting of taxes.[46]

Thus seals and coins provided miniaturized access to the body of the king and the nude youthful beardless male form with which the king was associated – but that contact was restricted by the fact that the designs of these objects were dictated by the palace and their primary use was subject to palace supervision and intervention. In contrast, the creation and use of figurines was comparatively unsupervised and uncontrollable, outside of any official connection to the royal court. Such freedoms could have allowed figurines of the king and associated body types to flourish in whatever form people preferred. The fact that they did not – indeed, they were scrupulously avoided – further supports the notion that Hellenistic Babylonian figurines operated as unofficial regulators and enforcers of the broader social contract. The kind of personal connection with a miniature human body that figurines allowed was likely not considered an appropriate relationship for an everyday person to have with the body of the king. Even bodies that could be directly associated with the king, such as the generic youthful beardless nude male, might have been too close for comfort.

Fragmenting the Active Male Body: Athlete Figurines

Athletes were one of the few Hellenistic Babylonian figurine motifs in which the youthful beardless male body could be depicted. However, just because such figurines of the nude youthful male body in action were possible does not mean that they were uncritically accepted or viewed as unproblematic by all members of Hellenistic Babylonian society. Indeed, the athlete figurines bear material evidence of the contested social space that they occupied and the cross-cultural negotiations in which they were involved. In particular, I argue that the ways in which the terracotta bodies of athlete figurines were constructed – especially the mid-limb joins of their arms and legs, and the fragmented appearance of the body that resulted from such joins – distanced them from a completely mimetic relationship with real life in Hellenistic Babylonia.

With their torsos twisted and backs arched, the athlete figurines were depicted in energetic poses indicative of agile physical exertion. The use of separately added arms and legs further accentuated the dynamic contours of these splayed poses, giving a greater sense of flexibility and exercise than what could easily be achieved using a standard double mold. Yet, while the use of separately made limbs was a practical choice for depicting athletic activity, the selection of juncture spot was less so. Many of these athlete figurines were made with the upper arms and upper legs molded as one piece with the torso, and "finished-off" at a mid-point of the long bone. Most have the join placed at

DIVERSITY AND THE MALE BODY 163

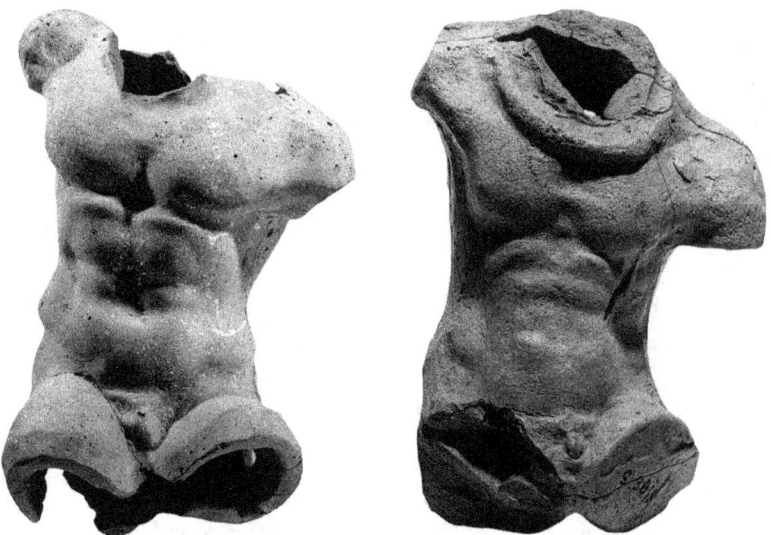

4.7 and 4.8. Nude male athlete figurines, terracotta, Seleucia-on-the-Tigris. Turin Excavations at Seleucia. (S8,525) height: 11 cm and (S3919) 6.5 cm, respectively. Photographs courtesy of Roberta Menegazzi.

roughly the upper one-third of the limb, with varying degrees of distance from the real joint of the shoulder or hip. For instance, only small portions of the upper arms are modeled with the figurine torso seen in Figure 4.7, while more substantial upper thighs are shown on the same figurine.[47] Alternately, the left upper arm of the figurine seen in Figure 4.8 is finished off at a lower point, corresponding to the one-third or one-half mark of the upper arm. Some joins could also be closer to the actual joints of the human body; for instance, the right arm and leg of the figurine seen in Figure 4.8 are severed quite close to the shoulder and hip positions, respectively. However, joins that mimic living human anatomy – the shoulder and hip, or, alternately, the elbow and knee – were less common than mid-limb joins. Note that both figurines share the same pose – with the left side of the body contracted and the spine curved in a sweeping arch – and yet their limb attachment points differ. This variation from figurine to figurine, even when the poses were remarkably similar, is an indication that more than just technical necessity was involved in the choice of where to place the seam between the torso and the separately made limbs.[48]

Since mimesis does not seem to have been the primary goal, and technical issues do not seem to have been the primary constraint, an alternate explanation must be proposed for the mid-limb joining places on the athlete figurines. The visual obviousness of such joins precludes assumptions that the viewer would not detect them; indeed, due to the material constraints of miniaturization, such seams would be more noticeable on a figurine than on a life-size marble statue. The physical properties of materials do not shrink with the scale of the whole object; thus the visible line of arm or leg attachment remains – with the slight concavity at the join, small pockets of dark empty space where the two sides do not quite fit perfectly together, and the bulkiness of any armature or adhesive used to affix the join – whether the arm is 10 cm or 10 mm in diameter. Thus, the seam *appears* bigger in the miniature scale, as it dominates a greater portion of the figure's arm or leg.

Two of the other properties of miniaturization – abstraction and exaggeration – further accentuate the appearance of a mid-limb seam. Because of their small size, miniature objects must always omit, condense, or abstract some anatomical details.[49] When the user's eye has few details to attract its gaze, non-anatomical joints become even more prominent; see, for instance, how the mid-thigh joints on the figurine in Figure 4.7 are even more noticeable when viewed next to the small and cursory depiction of the figure's genitalia. Conversely, the process of miniaturization also allows for the bodily details that *are* depicted to be emphasized, exaggerated, or distorted to a greater degree than would be visually coherent in a large-scale sculpture.[50] Such accentuated features call attention to points of interest in the figurine, such as the essential elements necessary to identify the figure depicted. This impoverished partiality of miniatures "evoke[s] and resonate[s] to" an experience and identity without aspiring to complete representation.[51] A similar reading of these figurines suggests that the oversized attention given to the noticeable mid-limb joining of the arms and legs emphasized both the limbs themselves and what the limbs signified in terms of identity and status – in this case, an athlete and his negotiated place within Hellenistic Babylonian society.

While the celebration of male physical prowess and sexual beauty was not new to Babylonia,[52] the specific glorification of the nude male body engaged in dynamic feats of athleticism was introduced during the Hellenistic period. As already discussed in this chapter, the nudity of the male figure would have been particularly difficult for the Babylonian audience. Athletic nudity and male homoeroticism, including pederasty, were deeply connected in Classical Greece[53] – a fact which, if understood in Hellenistic Babylonia, would have made Greek athletics specifically challenging for Babylonians to culturally accommodate. Although less problematic, the display of physical agility and strength for its own sake, rather than in the context of hunting or war, would also have been an unfamiliar artistic subject to a Babylonian viewer.[54]

Yet, rather than downplay the novel features of the athletic male bodies they portrayed, these figurines emphasized them. Whereas many Hellenistic

Babylonian figurines, even those made in the double mold, have little detailing on the back, athlete figurines were elaborately detailed on all sides with rippling musculature that mimicked a Hellenistic *koine* ideal, posed in the midst of their exertions in dramatic Baroque style.[55] Such vigorous movements of the limbs were accentuated through the placing of prominent mid-limb joins. Intensified attention was thus also directed to the spectacle and bodily performance of this relatively new, Greek form of identity. Rather than shy away from an acknowledgment of cultural difference, these figurines — and the techniques used to join their limbs — aggressively sought visual recognition as novel, different, and, when compared to a living human body, artificial. The inability of the body depicted to release this contorted posture of athletic activity or flex the real joints of the human body, such as the hips or shoulders, generated a pose that was permanent and intensified beyond what a living body could achieve.

Ironically, as the figurine became a perfected icon of athletic identity, it lost its ability to index athletic movement and action. Unlike the bodies of real athletes, the bodies of the athlete figurines are not in motion, and their actions are not performed. It is clear from the mid-limb joins that these bodies were *made* in this pose, rather than needing to move and stretch in order to attain it. The plaster "seat" under the buttocks of some athlete figurines, used to form a stable base, also gives a sense of posed permanence.[56] Such features encouraged distant engagement and admiration, rather than intimate tactile exploration of — and self-identification with — the figurine.[57] The athlete identity was made to seem foreign and detached — not just from a Babylonian viewer, but from all living bodies, even Greek and Macedonian ones — as it was simultaneously emphasized and explored. As a result, the athlete figurines skewed "the experience of the social by literally *deferring* it"[58]; engaging their viewers in an intriguing visual spectacle through indirect and unaggressive means.

This slow and circuitous introduction of Greek athletic tradition via the artificial bodies of the athlete figurines may have paralleled — and, indeed, prefigured — the actual adoption of Greek athleticism (or, at least, purpose-built spaces for the practicing of Greek athletics) into Hellenistic Babylonia. Although athlete figurines were found in early levels at Seleucia-on-the-Tigris,[59] archaeological and textual evidence both indicate that gymnasia were not introduced into Babylonia until late in the Hellenistic period, and even then were only founded at Babylon and Seleucia-on-the-Tigris. The earliest evidence for a gymnasion at Babylon is a Greek inscription "giving a victory list of ephebes and youths in gymnastic contests" that dates to 109 BCE, over two centuries after Alexander the Great, as well as three decades after the Parthian conquest of the

Seleucid Empire.[60] The archaeological evidence for a Babylon gymnasion is contested: the palaestra that some have identified as part of the gymnasion may actually be a part of the theater or another building.[61] However, even if it was a gymnasion, its architectural remains are even later in date than the Greek inscription.[62] Textual evidence for the gymnasion at Seleucia-on-the-Tigris is similarly late: a stamp of unbaked clay referencing the civic office of gymnasiarch dates to 72/1 BCE.[63] In addition to their delayed introduction to Hellenistic Babylonia, such gymnasia may also have operated quite differently from their Classical Greek prototypes. Both the unconventional architecture of the Babylon gymnasion (if it was such), as well as comparative evidence from gymnasia in Hellenistic Central Asia (such as at Ai Khanum[64]), indicates that gymnasia membership, activities, and rules for participation differed substantially from the Classical Greek gymnasion (in its most common practice), reflecting the multicultural communities in which they operated.

As with actual gymnasia, the athlete figurines discussed here were similarly restricted and unpopular: these figurines have only been found at Seleucia-on-the-Tigris, and even there were only recovered in limited numbers.[65] Thus the poses and the bodies seen in these figurines may indeed have been alien to the lived reality of athleticism and physical exertion in Hellenistic Babylonia. In fragmenting their limbs and thus appearing artificial, these figurines introduced general ideas about the Greek gymnasion even as they emphasized the distance between the potentially contested Greek identities that they represented and actual Hellenistic Babylonian social practice.[66] In other words, it was through their own fragmentation that these figurines were able to avoid fragmenting the social fabric of the communities in which they circulated.

COHESIVENESS AND THE FEMALE BODY

In contrast to the diversity of male ages and social roles depicted in the Hellenistic Babylonian figurine corpus, figurines depicting female bodies represented an almost monolithic ideal. Poses and activities could be varied: sexualized, possibly votive, female figurines with interactive movable arms; involvement in a spectrum of social relationships (with children, lovers, husbands, and musicians); and the banqueting, reclining figurines that will be presented in Chapter 5. Despite that moderate variety, the age range and body types of almost all those figures were fairly consistent, and link those examples with the largest category of female figurines in Hellenistic Babylonia: the frontal female figure, standing or sitting alone. It is to those figurines that my attention now turns.

Nudity and Clothing

One of the sharpest visual distinctions in the corpus of Hellenistic Babylonian female figurines is the divide between clothed bodies and bodies that are partially or (more often) fully nude. Much has been made of the existence of both groups of figurines – particularly the nude female figurines, which are usually given first position in catalogues and are often discussed extensively.[67] Although the reasons for such scholarly attention are not always explicitly articulated, the large number of these figurines in the corpus suggests their widespread importance in the Hellenistic Babylonian communities.[68] Nude standing female figurines also have a very deep history in Mesopotamia, and particularly the motif of a female figure displaying her breasts in her cupped hands has Mesopotamian precedents going back to the Sumerian periods.[69] This history makes such figurines a logical starting point for discussion of the Hellenistic-era tradition in the same region. Although I have framed my exploration in this volume in very different terms, using the affects of miniaturization as a driver of the discussion rather than a more traditional typological undertaking, I recognize the logic – and the significance of the continued use of this ancient Mesopotamian motif in a "Hellenic" age.

As seen in Figure 4.9, the nude female figure stands frontally, facing the viewer directly. Her hair is often elaborately coiffed in seeming anticipation of viewership; she is not caught in a delicate moment, but rather is fully prepared for our gaze. The pose of her bent arms, which are tightly crooked so that her hands can support her breasts, echo this impression of the nude female body confidently displayed. Other options for arm and hand positioning included just one hand held to the breast (see Figure 4.10) or both arms held at the sides (see Figure 4.11). This variety makes the precise meaning of the gestures unclear. Yet the direct presentation of the nude female body is consistent. The body itself is depicted in detail, with the breasts, rolls of flesh on the abdomen, navel, pubic creases, and tapering legs fully modeled. The level of detailing given to the genitalia varies. Most of these figurines do not mark a slit for the labia. Those that do, such as seen in Figure 4.9, are a tiny minority of the overall corpus.[70] However, it is worth pointing out that the standing frontal nude female figurines are among the *only* Hellenistic Babylonian figurines in which such female genital elaboration is provided.[71] Other poses for the nude female body do not seem to have been compatible with such a straightforward depiction of female anatomy. The proportions of the standing female nude body varied, particularly in the ratio of waist to hips: some, such as the figurine in Figure 4.9 have markedly wide hips, while others depict almost no curvature on the abdomen at all.[72]

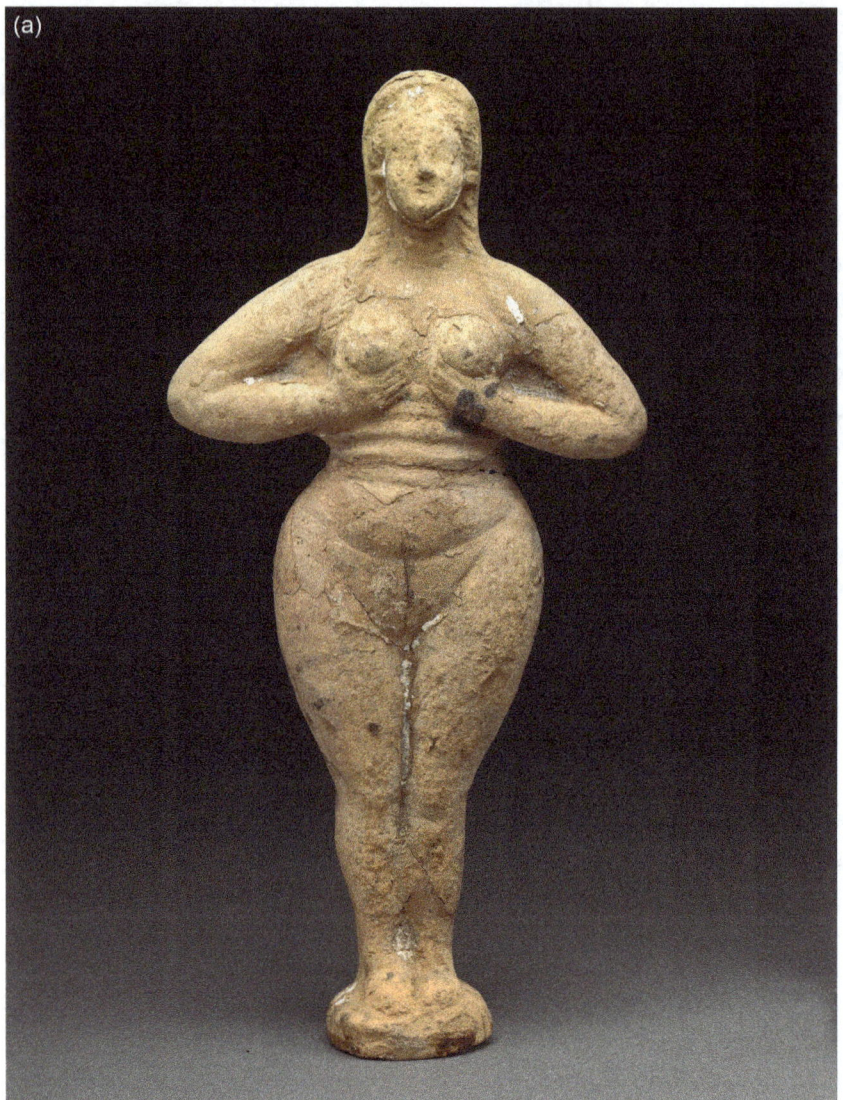

4.9a and b. Front and back of standing nude female figurine, terracotta, Babylon. Height 38 cm. British Museum (BM 80–6–17–1713=92215)
Photographs © The Trustees of the British Museum.

Many scholars have proposed divine identifications for such nude female figurines, both in the Hellenistic period and earlier in Mesopotamian history, labeling them as "mother goddess" types[73] indicative of "popular religiosity."[74] Yet, there is nothing necessarily supernatural about any of these female figurines; they do not sport wings or features of divine anatomy, nor any iconography (such as headgear or attributes) that definitively link them to a particular goddess. The association of the breast-supporting gesture with maternity or

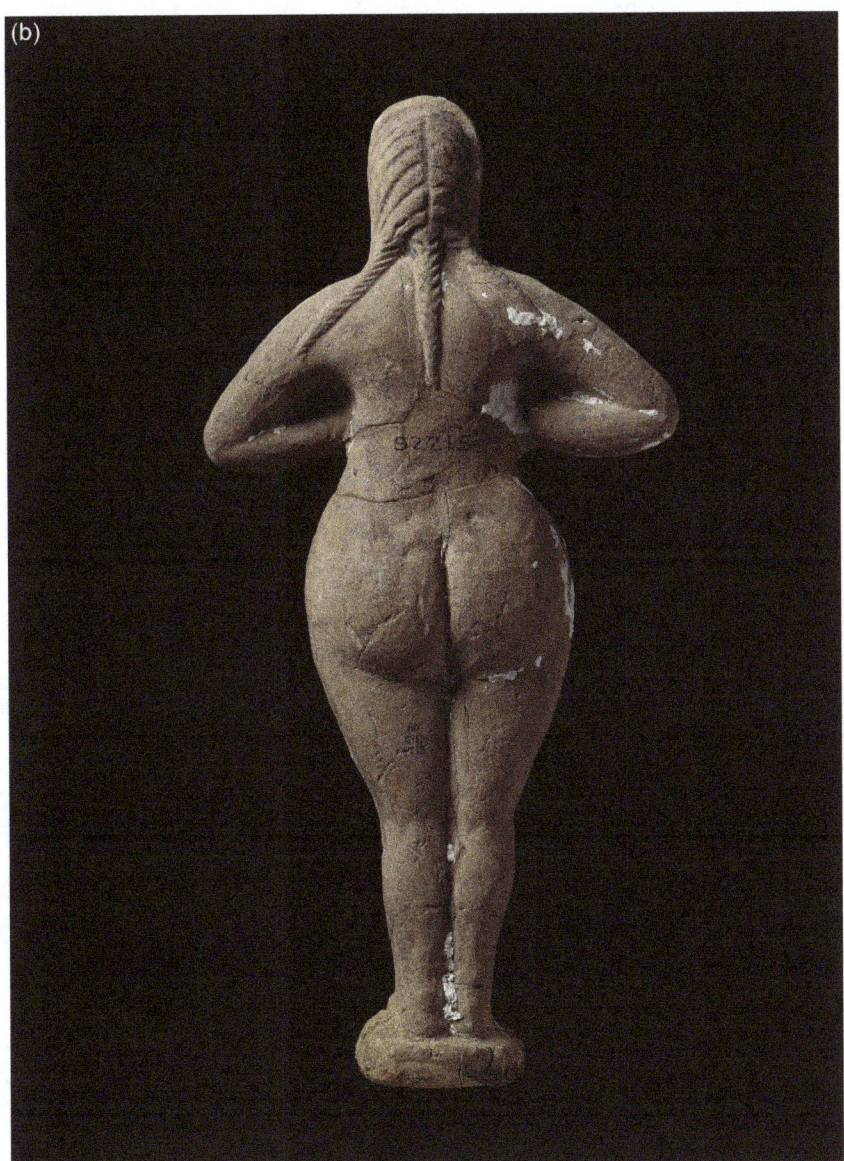

4.9b. (cont.)

fertility has similarly been called into question.[75] Thus, rather than rely on the notion of supernatural or maternal status for this motif, I find it most worthwhile to point out how the persistence of this very ancient Mesopotamian motif likely indicates a continuity of practice, with the purposes and meanings of such figurines persisting in at least some spheres of Hellenistic Babylonian life.

It might have been difficult for someone raised in Greek traditions and modes of viewing to be immediately comfortable with the vision of straightforward

170　IMAGES OF THE SELF: IDENTIFYING WITH FIGURINES

(a)　　　　　　　　(b)

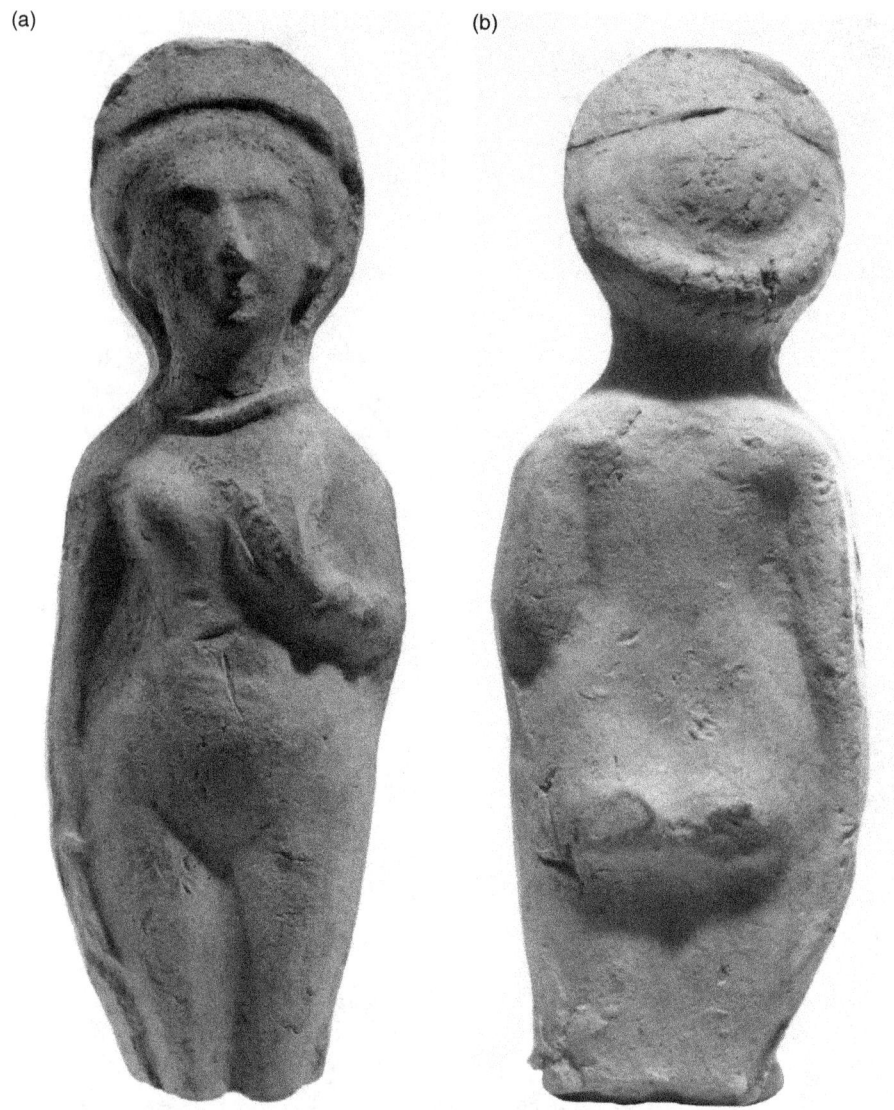

4.10a and b. Front and back of nude standing female figurine, terracotta, Seleucia-on-the-Tigris. Height: 11.45 cm. Turin Excavations at Seleucia (S6,720) Photograph courtesy of Roberta Menegazzi.

female nudity presented in Figure 4.9 (or, especially, the female sexual agency and display seen in Figure 1.15, in which the figure touches her labia with her fingers). Despite the greater acceptance of and interest in the female nude body in the Hellenistic period, Greek artistic conventions still dictated that female genitalia be left unelaborated – as seen, for instance, in the famous Knidian Aphrodite (Figure 4.12).[76] Aphrodite was a popular subject of sculpture throughout the Hellenistic *koine*, many examples of which derive from the Knidia and

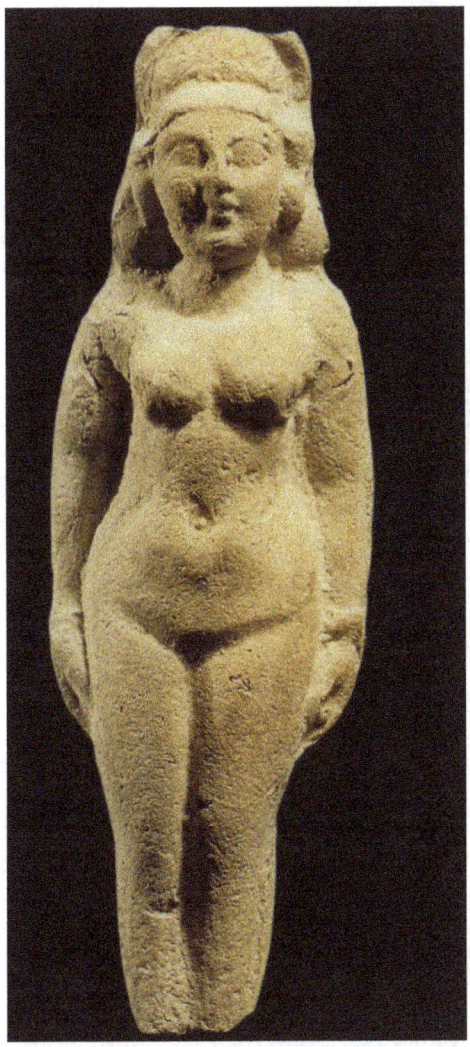

4.11. Nude standing female figurine, terracotta, Seleucia-on-the-Tigris. Height: 9 cm. Turin Excavations at Seleucia (S9,739)
Photograph courtesy of Roberta Menegazzi.

similarly position the hands to cover the genitalia and breasts.[77] To a viewer accustomed to that tradition, Hellenistic Babylonian figurine poses and gestures might have been difficult to appreciate. The presentation and display of the female breast had a complicated history in Greek art, where it was usually associated with imminent danger and violence.[78] The figurine seen in Figure 4.9 does not seem to shrink in the face of that potential for Greek unease; indeed, her scale is significantly larger than many other Hellenistic Babylonian figurines, measuring 38 cm tall, and her body is literally elevated on a small plinth. Overt celebration of Babylonian traditions seems to be suggested here.

172 IMAGES OF THE SELF: IDENTIFYING WITH FIGURINES

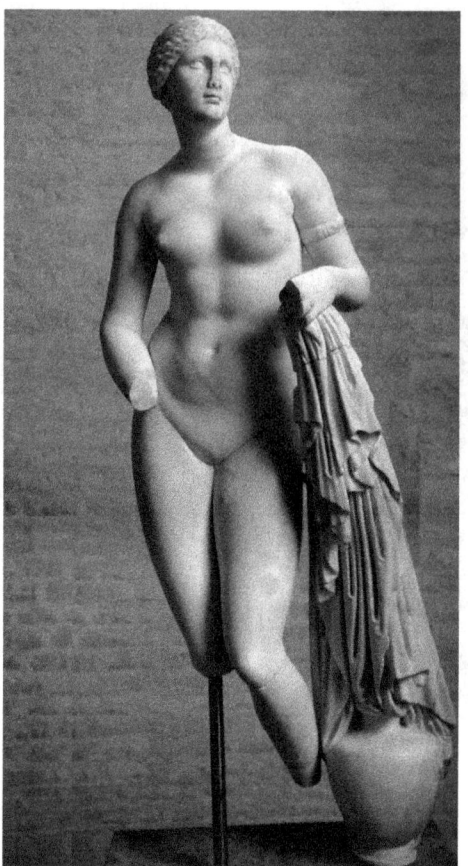

4.12. The Knidian Aphrodite, by Praxiteles (Reduced scale Roman copy, known as the Braschi Venus), marble, original from Knidos, fourth century BCE. Munich Glyptothek.
Photograph by Privatarchiv Foto von MrArifnajafov fotografiert (Creative Commons license).

Yet there were significant ways in which these nude female figurines also demonstrated their participation in the broader Hellenistic Babylonian figurine corpus and the modes of viewing and interacting with figurines that dominated that place and time. Many of the nude standing female figurines were made in double molds, thoroughly exploiting that technology's sculptural potential to create fully elaborated backsides with intricate details of hairstyle and anatomical form. This use of Greek double-mold technology to create a figurine in a very ancient Babylonian motif implies not just cross-cultural interaction, but sustained communication and a desire to reshape one's own traditions in response to the contemporary social environment.[79] While the molds themselves would have been relatively simple to exchange, the methods by which single and double molds are used to create figurines differ substantially.[80] Adapting a figurine design made in one mold technology to be produced in the other mold technology is a complicated process. Prior to the Hellenistic period, no one had ever seen the back of a Babylonian-style nude standing female figure, because these figurines were all made as solid flat-backed objects. Thus, the creators of the nude figurines seen here would have needed to conceptualize, from scratch, what their backs should look like.[81] This might indicate a new Greek user base for the nude female figurines, or perhaps a sustained cross-cultural interaction across boundaries of both manufacture and style, creating a multicultural product for a multicultural audience.

On the other hand, as I have previously argued, hybridities like this in Hellenistic Babylonian figurines were not simply happenstance amalgamations, but purposeful in their intent.[82] In this case, the use of a Greek technology and style intensified the original Babylonian ideas of bodily access and sexual directness embodied in this motif. As seen throughout this volume, the double mold could easily be used to create a figurine that was unmodeled or only schematically shaped on the back. The deliberate choice to create a fully modeled backside for the figurine in Figure 4.9 had enormous consequences for how the nude female body could be presented and viewed in Hellenistic Babylonia. Still frontal in pose and direct in affect, her body was nevertheless available to be viewed and handled in the round. Potentially seen from all angles, such figurines could now be explored in ways that previous Mesopotamian iterations of this motif, with their nonexistent backsides, did not allow, regardless of how sexually direct their poses would seem. Note that this was not necessarily what all users of this figurine motif wanted, as can be seen by the fact that many Hellenistic Babylonian examples of this motif were still made in single molds.[83] But the existence of many double-molded and elaborately modeled examples of nude standing female figurines suggests a market for this particular combination of Greek technology and style in service of Babylonian modes of viewing and ideas about the female body.

Issues of vision and access to the body also carry across the distinction between "nude" and "clothed" that is often considered to fundamentally divide the female figurines of the Hellenistic Babylonian corpus.[84] As seen in Figure 4.13, clothed female figurines were usually depicted in garments derived from Greek tradition and associated with the Hellenistic world. Thickly swathed in a mantle worn over a long *chiton*, this female body is almost entirely obscured, except for her head and the dynamic cross-body posture of her right arm. This sense of a female body hidden from view and impenetrable to tactile access fits well with traditional Greek approaches to thinking about the female form.[85] Yet Babylonian manufacturing techniques and styles could also be recruited to serve this mode of vision. In an almost perfect inversion of the situation seen in Figure 4.9, the figurine seen in Figure 4.13 is ostensibly Greek in motif, yet the Babylonian single mold has been utilized to create it. This was

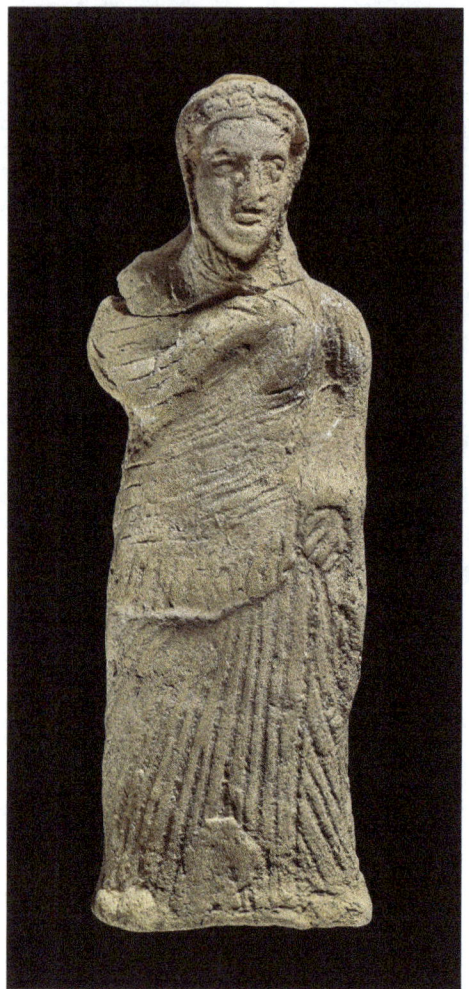

4.13. Clothed standing female figurine, terracotta, Babylon. Height: 16 cm. British Museum (BM 80-6-17-1702)
Photograph © The Trustees of the British Museum.

clearly a choice with some effort involved. The conversion of a double-molded Greek figurine motif into a single-molded figurine involved a reworking of the artistry of the object in order to indicate the complete head and facial details of the woman on only one mold, as these would be lacking with the use of just the front half of a double-mold set. The adaptation of the single mold technology usually led to a flatter female form, lacking shape or detail on the sides and back of the body – which, in turn, made those bodily regions even more impenetrable than the thick drapery implied them to be. Additionally, the folds of drapery in the figurine pictured in Figure 4.13 have been reduced in volume, adhering them to the body but also flattening them. As the ridges of cloth traverse the legs, the overall lack of depth to the figurine almost totally denies the existence of any organic limbs beneath. Thus the body has been made more hidden, with the viewer's agency even more constrained, than the original Greek motif made possible.

Yet, as much as this figurine would seem to conform to, and even intensify, Greek tradition, the choice to use a single mold also brought with it some aspects of a Babylonian perspective on the female body. As described by scholars who theorize the intersections of technology and art, no technology can be fully removed from the cultural environment that produced it, and the cultural forms and biases that it perpetuates.[86] In this case, the elaborately draped women derived from Greek tradition were now situated in frontal positions more familiar from the Mesopotamian figurine repertoire. Gone were the elaborate contrapposto poses and dynamic movement of the Tanagra tradition.[87] In their place, the swathed miniature women of Hellenistic Babylonia encouraged their users to have a more direct encounter with the female body. Indeed, even when these clothed standing female figurines were made in double molds (as seen in Figure 4.14), and thus the complexities of pose so vividly expressed in female figurines used elsewhere in the Hellenistic world would have been possible, a strongly frontal form was still preferred. This stands in stark contrast with the way that double molds and piecing techniques could be used in other Hellenistic Babylonian figurines,

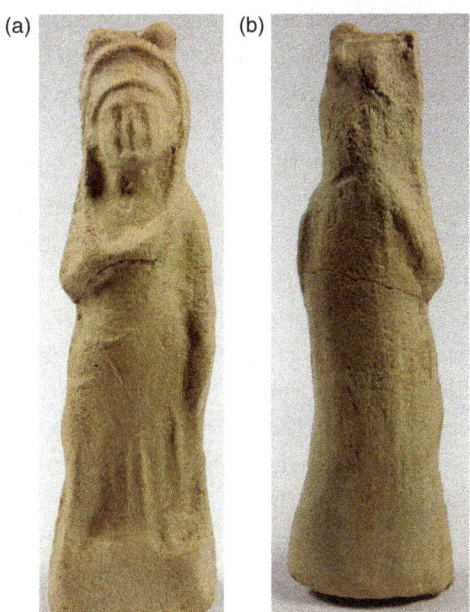

4.14a and b. Front and back of clothed standing female figurine, terracotta, Seleucia-on-the-Tigris. Height: 13.2 cm. Turin Excavations at Seleucia (S2920)
Photograph courtesy of Roberta Menegazzi.

such as the athletes modeled in dynamic poses. Viewing the body in motion was possible in the Hellenistic Babylonian figurines – but not for the standing female form.

The ways in which deep engagement and experimentation across cultural lines were used in the examples just discussed – employing the Greek mold to exaggerate the revelatory possibilities of the Babylonian nude, while utilizing the Babylonian mold to intensify the secretive swathed bodies of the Greek draped women – can also be more broadly seen across the Hellenistic Babylonian corpus of female figurines. Whether nude or clothed, depicted in motifs derived from Mesopotamian or Greek tradition, the female bodies seen in the Hellenistic Babylonian figurines are a very cohesive corpus. Substantial similarities of body morphology existed beneath superficial disparities of dress or hairstyle. This can be seen with the female figurines in Figures 4.11 and 4.14. Despite one of these figures being naked and the other clothed, the *body* of each bears a striking resemblance to the other, with a full, rounded face, elaborately coiffed hair, thick headband, and frontal posture. Both share a sexually mature, but otherwise youthfully unspecific, physique, which gives each female figure an idealized, ageless quality. Almost all female figurines in Hellenistic Babylonia share this adult, but youthful, age, whereas depictions of female children or older women are virtually nonexistent. This is in contrast with the broader Hellenistic *koine* female figurine tradition, which could depict a considerable span of age differences, ranging from girls to teenagers to mature matrons.[88]

This situation of marked cohesiveness in the Hellenistic Babylonian female figurine corpus also differs sharply from the manner in which the distinction between nudity and clothing seems to have been particularly meaningful when applied to the male body. Figurines of men were posed very differently when they were clothed versus when they were nude and, thus, would seem to have meant something different in those two costumes.[89] In contrast, figurines of women had the same bodies and often the same poses and activities whether clothes were depicted or not. This cohesiveness of the female figurine corpus further problematizes the presumed cultural distinctions between nude figurines as deeply Mesopotamian and clothed figurines as more overtly Greek. *If* the distinction between clothed and nude female figurines was indeed a cultural one, then some of those cultural messages and traditions were clearly being communicated, exchanged, adopted, and adapted across cultural lines in ways that do not seem to have been as fluid or possible in the male figurines.

Active Arms: Breasts, Maternity, and Music

The cohesiveness of body type and willingness to cross cultural boundaries in approaches to the female body was further intensified in how the female figurines' arms were often shown to be active. As can be seen in Figures 4.10 and 4.14, the female bodies are similar, despite their difference in clothed/nude status, in not just their shape but also in the poses of their arms. Bent sharply at a forty-five-degree angle, each figure stands with one arm brought sharply to her chest. In the case of the figurine in Figure 4.10, that arm is clearly posed so that her hand can support one of her breasts. In the case of the figurine in Figure 4.14, the connection between hand and breast is not immediate, if it even exists. The hand might simply be resting on the chest or, in some other examples, it appears to be holding a small object that is positioned between the breasts.[90] This difference in activity may have been quite meaningful. The self-offering of the displayed breast is a gesture forward, toward the audience, whereas the self-restraint of the wrapped arm is a gesture backward, keeping the body pinned down and under control.[91] These would seem to be very different ideas indeed.

Yet it is hard to dismiss this similarity in the arm poses as a fantasy of modern eyes, making connections where none existed. These women's arms were emphasized to the viewer – not just in the nude figurines, where the arm stands out boldly as it crosses the bare chest, but also in the clothed figurines. It would be easy to make the arm of a draped figure almost entirely disappear; indeed, to some degree, the binding, containment, and almost complete concealment of the arm was the purpose of the wrapped-arm pose in Greek statuary.[92] But instead of obscuring the arm and its gestures (real or potential), the figurines highlight it. The arm of the figurine in Figure 4.13 stands out as a bold ridge of clay against the almost flat plane of the body to which it is attached. In similar examples, the lines of drapery do not clearly cross the arm, calling into question whether the arm was really meant to be wrapped and hidden or if it was bare and free to move.[93] The attention-grabbing aspect of the bent arm (usually right arm) can clearly be seen when contrasted with the other arm (usually left arm) held at the figure's side. It is the relaxed arm, not its bent compatriot, which disappears into the folds of the fabric and the modeling of the figure's body, fading from both sight and notice.

An additional argument for linking the bent arms of both clothed and nude figurines is the choice to bend the elbows and pose the hands in nearly identical ways. It is the relatively rare figurine (one example of which is seen in Figure 4.15) that has the figure's arm positioned somewhere other than at her breast or by her side. This similarity is particularly striking when compared with the male figurines discussed earlier in this chapter, which were also commonly shown with bent arms. However, the positioning and angle of their arms is quite distinct from the female figurines. The offering-bearer in Figure 4.2 holds his arms at a ninety-degree angle. His activity might have been similar to that of many of the female figurines holding an arm to the chest – and yet, the posture and attitude is distinct. The male figurines in Figures 4.4 and 4.5 offer yet a different arm pose, with their elbows bent only slightly and their hands hooked around their belts. The nude mature male figurine in Figure 4.3 also has a slightly bent arm, although it is held to

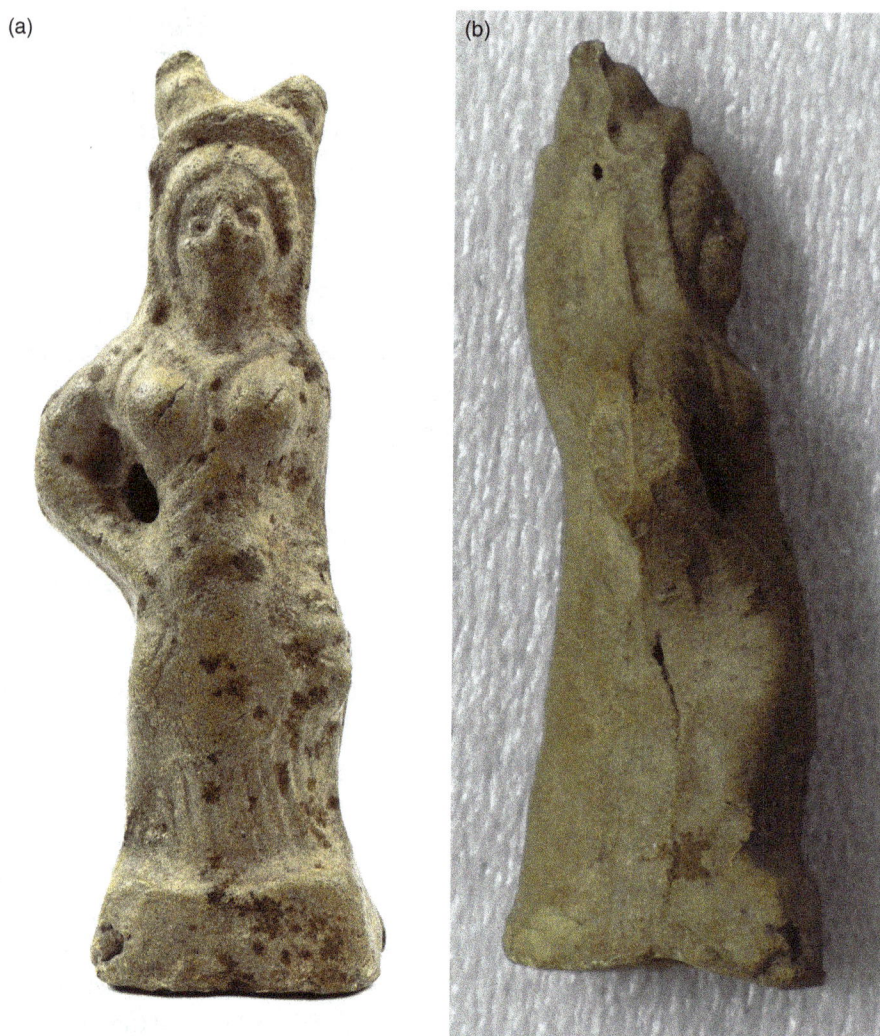

4.15a and b. Front and side of clothed female figurine, terracotta, Nippur. Height: 11.7 cm.
University of Pennsylvania Museum of Archaeology and Anthropology (B 1667)
Photographs courtesy of University of Pennsylvania Museum.

his side; additionally, his right arm is bent behind his back. Compared with this male variety in arm poses, the female figurines look even more unified – and their arm postures potentially meaningful.

What might those meanings have been? One of the most immediate ideas conveyed by this similarity of pose is that all women look similar and act in similar ways, varying only in slight details. This reductive and somewhat misogynistic outlook on female bodies and female identities is reinforced by the similarities in their ages and body types (whether nude or dressed), and supported by the evidence that figurine users in Hellenistic Babylonia were quite comfortable with female figurine motifs crossing cultural and technological boundaries. Indeed, even those few female figurines with arms posed in different ways, such as seen in Figure 4.15, share the same body types, clothing styles, and elaborate coiffures that unite the rest of the corpus.

Yet, beyond that initial idea, other possibilities were also opened by that shared pose. One was simply the notion that women could, indeed, *act* – their arms were not always held fixedly by their sides, waiting patiently to be acted upon rather than taking their agency in their own hands. This sense of an "active arm," in addition to the precise pose, also linked these standing female figurines to other figurines of women more obviously shown "in action," such as the sexualized figurines with separately made and attached bent arms. Two other groups of female figurines – women with children and musicians – also visually echoed this idea of an active arm. Regardless of which arm they use, the standing female figurines almost exclusively gesture toward their left breasts.[94] This preference for the left breast is potentially important. It parallels the left-side placement of the child and the nursing of the infant in the maternal figurines. Emphasis on the left side of the mother's body not only represented a stylistic continuity with pre-Hellenistic figurine traditions, but was also likely connected to positive infant social development, as discussed in Chapter 3.

Musicians could have similar arm placement; the figurine playing a tambour-style drum seen in Figure 3.13 is a particularly close parallel. In her reach across the body with her right arm to play the drum held against her left shoulder, her right hand rests immediately next to her left breast. In some instances, such as with the figurine pictured in Figure 4.16, the right hand sits virtually on top of the left breast. A similar reach toward the left breast can be seen in many female figurines who play the harp. Indeed, in these examples, the arm posture seems

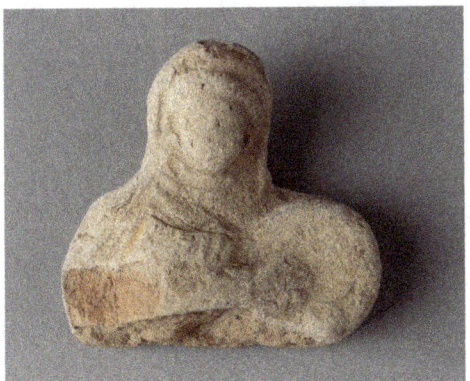

4.16. Clothed female figurine playing a tambour-style drum, terracotta, Seleucia-on-the-Tigris. Height: approx. 7 cm. Kelsey Museum of Archaeology, University of Michigan, Ann Arbor (KM 15190)
Photograph courtesy of Kelsey Museum of Archaeology.

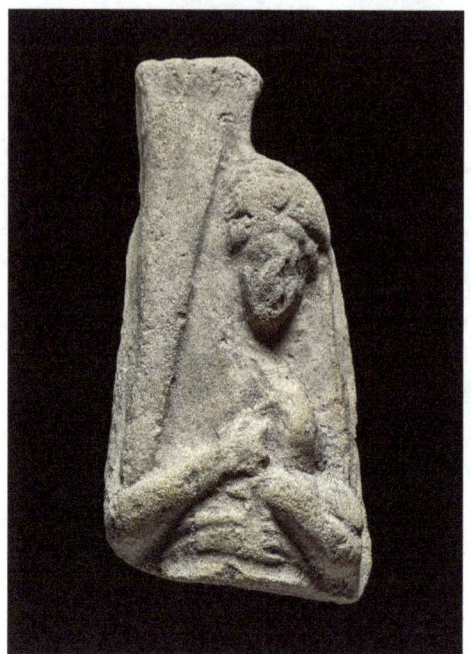

4.17. Clothed female figurine playing harp, terracotta, Babylon. Height: 7.5 cm. British Museum (BM SP. III 47+ = 127337)
Photograph © The Trustees of the British Museum.

even more deliberate; as seen in Figure 4.17, the figure's two hands frame and highlight the left breast, even though this is not an ideal posture to allow the right hand to strum the instrument's strings. This similarity was certainly not a rule: female figures alone could be depicted with a variety of instruments, such as the hand cymbals or double-pipes, which required different postures and gestures.[95] Male figurines too could be shown as musicians, although less commonly.[96] However, amidst this variety of musician figurines, the tambour-drum and harp players were among the most popular in Hellenistic Babylonia.[97]

It might seem tenuous and superficial to draw a connection between figurines of musicians, mothers, and other women on the basis of their active arm postures. Yet the potential for this link might have already been present in the minds of many Hellenistic Babylonian figurine users. The cult of the mother goddess Cybele was very popular in the Hellenistic period, particularly in Macedonia, Greece, Asia Minor, and the Eastern Mediterranean. The standard Hellenistic *koine* iconography for Cybele depicted the goddess seated on a throne, with lions, wearing a tall crown and holding a *tympanon* with her left arm.[98] Although adapted and reinvented in Archaic and Classical-period Greece, this iconography reflected, in part, the goddess's Anatolian (and thus, Near Eastern) origins.[99] For the purposes of this discussion, it is particularly notable that one of the most maternal figures of the Hellenistic *koine* pantheon was also a musician, who carried a Near Eastern instrument (that was otherwise not especially popular in Greece) positioned on her left side in such a way that it would be played by her right hand. Identifiable, unambiguous depictions of Cybele herself are not found in the Hellenistic Babylonian figurine repertoire. Yet given the popularity of Cybele elsewhere in the Hellenistic world, it would be difficult to imagine that her vivid combination of maternity and the tambour-style drum – as well as her portrayal of female agency and power[100] – did not inflect the viewership and reception of Hellenistic Babylonian figurines.

In addition to this connection with Cybele imagery, a link with Mesopotamian traditions was also emphasized by the substantial similarities in the Hellenistic Babylonian figurine corpus between the arm poses of the standing female figurines with those of the mothers and the musicians. Both the nursing woman and the drum player motifs were closely connected with pre-Hellenistic traditions in Babylonia – and, crucially, almost entirely absent from Classical Greek tradition, outside of Cybele iconography. Through the figurines, Greek-clothed women holding their hand to the left side of their chests were brought into the Hellenistic Babylonian fold, so to speak – closely entangled with the nude women supporting their breasts, the nursing mothers, and the tambour-drum playing musicians, all of which represented ancient and enduring concepts of female identity in Babylonia. The clothed women, regardless of the ethnic origins of their dress (or even their own ethnic origins), had now joined these ranks and signaled, through their poses, their participation in the sisterhood.

Women in Society

Extrapolating from this sisterhood of figurines to women's roles in the real-world society of Hellenistic Babylonia is not a straightforward process – just as it is not straightforward for any group of figurines. Figurines do not present complete, complex personhoods that are fully realized; rather, they present visions of person-like bodies, whose identities have been both abstracted and intensified. Real women's identities, as experienced and lived, must have been far more multifaceted, varied, and complex than their figurine counterparts implied through their comprehensive similarity.[101] However, the figurines do provide insights into how Hellenistic Babylonian society thought about women's identities, women's bodies, and what kind of female "being" was ideal. Although this is not the same as accessing real women's lives – and the two should never be confused for one another – this information provided by "figurine women" is nevertheless valuable.

Despite the fact that female figurines are a substantially larger proportion of the Hellenistic Babylonian figurine corpus than are male or child figurines,[102] their age ranges and actions were more circumscribed than their masculine counterparts. This is not entirely unexpected, given the greater agency of men throughout the ancient world. What is surprising is the absence in the Hellenistic Babylonian figurine corpus of the depiction of female bodies engaged in particular social activities that were represented in figurines across the broader Hellenistic world. Social relationships were limited in the Hellenistic Babylonian figurines to an adult woman (presumably a mother) with a child that is usually male[103] or an adult male-female pair. Absent are any depictions of two or more women together, such as are well known from Hellenistic *koine* figurines, including those of the Tanagra tradition, as well as earlier Greek representations (such as of the mother-daughter deities Demeter and Persephone).[104] Outside of the professional sphere of musicians, Hellenistic Babylonian figurines do not show female bodies in contact with one another – rather, they are seen in association with male bodies, usually as mother or wife.

Yet despite this seeming lack of opportunities for activity or female interaction, the standing female bodies of the Hellenistic Babylonian figurine corpus do exhibit a remarkable level of agency. This can particularly be seen when comparing the female figurines in this chapter with the sexualized figurines with separately attached arms discussed in Chapter 2. Despite the fact that many of the figurines discussed in this chapter are nude, as are the figurines seen in Figures 2.10 and 2.12, their body shapes, particularly in the hip to waist ratio, are different.[105] The figurines discussed here additionally differed from their more sexualized counterparts in the agency of their gestures and the stability of their manufacture. Although many of the standing female figurines call attention to their breasts, and sometimes even display one or both breasts to the viewer, the sexualized helplessness seen in the separately attached arm figurines is completely absent. Indeed, it is possible that the gesture was not meant to be sexual, given its close connection with postures of nursing. Regardless of her intent, the figurine seen in Figure 4.9 gives the illusion that the woman depicted is *deciding* to pose in this fashion; any sexual activity that might result would seem to be her choice.

The manufacture and materiality of the figurine itself reinforced this impression of her agency. Her hands prevent the user, even a tactile interlocutor, from completely accessing her breasts. Despite the detailed depiction of her sexual anatomy, the figure would need to move in order to allow the user to have full contact with her breasts – or, indeed, any contact with the more sexual (and procreative) regions of her body, such as the inner labia and vagina. Though this figurine looks to be baring all, much is actually left outside the vision and grasp of the user.

A sense of female agency similarly characterizes the clothed female figurines with one hand to their chest, a pose linked with *sophrosyne* or self-control. This was primarily a masculine virtue in Classical Greece; women, even those of the upper classes, were depicted in Classical Greek art as having less control over their bodies, facial expressions, and gestures – as a reflection of their relative lack of self-wisdom and emotional control.[106] None of this gendered nature of the pose seems to have been expressed in the Hellenistic Babylonian figurine tradition. This was not unique to Hellenistic Babylonia; indeed, this arm posture was one of several popular poses for depicting respectable women in figurines and statues across the Hellenistic world.[107] However, in their direct gazes, frontal body postures, and (in nude versions) unabashed sexuality, the Hellenistic Babylonian figurines were among the more extreme examples of female self-possession and agency.

In contrast, the most popular Hellenistic *koine* women's pose, the *pudicitia* pose (one hand held to the head, one across the body),[108] is almost never found in the Hellenistic Babylonian figurines. As the *pudicitia* pose was linked to ideas of female subordination, stillness, and detachment – rather than self-mastery and agency – the unpopularity of the pose in Hellenistic Babylonia further reinforces the argument that women's poses were selected, at least in part, because of the level of self-determination they conveyed. By taking control of their own bodies and emotions, indicative of a level of self-mastery untinged with shame that was usually reserved for men in the Classical Greek mindset, the female figurines of Hellenistic Babylonia (and perhaps their real-life counterparts) demonstrated their agency and power.[109]

Additionally, these female figurines were very sturdy, with thick walls and flared bases. Although they did not necessarily encourage tactile contact, most could be handled roughly and did not break easily. Strong construction was favored, even when it entailed the creation of double-molded figurines so thick that they contained internally trapped air pockets, which risked rupturing during the firing process. Such durability also threatened the mimetic potential of many such figurines; as can be seen in the side view in Figure 4.15b, the use of thick walls on double-molded figurines often rendered bodies that were far deeper front to back than an actual human body should be. The manufacture of such figurines despite the design "flaws" that threatened structural and visual integrity indicate that stability and durability were prized. Most female figurines were more durable than male figurines, and more of them survive relatively intact. This tendency toward robust manufacture further intensified the sense of agency implied by the poses, suggesting that the female figures controlled their own bodies and did not exist for the purpose of being violated and broken at the will of their user. Thus while the figurine-influenced ideal for a Hellenistic Babylonian woman may have been lacking in variety, it was not lacking in strength or resiliency.

From this understanding of female agency as conveyed in the figurines, a new perspective on the cohesiveness and similarity of the female figurine corpus might be reached. The overlap between the arm poses, the adaptations of the single mold for clothed figurines and the double mold for nude figurines – all of these features indicate not simply the existence of substantial cross-cultural hybridity within the female figurines of Hellenistic Babylonia, but also (and crucially) the striking depth and richly experimental nature of that hybridity. If one were to read this extensive hybridity in the female figurines as a direct reflection of Hellenistic Babylonian social life, a difference in male versus female gender roles could be posited. Women, while restricted to a limited ideal of ages, activities, and social relationships when compared with their male peers, might have been considered more adaptable and better able to cross Greek-Babylonian cultural lines. Of course, as I have extensively argued elsewhere, figurines should not be read as a comprehensive and faithful reflection of real social life[110]; undoubtedly there were men in Hellenistic Babylonia whose identities and activities also crossed cultural boundaries, just as women likely had interpersonal relationships with one another. Yet it is noteworthy that the Hellenistic Babylonian ideal was for women to be more fluidly multicultural than men, and to serve as the conduits and mediators of male social relationships.

This power to smooth over potential differences and facilitate the societal bonds of Hellenistic Babylonia suggests a certain level of agency for the female body, which accords well with the visual features and physical construction of the standing female figurines. Yet the use and control over miniature female bodies should also be taken into account here. Indeed, it is possible that multicultural identities for *all* members of Hellenistic Babylonian society, regardless of gender, were being negotiated through the hybrid female figurines. The idealized sameness of their bodies and the limitations on their activities allowed these female figurines to provide a generic canvas onto which cross-cultural interactions and hybrid experimentations could be inscribed.[111] Female bodies likely provided this "blank slate" for multiculturalism because the power and status of women in Hellenistic Babylonian society, while not negligible, was usually less than that of men.[112] Mistakes in these experiments would have had fewer social consequences, because they could be distanced from the dominant gender group. Yet the connections between the hybrid female figurines and masculine identities were still strong enough to be effectual. As lovers, spouses, co-musicians, or children of women, male bodies, no matter how culturally singular, were depicted in the figurines as intimately and inextricably tied to female bodies – and, thus, were invited to join in their multicultural hybridity by association or by proxy. Women's bodies, as represented in figurines, were a landscape upon which the movement of people of all genders toward a more multicultural society could be written – a society over which the individual user had little direct control. In preventing the user from moving the figurine's hands, touching her body beyond what her construction

EXPERIMENTATION AND THE CHILD'S BODY

permitted, or casually breaking her body through rough handling, the female figurines – like many of their group figurine counterparts – enforced the durability of this vision of the community. Upon this visually cohesive group of miniature female bodies were molded the ideals of Hellenistic Babylonian society: the smoothing over of cultural difference to create a monolithic, timeless unity.

EXPERIMENTATION AND THE CHILD'S BODY

Rounding out this chapter's discussion of "real life" identities in the Hellenistic Babylonian figurine corpus, I conclude with examining the children figurines. At the opposite end of the age spectrum from which this chapter began, masculinity in childhood (at a variety of ages, from infancy to adolescence) also seems to have been a site of fascination. Unprecedented in the figurine traditions of either pre-Hellenistic Greece or Babylonia, depictions of boys proliferated in Hellenistic Babylonia. This discussion is an effective bridge between the female figurines just discussed and the Hellenistic *koine* figurines (particularly those of gods and goddesses) which will be explored in the following chapter. Like the figurines depicting women's bodies, the children figurines seem to have been the locus of intensive negotiation regarding social roles and norms. However, that negotiation proceeded differently in the child figurines because of the unique status of the child's body. On the one hand, children are inconsequential, not fully social beings, trapped in a liminal state of becoming – thus, as with the bodies of women, figurines of their bodies could be places for less risky social experimentation.[113] Yet at the same time, almost all Hellenistic Babylonian figurines of children were overtly sexed as male[114] and thus represented the next generation of adult men.[115] Mistakes in such experimentation had the potential to be highly consequential in some future place and time. Thus, as I will argue in this section, the negotiation with childhood identities that took place in the figurines was distanced from reality by being located primarily in the world of the supernatural. This entanglement with the divine, as well as the general subject matter of childhood (which was especially popular throughout the Mediterranean and Near East during the Hellenistic era), links the Hellenistic Babylonian figurines of children with the broader *koine*. The implications of this melding of "local" and "global" will be explored further in Chapter 5.

Servants and Slaves

An emphasis on masculinity and a shared sense of activity unite the children and the adult men in miniature. However, remarkably few of the child figurines seem engaged in ordinary activities and everyday social identities. Those that do are predominantly found at Seleucia-on-the-Tigris, where children draped in styles similar to their elders[116] or pudgy babies with arms at their sides in a swaddled position[117] met the gaze of users who could imagine the children to be members of their own social class and community. The child figurine pictured in Figure 4.25 is one of a handful of examples that show the boy wearing a *chlamys*, in a likely statement of class status as well as Greek identity.[118] In contrast, most of the figurines of children are clearly marked in ways that differentiate their bodies, as either belonging in positions of servitude (which, for the ancient world, most likely meant slavery) or elevated to the level of gods.

The figurines that show the child at work in a slave or servant-like capacity were most popular at Seleucia-on-the-Tigris,[119] although they were found at Babylon as well,[120] and often demonstrated links to Greek culture. For instance, a figural plaque, which was later embedded as temper in a mudbrick used to build a house, depicts a child carrying a long-necked, handled jar (similar in form to a Greek *lagynos*[121]) on his left shoulder (see Figure 4.18). Another figurine depicts a girl carrying a jewelry box, in a manner closely reminiscent of the domestic slaves attending their mistresses on late Classical Attic tombstones.[122] Still others show the child carrying an animal slung over his shoulders, in a pose and activity similar to Archaic and Classical Greek depictions of young men transporting sacrificial offerings to temple precincts.[123] The limited number of such figurines and the restriction of their use primarily to Seleucia-on-the-Tigris suggests that they appealed only to a small, likely Greek, subset of the population. This limitation was correlated

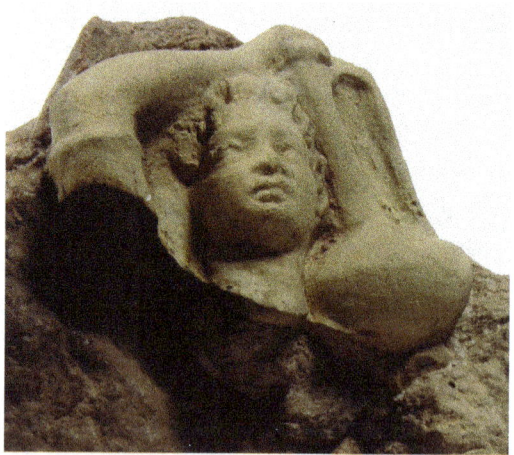

4.18. Mudbrick with embedded figurine of boy carrying a long-necked jar (*lagynos*?), terracotta, Seleucia-on-the-Tigris. Height of figurine 4.8 cm. Kelsey Museum of Archaeology, University of Michigan, Ann Arbor (TM 1930.149/KM 2018.01.0102)
Photograph courtesy of Roberta Menegazzi and the Kelsey Museum of Archaeology.

with the other material culture implicated in these figurines; for instance, Seleucia-on-the-Tigris was the only Mesopotamian city where *lagynos* pottery has been found.[124] In some cases, corroborating material culture does not even exist – for instance, no Greek-style temple has yet been discovered in Babylonia that would indicate the sacrificial offering scene referenced by the animal-carrying boys was practiced locally in this manner. Rather than referring to the real world of the local social community, such figurines instead seem to be nostalgic fantasies that invoked the customs of a different time and place – namely the Classical Aegean. That these remembrances were particularly concentrated on the bodies of slave children, some of the weakest members of society, suggests a desire for literal power over the recollection – and perhaps reflected the users' sense of relative powerlessness over the actual real-life situation in which they found themselves. One might imagine a homesick recent immigrant to the region would be comforted by being attended on by a slave boy or girl in traditional Greek fashion – if only in miniature.

Slave status is also a possible reading of the unusual figurines of male children with erotic features. While most figurines of children are depicted nude, a few rare examples from Seleucia-on-the-Tigris show the naked boy's body with his limbs widely splayed.[125] Vigorous activity is also seen in the figurines of adult athletes, but the style of the child's pose is not an obvious parallel and the exertion of the boys is without a clear purpose in the gymnasion. Indeed, a much more compelling comparison can be drawn to the figurines of women with separately made arms. Although the legs of the women are more tightly held together than those of the boys, the open postures, the widely flung arms, and the ability of the user to both gaze and caress the nude form is similar. The version of this pose seen the boy figurines more tightly parallels Greek sculptural styles than the adult female figurines do; for instance, as seen in Figure 4.19, the pose of the boy's body echoes the seductive S-curve of Praxiteles's Knidian Aphrodite(see Figure 4.12).[126] His body is elaborately modeled on both front and back, with care taken to depict the genitalia and the softly rounded buttocks. The head of the boy tilts downward, avoiding or unaware of the user's gaze, and thus allowing the user's pleasurable exploration to continue unchallenged. His chubby face emphasizes his childhood, while his charming expression evinces pleasure. The thick wreath that adorns his head positions this figure outside the realm of the every day, and makes additionally clear that this is not an ephebe diligently exercising in the gymnasion. Rather, a sense of celebration is suggested. In many ways, this erotically charged image of a beautiful youthful male body would be at home in the Greek symposion, where boy slaves were required to add to the festivities by performing servant-like work and being available as sexual partners.[127] Like the figurines of children at work, the figurine seen in Figure 4.19 may have been prized by its user for its ability to nostalgically evoke that distant place and time, as well as allow power

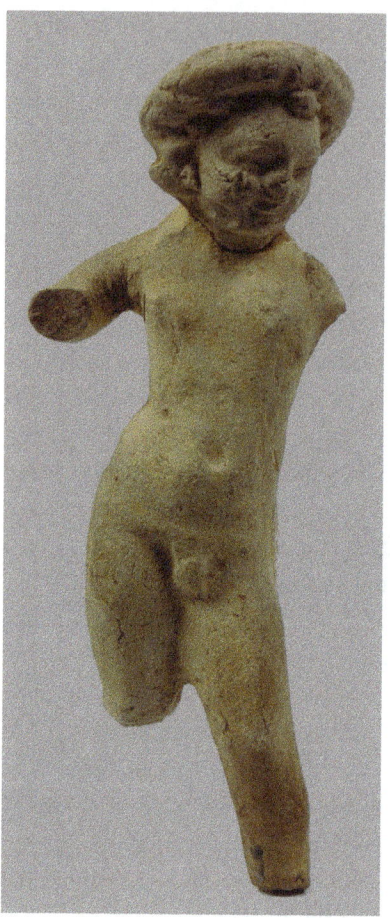

4.19. Nude boy figurine, terracotta, Seleucia-on-the-Tigris. Height: 11 cm. Kelsey Museum of Archaeology, University of Michigan, Ann Arbor (KM 15899)
Photograph courtesy of Roberta Menegazzi and the Kelsey Museum of Archaeology.

and control over it. However, in the case of the erotic boy figurines particularly, any such reminiscences seem to have been extremely unpopular with the Hellenistic Babylonian figurine clientele generally. This might be explained by the fact that while slavery, including child slavery, was not uncommon in Babylonian culture,[128] sexual attraction to children was not celebrated in Mesopotamian tradition.[129] The bodies of these boys and the kinds of looking and touching these figurines encouraged were sharply out of place, and perhaps even offensive, in a Babylonian community.

Although not slaves, mortal – or, at least, not obviously divine – children also appeared as part of woman-and-child figurines, which were discussed in Chapter 3. In those figurines, the children were generally shown as human babies or toddlers with no indication of supernatural features nor slave status. In contrast, children depicted alone on figurines were almost always shown either with marks of servitude, or with wings, crowns, and other supernatural attributes. This disparity is striking and in need of explanation. It is possible that we should not regard a child with an adult woman and a child on his or her own as the same kind of "children," as viewed by an ancient audience. Orphans or foundlings who survived their abandonment were a trope of hero myths in the Greek world,[130] which may be evidence of an ancient perspective on the unlikelihood that children without structured adult care would survive (or at least would be worth thinking about) if they were not otherwise supernaturally endowed. Slaves or god-heroes – there seems to have been little room in between these two identities for a child alone in the miniature world, just as there were likely few options in between those extremes for real children who were abandoned or otherwise alone in the life-size world.[131]

Children and the Supernatural

Most of the Hellenistic Babylonian child figurines depict gods – or, at least, children with supernatural attributes, as the precise identities of many of the figures are ambiguous. Of those figurines that can be somewhat confidently identified, Eros and Harpocrates were the two most popular gods. However, the attributes of the child figurines do not always clearly align with how either of those two child gods were depicted elsewhere in the Hellenistic world. Blending of imagery, adding elements that were not part of either god's repertoire, or omitting attributes that were, also characterizes the corpus. Even if a figurine did align clearly with the Hellenistic *koine* depiction of a god, it does not mean that every user would have interpreted, named, or used the figurine as its motif indicated. For instance, even if a winged boy was seen as Eros by some users, others could have associated it with another popular Hellenistic child god, such as Attis.[132] Such imagery could also have tapped into the long history of winged human bodies in Mesopotamian art, particularly that of Assyria, where such figures were often protective deities.[133] Overall, it seems to have been most important that these children were overtly supernatural, rather than unambiguous representations of particular gods.

Wings were one of the most common supernatural features to appear on figurines of children, linking them with Hellenistic *koine* depictions, including extensive figurine examples, of the Greek god Eros.[134] The Hellenistic Babylonian versions were generally shown with naked bodies on which the male genitals are clearly visible, providing incontrovertible evidence of their sex, while the large heads, round faces, and pudgy bellies of the figures situate their age in childhood or early adolescence. The wings, patterned after those of birds, were attached high on the child's back and arch up over the shoulders. These winged boys were often shown standing in a front-facing position, with their arms at their sides, and sometimes elevated on a base. This positioning

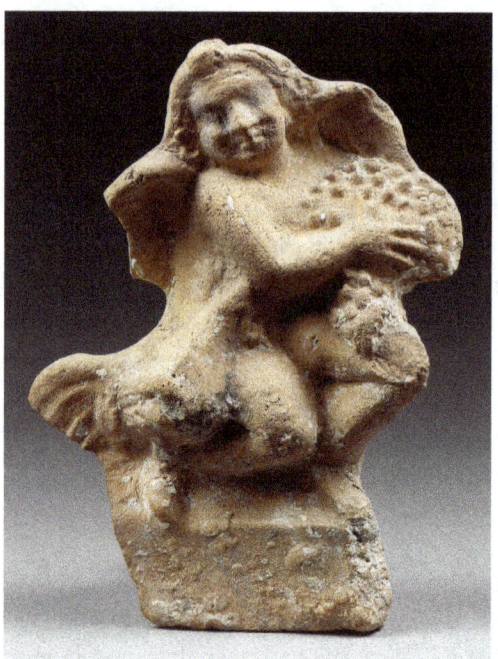

4.20. Figurine of nude winged boy with grapes and bird, terracotta, Babylon. Height: 14 cm. Musée du Louvre (AO 25928)
Photograph courtesy of Art Resource and the Musée du Louvre.

encouraged a direct encounter with the user, and stands in contrast with many Hellenistic *koine* depictions of children (especially depictions of Eros from so-called "Rococo"-style statuary) in which the child's body has a posture more natural to an active toddler.[135]

Also complicating the identification with Eros is the depiction of winged children in joyful attitudes of teasing a bird with grapes. Active and teasing postures were typical of Eros imagery throughout the Hellenistic *koine*; however, the particular activity of taunting a pet bird was more commonly associated with mortal children.[136] Yet, in many of the Hellenistic Babylonian figurines, bird teasing was perpetrated by a boy who was either winged or sat upon a throne. For instance, the figurine seen in Figure 4.20 depicts a winged boy who faces the viewer, but who turns his body away to his left. He is hunched over and clutching to his chest a disproportionately large bunch of grapes. He stares down at a bird, possibly a rooster, which is leaning across the boy's right hip in an attempt to peck the grapes. The boy's knees are deeply bent, with one knee almost touching the ground, as if he were squatting and turning at the same time. The squatting, turned-away pose of the body, and the motif of grapes and birds, is shared with many terracotta figurines across the Hellenistic world,[137] as well as statuary[138] and even a child's grave relief from Smyrna.[139] Yet most of those were clearly meant to depict mortal children.

Other divine features can also be found on the bird-teasing boys in Hellenistic Babylonian figurines. An elaborate throne elevates the boy on a figurine from Nippur which depicts the same genre scene.[140] In other cases, the child rides an abnormally large bird in a straddling/reclining position.[141] Such an activity is clearly not within the realm of mortal behavior and may further indicate an Eros identification for these boys, as Eros's mother, Aphrodite, was sometimes shown in Classical Greek vase painting as riding a bird in a similar manner.[142] In many cases, these god-children are shown with glimpses of playful, child-like joy. Nevertheless, such figurines distance their subjects – through divine attributes, activities, and thrones – from the everyday world inhabited by the mortal version of this cheeky toddler in the figurines' Hellenistic *koine* counterparts.

However, the most popular version of this bird-and-grapes genre scene in the Hellenistic Babylonian figurine corpus was characterized by severe formalism and distance. In such figurines, the grapes and bird were reduced to attribute-like objects, clutched lifelessly to the boy's chest, rather than depicted as active elements of a playful plot. As seen in Figure 4.21, the boy holds both the grapes and a small bird, one in each hand. Notable with many of these boys,

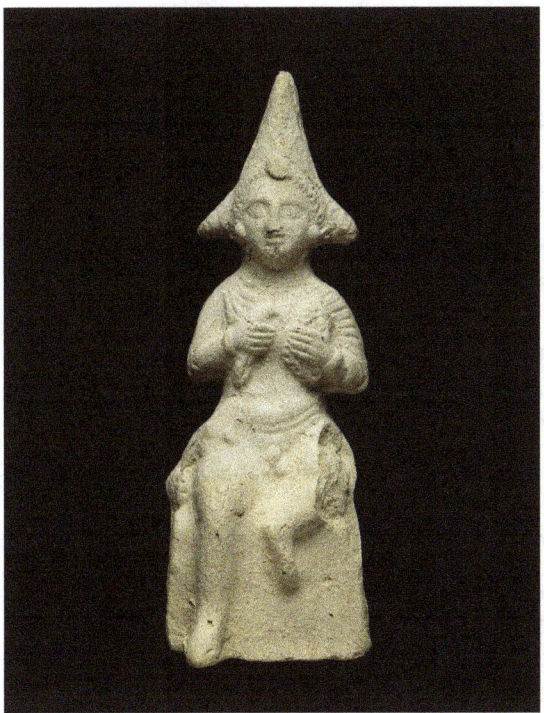

4.21. Figurine of nude boy wearing three-peaked hat and holding bird and grapes, terracotta, Babylon. Height: 16.5 cm. British Museum (BM 91814); note this figurine is published in Karvonen-Kannas 1995, No. 214; but is incorrectly pictured as No. 218 on Plate 38. Photograph © The Trustees of the British Museum.

particularly those seated on thrones, is that their genitalia are often clearly depicted despite their seated positions. This was accomplished through the contrived pose of the bent left leg held with the knee splayed away from the body and the foot resting near or against the inner right leg. In most Hellenistic *koine* art, this leg pose was reserved for bodies and identities outside the normal citizen classes, such as mythological figures or subjects of parody.[143] The significant effort undertaken to be clear about these figures' male gender thus also removed them from the everyday world of mortals, and so paralleled the manner in which these figurines stripped all sense of childhood playfulness from the duck and grapes motif. These boys are not particularly child-like, but rather appear calm, collected, and intent on communicating with the audience who is observing them with their object-attributes. Poised, serene, and in control, they almost seem as future men – except for the fact of their supernatural elevation and separation from the everyday world of Hellenistic Babylonia.

The three-peaked headdress worn by the boy in Figure 4.21 is another major component of that supernatural identification. In this case, it is to Harpocrates, a Hellenistic-era version of the Egyptian god Horus in his childhood guise, that the figurine was likely referring.[144] The use of the three-peaked hat was very popular in Hellenistic Babylonian figurines, although these miniatures rarely have the full spectrum of Harpocrates iconography found in Egypt, such as the finger held to the lips.[145] Rather, the three-peaked hat seems to have been integrated into the Hellenistic Babylonian child figurine corpus as yet another supernatural attribute that could be used interchangeably with features already discussed: holding birds and grapes, riding a bird, sitting on a throne, and so forth. Indeed, the only indication that any clear distinction was made between "Eros" and "Harpocrates" is the lack of boy figurines sporting both wings and three-peaked hats. Nevertheless, the elaborate hairstyles seen on some winged boy figurines, such as that in Figure 4.20, which features a prominent central ridge of curls, curiously evokes the central (usually the largest) peak of the three-peaked headdress – suggesting through vague visual similarity a certain manner of kinship between these divine children.[146] Children wearing three-peaked hats were also occasionally shown as rider figurines from horse rider sets, with their legs splayed wide to accommodate a separately fashioned mount.[147] This connection with the real-life activities of mortal, grown-up men further reinforced the seriousness of these boy figurines as juvenile versions of real adult male identities – with the divine three-peaked hat as the lone reminder of their otherworldliness.

Overall, the formality and earnestness of these supernatural child figurines may seem surprising compared with charming and playful Hellenistic *koine* statuary. Yet, a sentimentalized view of childhood as amusing for its own sake was a relatively recent – and, in the context of the ancient world, somewhat singular and peculiar – invention of the Hellenistic era.[148] Having no Mesopotamian precedent (indeed, little pre-Hellenistic Greek precedent), it may not have been

EXPERIMENTATION AND THE CHILD'S BODY 193

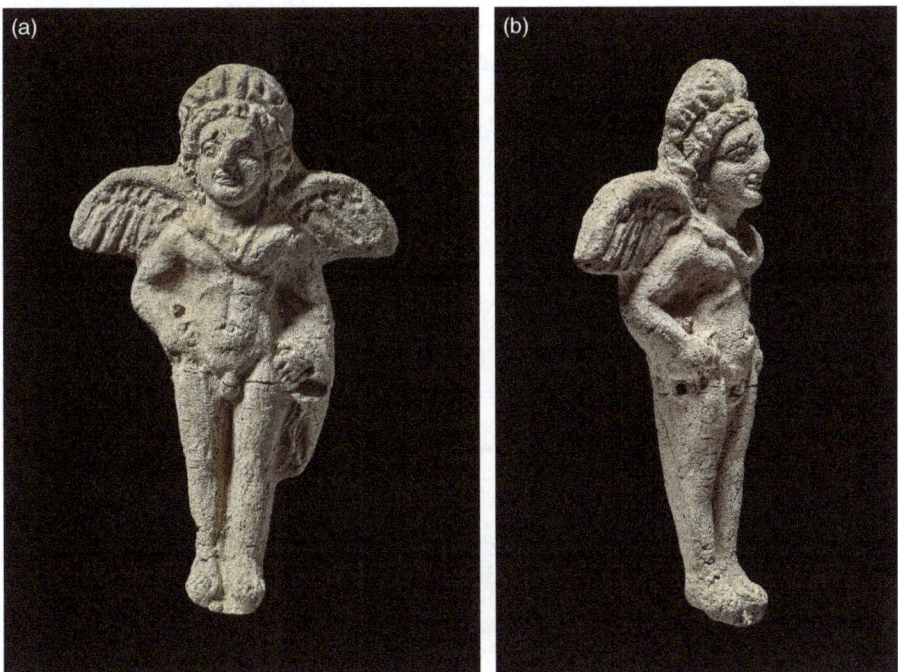

4.22a and b. Front and side of figurine of nude winged boy, pierced at hip level, terracotta, likely from Babylon. Height: 7.5 cm. British Museum (BM 84-2-11-581)
Photograph © The Trustees of the British Museum.

especially popular in Hellenistic Babylonia. Combining a popular Hellenistic image of childhood play with the supernatural repertoire of Eros and Harpocrates, popular Hellenistic child gods, may have rendered motifs like birds and grapes more understandable and broadly appealing.

Ritual and the Child's Body

Most of the figurines discussed in this book were designed solely to be miniature representations of human bodies. They likely had various purposes and uses for which they were employed – votives, devotional objects, pedagogical tools, decorative mementos, funeral offerings, and so forth – but as objects, they were simply figurines. Many of the child figurines were different. For instance, as already seen in Figure 2.18, some items could be both a functional object, such as a rattle, and a child figurine (in that case, a boy wearing a three-peaked hat and possibly holding the bird and grapes) at the same time. The close connection of that figural rattle with the popular iconography of Harpocrates endowed the entire corpus of supernatural child figurines with a sense of potential real-world use, such as musical performances in rituals, or to entertain small children.

Small figurines of winged boys wearing wreaths, such as that seen in Figure 4.22, may also have had ritual associations. While the general motif is very similar to other Eros imagery, the materiality of this figurine is distinct. This object was one of a series of figurines, likely from Babylon, which all have identical measurements and visual features, and thus seem to have all been produced in the same figurine mold with minimal to no modifications. While this kind of serial mass production was not unusual with mold-made figurines in other locales or periods of the ancient world,[149] Hellenistic Babylonian craftspeople rarely used molds in this way. There are exceptionally few Hellenistic Babylonian figurines that can be conclusively identified as having been made in the same mold; those that were seem to have undergone post-mold modifications in order to differentiate them from their peers. Thus, the fact that the figurine seen in Figure 4.22 is one of ten nearly identical objects is highly unusual.[150] The small scale of these figurines is also relatively rare, as they measure just 6–7.5 cm tall, depending on their degree of preservation. This small scale could help to reinforce that these winged figures were "actually" children – if these figurines were viewed next to most figurines of adults, they would be size proportionate, and thus look like real children in comparison. Note that this is not the case with many of the other figurines depicting children, which can be as large as most adult figurines, if not larger (see, for instance, Figure 4.25).

Perhaps the most important difference in the materiality of these small winged boy figurines is their structural design. They were single molded with slightly concave backs and a small (3 mm diameter) hole pierced entirely through the figurine from side to side. This hole transects the body of the figurine from one hip to the other, just below the spot where the boy's hands were shown resting on his hips. As these figurines cannot stand alone, it is possible that the hole was used to suspend the figurines by means of a string or pin threaded through it. But because the hole is placed so low on the boys' bodies, the suspended figurines would be top-heavy and quickly flip upside-down if hung freely. The location of the hole seems to have been intentional, rather than an accidental flaw, as all of the figurines are pierced in this position, as are similar examples from other cities.[151] Some sort of stable back support or very firmly clamped suspension would have been needed to keep these figurines upright.

Due to their small size, it is possible that these miniatures served as necklaces or other jewelry. Male children, including children who could be plausibly identified as Eros or Harpocrates, were popular motifs in Hellenistic Babylonian jewelry.[152] In that case, the user's body would serve as the back support; however, the figurines would be prone to flipping upside-down if the wearer were to move. This would seem to be a disadvantage to using such figurines as jewelry, at least if display were the primary motivation for wearing them. Alternatively, the movement and flipping of the winged boy as the wearer moved his or her body might have had a visual and sensory appeal, recruiting the user into continually readjusting and "playing with" an energetic and mischievous child.[153] Ritual activation, particularly if this figure was understood to have amuletic or apotropaic properties, might also have been facilitated by such twisting and turning, which would have seemed largely autonomous from the human will and choice of the wearer.[154]

The pierced boy figurines might also have been attached to an inanimate object or surface, like furniture or a wall – or possibly even to the sound boxes of stringed musical instruments. Larger figurines of wreath-wearing winged boys show the figure playing a stringed musical instrument similar to a Greek *kithara* (box lyre). An example from Nippur, seen in Figure 4.23, shows the winged boy playing a square-boxed *kithara*. The square-boxed *kithara* was a public performance instrument,[155] and Classical Greek *kithara* used in public performances often had decorated soundboxes.[156] Given that the motif of the winged boy was connected with the instrument in at least some Hellenistic Babylonian communities, it is perhaps not implausible to suggest that the pierced winged boy figurines – which seem designed to be used as ornaments or appliques of some sort – might have been physically connected to real-world instruments of this type. One might even imagine them "flying" through the air as the instrument itself was moved in time to the music and the swaying of the musician's body. This is, of course, speculative. But what seems certain is that the design of these small boy figurines, such as that in Figure 4.22, made them more than just figurines. As with the child rattles, these miniature boys were objects that were meant to move and to do things in the real world – and,

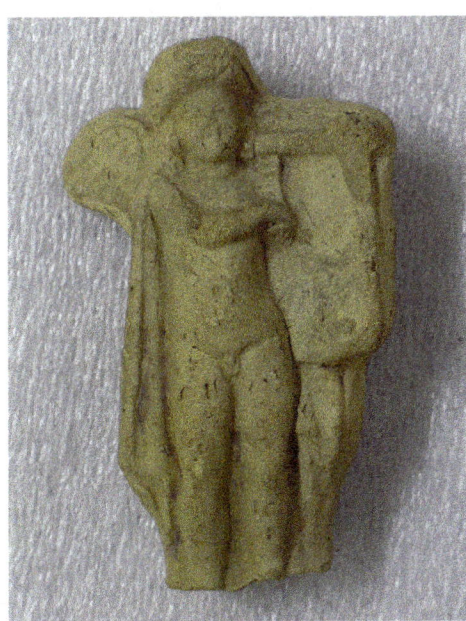

4.23. Figurine of nude winged boy playing a *kithara*, terracotta, Nippur. Height: 11.8 cm.
University of Pennsylvania Museum of Archaeology and Anthropology (B 9451)
Photograph by author, printed courtesy of the University of Pennsylvania Museum.

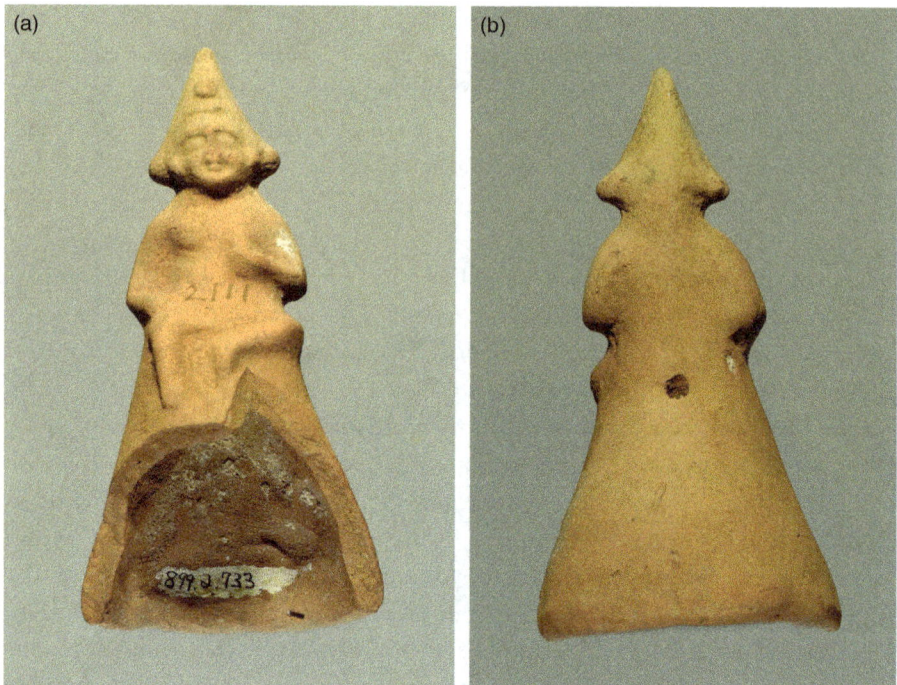

4.24a and b. Front and back of figurine (possibly incense burner) depicting child wearing three-peaked hat and sitting on cone, terracotta, likely from Babylon. Height: 13 cm. Harvard Semitic Museum (1899.2.733)
Photograph courtesy of the Semitic Museum, Harvard University.

as a result, they implicated the childhood body with activity and effects beyond the scope of most figurines.[157]

Efficaciousness, in this case with a more directly understandable ritual function, might also have been expected of figurines of boys sitting on cones. As seen in Figure 4.24, such children were often endowed with supernatural features; in this instance, wearing the three-peaked hat associated with Harpocrates and holding object-attributes clasped to the chest. One common difference in the attributes, however, is that many of the children seated on cones hold a small bowl or drum, rather than the bird and grapes. That difference in held objects may have been quite meaningful. The drum had a powerful association with ritual performance in Hellenistic Babylonia.[158] The use of the drum would also have linked these cone-sitting boys with the musical associations of the child rattles (who were also commonly shown wearing three-peaked hats) as well as potentially the pierced winged boys just discussed. If the object held by the boy was meant to be a bowl rather than a drum, the position of holding it centrally in front of the chest would echo the adult male offering bearer (as seen in Figure 4.2).

Beyond iconography, the materiality of these figurines themselves had potential ritual implications. The cone on which these boys sit may have been more than simply an odd, but vertically stable, perch. Most of the cones have round holes pierced in the back, in a position at the top of the open cone that would be ideal to allow smoke to escape (see Figure 4.24b). In light of this construction, I suggest that these objects might have been used as incense burners.[159] Further support for a sacral function may be indicated by the few instances where such objects were found in Parthian funeral chambers.[160]

The figures shown atop such cones were not uniquely children; women, men, and even apes were occasionally depicted in similar positions.[161] But the particular association of these cones with figures of boys, and the possibility that these cones were used as incense burners, seems to support the overall sense in the Hellenistic Babylonian corpus that the child's body was somehow special and different from the bodies of adults. Not only was it frequently given supernatural attributes, but it could also be used to "do" things in the real-scale world that other miniature bodies were less capable of – or less appropriate for. Indeed, through such uses, the bodies of boys were made almost infinitely liminal. Not only were they poised between infancy and adulthood (both of which were enshrined in other figurine motifs) but, with their supernatural attributes, they hovered between the human world which they occupied as objects and the divine realm to which their wings, headgear, and other features referred. As functional objects, they also teetered on the border between "true" figurines (and the illusion of a miniature world that such objects create) and life-sized efficacy in the real world. Such liminality was, perhaps, a fitting metaphor for the tenuousness and possibilities of youth. But it also put these child figurines significantly out of sync with the vast majority of the Hellenistic Babylonian figurine corpus. If the members of this community found it possible to identify with most figurines, seeing them in some sense as adequate approximations of real living adults, then by extension these child figurines that seem to occupy a different category altogether could easily be dismissed as *not* referring to real living children.

"Pick Me Up!": Coercing User Participation in Child Figurine Experiments

In the child figurines, distance from reality could also be intensified by the use of the visually noticeable piecing technique of figurine manufacture that was seen in the athlete figurines discussed earlier in this chapter. Hellenistic Babylonian figurines depicting children far outnumber those depicting athletes, and most of these ubiquitous child figurines were terracottas made in standard double molds (or, more rarely, single molds) without separately added arms. Among those examples which did have separately added limbs, there were a variety of poses in which the child could be positioned: seated, seated on

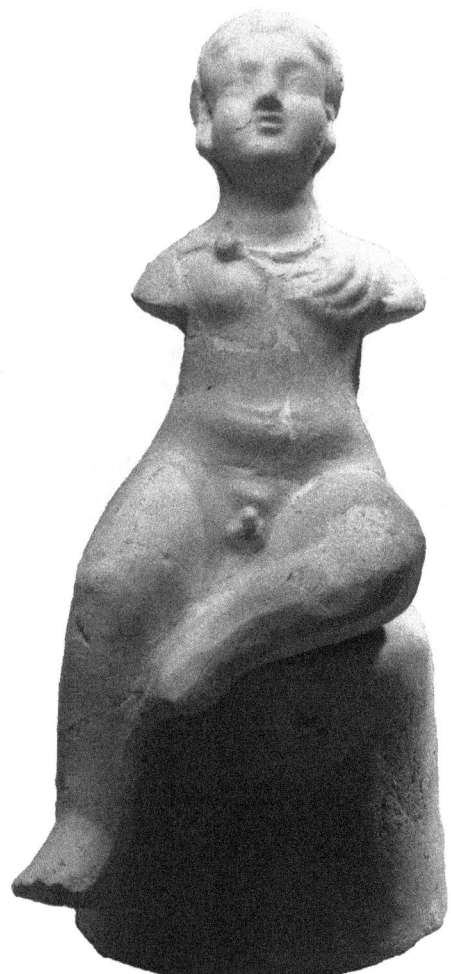

4.25. Figurine of nude boy with finished-off arms (for attachment of separately modeled arms), terracotta, Seleucia-on-the-Tigris. Height: 31.1 cm. Turin Excavations at Seleucia (S501) Photograph courtesy of Roberta Menegazzi.

a cone, twisting in dramatic movement, and standing frontally.[162] The child could be either male or female (although male was far more common), the scale could vary considerably,[163] and the figure could be depicted clothed, semi-clothed, or nude. Yet, despite this variety, there was a rigid uniformity in the joining of the separately made limbs: as seen in Figure 4.25, the arms were "finished off" in a characteristic triangular shape, at a point one-third to one-half way between the shoulder and the elbow, for separately made arms to be attached after firing. Legs could also be made separately from the molded torso, but these were usually attached before firing and the seam disguised. The fluid and unnoticeable joins of the legs present a strong contrast with the highly visible and artificial arm seams, suggesting that visual attention should be directed specifically to the arm gestures rather than the figure's posture or overall pose.

Yet, despite the depiction of these vivid arm gestures and the attention that was called to them, the construction of such figurines also distanced these images of children from reality. Just as with the athletes, the children depicted in these figurines were shown as active, but in artificially posed and predetermined ways. Due to the rigidity and predictability of their mid-limb joins, their arms do not offer even an illusion of the ability to flex at the real shoulder or elbow, and thus have no visual potential to move in the fluid and unpredictable ways characteristic of actual children. These figurines do not represent childhood as lived, but rather formally present a reified visual specter of "child-ness" to be contemplated and negotiated.

The standardized mid-limb fragmentation also provided a particularly secure attachment for an arm that was bent ninety degrees at the elbow and held frontally with the palm of the hand upward. Separately made arms in this position have been found; many of these are similar to the arms which might have been attached to female figurines (such as seen in Figure 2.11), while others, such as that in Figure 4.26, are larger and would likely fit only the bigger child figurines. As with the female figurine arms, the hands could vary in their activities; this example has an empty palm, others are holding objects such as fruit or bowls, or depict the hand balled into a fist. Regardless of the specific gesture, such arms position the figurine as reaching forward into the viewer's space, in a highly engaging invitation that echoes a toddler's pleas to "pick me up!" Exclusive visual emphasis on the arms, and the subtlety of the leg joins, reinforced that these enticing gestures should be the sole focus of the user's attention. Any sympathetic response a viewer might feel at seeing (the representation of) a child reach out his or her arms seeking adult care would potentially recruit that viewer into engaging with, and even feeling personally invested in, the cross-cultural negotiations of that child's place within the

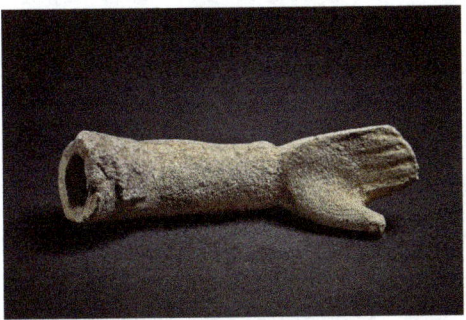

4.26. Right arm that is bent at the elbow and severed mid-humerus for attachment to a separately made figurine, terracotta, Borsippa. Length: 14 cm. British Museum (BM BN 2) Photograph © The Trustees of the British Museum.

community. An emotional bond with the miniature object was thus created, which situated the human user – perhaps unwittingly – as a participant in the broader community dialogue in which the figurine was engaged.

The outcome of such negotiations would likely have been both fraught and critical, as they concerned the social roles of the youngest (and thus the future) generations of Hellenistic Babylonians. Who those children would become may frequently have been an issue of widespread concern and interest, especially in the early days of the Hellenistic period. Due to cross-cultural marriage, as well as the effects of growing up in a multicultural society, many children in Hellenistic Babylonia had multicultural roots, which could be expressed in complex ways (such as combinations of Greek and Babylonian names for a single individual, or for siblings within one family).[164] The need to visually represent and work through the implications of those shifting identities for the next generation(s) may explain the popularity of child figurines and their variety. It may also explain their overt focus on the male gender, a feature of the corpus which is particularly odd given that the Hellenistic *koine* sculptural repertoire also included many depictions of girls – indicating that childhood generally, not just male-gendered childhood, was worthy of attention.[165] In contrast, the communities of Hellenistic Babylonia seem to have had little interest in depicting prepubescent girls, aside from a very few figurines at Seleucia-on-the-Tigris.[166] The importance of negotiating and determining the adult male roles that these Hellenistic Babylonian boys would soon inhabit seems to have outweighed any significant desire to participate fully in the *koine* sculptural trend.

Finally, and perhaps most crucially, the urgency of the identity negotiations surrounding children may explain the overarching theme throughout all the child figurines: namely, their distance from reality. Almost every figurine of a child known from Hellenistic Babylonia is somehow "out of the ordinary." The figurines just discussed used fragmented limbs and noticeable joins to impose vivid reminders that the miniature was not a true replica of a living child. But whether it was degraded to the status of a slave or elevated to the status of a god, placed in uncharacteristic childhood solemnity on a cone or throne, made to operate both as a miniature figure and a rattle or incense burner, figurine versions of the child's body were consistently separated from everyday modes of living and existing in Hellenistic Babylonia. Thus, any experiments or mistakes made in their negotiation would be less likely to be indelibly linked to reality, and thus less likely to have permanent and potentially dire effects. Making the process seem less "real," less emotionally fraught, allowed the members of the community to work through the new (and evolving) social and cultural identities of their children without being overwhelmed about the personal and familial implications of their negotiations.

CONCLUSION

This chapter began with the notion that figurines, particularly figurines of solitary individuals who face their users in uninterrupted interaction, allowed people to identify with them. Such idealized yet relatable manifestations of social personas could be easily taken up (if one shared sufficient personal characteristics, such as gender or age, with the figurine, a concept also known as the "constraints of candidacy"[167]), experimented with, and presented to the outside world, using the figurine itself, with its display-oriented materiality, as mediator. This display of idealized identities thus took on ramifications beyond the personal; indeed, miniature representations of commonly shared identities and interpersonal relationships could saturate communities with "particular image/senses" of social existence.[168] As commoditized, externalized packages of social identities, miniature objects provided visual cues about acceptable and available roles within society – educating the viewer about the social space allowed to him or her.[169] Miniatures also participated in reshaping that social space; if people no longer found a particular miniaturized identity to be relevant or compelling, it could be altered or remade in future figurines to more adequately reflect contemporary norms. The new miniature embodiment of social ideals would, in turn, influence the development of new human identities among its users.[170] This recursive process of human and object agency is similar to what Hodder refers to as "chains of entrapment,"[171] in which the cycle of human dependence on objects means that objects can demand certain behaviors and identities from humans, and vice versa.

Because of these figurines' particular link to "the self," this chapter is also where we might have expected to find the best expressions of cultural identity – be it a singular focus on dividing groups (such as Greeks, Babylonians, Parthians, and others) from one another or evidence for consistent hybridity. Instead, these figurines revealed a more complicated situation. Some groups of figurines, such as those depicting female bodies, demonstrate a thorough interpenetration and sharing of culturally associated styles, motifs, and technologies. Others, such as the male figurines, could be more culturally isolated – at least in the depiction of certain motifs. Overall, I have shown throughout this chapter that neither cultural singularity nor hybridity seems to have been an automatic or reactionary process, neither an "oil meets water" repulsion nor an "add two cultures and stir" recipe-like blending. Instead, to echo a phrase I have used elsewhere, we see "hybridity with a purpose":[172] a deliberate utilization of the rich visual repertoires of multiple cultural traditions to craft images of the human body that were both appealing and acceptable to many members of the community, and served the purposes of identity expression which were most desirable to that community. What constituted a desirable identity and a desirable body differed according to the specifics of age and gender. The degree to which bodies could be experimented with also differed depending on the power of those bodies in the real world and the degree to which people cared whether or not that experimentation would imperil the selfhood of real-life members of the community. Discussion of this selective, purposeful engagement with the artistic legacies of both Babylonia and the Hellenistic *koine* will take the forefront in Chapter 5, the final chapter of the volume.

CHAPTER FIVE

THE GLOBAL AND THE LOCAL: MAKING CULTURAL AND SOCIAL CHOICES WITH FIGURINES

OVER THE COURSE OF THIS VOLUME, ANALYSIS HAS EXPANDED from the most personal interactions with figurines, to the process of observing and identifying with figurines as coparticipants and shapers of the social world, to this chapter, in which I make clear the regional and cross-regional implications of those figurine choices. Yet if the preceding four chapters of this volume have shown anything it is that most, if not all, Hellenistic Babylonian figurines reflected cultural and social choices. Their motifs, forms, styles, and functions were selectively adopted and engaged with, or marginalized and discarded, due in part to the cultural and social practices that those figurines reflected and stimulated. The difference with the figurines discussed in this chapter is not uniquely intrinsic to these case studies. Rather, I have chosen these particular figurines to discuss here because I believe they shed the most productive light on the broader implications of those choices, either for the way in which Hellenistic Babylonian communities engaged with ideas, forms, and motifs circulating throughout the contemporary societies of the Hellenistic world, or the ways in which Hellenistic Babylonian figurine users made choices that were more distinctive.

Despite the oppositional framing of this chapter as "global" versus "local," all of the examples will reveal their "local-ness" as figurine traditions. Whether expressing the selective adoption of Hellenistic *koine* motifs with appeal to Mesopotamians, the adaptation or restriction of *koine* genres to change the nature of the conversations that those figurines encouraged, or the refusal to adopt some motifs at all, every figurine discussed in this chapter – even those that look like textbook Aphrodites or Apollos – were, in their way, local. Yet, as will be seen in the last case study of the chapter, this local-ness was, in itself, not homogenous throughout all the communities of Hellenistic Babylonia, nor was it ethnically or culturally targeted simply to reduce the impact of Greek ideas and forms. Rather, in many ways, the figurines resist any urge we might have to expand our sights to the macro level and summarize their corpus and tradition writ large. In the end, these personal objects insist on being just that – personal and individual to the users and the communities that valued them.

THE "GLOBAL": DEITY FIGURINES ENGAGED WITH THE HELLENISTIC *KOINE*

Figurines representing gods and goddesses are among the most *koine*-specific motifs seen in the Hellenistic Babylonian corpus. Some of these motifs have already been discussed, such as the child gods Eros and Harpocrates that were explored in Chapter 4. My choice to place the discussion of Eros and Harpocrates within the discussion of figurines depicting children, yet single out other deity figurines to discuss here as representatives of the Hellenistic *koine*, is not indicative of my sense of their importance, meaning, or their respective concentration of cultural identity (their "Greek-ness" or "Babylonian-ness"). Indeed, all the *koine* motifs that appear in the Hellenistic Babylonian figurine corpus illustrate both the connections to the wider Hellenistic world and an engagement with very local Hellenistic Babylonian concerns. As such, the exploration of Aphrodite figurines could just as easily have been placed with the discussion of female figurines generally. The boundaries between the "mortal" and the "divine" were not firmly fixed in Hellenistic Babylonian imagery: the embracing couples might have been seen as Eros and Psyche, the women with children might have been seen as Isis or Cybele. Similarly, the scale at which gods and goddesses were depicted in figurines was the same scale as mortal bodies in miniature – thus, the expected size differential between gods and humans created by the lived experience of cult statues was not played out at miniature scale. This leveling of the field, so to speak, likely contributed to the figurines' appeal, as these objects were capable of making the gods more accessible.[1] Ambiguity and multifunctionality were a part of this accessibility, eliding the worlds of mortal and divine to bring those spheres into greater contact and, perhaps, harmony. Caution must therefore be exercised in assigning a purely "divine" identity to such figurines. Imagery that reads as "Aphrodite" to modern scholarly eyes trained in the legacy of Praxiteles might have been seen very differently by Hellenistic Babylonian consumers.

I am also not intending to be comprehensive here, searching out every last Hellenistic Babylonian figurine that might have echoed *koine* deity imagery. As is to be expected, Seleucia-on-the-Tigris, as a cosmopolitan capital and Greek foundation, had more such figurines than the other Babylonian cities, both in quantity and in type – with a handful of examples of figurines depicting deities such as Serapis who seem to have had little resonance elsewhere in Babylonia.[2] Rather than attempting a comprehensive survey of all such exemplars and variations, a few examples of general trends serve here to illustrate how the global influence of the Hellenistic *koine* was not received via passive absorption, but rather selectively engaged with, adapted, and deployed to meet particularly local Hellenistic Babylonian needs.

Aphrodite (and Athena)

It comes as no great surprise that Aphrodite was among the most popular of the Hellenistic *koine* deities to be depicted in figurine form in Hellenistic Babylonia. Indeed, given Aphrodite's widespread popularity throughout the Hellenistic world, it is somewhat unexpected that her figurines were not *more* common in the Hellenistic Babylonian corpus. A handful of examples are known from Babylon and Uruk, while a few dozen were excavated from Seleucia-on-the-Tigris. Of those that do exist, most show a nude or seminude Aphrodite in a crouching pose (sometimes bathing or grooming; see Figure 5.1) or wrapping her drapery around her body.[3] While not always the finest or most well-crafted examples, the Hellenistic Babylonian figurines generally replicate imagery known from elsewhere in the Hellenistic world and demonstrate an appreciation of Aphrodite's cult and powers in Hellenistic Babylonian society, particularly at the Greek foundation of Seleucia-on-the-Tigris.

Yet, as tempting as it might be to conclude this discussion of Aphrodite simply and neatly, interpreting the figurines that depict her as straightforward evidence of Hellenistic influence in Babylonia, a few Aphrodite figurines suggest a somewhat more complex situation. The figurine seen in Figure 5.2, one of the rare figurines depicting Aphrodite found at Uruk, is one such example. It portrays Aphrodite – if it is indeed Aphrodite, a point to which I will shortly return – standing and fully clothed. Her left arm is held tightly at her side, with her left hand emerging at hip level from the complex folds of her clothing. Her right arm is bent and wrapped, with her hand held to the center of her chest. This pose, likely indicative of self-restraint, is shared with many of the figurines that most probably depicted mortal women; the particular meaning of the pose and examples were discussed in Chapter 3 (see particularly Figure 3.7) and Chapter 4 (see particularly Figures 4.13 and 4.14). Her delicately modeled face is surrounded by a thick band of hair, which terminates in balls of curls over her shoulders, and is in turn surmounted by an elaborate

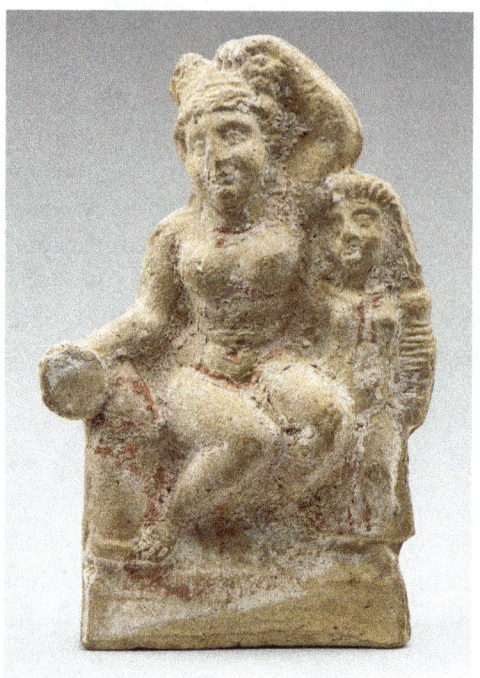

5.1. Figurine of crouching Aphrodite with Eros, terracotta, Babylon. Height 12 cm. Musée du Louvre (LO MNB 1840)
Photograph courtesy of Art Resource and the Musée du Louvre.

crown or wreath. Hovering over her right shoulder flies Aphrodite's son, the child-god Eros. His identity is made clear through his wings and child-like body proportions (particularly his chubby, short legs); however, his gesture is more ambiguous. Hellenistic Babylonian figurines connected to the iconography of Eros or Harpocrates sometimes hold their arms bent with the hands pressed tightly to the chest. Yet, this pose and gesture were more typically associated with figurines depicting adult women.

Is this, in fact, Aphrodite? The elaborate crown and presence of a flying Eros certainly suggest that identification.[4] Yet, if Eros were not depicted on this figurine, the female figure could easily have been seen as a mortal woman. Her reserved posture and completely clothed body certainly suggest a more human ideal; neither self-restraint nor demure modesty had much role in Aphrodite's persona as it was understood in the Hellenistic period. If Aphrodite could dress and pose this way in Hellenistic Babylonia, then virtually any Hellenistic Babylonian female figurine could be Aphrodite, if the occasion called for it and the user wanted to see it in that way. The inverse implication would also hold true: Hellenistic Babylonian users might have seen mortal women – for men, perhaps their wives, for women, perhaps themselves – in figurines ostensibly depicting the goddess.

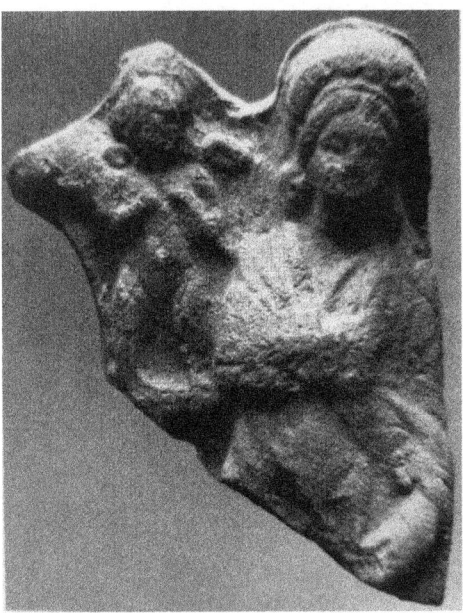

5.2. Figurine of Aphrodite with flying Eros, terracotta, Uruk. Height 11.5 cm. Baghdad (W 18 424)
Photograph reprinted from Ziegler 1962: Abb. 339, with permission of Gebrueder Mann Verlag.

Direct evidence for this interplay between goddess and mortal comes from the hairstyles of other Hellenistic Babylonian female figurines. Many head fragments from broken figurines preserve female faces crowned by an elaborate double-bun hairstyle. Although it has become flattened and distorted in its Hellenistic Babylonian use, this double bun derives originally from the topknot or bow of hair seen on several famous statues of Aphrodite.[5] Yet it seems unlikely that all of these heads originally belonged to Aphrodite figurines. Not only do very few Aphrodite figurines in Hellenistic Babylonia wear this hairstyle (see Figure 5.1 for a rare example), but the many figurines that *do* show the hair worn in this way also predominantly appear to depict the bodies of ordinary mortals (see Figures 3.1, 4.14, and 4.15). Other female figurines that could wear this hairstyle, such as those with separately attached arms (see Figure 1.1), are neither obviously Aphrodite nor unmistakably human. Clearly a significant crossover of iconography was possible between figurines intended to unambiguously depict the goddess, and those whose identities were less specified.

While this lack of clarity can be a frustration for modern scholars, it might have been seen as an advantage in the eyes of the ancient users of these objects. The appeal of a goddess of sex and love could easily transcend the specifics of Hellenistic *koine* imagery. Rather than seeing the limited number of *koine*-style figurines as the only evidence for Aphrodite in Hellenistic Babylonia, it may be more accurate to see Aphrodite (or at least the potential for Aphrodite) in many of the other female figurines. This flexibility was not an invention of Hellenistic Babylonia, but common throughout the Hellenistic world. Hellenistic statues of mortal women are also notoriously difficult to distinguish from Aphrodite statues, due to the significant influence that images of the goddess had as a role model of beauty.[6] Thus this "global" *koine* phenomenon was, in a way, almost purposefully "local," in that it easily reflected and engaged with the identities, appearances, and self-presentations of local women in whichever context it was deployed.

The specific ways in which the figurine seen in Figure 5.2 is "local" are complex; in using the term "local" I do not simply mean "Babylonian." Rather, I mean "Hellenistic Babylonian," reflective of all of the multifaceted interweavings of distinct cultural traditions characteristic of that place and time. The technique in which the figurine was made bridges cultural boundaries. The flatness and frontality of the depiction fits within a Babylonian mode of viewing, in striking contrast with the dramatic torsion in which Aphrodite's body is often shown in Hellenistic sculpture. Yet, the object was created in the Greek double mold. The basic motif was Hellenistic, the style of Aphrodite's clothing is clearly Greek, and the arm pose is of Hellenistic derivation. However, that pose was deeply entangled with traditional Mesopotamian poses of women holding, or displaying, one or both breasts. The Eros figure assumes the more typical Mesopotamian version of the pose, highlighting the connection between the two gestures. That the two Hellenistic gods most connected with sex and love demonstrate both poses – giving the gestures almost equal attention – seems fitting. This negotiated harmony between Mesopotamian and Greek ideas about female bodies and female beauty could hardly find a more apt personification.

A similar effect, albeit compressed onto one figurine body, can be seen in Figure 5.3. In this instance, it is Aphrodite herself who is posed in the Babylonian gesture of holding one hand up to the chest in order to support or display the breast. The one-handed variant of the pose can be seen in many Hellenistic Babylonian figurines, such as that pictured in Figure 4.10. In such figurines, it is the left breast particularly that is emphasized – a preference also followed in the Aphrodite seen here. This pose and the value system it expressed had deep roots in Mesopotamian visual traditions, particularly figurines. Indeed, it is difficult to be certain that Aphrodite was intended, given that there is so much about this figurine that is Babylonian: not just the gesture of the left arm, but also the frontal posture, the placement of the right arm pressed against her side, the full female nudity including genital region, and the ridge of clay around the body that gives the impression of a "tongue relief,"[7] despite the fact that it was made in a double mold. It is important to note that this figurine, which was so engaged in a sophisticated way with Babylonian ideas about the female body, was found at Seleucia-on-the-Tigris. For all the examples in this

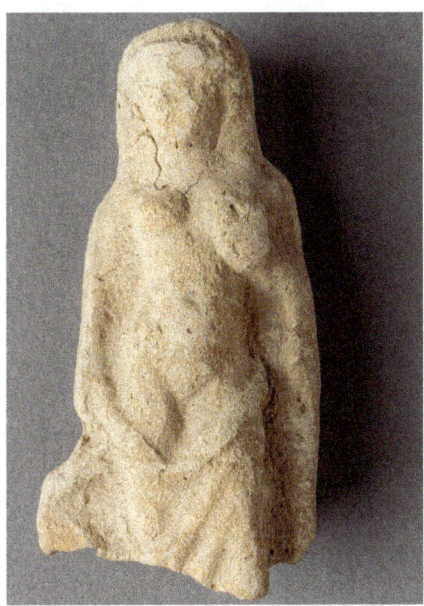

5.3. Standing Aphrodite figurine, terracotta, Seleucia-on-the-Tigris. Height 7.4 cm. Kelsey Museum of Archaeology, University of Michigan, Ann Arbor (KM 15043)
Photograph courtesy of the Kelsey Museum of Archaeology.

volume in which Seleucia-on-the-Tigris differed in the figurine motifs and styles its community preferred, it is important to note that this city was not a Greek island, adjacent and apart from its neighboring cities. It was very much a part of Babylonia, albeit a part that also had a more significant tie to the rest of the Hellenistic world.

This is not to say that this object bears no trace of Hellenistic inspiration: the figure's subtle contrapposto and the use of the double mold (despite the lack of detailed modeling on the back of the figurine) speak to influence from the Greek world. But the most compelling detail, which links to the Hellenistic *koine* and suggests that this figurine was intended to be Aphrodite, is the treatment of the drapery. The folds of cloth, swooping down from the figure's left hip to wrap tightly around her thighs, are then caught and held upward by her otherwise inactive right hand. Is she robing or disrobing? The meaning and intended resolution of her gesture remain unclear, just as they are in the famous Knidian Aphrodite statue from which this motif was originally derived (see Figure 4.12). Because of the female figure's ambiguous pose, the viewer is left to wonder whether he or she is an interloper or an intended audience. A coquettish play is thus created, intended to delight and seduce.

Yet, despite the presence of potentially concealing fabric, neither the Knidian Aphrodite nor this figurine hides the female genital region – unlike many semi-draped Aphrodite statues from the Hellenistic period, in which the clothing skirts the top of the hips and does conceal the genitals.[8] In the case of this figurine, I would suggest that the depiction of cloth has an opposite, almost framing, effect, similar to the swaths of drapery around the thighs of Hellenistic *koine* statues depicting young male gods, such as the Cyrene Apollo.[9] When coupled with the Babylonian breast-supporting pose, the coquettishness seems to fall away almost entirely: this is a woman who wants to be seen, who is self-possessed and proud to display her naked body, with all of its powers and charms. So, while an Aphrodite identification seems logical here, this is an Aphrodite transformed – a "Babylonian-ization of Aphrodite," as it were, to invert Zainab Bahrani's famous claim about the "Hellenization of Ishtar" in describing the initial Greek incorporation of a nude female goddess into their pantheon and visual imagery.[10] Bahrani's point is a valid one here, for in many ways Aphrodite and her imagery was never truly isolated from the Near Eastern traditions from which they came; a point also explored by S. Rebecca Martin in her masterful discussion of the so-called Slipper Slapper Aphrodite statue from Delos.[11] Thus, despite our modern desire to see figurines of Aphrodite in Uruk or Seleucia-on-the-Tigris as "global" influence from the wider Hellenistic world, in many ways the goddess was already at home.

There is also a possibility that some viewers might have used figurines like that shown in Figure 5.3 specifically to depict Ishtar or another deity. Many options for powerful female deities existed in the Hellenistic Near East, with Aphrodite, Astarte, Ishtar, Isis, and Cybele only among the more popular selections. Imagery that defied conventional categorization, as most of the Hellenistic Babylonian figurines of "Aphrodite" do, opened up such possibilities, allowing the female figure's specific identity to be decided by the eye of the beholder.[12] However, these deities were not identical in their powers, attributes, and mythology. In particular, some of the martial prowess and violence connected with the cults of Ishtar and Astarte might not have been fully satisfied by Aphrodite figurines. In many of the Hellenistic Babylonian cities, this insufficiency (if it was indeed regarded as such) might simply have led to an unpopularity of figurines that were too closely identified with Aphrodite. Obvious representations of Aphrodite are not common, even at Seleucia-on-the-Tigris, when compared to the innumerable female figurines whose imagery (such as the knobbed hairstyle) engaged with Aphrodite's iconography but whose identities were less fixed.

Other options for those in want of a more Ishtar-like goddess also existed, particularly at Seleucia-on-the-Tigris: figurines of Athena, Greek goddess of wisdom and war, or Nike, the winged Greek goddess of victory.[13] Known only from a handful figurines, these deities nevertheless had a small place in the relatively restricted pantheon of Greek gods found in Hellenistic Babylonian figurines. As seen in Figure 5.4, Athena is always seen in a guise that explicitly invokes her martial powers (usually wearing a helmet and carrying a shield), as well as her clothed modesty. The substantial plinth base on which Athena stands

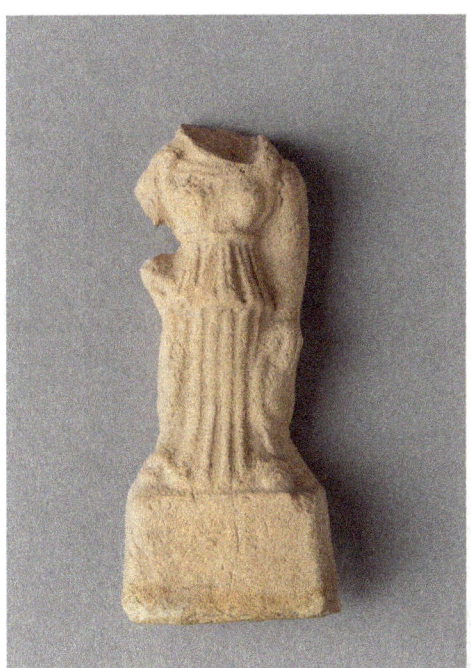

5.4. Standing Athena figurine, terracotta, Seleucia-on-the-Tigris. Height 7.6 cm. Kelsey Museum of Archaeology, University of Michigan, Ann Arbor (KM 15233)
Photograph courtesy of the Kelsey Museum of Archaeology.

also emphasizes her power and inaccessibility – this is a goddess to be regarded from a respectful distance, not to gawk at too closely nor to touch. Yet, her feminine body was also carefully depicted – particularly her breasts, which stand out individually as full and round despite the clothing that covers them, rather than disappearing into a vague lump underneath swaths of drapery. Perhaps this emphasized femininity was simply a technique used to ensure that the goddess's identity was clear and that these figurines would not be confused with male soldiers. But to Babylonian eyes, the dual powers of Ishtar as master of both sex and war might have been called to mind. Nike figurines might have similarly evoked this duality of ideas – as she likely would have for Greeks as well, given the overt sexualization of Nike figures on famous Classical Greek monuments, done in order to make victory seem appealing and attractive.[14]

I hesitate to argue that figurines of Athena or Nike were used in Hellenistic Babylonia because of a perceived connection with Ishtar. Both figurine motifs were extremely rare and confined to Seleucia-on-the-Tigris. If this was a way for Hellenistic Babylonians to combine their interests in a Greek goddess and a Babylonian goddess, it was not a popular strategy. Perhaps the use of Athena or Nike figurines was restricted to those who wanted a more direct connection with Greek traditions and deities. Yet given the limited pantheon of Greek gods who were incorporated in the Hellenistic Babylonian figurine corpus, it seems worthwhile to ask why some gods were adopted, even on a limited scale, while others were shunned. Local concerns likely played an important role,[15] even when these figurines do not look obviously "hybrid." Such blending of local values with Hellenistic *koine* figurine traditions will be further explored in the next case study.

Herakles, Lion-Hunting Hero

Many of the bearded, mature nude male figurines discussed in Chapter 4 were likely intended to represent the Greek hero-god Herakles, and thus I return to them here, in this discussion of Hellenistic *koine* deities. As seen in Figure 5.5, such figurines often depicted the male figure carrying the club and the lion pelt that were Herakles's distinctive attributes. Other examples, such as that seen in Figure 4.3, more explicitly evoked the Lysippian "Weary Herakles"

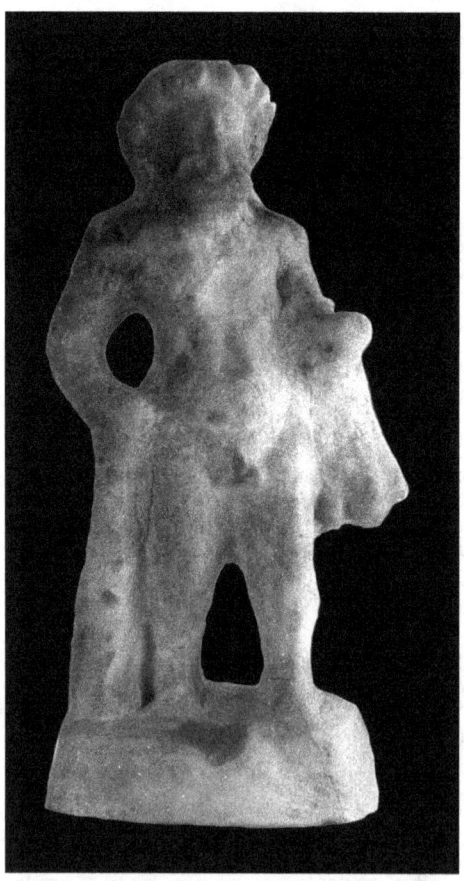

5.5. Standing Herakles figurine, terracotta, Seleucia-on-the-Tigris. Baghdad (B16934) Photograph originally published as Van Ingen 1939, No. 251.

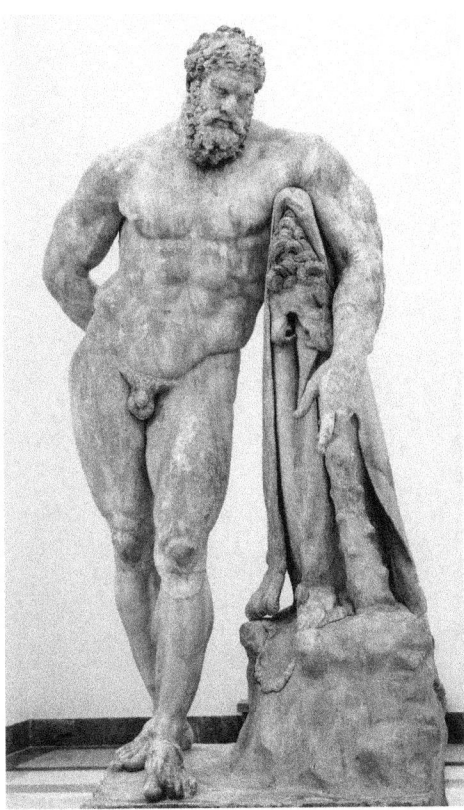

5.6. Weary Herakles, by Lysippos (Roman copy, known as the Farnese Herakles, by Glycon of Athens), original bronze, fourth century BCE. Museo Archeologico Nazionale, Naples. Photograph by Marie-Lan Nguyen (Creative Commons license).

(see Figure 5.6), with his downturned head, right arm held behind the back, and club resting in the left armpit to support the weight of the upper body. Clearly figurines such as these were directly influenced by the visual traditions of the broader Hellenistic world.

Yet, in their eagerness to adopt the Hellenistic motif of Herakles, the Hellenistic Babylonian craftspeople seem to have been less obviously interested in imitating Hellenistic *koine* art. The figurine seen in Figure 5.5 does indeed reflect the Herakles motif, and Greek motifs generally: he wears a thick wreath on his head, has an elaborately muscled torso and full male nudity (including carefully depicted genitalia), holds the lion pelt draped over his left arm, while his right hand rests casually on his club. The figurine was also made in the double mold, and stands easily on its plinth base. Yet, unlike with the figurine seen in Figure 4.3, the maker of this object demonstrated no familiarity with the art of Lysippos – or with much of Greek art generally. The legs are far too short in proportion to the torso, with their wide stance and openwork crafting only

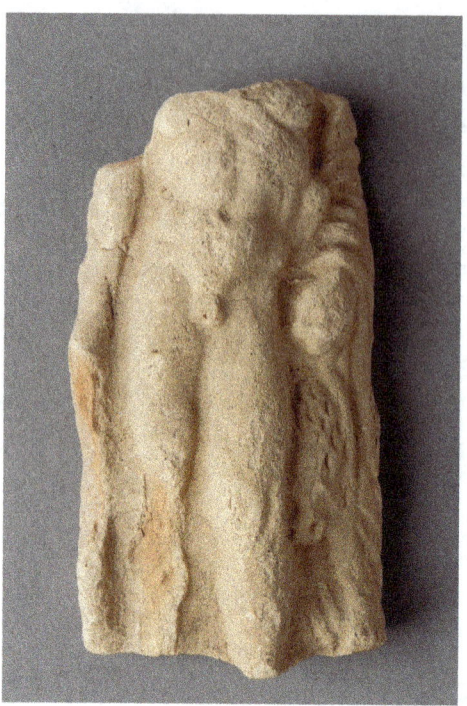

5.7. Standing Herakles figurine, terracotta, Seleucia-on-the-Tigris. Height 9.5 cm. Kelsey Museum of Archaeology, University of Michigan, Ann Arbor (KM 15544)
Photograph courtesy of the Kelsey Museum of Archaeology.

accentuating their stubby awkwardness. The openwork of the right arm similarly calls visual and tactile attention where none is needed to convey the meaning of the motif. The large head, staring up and outward, evinces a confidence more in common with statues of Zeus than of Herakles, and the proportions are almost anti-Lysippian, given that artist's fame for creating smaller heads on more elongated bodies.[16] A better comparison for this figurine can be found in the stocky Herakles depictions on monumental reliefs at Nemrud Dagh and other Commagene sites.[17] Made in eastern Asia Minor in the mid-first century BCE, the Commagene Herakles reliefs were created as part of a monumental program by King Antiochus of Commagene in order to celebrate his combined heritage from both the Persian/Near Eastern and Greek traditions.[18] The figurine seen in Figure 5.5 seems similarly engaged, if perhaps not on so grand a scale or with such a political goal in mind.

In contrast, the figurine seen in Figure 5.7 appears much more Greek in style. In addition to portraying the Herakles motif, the body of the hero-god is posed in a striking contrapposto, with a sinuous S-curve to his body. The muscles of his torso and his genitalia were elaborately modeled, as was the stippled lion pelt that drapes over his left arm and dangles below his hand.

Although the figurine is broken, his legs are clearly long in proportion to his torso, following a more Lysippian model. Yet, unlike the figurines seen in Figures 4.3 and 5.5, this figurine was made in a single mold and is flat on the back, just like many Babylonian figurines. In comparing these three examples, it becomes clear that the people of Hellenistic Babylonia were deeply engaged with Herakles imagery and the idea of Herakles as represented in figurine form. This was not a casual adoption from the wider *koine*, to be replicated in a few, relatively unpopular objects. Rather, this was a sustained process of replicating, remaking, adapting, and incorporating Herakles into the Hellenistic Babylonian figurine tradition on a wide scale. Indeed, figurines of Herakles were popular across Hellenistic Babylonia,[19] and were used well into the centuries of Parthian control (a period in which this motif was, in fact, particularly well liked[20]).

One of the theories commonly offered for why Herakles figurines were so popular suggests that it was due to their use as votives by members of the Seleucid army. However, while one such figurine was found at the Faïlaka fortress,[21] many similar figurines were found in various non-military domestic contexts in cities such as Seleucia-on-the-Tigris and Susa.[22] Additionally, a connection with a Greco-Macedonian military does not adequately explain why the particular prevalence of such figurines in the Hellenistic Near East (Babylonia, Susa, and the Persian Gulf)[23] outpaced the popularity of similar figurines in Hellenistic Greece and Egypt – regions that also supported massive military forces.

A more productive explanatory avenue is offered by the Hellenistic Babylonian evidence for giving multiple names and multiple cultural identities to imagery ostensibly of Herakles. For instance, Herakles would seem to be the subject of a larger-scale bronze statue, measuring 85.5 cm high, that was created in Babylonia during the Parthian period. As seen in Figure 5.8, this statue depicts a mature male, wearing a rounded full beard, standing in a contrapposto pose with his hand on his right hip.[24] Named in its secondary inscription as the god Herakles/Verethraghna,[25] it may have represented the Babylonian god Nergal in its original context of Mesene (southern Babylonia),[26] before being relocated via conquest to the Temple of Apollo at Seleucia-on-the-Tigris.[27] Clearly this male body type was capable of filling several different divine roles within the Hellenistic Babylonian imaginary.[28]

The "Herakles" figurines themselves support this idea of multiple divine identifications in their accommodation to both Greek and Near Eastern priorities. Lion-hunting attributes, such as the club and lion pelt, consistently appear in Hellenistic Babylonian Herakles figurines. In contrast, other details of Herakles iconography from the Greek tradition – such as the Apples of the Hesperides (seen, for example, in the Farnese Herakles statue)[29] or even the more ubiquitous Late Classical and Hellenistic Greek focus on Herakles's

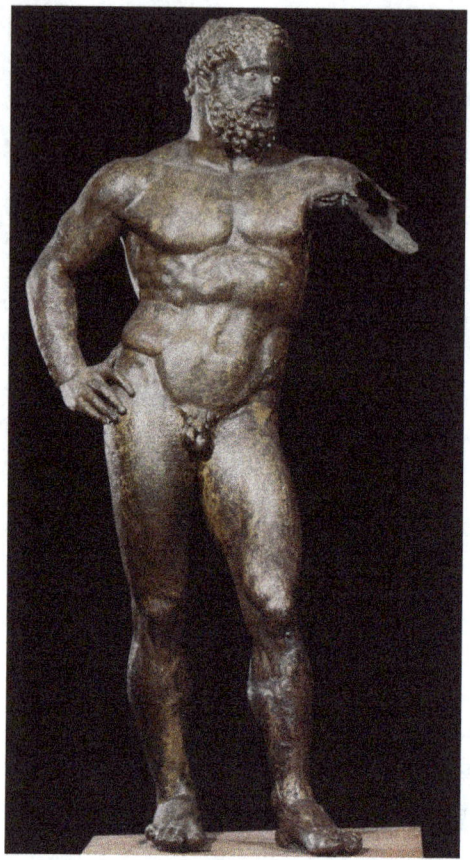

5.8. Weary Herakles (also known as the "Herakles of Mesene"), named in inscription as the god Herakles/Verethraghna, late second century BCE–first century CE, bronze, Seleucia-on-the-Tigris. Height 85.5 cm. Baghdad, National Museum of Iraq, inv. no. 100178. Photograph courtesy of Roberta Menegazzi.

downturned head as an expression of his exhaustion and vulnerability – were much less commonly employed.[30] While the physical fatigue of semi-divine bodies or magical apples had little or no resonance in Babylonian tradition, a virile, bearded, lion hunter fit comfortably within very ancient Mesopotamian traditions of lion-hunting heroes.[31]

Earlier monumental images of lion-hunting men survived into the visual world of Hellenistic Mesopotamia through multiple avenues. Variations on the ancient nude belted hero motif – depicting the king or other heroic figure grappling with lions – were portrayed on Mesopotamian palace walls throughout the first millennium BCE. These included the reliefs depicting the *lahmu*, or "Hairy one," at the Neo-Assyrian palace at Khorsabad, as well as images of the Assyrian king hunting lions depicted both on palace wall reliefs and seals.[32] Similar imagery existed in Persia: reliefs of the "Persian Royal Hero" were carved on the doorjambs of Darius's palace at Persepolis; both the Royal Hero and other lion-hunting figures were popular on Achaemenid stamp and cylinder seals.[33] The reliefs at Persepolis, as well as the small-scale Achaemenid arts, would still have been accessible as media for the circulation of ideas throughout Hellenistic Babylonian society.[34] "Herakles" figurines would present striking similarities to these older Near Eastern images, through the shared upright posture, bearded face, well-muscled mature male body, and lion-hunting attributes.

The existence of an earlier Mesopotamian tradition of a specific kind of heroic nudity may have been one of the reasons why Babylonians felt interested, or even just comfortable, engaging with the "Herakles" figurines. Outside the realm of the nude belted hero and the associated contest scenes and hunting motifs, male nudity was usually not considered a positive attribute in Mesopotamian art.[35] The concordance of the Greek idea of Herakles with several of the attributes of the Mesopotamian nude belted hero provides one possible explanation as to why the "Herakles" figurines became accepted and popular, whereas depictions of other nude males derived from the Greek tradition (such as Apollo or Dionysos) were less prevalent. Thus, while it is tempting to see the Herakles figurines as one of the most significant engagements that Hellenistic Babylonia had with the broader *koine* tradition, these objects were also intensely local. Even figurines that seem at first glance to suggest a display of cultural difference could be the "hybrid" product of cross-cultural exchanges.

Apollo

Besides Herakles, figurines depicting other male gods popular in the Hellenistic world, such as Apollo or Dionysos, were uncommon in Hellenistic Babylonia.[36] Other scholars have already observed the contradiction between the official popularity of several Greek gods – Apollo, for instance, was worshipped as an ancestor of the Seleucid kings – and the "all the more surprising" fact that figurines of these gods "have not been discovered in greater numbers."[37] This seeming paradox also encompasses the bronze statue from Seleucia-on-the-Tigris, seen in Figure 5.8. This statue was explicitly given the Greek name of Herakles as well as a Parthian god name, yet was dedicated in a temple to Apollo.[38] Clearly Apollo could be, and was, worshipped and admired in Hellenistic Babylonia, but rarely represented in sculptural form. Reasons for this lacuna have already been posited in Chapter 4; namely, that figurines of Apollo might have been too visually similar to the images intimately associated with the Seleucid king (and the Parthian kings which followed them and who continued to use Apollo imagery on their coinage) to be comfortably owned and handled by members of the broader public.

This is not to say that figurines of Apollo are completely absent from the Hellenistic Babylonian corpus. The rare examples emphasized Apollo's less royal and military aspects by depicting him as the lyre-playing god of music. Both a military and a musical Apollo would likely have appealed to Near Eastern audiences, including Babylonians and Iranians. The Apollo *Toxotes* (offering/holding a bow or arrows) seen on coins such as that pictured in Figure 4.6b likely derived from Achaemenid Persian coinage[39] – objects which were themselves designed to draw upon earlier Mesopotamian imagery of royal and divine power,[40] especially from Babylonian and Assyrian cylinder seals.[41] The adoption of the archer motif was likely a deliberate strategy on the part of the Seleucids to make their rule locally palatable across the Near East and to imply the support of locally recognized deities[42] – a numismatic tactic also employed by the Parthian kings who succeeded them.[43]

The figurines, in contrast, would have been appealing for entirely different reasons. Figurines of musicians were popular in Hellenistic Babylonia, and so a deity linked to musical performance might also have been welcome – or, at least, accepted. In addition to singling out one of Apollo's less aggressive attributes (the lyre) and roles (god of music), the figurines also depict a very different body type than the Apollo on coinage was given. The Apollo *Toxotes* of Hellenistic Babylonian coinage not only assertively proffers the instruments of war, but also lounges nude, confidently displaying his overtly masculine body and genitalia. In contrast, the figurine Apollo, an example of which is seen in Figure 5.9, appears feminized. Despite wearing a tunic, typically a male garment, Apollo's clothes are tightly cinched at the waist, puffing out above the belt to create the illusion of female breasts.[44] The face is round and unbearded, and long hair is softly swept back under the elaborate headdress.

This feminizing or androgenizing of Apollo was not unique to Hellenistic Babylonia; indeed, it parallels iconographic developments in the seals of the Hellenistic Levant[45] and it fits comfortably within a Hellenistic *koine* trend, seen especially in statues of the Greek gods Apollo and Dionysos, in which bodies that are male sex have female gender characteristics (such as softened facial features and long flowing hair).[46] In this way, figurines such as that seen in Figure 5.9 are reflective of the "global" style of the broader Hellenistic world. Yet they are also very "local," in that the choices made in their creation and use – both to depict a nonmartial Apollo, as well as the general disinterest in Apollo figurines regardless of their appearance – reflect concerns particular to Hellenistic Babylonia. Those concerns seem to have been political, not cultural, and yet I would argue that these figurines were nevertheless "hybrid" in that they were engaged with the community in which they operated and expressive of its negotiated multicultural stances on the use of miniature imagery of all kinds. Despite representing a specific Greek god, these figurines were also entangled with another, broader

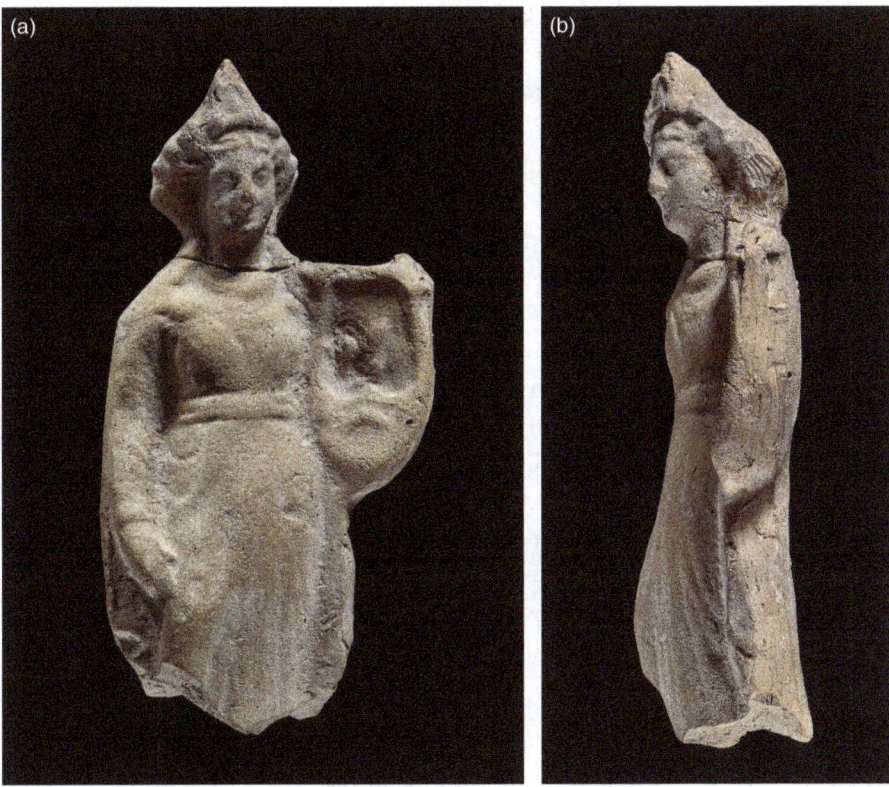

5.9a and b. Front and side of standing Apollo figurine holding instrument, terracotta, Babylon. Height 13 cm. British Museum (BM Sp. III 16+ = 91817)
Photographs © The Trustees of the British Museum.

negotiation about the limits and category-crossing potential of human bodies, such as the boundary between male and female, as will be discussed in the next section of this chapter.

AT THE BOUNDARIES OF THE (SOCIAL) WORLD: FIGURINES OF OTHERNESS

Turning from the figurines depicting Greek gods and goddesses, I now examine another group of Hellenistic Babylonian figurines that were engaged with the motifs of the Hellenistic *koine*. These figurines of "otherness" depicted bodies and identities on the margins of the social world, whose presence had not always been acknowledged in pre-Hellenistic artistic traditions, but which had become newly interesting in an era when societies were incorporating an unprecedented diversity of different people. This broader visual conversation about personhood was taking place across the Hellenistic world, and Hellenistic Babylonia's participation in that discussion happened through dialogue with the *koine* – and likely for the same reasons. Indeed, Hellenistic Babylonia, as a particularly diverse region of the Hellenistic world, might have had a more pressing need for such conversations than other locales and communities did.

Yet, Hellenistic Babylonia engaged in this visual discussion only selectively. Some Hellenistic *koine* figurines depicting marginal or "othered" bodies were accepted, replicated, and adapted for local use. Others were rejected, occupying only a restricted place in the Hellenistic Babylonian corpus, or none at all. Through this exploration of these selective engagements with otherness, two ideas will emerge. First, to echo the discussion on *koine* gods and goddesses, despite often appearing to be straightforward adoptions of Greek (or, rather, Hellenistic) culture, these figurines reflected firm local preferences, modes of vision, and social concerns. They were, in short, "local" despite being "global." Second, the hybridity seen in these figurines – as with so much of the cross-cultural hybridity seen throughout this volume – was experimental, and often concerned with ideas and issues other than cultural identity. In particular, figurines of "otherness" were, I argue, used to negotiate the place of all people in Hellenistic Babylonia, regardless of whether or not their bodies looked "normal."

Hermaphrodites, Intersex, and Ambiguous Gender

One of the most striking examples of "otherness" in Hellenistic Babylonian figurines can be seen in objects that explicitly depicted bodily characteristics usually associated with both male and female sexes. Such figures are often labeled "hermaphrodites"; however, the culturally neutral terms "intersexed" or "intergendered" seem more appropriate within the Hellenistic Babylonian context.[47] Such figurines were rare within the Hellenistic Babylonian figurine corpus, and thus the experiments that they reflected likely concerned the very margins of society, rather than the more popular ideals of "normalcy" at its core.[48] Although such figurines may reflect real anatomically intersexed bodies or transgendered identities, I argue that they also were a conceptual toolkit used to negotiate and experiment in a broader way with the boundaries of humanness in Hellenistic Babylonian society.

The richly experimental nature of Hellenistic Babylonian intersexed figurines is evident from their diversity of motif and pose. They do not form a coherent corpus of objects that can be classified together according to formal properties, other than by the depiction of both male and female sex. Even the ways in which they show combinations of male and female features differ from object to object. For instance, two nearly identical terracotta figurines from Hellenistic Uruk, one of which is pictured in Figure 5.10, present primarily female bodies: rounded breasts, elaborate headdresses of vertically ridged curls,

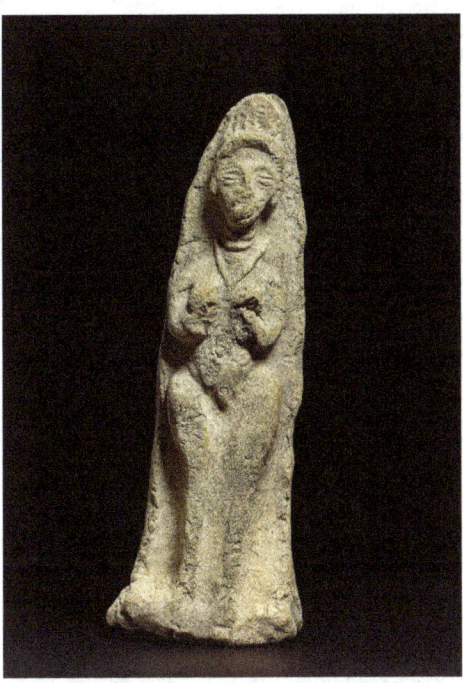

5.10. Intersexed figure supporting breasts, terracotta, Uruk. Height 17.7 cm. British Museum (BM 51–1–1–107)
Photograph © The Trustees of the British Museum.

necklaces, the position of the arms to support the breasts, narrow waists, and wide hips. All of these features are shared with Hellenistic Babylonian figurines that are unambiguously female. The pose of hands supporting the breasts had particularly ancient roots among Mesopotamian figurines depicting nude females, and remained common in Hellenistic Babylonian figurines. The pose may have had some connection to Ishtar,[49] as may the idea of intersexuality, although the evidence for seeing this as an image of the goddess herself is slim.[50] Regardless of identification, the earlier Babylonian figurine form was altered in these miniatures – instead of female genitalia, these figurines from Hellenistic Uruk were depicted with male sex organs.

Similarly intersexed imagery can also be seen in two alabaster figurines from Babylon, pictured in Figure 5.11. Like the Uruk figurines, these alabaster miniatures wear elaborate feminine hairstyles (albeit of the double-knobbed type) and support their breasts with their hands. Of the two, the standing figurine in particular shares the hypersexualized body type, with narrow waist and wide hips, seen in female figurines with separately added arms. Despite these female characteristics, male genitals (flaccid penis and scrotum) are clearly shown on both figurines, which are usually described as male children.[51] However, I suggest that any gender determination should not rest on primary

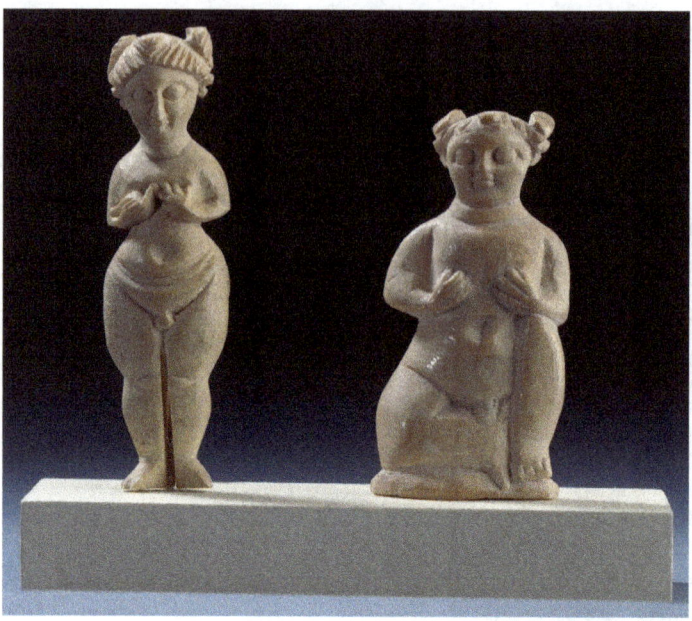

5.11. Figurines of intersexed figures, alabaster, Babylon. Vorderasiatisches Museum Berlin (Left: VA 10087; Right: VA 10088). Height of VA 10087: 5.4 cm; height of VA 10088: 4.8 cm. Photograph © Staatliche Museen zu Berlin-Vorderasiatisches Museum, Foto: Olaf M. Teßmer

sexual characteristics alone, especially as details of these figurines' poses indicate sophisticated play with the boundaries of masculine and feminine imagery. Because of its female body shape, the standing figurine might be expected to hold or display its breasts in its hands. Instead, a small bird is shown held in the figure's right hand, while what look like the splayed fingers of the left hand, which appear to be six in number, may instead represent grapes. This iconography of the bird and grapes aligns the figurine quite closely with Hellenistic Babylonian figurines of male children, seen for instance in Figure 4.20. Conversely, the squatting figurine, which has a body type more expected for a male child – including the pose of one bent leg splayed outward, with the side of the foot visible – does not appear to hold any objects. Instead, its pose of open hands placed on the chest, perhaps even supporting the breasts, aligns this object more closely with female figurines. The use of the more female hand/chest action for a more masculine body in the squatting figurine, and vice versa in the standing figurine, indicates that these objects were not primarily intended to create a cohesive category of intersexed or intergendered imagery. Rather, experimentation with traditional gender norms seems to have been the aim of these figurines.

Further play with gender boundaries using pose can be seen in a reclining bone figurine from Seleucia-on-the-Tigris, pictured in Figure 5.12. Reclining figurines such as this are almost exclusively female in Hellenistic Babylonia, as

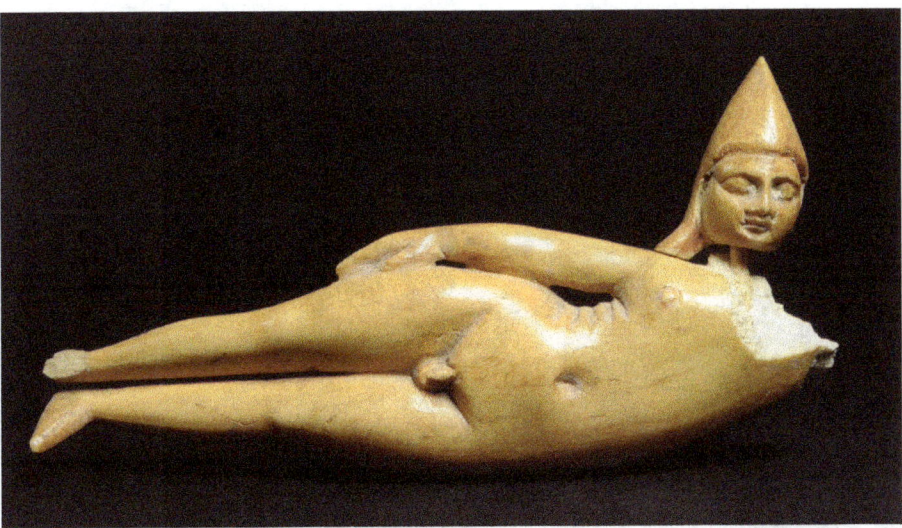

5.12. Figurine of reclining intersexed figure, bone, Seleucia-on-the-Tigris. Length: 10.6 cm. Kelsey Museum of Archaeology, University of Michigan, Ann Arbor (TM 1931.483+1931.461/ KM 2018.01.0528 + 2018.01.0528)
Photograph courtesy of Roberta Menegazzi and the Kelsey Museum of Archaeology.

will be discussed in the last section of this chapter. This object similarly presents a predominantly female body, with a soft curving waist flowing to wider hips. Although the chest is smooth and seems to lack the swelling of breast tissue associated with female bodies, the detailed depiction of a nipple may indicate female breasts (particularly if the natural contours of the bone did not leave sufficient material from which to carve breasts). Such elaborate depictions of nipples are uncommon on Hellenistic Babylonian figurines of either gender, so the inclusion of this unexpected and eye-catching detail may perhaps have served as a way to draw the user's attention to the ambiguity of this intersexed body, with its female proportions and pose, but male genitalia. From an anatomical perspective, this figure may be entirely male – yet, the significant overlap with female imagery indicates a blurring of gender boundaries.

Similar gender fluidity can be seen in figurines from Hellenistic Babylonia that might be identified with the Greek god Apollo, which depicts a draped figure holding a lyre. Hellenistic Babylonian figurines generally emphasized an androgynous or feminine form of Apollo that was also popular elsewhere in the Hellenistic world. However, as with the hermaphrodite figurines, the communities of Hellenistic Babylonia seem to have taken this play with gender boundaries a step further. The figurine seen in Figure 5.13 shares the Apollo pose and lyre, but with explicitly female garments – the long *chiton* and wrapped *himation* draped to the ground, traditionally worn by Greek women. The

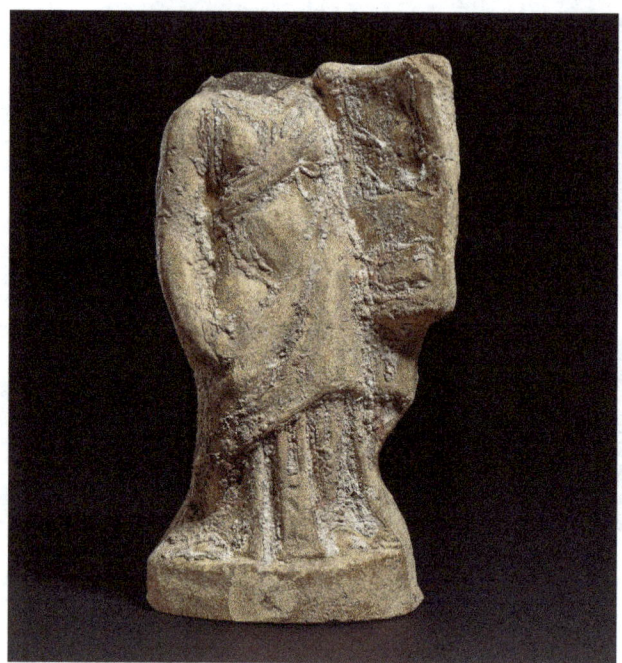

5.13. Figurine in posture of Apollo, wearing female garments, terracotta, Uruk. Height: 16.4 cm. British Museum (BM 91813)
Photograph © The Trustees of the British Museum.

breasts that can be seen high on the figure's chest are not ambiguous, possible optical illusions, but are rather the expected body type for this garment. Although the head of the figurine is missing, the body posture and wide base clearly indicate that this figurine was intended for vertical display, directly offering this unexpectedly gendered body for the viewer's immediate inspection.

Were such miniature bodies, exhibited and visually consumed, intended to reflect the biological and social realities of real individuals in Hellenistic Babylonia? Undoubtedly there were people in Hellenistic Babylonia whose body morphology or gender identities fell outside scholarship's usual assumptions of binary cisgender normativity. While gender distinctions often appear to be part of the "natural, eternal order of things,"[52] feminist theory (including in art history) has long since shown that gender is a contested concept that is culturally constructed and that, even within a particular culture, gender roles and performances are continually renegotiated as they are enacted.[53] Mesopotamian society recognized third and fourth genders at various points in its history,[54] and some cultic professionals, palace eunuchs, and others were expected to operate outside binary gender norms.[55] Nevertheless, it seems unlikely that there were many intersexed people in the population of

Hellenistic Babylonia,[56] nor that their numbers had increased substantially from earlier periods of Babylonian or Greek history.

Given the rarity of the figurines, it is especially striking – and potentially significant – that the miniature versions of intersex and intergender bodies differ so widely in pose, hairstyle, body type, and use of secondary sexual characteristics. Rather than presenting a cohesive corpus of imagery – or reflecting a cohesive social identity – these figurines instead seem to be experiments. I therefore propose that it is more useful to see the sudden appearance of intersexed and intergendered figurine imagery in Hellenistic Babylonia less as mimesis, and more as an attempt to negotiate in very direct ways with the boundaries between female and male – done in order to negotiate the overarching boundaries of what it meant to be human in Hellenistic Babylonian society.

As experiments, these figurines likely fit within pan-Hellenistic explorations of the boundaries of gender and sexuality, seen in Hellenistic *koine* sculpture and figurines throughout the Mediterranean, such as the "Hermaphrodite" sculptural type. Yet Babylonian tradition also influenced these figurines; all depict the intersexed figure using poses and iconography drawn from a Babylonian approach to visualizing the female body. The pose of hands displaying the breasts, and the reclining, outward-facing female figurine – these are Hellenistic Babylonian, rather than simply a duplication of Hellenistic *koine* tradition. The use of these Babylonian poses means that all of the figurines face the viewer directly, presenting their mixed sex for the viewer's unmediated inspection. Through the positioning of the figures' hands, it is usually the female characteristics of the body to which the user's gaze is pointed. Larger-scale statues of hermaphroditic figures from elsewhere in the Hellenistic world could likewise direct the viewer's attention; yet, in such statues, it was usually the male genitalia, not the female breasts, which were emphasized by the figure's posture, gesture, or garments.[57] The emphasis on the female sexual anatomy and female gendered markers of the Hellenistic Babylonian intersexed figurines suggests a more Babylonian inflection to these images. Paralleling the discussion of female figurines in Chapter 4, here too we see that these social experiments within the Hellenistic Babylonian intersexed figurines were overlaid onto the landscape of (predominantly) female bodies. The association of such mixed-sex or mixed-gendered bodies with traditional, even divine, imagery (both Greek and Babylonian) also ensured that such negotiations were taken seriously within the community that viewed and used these figurines.

Figurine experiments that tested the boundaries of humanity could also focus on identity issues other than gender. For instance, in Figure 5.14, an ape body, rather than a female body, has been substituted for Apollo. This simian figure is shown in Apollo's pose, holding his instrument, and wearing a festive wreath.

226 THE GLOBAL AND THE LOCAL

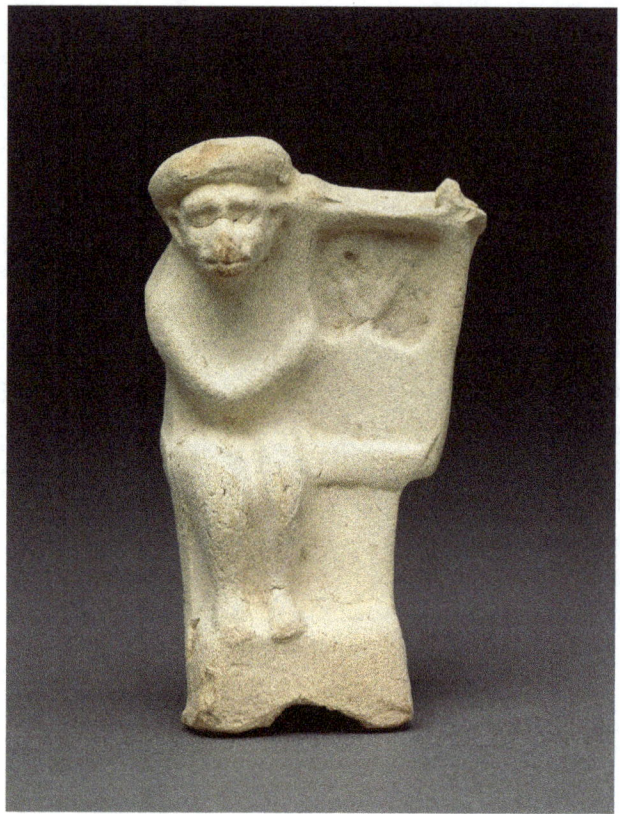

5.14. Figurine of ape in posture of Apollo, terracotta, Babylon. Height: 11.3 cm. British Museum (BM 91796)
Photograph © The Trustees of the British Museum.

This ape figurine represents a common Hellenistic Babylonian exploration of the boundaries between ape and human, and may tap into broader trends in the ancient world of negotiating a "properly human" body by incorporating animal forms and utilizing animal–human hybrids.[58] Ape figurines were often made so that the face appeared human from the front, and was only easily distinguished as simian in the profile view.[59] Such negotiations would not have been new to Babylonia; indeed, Mesopotamia had a long history of figurines that blurred the somatic distinctions between monkeys as musicians and humans as musicians, reflecting the ambiguous status of human musical performers, many of whom were members of low social classes or even marginalized outcasts.[60] The figurine seen in Figure 5.14 thus might have appealed to members of both Greek and Babylonian cultural traditions, incorporating aspects familiar to both – yet might also have been challenging to all viewers, compressing as it did identities that spanned from animal to deity, from marginalized to privileged, and refusing to resolve this tension in favor of excluding any cultural or other social groups.

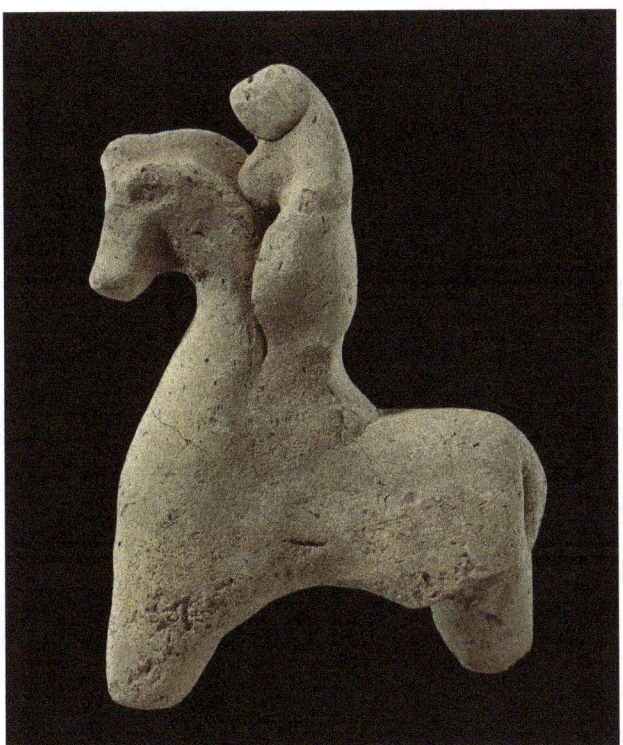

5.15. Horse and rider figurine, terracotta, Uruk. Height: 11.9 cm. Vorderasiatisches Museum Berlin (VA 12137)
Photograph © Staatliche Museen zu Berlin-Vorderasiatisches Museum, Foto: Olaf M. Teßmer.

Similar explorations of the boundaries of humanness might also explain the sudden Hellenistic Babylonian interest in figurines of children (discussed in Chapter 4) and people with dwarfism (discussed in the next section of this chapter), as well as in figures with amorphous bodies that do not clearly display gender or age. Many of the horse riders fall into this latter group. While some Hellenistic Babylonian horse rider figurines, as seen in Chapter 2, clearly present a human body riding a horse body, others have vague or ambiguous bodies. In many cases, the body of the rider seems to be merged into the body of the horse, with no separate legs or arms given to the human at all (see Figure 5.15). In other cases, the rider figure appears to be attached to a horse body and legs, but with no corresponding horse head; in some of these figurines, the rider is playing a musical instrument, usually a tambour-style frame drum.[61] The complete merging of human and horse features was relatively rare, but it did occupy a place on a broader spectrum of horse rider bodies that were more or less blurred and ambiguous in their depiction of bodily details.

In most cases, the specificity of the horse and the posture of the human body meant that the activity of horse riding was the *only* part of the figure's identity that was "fixed and not open to negotiation or alteration," while other parts of the body were left undefined to "invite consideration and imagination."[62] Removing or abstracting the features required for the depiction of a corporeal human being "denaturalizes that body and thus lays it open to reconstructions."[63] The viewer is encouraged, or even required, to reconstruct the missing pieces, but with the flexibility that "many different whole bodies can be built from the same isolated part and no one reconstructed body need be the correct whole."[64] Unspecific bodies and costumes resulted in vagueness about aspects of these figures' identities, including their age, social class, ethnic identity, profession, and rank. Gender, too, was often left indeterminate[65] – and, thus, these figurines form an almost "ungendered" balance to the explorations of personhood that concerned the addition of "extra" sexual characteristics on the intersex figurines just discussed. The user of a horse rider figurine, such as that seen in Figure 5.15, could have selected whichever gender he or she preferred for the figurine – or, perhaps the user even changed the gender selection based on the activity in which the figurine was being used or the context in which it was displayed.[66] In other instances, the user might have preferred a "blank," ungendered or unsexed, figurine. The presence of a sexed body, or a sex identification, could be a hindrance: "sexual regions of the body are highly charged and potentially disruptive in character,"[67] thus a non-sexed body could be less contested and allow for other identities to be explored without having sexual or gendered implications.

The activity of horse riding might have been a particularly important subject for the people of Hellenistic Babylonia to negotiate without the burden of simultaneously engaging with issues of sex and gender. As already discussed in Chapter 2, many of the horse rider figurines – including those with more detailed bodies – were usually given unspecific or multiethnic costuming so as to reflect the diversity of the Seleucid and Parthian armies, as well as to avoid giving militaristic associations to cultural and ethnic differences. There is no reason, however, to assume that horse riding was restricted to the military; elites and others able to afford horses likely rode. Within this context, the depiction of women on horseback might have been a challenging point of negotiation. Some Hellenistic Babylonian figurines depict women in litters or riding sidesaddle on horses, in what was likely an overtly gendered pose.[68] That figurine motif originated in the Achaemenid period; however, such postures would also have been at home among a Greek audience, echoing Classical and earlier depictions of women riding animals, such as Europa abducted by Zeus disguised as a bull.[69]

In contrast, women riding horses in active, astride postures were typically associated with Amazons (often dressed as, and used as proxies for, other types of "barbarians") in Classical Greek art. However, such value judgments about women as astride horse riders were likely unpalatable even to the Macedonians, among whom many elite women were active riders and warriors, as demonstrated by their grave goods.[70] Some Hellenistic queens may have fought on horseback in battle, riding in an astride position.[71] Women in the Near East were also horse riders, especially in the nomadic or seminomadic groups of the Black Sea region, Caucasus steppes, Central Asia, and Iran.[72] Several of these regions were part of the Seleucid and/or Parthian Empires; others were connected to Babylonia via trade, particularly early versions of the Silk Road. At one such Silk Road trade center, Begram (ancient Alexandria-of-the-Caucasus, in modern Afghanistan), an ivory carving of a seminude woman riding astride a mythological creature was found in the same room as Hellenistic-style statuettes of Herakles-Serapis, Eros, and Harpocrates.[73]

Within this diverse landscape of possibilities for women as horse riders, assigning a gendered status to all Hellenistic Babylonian horse-rider figurines would have been laden with potential pitfalls. A choice to show these astride riders as women would have involved wading into cultural preferences, some of which were very ideologically charged, while specifying male gender would have closed off the possibility of female riders entirely. The abstraction and vagueness already inherent in the creation of miniature objects allowed for another, seemingly more satisfactory choice: to make the body ambiguous, and thus concentrate attention on the act of horse riding while allowing the gender of the rider to be determined by the imagination of the user or, perhaps, be left entirely unconsidered and unspecified.

To return to this section's broader discussion: regardless of whether a figurine intensified focus on sex and gender by depicting aspects of multiple body morphologies, or eliminated gender markers altogether, all such figurines experimented in some way with the presentation of the anatomical features of a human body. Thus they all may have been a way to publicly "think through" what it meant to be a human member of society, using nonthreatening, tactile, and engaging miniatures as proxies. Interestingly, these proxies do not directly refer to cultural difference, especially the differences between Greeks and Babylonians, and the pressing question of how people from such diverse backgrounds could be integrated into one community as participants, rather than outsiders. Instead of tackling that problem head-on – by, for instance, depicting a nude female displaying her breasts in the lyre-playing guise of Apollo – the figurines discussed here were more sideways negotiations of difference that substituted gender, species, age, or other bodily differences in place of more high-stakes cultural differences.

In so doing, these figurines were hardly "others" at all, but rather fit securely and centrally within broader Hellenistic Babylonian figurine trends. The bodies of women, as well as the bodies of supernatural children, were also used as landscapes of social experimentation. Intersexed and hermaphroditic bodies might have been seen as similarly ideal locales on which to test new ideas because such bodies were conceptually relevant to members of both Greek and Babylonian cultures: reflecting Hellenistic *koine* explorations of the

"Hermaphrodite" and the boundaries between genders, as well as Babylonian traditions that accepted gendered identities beyond male and female. As a result, not just gendered bodies but also the idea of gender itself might have been an acceptable topic for people of both cultures to test the boundaries of humanness in the post-Alexander world. The existence of this dialogue across several Hellenistic Babylonian communities indicates a Babylonian reception of – as well as a strong Babylonian influence on – the messages these figurines were conveying and the negotiations which they embodied.

Dwarfism, Disability, and the "Grotesque" Body

Yet, how do we know that Hellenistic Babylonian figurines depicting marginalized or atypical bodies were engaged in serious social commentary, rather than being used strictly for amusement? A useful comparison is presented by the so-called grotesque figurines from the broader Hellenistic *koine* tradition. These figurines, often considered a part of the Hellenistic Rococo style and linked with a limited corpus of life-size statues,[74] are characterized by an extreme exaggeration of bodily difference, coupled with contorted poses and distorted facial expressions.[75] Particularly popular in the Hellenistic figurine traditions of Greece, Asia Minor, and Alexandria,[76] these figurines have often been linked to characters in the Hellenistic New Comedy.[77] Their distorted bodies, enlarged facial features, and contorted poses may have been intended to amuse, evoking emotionally charged laughter that was perhaps more about fear, shame, contempt, and a desire to distance and distinguish oneself from a nonideal body, rather than primarily about pleasure.[78] Apotropaic powers, as well as use as "good luck charms,"[79] are also possible interpretations of this genre; indeed, such functions could have been intermingled in the same object and by the same users.[80]

Such interpretations of the Hellenistic "grotesque" tradition likely have some resonance with the ancient reality. However, it is also important to note that the modern label of "grotesque" is applied to a wide variety of Hellenistic *koine* figurines that depicted bodies with deformities, disabilities, or other nonideal features. As other scholars have recently pointed out, the term "grotesque" elides important physiological and experiential differences between bodies.[81] The somatic effects of temporary conditions such as drunkenness, hard work, or extreme hunger are often grouped with figurines that depict permanent conditions. Similarly, catalogues of figurines often lump together objects that depict pathologies with those figurines that show physical symptoms of sustained manual labor and old age – in other words, the impacts of social conditions and time on otherwise "normal" bodies. The effects of illness are usually not carefully separated from the effects of trauma, nor from genetic conditions and birth defects, when creating the category of the "grotesque."[82]

It is fair to question whether ancient audiences would have regarded these figurines in the same way that scholars categorize them. Certainly, diagnoses of disability in the Hellenistic period would not have had the comprehension of genetics, physiology, and disease upon which modern medical practitioners rely. Nevertheless, the available evidence – from philosophical, medicinal, religious, and legal perspectives – strongly indicates that multivalent ways of thinking about disabled or atypical bodies existed in the ancient world.[83] This complexity was likely paralleled in the visual culture: some of the "grotesque" figurines of the Hellenistic *koine* seem to be generalized caricatures, whereas others show a medical-like attention to the details of specific pathological conditions.[84] It is therefore possible that our ways of thinking about the so-called grotesque figurines of the Hellenistic *koine*, particularly in grouping all such miniature bodies together into a single category, may be shortchanging the sophisticated ways in which the people of the ancient world thought about bodily difference.

Perhaps the best illustration of this complexity comes from Hellenistic Babylonia itself. As in the rest of the Hellenistic Near East, Hellenistic Babylonia had relatively few "grotesque" figurines in its corpora. Completely absent from Uruk and Nippur (as far as is known), most examples come from Seleucia-on-the-Tigris, with a few also discovered at Babylon. This geographic distribution is not, in itself, remarkable; Seleucia-on-the-Tigris, as a new Greek foundation, and Babylon, as a site of significant Greek-style building activity, both tended toward greater engagement with Hellenistic *koine* figurine motifs. But what is particularly distinctive about the use of the "grotesque" at Seleucia-on-the-Tigris and Babylon is the selective manner in which this genre was deployed. The vast majority of the body types found in the Hellenistic *koine* "grotesque" tradition are completely absent in Babylonia. These lacunae include an absence of the depictions of old age, drunkenness, manual labor, contorted bodily poses, emaciation, exaggerations of ethnic differences, skeletal deformities (other than bow-leggedness associated with dwarfism), and most facial deformities – all of these seem to have been completely unpopular among the communities of Hellenistic Babylonia. Similarly absent were the detailed studies of particular pathologies, which elsewhere in the Hellenistic world can be so specific as to allow for modern medical diagnoses. Perhaps four or five figurines showing mouth deformities, depicted as enlarged lips with a hole pierced through the partially open mouth, are known from Seleucia-on-the-Tigris.[85] But the vast range of bodily exaggerations, deformations, and manipulations that are seen in figurines elsewhere in the Hellenistic *koine* seem to have had no place in the Babylonian visual landscape.

Instead, the only type of "grotesque" body to have any significant role in the Hellenistic Babylonian figurine tradition was the figure of the dwarf. Scholars have recently critiqued whether figurines exhibiting bodily features of

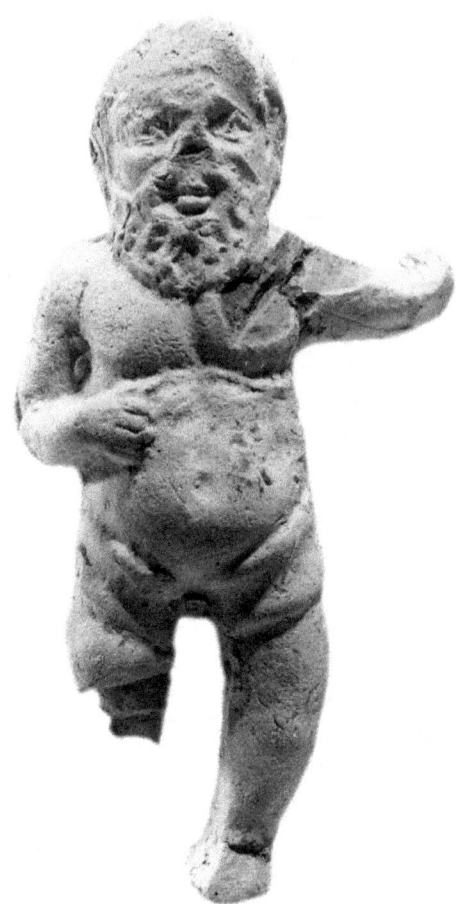

5.16. Standing dwarf figurine, terracotta, Seleucia-on-the-Tigris. Height 10.6 cm. Turin Excavations at Seleucia (S 9,651)
Photograph courtesy of Roberta Menegazzi.

dwarfism should be grouped with other "grotesques," as dwarfism seems not, in itself, to have been considered a "disability" in the Hellenistic world.[86] Such individuals could be fully functioning members of society, participating in community and economic life with few, if any, necessary accommodations. It is therefore possible that figurines depicting them were simply representing the full spectrum of lived personhood in the community – in much the same way that figurines of children suddenly became popular in the Hellenistic period. Many of the Hellenistic Babylonian figurines support such an assertion; examples such as that seen in Figure 5.16 show no traces of somatic exaggeration and can be distinguished as "dwarves" only by the difference between their proportions and those of a typical depiction of an adult man or child. It seems somewhat disingenuous to label such a figurine "grotesque" and suspect its users of delighting in mocking its alterity. While scholars must always be wary of ascribing our modern sensibilities and compassion to ancient audiences, in this case, the material itself gives no hint that this figure was considered with anything other than a frank and straightforward openness to bodily variation.

More exaggerated bodily forms are shown in other Hellenistic Babylonian figurines portraying dwarfism. These include the depiction of dwarves with extreme bow-leggedness, exaggerated satyr-like facial features (including snub nose, contracted brow, and balding head), and/or enlarged male genitalia (including some extremely priapic figures[87]). Such figures more closely approach ancient Greek categories of disability. Figurines with these features were not only used as freestanding objects,[88] but also as puppets. As discussed in Chapter 2, such miniature performers would have permitted their users to manipulate their nonideal bodies, which were forced to perform on command according to the whim of the user, who was allowed to distance himself or herself by taking on the powerful role of both theater director and audience member. Some of the ideas of laughter and derision usually used to describe the Hellenistic *koine* "grotesque" tradition may indeed have applied to such objects.

However, the fact that bodies with dwarfism were almost uniquely chosen for this role in Hellenistic Babylonia, out of all the myriad possibilities offered by the Hellenistic *koine* "grotesque" genre, also suggests that these figurines are evidence of something slightly different than a desire for lowbrow humor.[89] The dwarf body proportions, the squatting posture created by bow legs, and the contorted facial features were also all shared in common with another figurine tradition: that of the Egyptian dwarf-god Bes.[90] A protective deity, Bes was associated most commonly with children and women in childbirth, although he could also safeguard individuals in other dangerous or liminal states, such as sleep, warfare, dying, or under the influence of music or alcohol.[91] Bes was particularly beloved in the Hellenistic world[92] – however, his cult had already spread to Babylonia prior to this era, and was commonly practiced during the Achaemenid period.[93] In his role as protector, Bes's bodily differences were seen less as amusing disabilities and more as strengths, guarding his devotees through their apotropaic power. Such a functionality was at home within Mesopotamian concepts of protection, which had formerly relied on depictions of Humbaba or Pazuzu, distinctively monstrous creatures who were nevertheless fearsome allies capable of warding off evil, such as the baby-snatching Lamaštu/Lilitu.[94] Bes's iconography may be seen in many of these Hellenistic Babylonian dwarf figurines; for instance, the headdress worn by the dwarf figure seen in Figure 5.17 is similar to Bes's feathered crown.[95] An association with this god might explain this figurine's other characteristics as well, such as his wrinkled face, or the extreme bow-legged posture seen on other examples.

Of course, other, non-dwarf figurines of the Hellenistic *koine* "grotesque" genre might also have had apotropaic functions. However, such figurines did

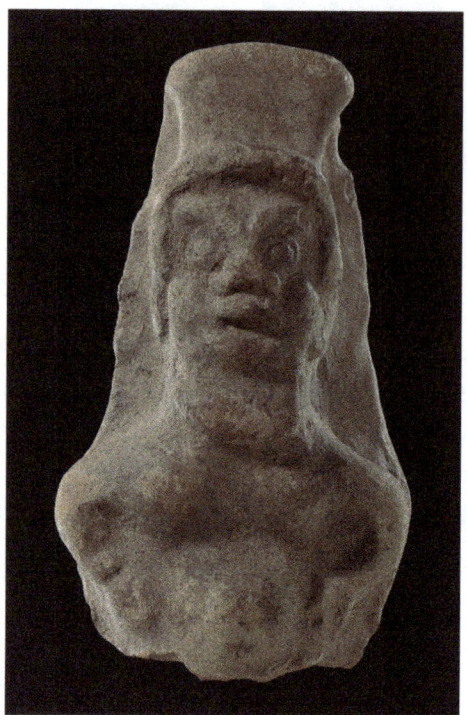

5.17. Dwarf figurine wearing flared headdress, terracotta, Babylon. Height 9 cm. Vorderasiatisches Museum Berlin (VA Bab 3534)
Photograph © Staatliche Museen zu Berlin-Vorderasiatisches Museum, Foto: Olaf M. Teßmer.

not as obviously overlap with a motif and a deity that was already widely accepted in Babylonia. Since the worship of Bes was established in Babylonia prior to the Hellenistic period, it seems logical that the communities of Hellenistic Babylonia might have been willing to accept "updates" to the iconography. From modern scholarly perspectives, such figurines seem reflective of *koine* motifs and styles; yet, in all likelihood, they would not have been seen as particularly "Greek" to the Babylonian people,[96] for whom Bes was already a somewhat "local" god.

This is not to say that every Hellenistic Babylonian figurine depicting a body with dwarfism was used as a depiction of Bes. Many figurines do not explicitly bear Bes iconography; others, such as the puppets, seem a somewhat unlikely use for the body of a god (although it is certainly possible that enlivening the god's movements might have been thought to give him greater protective power). However, what these figurines, whether Bes or not, do indicate about Hellenistic Babylonia is that these communities were generally uninterested in experimentations with "otherness" which concluded that marginalized bodies were, in fact, outside the boundaries of humanness. The strong linkage of dwarf bodies with a powerful and protective god suggests a recognition of the value of such individuals, who could play an important social role. Mocking and excluding, on the other hand, does not seem to have been a primary goal – thus, figurines of the Hellenistic *koine* "grotesque" tradition which had ridicule as their major aim were not appealing in Babylonia.

This data seems to paint a rosy picture. However, we should not assume that Hellenistic Babylonians were more enlightened and humanitarian than their Hellenistic peers – or, if they were, that such noble impulses were motivated by disinterested kindness alone. Rather, as with so many features of the Hellenistic Babylonian figurine tradition, I propose that this aversion to the mockery that was entailed in the Hellenistic *koine* "grotesque" genre may have been spurred more by self-interest. Mesopotamian texts preserve a long history of concern with disability and deformity, both as medical conditions and as negative omens.[97] Careful recording of a variety of conditions was accompanied by judgments about the likelihood of curing these ailments, as well as the danger that the afflicted individuals posed to the community and social order due to their role as portents of ill futures. Possible steps could be taken to quell the danger, including rare cases in which extreme "remedies," such as burying alive or throwing in a river, were used to kill infants born with particular unusual symptoms.[98] What many of these solutions had in common was that not only was the life within the offending body extinguished, but the body itself was removed from the sight and presence of the community. Disabled infants in the Greek world could also be killed or exposed,[99] and so it was not the action per se but its motivation which may have differed in a Babylonian context. To what degree such perspectives and concerns were still operational in Hellenistic Babylonia is not clear; however, ritual and religious texts such as these continued to be copied and read, if only by a few specialists, well into the Hellenistic period.

Babylonians raised in this tradition might have been particularly loathed to depict deformed or disabled bodies in miniature.[100] Any potential apotropaic benefit of such imagery could have been accomplished in a more familiar form by figurines reflective of the Bes motif, while the idea of protection-via-laughter might not have held as much sway in Babylonian communities.[101] Instead, such bodies might have been seen as more overtly dangerous and in need of removal from the community, not replication in handheld form to be treated as a joke. Subtle differences in the way that Greek and Babylonian communities regarded the origins of disability and deformity may explain this divergent perspective: whereas the common Greek perspective considered such impairments to be punishments, usually for a fault of the individual or their family,[102] the Babylonian omens imply that the birth of such individuals could be an indictment of broader problems in society, including its political structure or rule.[103] It would be difficult to laugh if one was worried about dangerous consequences; it would be doubly so if one was worried that one's own community or king was at fault.

In addition to the potential for existential threat posed by some disabled bodies, a less potent – but perhaps no less pressing – concern with community membership might also have discouraged the adoption of Hellenistic *koine* "grotesque" forms. Ridicule of alterity and physical difference might have had significant social consequences in tremendously diverse communities such as those of Hellenistic Babylonia – and throughout the Hellenistic Near East generally, where "grotesque" figurines were similarly unpopular. As this volume has shown, most of the figurines of Hellenistic Babylonia seem to have been well-liked precisely because they smoothed over cultural and other differences, not highlighted them. Within such a delicate social balance, ostracizing one group based on their somatic differences might have opened up the possibility of ostracizing others. This seems not to have been an outcome worth risking, especially not with humor as the primary reward. The careful depiction of bodies with dwarfism evinces a level of respect for the social participation and usefulness of the individuals who inhabited such bodies. This parallels the frank and unamused depiction of intersexed and intergendered bodies discussed earlier in this chapter. These choices made in how to display "different" bodies in miniature had the potential to expand the visual world (and through it, the social world) of Hellenistic Babylonia to accommodate all kinds of human differences – gendered, somatic, and otherwise.

HYBRIDITY WITHIN THE LOCAL

This section concludes the figurine case studies of this chapter, and of this volume, with a final exploration of the "global" and the "local," this time focused specifically on the "local." As in the previous sections of this chapter, these figurines will show that in Hellenistic Babylonia there was no clear and consistent opposition between these concepts. In the deity figurines related to trends of the Hellenistic *koine*, almost every figurine that seems superficially to have been an ambassador for pan-Hellenistic traditions also insistently reflected and responded to local concerns. Figurines of potentially marginalized bodies, such as intersex or dwarf figurines, engaged with both *koine* and local traditions in order to work through issues of "otherness." These objects expressed and negotiated a preoccupation with the boundaries of humanity that conceived of outsider status as something embodied rather than geographical or cultural – but explored those issues in such a way that the "othered" bodies were ultimately incorporated, rather than ostracized. In this last section of the chapter, I demonstrate that the idea of the "local" is, itself, a construct.

Certainly, some figurine ideas and motifs were more deeply embedded in Mesopotamian history than others, and emerged from (or at least seem to have been at home within) that tradition. How those Mesopotamian traditions intersected with new Greek ideas and forms was expressed in general trends within the figurines of Hellenistic Babylonia, and many of those trends have been explored in this volume. However, in this last case study of the book, I want to push in the opposite direction: rather than exploring commonalities within the figurine practice of Hellenistic Babylonia as a whole, I wish to point out just how specialized and individualized those practices could be. Each city and community – indeed, if our archaeological evidence were granular enough, I suspect each neighborhood and household – had its own traditions, preferences, and ideas about figurines. There were many kinds of "local" simultaneously operational in Hellenistic Babylonia. As a result, cross-cultural hybridity – often taken to be one "thing," one process of interaction between one defined pair of cultural groups (in this case Greeks and Babylonians) – differed even between the communities of Hellenistic Babylonia.

In this last example, my analysis focuses on how hybridity could be created on a local stage, and how the particular concerns that hybridity expressed were not always exclusively cultural in nature (i.e. concerning the acceptance or rejection of Greekness, per se). I could have selected any number of case studies through which to explore this idea; indeed most of the figurine groups in this book would fit the bill. The case study I chose concerns reclining female figurines and their absence from Hellenistic Nippur.

The Reclining Female Figurines (Not) from Hellenistic Nippur

Despite the fact that two scholarly publications purport to document the existence of reclining female figurines at Hellenistic Nippur, I have recently demonstrated that those provenience attributions were made in error.[104] There are no securely attributed reclining female figurines from Hellenistic Nippur, despite the utilization of this figurine motif and form at Babylon, Seleucia-on-the-Tigris, and Uruk. In general, the Hellenistic figurine corpus from Nippur is similar to that of these other three Babylonian cities, sharing many motifs and manufacturing techniques. Many of these Nippur figurines reflected Greek traditions and influence, as was seen in the Nippur figurines depicting couples discussed in Chapter 3 and pictured as Figures 3.5 and 3.7. Others engaged more heavily with Near Eastern traditions, such as the large numbers of musician figurines, particularly women playing tambour-style drums, found at Nippur (see Figure 3.13). Based on this substantive overlap of the Hellenistic terracotta figurine corpus of Nippur with that of the other major Babylonian cities, the excavators at Nippur could reasonably have expected to discover reclining female figurines in Hellenistic era contexts at their site – and yet they seem not to have made such a discovery, a fact which led to the purchasing of reclining figurines from other Babylonian sites, as documented in detail in my earlier work.[105]

The reclining female figurines found at other sites, such as the figurine from Uruk seen in Figure 5.18, generally depict a female figure reclining on her left side, with her upper body propped upright by the left arm. The right arm, which drapes against the right side of the body, is always modeled with the torso. In terracotta examples like this one, the whole figurine body, including legs and head, was created as one piece using a standard double mold. In stone examples, the head was sometimes carved and added separately, but the rest of the body, legs, and the right arm were carved together. The fusing of the right arm to the side of the body on which it rests sometimes presented a striking visual contrast with the left arm. Some reclining figurines were made with the left arm held closely to the body and modeled as one with the rest of the object (see, for instance, Figure 5.19). In their left hands, such figurines often held a banqueting cup. Other figurines, as seen in Figure 5.18, featured a separately made lower left arm that was joined to the body at or just above the elbow. Such arms extended outward toward the viewer, and probably held a banqueting cup like their compatriots without separately added arms.[106] Owing to the fragility and precariousness of this join location, the joined lower left arms of such figurines are generally not preserved with the bodies. Yet separately made arms in this posture have been excavated, supporting the plausibility of such reconstructions.[107]

The absence of reclining female figurines with secure Nippur provenience suggests the lack (or at least the unpopularity) of this particular product of Greek-Babylonian cross-cultural hybridity within the Nippur community. Such reclining female figurines drew upon Greek imagery of symposion participants[108] (including in their frequent depictions of naked or semiclothed figures), have the sensitive naturalism characteristic of Greek artistic styles, and

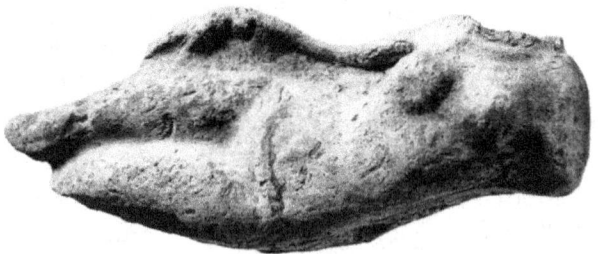

5.18. Nude reclining female figurine, terracotta, Uruk. Length: 13.8 cm. Baghdad (W 15044) Photograph reprinted from Ziegler 1962: Abb. 400, with permission of Gebrueder Mann Verlag.

HYBRIDITY WITHIN THE LOCAL 239

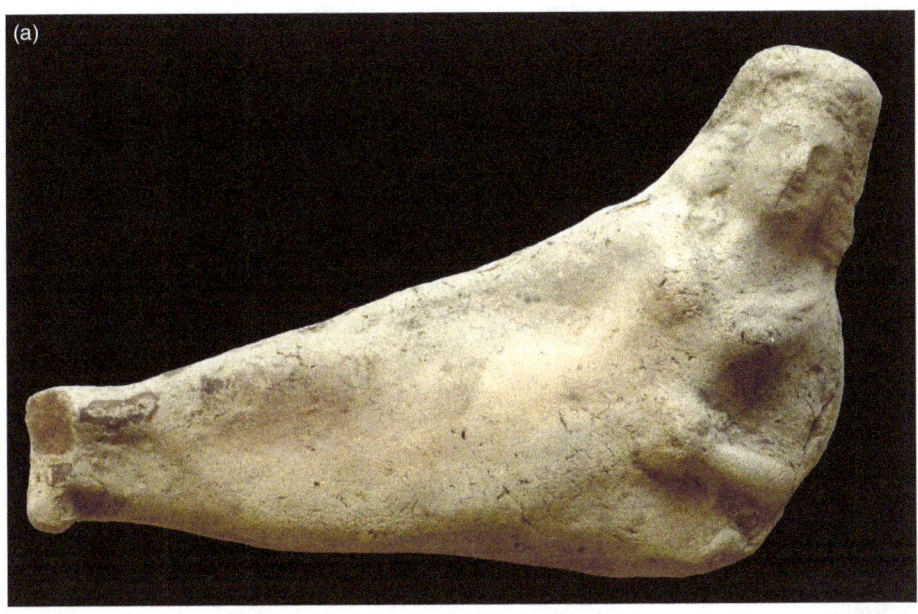

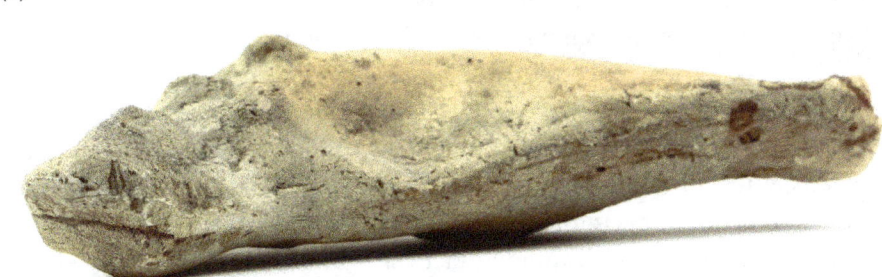

5.19a and b. Front and top of reclining female figurine, terracotta, probably from Babylon. Length: 13.5 cm. University of Pennsylvania Museum of Archaeology and Anthropology (B 9122)
Photographs courtesy of the University of Pennsylvania Museum.

were often made in the Greek double-mold technique. However, most of these figurines transformed the reclining banqueter from male (as would be expected in the Greek figurine tradition[109]) to female, and present this female figure with a strongly frontal body posture and gaze. Female participants in feasting and revelry scenes were not unknown in pre-Hellenistic Greek art; examples include Archaic and Classical Greek depictions of *hetairai* at symposia[110] and wives sitting or reclining near their banqueting husbands' legs or feet.[111] Hellenistic figurines from the Greek site of Myrina portray the woman in closer proximity to her husband, often affectionately wrapping her arm around him; yet the roles of the two figures are still clearly differentiated, with the husband reclining while the woman is sitting.[112] The reclining figurines from Hellenistic Babylonia differ significantly from these Greek precedents in that the female figure replaces, rather than adjoins, a male figure.[113] These solitary reclining female bodies are more closely modeled on Greek imagery of a *male* banqueting participant occupying his own couch – suggesting that the reclining woman seen in the Hellenistic Babylonian figurines is a banquet participant in her own right, entitled to her own "seat at the table."[114] The strong preference for female bodies in these reclining figurines might have been a concession to Babylonian cultural norms, which were more comfortable with depicting naked females than naked males.[115] Yet, an aversion to male nudity cannot completely explain the rarity of male reclining figurines in Hellenistic Babylonia, since many of the female reclining figurines are depicted either partially or fully clothed.[116]

Depictions of female banqueters reclining alone cannot be interpreted as straightforward representations of the male-dominated Greek symposion[117] – at least, not as we understand its practice in the Classical period on the Greek mainland. But I suggest that these figurines could have served as negotiated, Babylonian-sensitive enticements into broader Greek social practices of banqueting. Hellenistic *koine* ceramic vessels spread across the Near East in the wake of Alexander, becoming one of the Hellenistic world's most widely shared forms of material culture.[118] The Greek vessels most consistently adopted and imitated in Babylonia by local potters were fine serving wares used for presenting and eating, rather than preparing or cooking.[119] This preference for Greek tableware, which would have been conspicuously visible[120] especially to visitors and dinner guests, implies that the appearance and performance of Greek dining practices – including a reclining, leisurely banqueting style – may also have been appealing. Reclining female figurines would have reinforced the social status and pleasures of such Greek-style banquets – and suggested the alluring prospect of beautiful female companionship during feasting – by presenting this dining practice within the pleasingly tactile format of the terracotta figurine.

Openness and accessibility to touch are common qualities among the Hellenistic figurines of Babylonia; as has been discussed throughout this volume, these figurines' smooth surfaces, relatively sturdy construction, and handheld size encouraged their users to grasp, handle, and caress many of them. Reclining female figurines were especially likely to encourage such tactile encounters. Some versions of these reclining female figurines included modeled couches or cushions that serve as figurine bases and thus the object can stand alone on a flat surface; yet, most reclining female figurines lack an obvious couch support and cannot stand alone. Nude or partially nude (from the waist or hips upward) reclining female figurines were especially likely to lack a modeled couch and the vertical stability it supplies[121] – thus, in order to be viewed upright and inspected closely,

HYBRIDITY WITHIN THE LOCAL 241

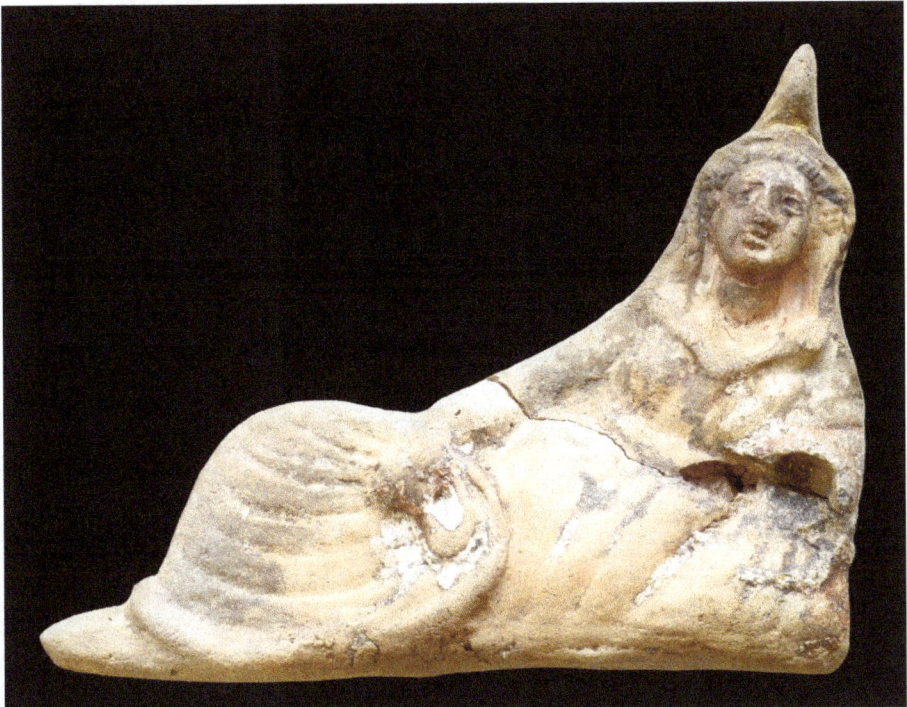

5.20. Reclining female figurine, terracotta, Babylon. Length: 16.2 cm. University of Pennsylvania Museum of Archaeology and Anthropology (B 9121)
Photograph by author, printed courtesy of the University of Pennsylvania Museum.

such figurines needed to be held in the hand. The female figure's nudity or, if clothed, the depiction of tight or revealing clothing added an erotic dimension to tactile interactions. Examples of such revealing clothing can be seen in the figurine pictured in Figure 5.20, with its low V-shaped neckline and suggestive gathering of cloth in the hand placed near the genital region, as well as in the pinched, narrow waist and wide hips seen through the clinging garment of the figurine pictured in Figure 5.19.

The particular materiality of many of these figurines also added to their erotic quality. For instance, to return to a stone figurine discussed in Chapter 1 and pictured in Figure 1.6, we see a reclining, nude female figure. Her pinched waist and wide hips are accentuated by carved lines, painted pink, that indicate sensuous folds of flesh. The spaces underneath her right arm, which rests languidly along the contour of her supine body, have been carved away at her waist and thigh, granting visual (as well as potentially tactile) access to both. Her calves are similarly carved with space between them, providing a sexually suggestive visual entry point to the division between the legs – a focusing of user attention that is compounded by the painted pink lines between the thighs and in the pubic creases. Despite the age and poor preservation of the figurine (for instance, part of the hair and left lower arm are missing), the stone still emits an enticing luster, encouraging the user to manually explore the supple curvatures of breast, waist, and thigh that the carving of the stone and the motif of the reclining nude female figure have made accessible and available. The elaborate painted sandals and beaded necklace emphasize that this figure is not accidentally caught in a state of undress, but rather inhabits a deliberately constructed nudity that anticipates viewership.

This sexualization of the reclining, banqueting body – a formulation which would have been very much at home in Greek ideas of the symposion – may explain why such figurines needed to depict female bodies, rather than male ones, in order to be acceptable in Hellenistic Babylonia.[122] Yet more than just cultural concessions to Babylonian eyes may have been at work here. The lack of vertical stability seen in so many of the Hellenistic Babylonian reclining female figurines is in contrast with many reclining male figurines excavated in mainland Greece,[123] which were often made with supportive bases that enabled them to stand alone. Even though the male body was often presented as nude or partially nude in the figurines from Greece, the inclusion of a firm base meant that such figurines did not solicit the same kinds of tactile interaction – and thus were visually, rather than experientially, sexualized – when compared with what was encouraged by the reclining female figurines of Hellenistic Babylonia. This indicates that the specific kind of tactile sexualization seen in the Hellenistic Babylonian reclining figurines may not have been simply an adoption of Greek symposion tradition, but also a response to Babylonian preferences. Overlap of Greek and Babylonian cultural traditions may also explain the directly frontal (albeit reclining) postures and straightforward gazes of these solitary reclining female figures, which echoed both Greek imagery of male symposiasts and earlier Mesopotamian imagery of assertive, frontal, display-oriented (and possibly erotic) female figures. The Babylonian viewer may also have recognized an invitation to sexual encounter in the female body's solitary resting posture, which drew upon deeply rooted local precedents including, but not limited to, Old Babylonian erotic plaques.[124]

The seduction effect of the Hellenistic Babylonian reclining female figurines might have been enhanced in those examples that had a separately molded left arm that originally extended outward toward the viewer and likely held a banqueting cup. A sizable number of these reclining figurines were equipped with such separately made limbs, the meanings and effects of which were almost certainly complex. Unlike with the mid-limb seams on the athlete and child figurines discussed in Chapter 4, the elbow placement of the arm join on the banqueting figurines is a closer approximation of a living human joint. The illusion of potential movement, rather than frozen immobility, was conveyed as the banqueter extended her cup into the viewer's space. However, these separately made arms were often attached using clumsy affixing techniques, resulting in a bulky and noticeable jointing of the added arm. The arm socket of the figurine seen in Figure 5.20 still bears substantial traces of bitumen in the join and painted plaster surrounding it, both of which would have created a clunky and visually distracting bond between the figurine body and its fragmented appendage. Such a noticeable join counteracted the elbow joint's illusion of corporeal wholeness by intensifying visual interest in the seam, and highlighting its artificiality. Once attention was directed to the attached arm, the viewer was likely to notice that this was the only limb made separately and appended after firing. While the other limbs were modeled seamlessly and elegantly with the body, the extended banqueting arm feels like a disconcerting afterthought that both intrudes outward into the viewer's space and is visually alienated from the body to which it is attached. The fragmented arm thus creates a visual bridge – or alternatively, occupies a visual no man's land – between the object and the viewer.

Both readings seem possible, perhaps simultaneously. The fragmented and rejoined arm, reaching out into the user's space to offer a drinking cup, enthusiastically and overtly makes a statement of inclusion. The tactility and inclusive gestures of such figurines encouraged the user to envision himself or herself as a coparticipant in banqueting, with this festive and assertive female figure as a companion. These figurines reinforced the visual enticement and exotic luxury that Greek ceramic tablewares already provided, yet more explicitly invited inclusive cross-cultural participation in Hellenistic banqueting practices. The illusion of potential movement added to the reclining figurine's affect, powering the thrust of a banqueting invitation into the user's space, and forcing him or her to consider it – even if the invitation was ultimately declined. The highly noticeable, outward-jutting, cumbersome yet seemingly movable, separately made arm makes a strong point that the cross-cultural negotiation which the figurine represents will not be ignored.

However, the more estranged reading of the separately made arm may also have been an important part of how these figurines signified to a Hellenistic Babylonian viewer. The awkwardly bulky join at the elbow could convey the unsettling sense that the solitary fragmented arm was not fully connected either to the figurine body or to the viewer it gestured at but, rather, occupied an alienated middle ground in between the two. This unanchored appendage could also evoke a terror of trauma: the fragmenting of just one limb (rather than all four, as seen in the athletes, or both arms, as seen in the children), as well as the attempt to mimic a living elbow joint, gives less of an impression that the miniature body was artificially made and more of an impression that living flesh has been gruesomely severed and reattached. This visual estrangement of the fragmented arm renders its joint, and its action, more tenuous than the reality of its fragile seam had already made it. What might have been a flirtatious and captivating invitation to dine with a beautiful, leisurely woman takes on a grotesque and uncanny aspect, and is thus distanced from the viewer. Rather than being completely seduced, the user could feel in control of the incitement to participate in Greek banqueting practices. The banqueting arm could be rebuffed, or even rebroken and discarded, with ease[125]; even if the figurine's user did not actually damage the object, the option of doing so was vividly called to the imagination by the mere presence of such a tenuous join. The possibility of such power might have been appealing to the communities that used these figurines. Babylonian users, in particular, might have preferred the idea that engaging with the social customs of the broader Hellenistic world was an optional choice left to individual or community discretion.

There seems to have been some factual basis to this notion that individuals and communities had agency in choosing whether or not to accept such (figurine) invitations to participate in Hellenistic *koine* practices. In choosing not to create or use reclining female figurines, the community of Hellenistic Nippur may have been rejecting not just a miniature motif but also an entire social practice of Greek-Babylonian negotiated feasting traditions. The Hellenistic *koine* ceramic tableware made and used at Seleucia-on-the-Tigris, Babylon, Uruk, and (further afield) at Faïlaka is relatively rare at Nippur.[126] When "Hellenistic" styles did appear in the Hellenistic Nippur ceramic corpus, they usually consisted of Greek motifs added as superficial surface ornament to local Babylonian ceramic forms,[127] rather than substantial alterations reflecting deep engagement with Greek ceramic tradition. A greater use of Hellenistic *koine* ceramics is to be expected at Seleucia-on-the-Tigris and at Babylon. However, the contrast between Uruk and Nippur (both of which are generally considered to have been conservatively Babylonian during the Hellenistic period[128]) is particularly striking: "Greek origin" ceramics make up 24.5 percent of the Seleucid-period ceramic assemblage at Uruk[129] and are recovered "from all the major sanctuaries and residential structures so far excavated,"[130] whereas the numbers of similar ceramics at Nippur are negligible.[131]

The absence of reclining female figurines recovered from excavated contexts at Nippur, when considered in light of that community's parallel lack of a significant use of Hellenistic *koine* ceramics, suggests an almost total rejection by the Hellenistic Nippur community of certain Hellenistic foodways and banqueting practices, as well as a rebuff of the association of female sexuality and nudity with such feasts.[132] Indeed, the entanglement of reclining female figurines with Hellenistic *koine* ceramic types and Greek-inspired banqueting practices, as I have proposed it, may actually explain why reclining female figurines seem to have been unappealing to the people of Hellenistic Nippur – not because of their Greek associations generally, but rather because of their connections with Greek banquets specifically. Indeed, other figurine motifs that were deeply engaged with the Hellenistic *koine*, such as depictions of Aphrodite, Eros, and Herakles, were made and used successfully within the same community. Thus it seems that the people of Nippur were not rejecting "Greek-ness" per se, nor refusing all use of Greek cultural forms. Rather, the Nippur community seems to have been specifically uninterested in engaging in a particular kind of cross-cultural negotiation of the social activity of banqueting, including its attendant foodways, visual spectacles, and social performances.

It is also possible that the lack of reclining female figurines at Hellenistic Nippur may reflect regional differences in funerary tradition. Although the evidence is tenuous and disputed, there are some indications that such reclining female figurines in Hellenistic Babylonia held funerary significance. Robert Koldewey, excavator of Babylon, specifically mentions the grave contexts of several reclining female figurines in alabaster, in contrast to the domestic contexts in which most other figurines were found.[133] Evelyn Klengel-Brandt similarly remarks upon the "special connection" between "figurines of recumbent women" and burial rites in Parthian Babylon[134]; however, her more recent work seems to refute this evaluation.[135] Elizabeth Douglas Van Buren discusses Hellenistic Babylonian reclining female figurines as "reclining on a funeral couch."[136] Wilhelmina Van Ingen asserts that "it is generally agreed that they [i.e. reclining female figurines] sometimes have a funerary significance, for many have been found in graves"; yet, she goes on to note that most such figurines at Seleucia-on-the-Tigris were found in domestic contexts.[137] Antonio Invernizzi mentions reclining female figurines found associated with tombs at Seleucia-on-the-Tigris and Uruk.[138]

Roberta Menegazzi offers some of the most concrete evidence for a correlation between reclining female terracotta figurines and funerary contexts: "10 of the 41 figurines found in burials [at Seleucia-on-the-Tigris] represent reclining women," a high percentage (roughly 25 percent) which she argues is "of great significance in determining the function and meaning of reclining figurines."[139] However, the significance of this finding is somewhat lessened by the overall rarity of figurines found in tombs at Seleucia-on-the-Tigris (forty-one figurines out of a total of nearly 11,000 figurines excavated at the site[140]), as well as the very small proportion (approximately 1.4 percent) of the total number of reclining female figurines that were found in graves (ten figurines out of a total of 717 whole or partial reclining female figurines excavated at the site[141]). With such a limited number of Seleucia-on-the-Tigris's reclining female figurines being deposited in tombs, it seems likely that other, nonfunerary functions and meanings for these figurines also existed.

It is not my purpose here to resolve the issue of whether or not reclining female figurines had a particular connection with Hellenistic funerary practice in Babylonia – or, if they did, if such funerary associations were consistent across all the cities of Babylonia where such figurines were used.[142] Terracotta figurines of any form or motif are quite rare in such funerary contexts (even at Seleucia-on-the-Tigris) and, even for those figurines that are found with graves, it can be difficult to distinguish figurines that were deliberately placed in tombs from those belonging to the domestic spaces into which the tombs were usually dug. On the other hand, figurines (indeed, any objects) can have funerary, mourning, and commemorative meanings without physical placement in a tomb. With both of these possibilities in mind, I therefore offer the limited observation that if reclining female figurines in Hellenistic Babylonia did indeed have funerary functions or meanings, the absence of such figurines at Nippur points to an additional (and, indeed, an important) kind of regional difference between the community of that city and those of the neighboring urban centers. This funerary difference (if it existed) may have been intricately entangled with the banqueting differences between Nippur and its neighbors, as discussed above, especially given the widespread and longstanding history of a close association between banqueting practices (as well as banqueting imagery) and afterlife belief across the ancient Mediterranean and Near East.[143] The absence of reclining female figurines at Nippur may thus provide evidence of this Hellenistic period community's complete rejection of negotiated, Greek-inspired banqueting practices – both in this life and the next.

While perhaps surprising, such selective hybridities and regional differences in cross-cultural interaction are very common in the negotiated middle ground of multicultural contact and social change.[144] Interactions between cultural groups do not proceed along identical lines in every community, and the material culture and social practices produced as a result of such exchanges can take disparate forms.[145] A possible explanation for this particular situation of Nippur and its lack of reclining female figurines may be found in the limited evidence for Seleucid-period activity at Nippur, in contrast to more extensive habitation of the site during the Parthian period.[146] Reclining female figurines were made and used at other Babylonian cities during both the Seleucid and Parthian periods – thus, reduced Seleucid-period occupation at Nippur would not necessarily preclude their use. However, the specific connection of these figurines with Hellenistic *koine* ceramics and Greek banqueting practices may indicate that the cross-cultural negotiations with which they were involved were taking place soon after Alexander's conquests. Such negotiations may not have had a place at Nippur and, without a local, Seleucid-period precedent, may have been unappealing and unnecessary to Nippur's Parthian-period community.

It is this richly textured and individualized fabric of cultural identity and social life in Hellenistic Babylonia that over-reliance on terms like "hybridity" and "the local" risks oversimplifying and obscuring. Not only were there many different "hybridities" and many different forms of "local," but each of these was created with more than simply generic cultural concerns in mind. As this discussion, and almost every example in this book, has demonstrated, Hellenistic Babylonian figurines (and the cross-cultural interactions which they embodied) reflected a variety of specific, complex community concerns, played out at miniature scale.

CONCLUSION: LIFE IN MINIATURE

THIS VOLUME HAS SHOWN THAT FIGURINES HAVE AN IMMENSE AND particular power to inform upon the social imaginary of Hellenistic Babylonia. The vast numbers of figurines indicate that these objects experienced an enormous popularity, circulating throughout and penetrating the social landscape. The rich variety of figurines attests to their experimental and responsive nature. They do not represent a stagnant tradition unthinkingly copied, but rather formed an expressive toolkit for exploring, representing, and influencing the world around them. In the techniques used to create them, the kinds of bodies and identities that were depicted, and the choices of style and motif that determined their appearance and tactility, these figurines gave material form to the social conversations of which they were a part. Reflective of those community dialogues, the figurines also shaped their future trajectories.

The five chapters of this volume probed and explored that particular power of figurines to inform on social negotiations and identities as lived, rather than as simply idealized, in the cross-cultural communities of Hellenistic Babylonia. Common throughout this corpus was a selective engagement with Greek and Hellenistic *koine* motifs and ideas, and a particular acceptance of ideas that fit well within Babylonian tradition. It is important to note that the same process also operated, to some degree, in reverse, with Mesopotamian figurine forms and styles also being adapted to accommodate Greek modes of vision – or in some cases becoming diminished in popularity or even falling out of use entirely. Overall, those choices indicate that Hellenistic Babylonian society was host to extensive and intensive layers of negotiation, many of which were designed to create social cohesion – or, at least, to reduce social tension – between cultural groups, as well as perhaps between other groupings of people in this highly diverse community. Indeed, for all that scholarship focuses intensively on cultural tradition, and the residue of cultural contact in the object world, Hellenistic Babylonian people might not always have had issues of cultural identity foremost in their minds when making choices about the figurines they preferred to manufacture and use.

This rich complexity of the Hellenistic Babylonian figurine tradition reveals – and, indeed, was made possible by – the fact that "miniaturization" is not just one quality, one state of object being[1]. Just as there were many different ways that cross-cultural encounters could be given "hybrid" material form, so too there were different kinds of "miniatures," with a variety of affects, engagements, and social possibilities. One way of accessing these different intensities and valences of miniaturization is by recognizing that the intimacy that figurines seem to create with the human body is, in the end, an illusion. Describing all figurines as "intimate" based solely on their size flattens the corpus and reduces the usefulness of miniaturization as a descriptor or an analytical tool. This book used the concept of intimacy illusions to explore the different affective powers of figurines. Some of the figurines discussed, particularly in the earlier chapters, could be quite persuasive in the intimacy that they offered: allowing nearly full access to the figurine body, permitting the user to perform with the figurine in cooperation, parallelism, and play, only to curtail their accessibility in specific ways. Other figurines placed firm and immediately obvious stops on potential intimacy through features of distancing, such as the employment of plinth bases, sturdy vertical construction, inaccessible poses, or unwelcoming motifs.

These differences in how the miniature could be constructed and in how miniaturization, as a quality, was deployed into the object landscape, were agentive. They enforced social norms, enabled certain kinds of cross-cultural negotiations, and revealed the greater acceptability of some bodies, identities, and desires in preference to others. "Intimacy" was not something given freely or equally by each figurine – it was a seductive possibility and a complex tool, used to cultivate user interest, engagement, and "buy in" to the version of the social world that the figurines represented. We must treat miniaturization as complex and multivalent, seeing its expression differently in a range of different objects. Only then will we begin to recognize that miniature objects acted in a wide variety of ways on the human bodies they encountered and in the social milieu in which they operated. "Life in miniature" was vast indeed.

NOTES

INTRODUCTION

1. Concise overviews of these cities, along with many other sites in the Hellenistic Near East, can be found in Cohen 2013.
2. Many early excavators of Babylonian sites were primarily concerned with reaching stratigraphic levels from earlier periods of Mesopotamian history, as well as with finding larger-scale statues or cuneiform tablets, rather than figurines. For full discussion and examples, see Van Buren 1930, xxxvii–xli.
3. Several publications, ranging in date from the 1930s to 2014, have catalogued figurines from the different Hellenistic Babylonian sites; these catalogues use different typologies and classification systems, and vary in terms of how they "count" individual figurine exemplars. Some of the Hellenistic Babylonian figurines surviving in American and European museums have never been published.
4. The idea that Babylon was abandoned, or even forcibly depopulated in an effort to transfer inhabitants to Seleucia-on-the-Tigris, has been previously held by several scholars. This view has been amended through the work of Van der Spek (1993) on Seleucid-era astronomical diaries. For a full discussion of this scholarly confusion, as well as the evidence for the continued occupation of Babylon, see Sherwin-White 1987. For excavations of the Merkes neighborhood, including evidence of Greek inhabitants, see Reuther 1926; Wetzel, Schmidt, and Mallwitz 1957, 25, 51–57.
5. See Koldewey 1918; 1925; 1931–1932; Wetzel and Weissbach 1938; Schmidt 1941; Wetzel, Schmidt, and Mallwitz 1957; Bergamini 1988; Downey 1988; George 1992; Schmidt 2002; Kose 2004. For the interconnected Seleucid royal patronage of the major temples at Babylon and Borsippa, see Stevens 2014.
6. Downey 1988, 14.
7. Kirk 1935. See also discussion in Chapter 4 of this volume.
8. As argued by Ristvet 2014; 2015. See also McEwan 1981 and Linssen 2004 for discussion of Hellenistic-era cult practice in Babylon. A broader overview of institutions, history, and socioeconomic life in Babylon can be found in Boiy 2004.
9. Hadley 1978.
10. Invernizzi 1994.
11. Ponzi 1970–1971; Hopkins 1972; Downey 1988; Valtz 1988; Invernizzi 1993; Messina 2010.
12. Cohen 2013, 160.
13. See extensive discussion, plans, and photographs in Messina 2010.
14. As argued by Ristvet 2014, 260.
15. For a chart recording the use of different techniques across Hellenistic Babylonia, see Menegazzi 2014, 47.
16. Jordan 1928; Falkenstein 1941; Lenzen 1956; 1959; Schmid 1960; Schmidt 1970; 1972; Funck 1984; Finkbeiner 1987; 1993; Kose 1998.
17. For discussion of cultic and religious changes at Uruk during the Hellenistic period, see Krul 2018.
18. Falkenstein 1941, 52; Petrie 2002, 89.
19. Pedde 1993, 205–215.
20. Doty 1978, 1988; Langin-Hooper and Pearce 2014.
21. Wallenfels 1994a; 2016; Westh-Hansen 2011. For Seleucia-on-the-Tigris, see McDowell 1935b.
22. Valtz 1991; Petrie 2002; Westh-Hansen 2011.
23. Keall 1975; Downey 1988, 144–147; Van der Spek 1992; although note that it is difficult to

precisely distinguish Seleucid-period habitation at Nippur, due to its ceramic similarity with the Achaemenid period (see Gibson 1975; Hannestad 1983, 101).
24. McCown and Haines 1967; Keall 1975.
25. See, for instance, Legrain 1930, Plates 12–13; Fowlkes-Childs and Seymour 2019, 246–247.
26. The term *koine* is used by scholars to refer to the broadly shared traditions utilized throughout the Hellenistic world, as well as to that Hellenistic diaspora itself. When applied to figurines, *koine* specifically denotes motifs and styles that commonly appear in the corpora of the primary figurine producing regions of the Hellenistic world, including Alexandria, Athens, the Aegean, Asia Minor, and the Levant. There is often an implicit understanding that these figurine motifs originated in Greece, or in some way reflected Greek ideas and styles, in order to qualify as part of the *koine*. Nevertheless, the figurines of the Hellenistic *koine* tradition should not be confused with Greek figurines, as the complexities and preferences seen in the *koine* often developed outside of Greece and are distinctive of the Hellenistic world broadly, not mainland Greece and/or the Aegean specifically.
27. For one of these rare examples, see Karvonen-Kannas 1995, No. 85.
28. For technical explanation and discussion, see Menegazzi 2014, 49–58. Note that travel of craftspeople themselves, as well as travel of artworks in other media, such as seals, jewelry, and coins, likely also facilitated the exchange of ideas and object forms.
29. Uhlenbrock 1990; Karvonen-Kannas 1995, 22–25. For detailed photographs of the double-molding process, see Muller 1996, 9–13.
30. See discussion of regional variation throughout the chapters of Uhlenbrock (ed) 1990.
31. Langin-Hooper 2007; 2013b; also Westh-Hansen 2011; Menegazzi 2012.
32. Invernizzi 1985, 97; Ristvet 2011.
33. Gosden 2005, 203–205. Gosden (2011) also proposes that this is in sharp contrast with periods of more fixed social roles, which show a corresponding rigidity in miniature object types.
34. Assante 2002, 19–20.
35. Wilson 2012; see also Darby 2014b.
36. Langin-Hooper 2015, 62.
37. Langin-Hooper 2015.
38. Nelson 2007, 490 (emphasis original).
39. Geertz 1973, 93. Note that the original quote refers to the agency of cultural patterns and objects generally, rather than miniatures specifically.
40. For critiques of the concept of "Hellenization," see the foundational work of Kuhrt and Sherwin-White (eds.) 1987; Sherwin-White and Kuhrt 1993.
41. For these terms, their derivation from postcolonial theory, and their application to archaeology, see Gosden 2004.
42. For an excellent overview of hybridity and its conceptual flaws, including extensive citations of the relevant scholarship, see Martin 2017, 136–141. See also Moreiras 1999, 374; Feldman 2006, 63; Jiménez 2011, 114; Stockhammer 2012; Langin-Hooper 2013a; 2013b; Silliman 2015.
43. When applied to art historical objects from the Hellenistic period, "hybrid" is most commonly used to describe the blendings of visual forms from different cultures. For discussion and examples, see Langin-Hooper 2007; 2013a; 2013b; Herbert 2008, 272; Westh-Hansen 2011; Menegazzi 2012; Ristvet 2014.
44. Jimenez makes a similar argument with regards to mummy shrouds from Greco-Roman Egypt (2014, 170–171).
45. An argument also made by Menegazzi (2012, especially pages 159–160).
46. Differences in the execution of the modeling, physicality, and plasticity of the so-called "Herakles" figurines from Babylonia from similar figurines in Greece were also recognized by Klengel-Brandt (1993, 192).
47. Thus, such figurines do not satisfy what is often regarded as "a typical Hellenistic concern for multiple viewpoints" (Connelly 1989, 153).

1 A QUESTION OF INTIMACY: MINIATURIZATION AND FIGURINES

1. Much of the text of this section duplicates a discussion of miniaturization theory found in Martin and Langin-Hooper 2018. I thank Becky Martin for permission to adapt and reprint our work here.
2. See especially Bailey 2005; Joyce 2007, 2008.
3. Bailey 2005, 34.

4. Lloyd and Sloan 2008, 39, see also 40–41.
5. For foundational work on phenomenology and embodied subjectivity, see Merleau-Ponty [1945] 2012. For discussion, see Jay 2011; Fraleigh 2018.
6. For foundational work on materiality and thing theory, see Brown 2004; Miller 2005.
7. However, for excellent analyses of the intersection between recent figurine studies and adjacent theoretical fields, see Nakamura and Meskell 2009, 209–210; Robb 2009, 163–167.
8. Bennett 2010, xi.
9. Gell 1992, 47. It is especially revealing that Gell, in his groundbreaking 1992 article, constructs a theory of enchantment designed to encompass all art forms and aesthetic experiences, but chooses a miniature object (a scale replica of Salisbury Cathedral made from matchsticks, which many might hesitate to even label as an "artwork") as a primary example of the phenomenon. See also Mack 2007, 47.
10. Bailey 2005, 33.
11. Meskell 2015, 6.
12. Bachelard [1958] 1994, 148–182.
13. See, for instance, the examples in Van Buren 1930, 40–50.
14. Dillon 2012a.
15. Higgins 1967, 103.
16. As discussed by Meskell, figurines have the ability to "materially embody [people's] preoccupations and concerns" (2015, 11). Jones argues that miniatures are "active components of thought," giving physical form to human cognition and thus allowing those externalized thoughts to have broad social distribution and influence (2013, 370). Bennett discusses this power of objects as "moments of sensuous enchantment with the every-day world" that directly motivate people to translate their thoughts and principles into real-world behaviors (2010, xi).
17. Even two-dimensional portrait miniatures from more recent periods are generally talked about in terms of "intimate objects" (Coombs 1998, 117).
18. Lloyd and Sloan 2008, 23. A similar argument is made by Ng (2018, 79–81), as well as Richard: miniaturized "scale 'concentrates experience and memory' that can relate to distant places and times" (2019, 815; quoting Jones 2013, 369).
19. Siebert 2018, 26–27. Knappett makes a similar argument about the ability of the miniature to transcend time and space (2012, 92).
20. Joyce 2008, 37 (emphasis original).
21. Langin-Hooper 2015, 63. I have previously used concepts of human–object and object–object "entanglement" to discuss similarities and differences in the cross-cultural hybridities of Hellenistic Babylonian figurines (Langin-Hooper 2013b). In so doing – and in the slightly different construction of "entanglement" used here – I am drawing most explicitly on the work of Hodder (2012), as well as Thomas (1991), Renfew (2001), and Gosden (2011). In these usages, "entanglement" refers to the mutual entrapment of the human and object worlds, which come into being, shape, and ultimately depend upon one another. "Entangled" is also used, such as by Stockhammer (2012), as a substitute for "hybrid" in describing specifically cross-cultural objects.
22. For descriptions of the three different Classical Greek theories on vision, which differ significantly but all of which posited "that what one sees physically enters into the body and mind," see Stansbury O'Donnell 2011, 173.
23. For extensive discussion of the Mesopotamian concepts and vocabulary, see Winter 2000.
24. Prier 1989, 81–97.
25. Things that we see do not have the nature which we wish them to have but the nature which each of them actually has; and by seeing them the mind is molded in its character too. For instance, when the sight surveys hostile persons and a hostile array of bronze and iron for hostile armament, offensive array of the one and shields of the other it is alarmed, and it alarms the mind, so that often people flee in panic when some danger is imminent as if it were present ... many have fallen into groundless distress and terrible illness and incurable madness; so deeply does sight engrave on the mind images of actions that are seen.
   (Gorgias Encomium of Helen 16–17)

   I thank my former student, Autumn Garcia, for pointing out this text to me.

26. For discussions of the various and complex modes of figurine analysis, see Lesure 2011, Chapter 3.
27. As defined by the branch of figurine studies pioneered by Ucko (1968) and Voigt (1983). See also discussion in Graff 2013.
28. Moorey 2003, 7. For particular discussion about how almost any object can become a child's toy at some point in its life-cycle, see Crawford 2009.
29. Nakamura and Meskell 2009, 209 (emphasis original), citing Meskell 2007.
30. See discussion in Knappett 2012, 92–93; Richard 2019, 815.
31. Osborne 2001, 287.
32. See Feldman 2014.
33. See Miller 1997, 135–152.
34. Hughes 2008; Hughes 2018.
35. Langin-Hooper 2015, 65.
36. Many, but not necessarily all, miniatures invite the human touch. Some of the stone, shell, and metallic figurines of the Andean Wari culture strike me as particularly apt examples of deliberately nontactile miniatures, whose prickly appearance and sharp edges discourage touch (see especially the figurine pictured in Bergh 2012a, Figures 211a, 211b). Although my knowledge of the Wari material is minimal, it is my understanding that such figurines likely participated in the construction of authoritative elite power and intimidating warrior identities (Bergh 2012b) – as such, I would suggest that the nontactile (or, perhaps more accurately, *anti-tactile*) affordances of these figurines might have been specifically deployed to achieve an alienating affect. I thank my colleague Adam Herring for first introducing me to the Wari figurines and listening with interest to my non-specialist musings on them.
37. Grootenboer 2012, 180.
38. The scholarship of John Mack is an exception to this trend and, in his expert and wide-ranging consideration of miniaturization (2007), Mack's presentation of the different valences of miniaturization parallels the intentions of my volume. Particularly notable is that Mack similarly probes the wonder and awe inspired by miniatures that approach "the extremes of visibility" (2007, 47) and "evade complete comprehension" (2007, 207); however, crucially, he frames his discussion along an axis of possession and control rather than intimacy. Danielsson (2013, 335) also critiques the blanket application of "miniaturization" to small material, although along different lines than are presented here.
39. Lloyd and Sloan 2008, 14.
40. Green 1990, 53–55.
41. See, for instance, Ridgway 2001, 233–236; Stewart 2014, 166–168.
42. Bailey 2005, 32–33.
43. Knappett 2012, 100, following on the work of Clark 2010.
44. Clark 2010, 25–26, citing the work of Markman and Gentner 1993.
45. Bailey 2005, 32–44; see especially pages 35 and 38–39.
46. As discussed by Karvonen-Kannas 1995, 28; Menegazzi 2014, 55–58. It is possible that individual households were also involved in this system of manufacturing and sale, as evidenced at the site of Olynthus (Cahill 2002, 253).
47. For an exception to this, see Foxhall 2015.
48. For Greek sculpture, see particularly Neer 2010; for Mesopotamian sculpture, see particularly Winter 1989; 1996.
49. Van Buren 1930, xxxvii. For a history of Mesopotamian figurine tradition, as well as discussion of the meanings and resonances of clay as a sculptural material, see Graff 2013.
50. Martinez-Sève 2002, 763; Jackson 2006, 4; Menegazzi 2014, 69–70.
51. Van Ingen 1939, 33.
52. This facet of ceramic is still emphasized in contemporary artist practice and the art historical analysis thereof; see, for instance, Richards 1989; Favero 2010.
53. In the Mesopotamian myth of Atrahasis, for instance, all human beings are created from a mixture of clay and divine flesh (Dalley 2000, 15); in a similar fashion, the goddess Aruru creates Gilgamesh's uncivilized companion Enkidu from a pinch of clay (George 1999, 4–5). Greek mythology refers to clay as the formative material used in the creation of Pandora, as recounted in Hesiod's *Works and Days* (West 1999, 38–39). The story of creation in the biblical book of Genesis similarly describes the fashioning of human beings from clay.
54. While I will usually refer to the craftsperson in the singular to avoid grammatical complications, note that it is possible that many individuals were involved in the creation of an

individual figurine via an organized workshop production chain. In particular, it is possible that the painters who decorated the fired figurines were different specialists from the ceramic artists who formed them. For further discussion of painting on terracotta figurines, and the role of painting in workshop production, see Bourgeois 2010; Menegazzi 2014, 52–58; Passmore 2014.

55. The Greek term "coroplast" is a professional title for a ceramic artist who specialized in figurines; for a discussion of the practice of coroplastic arts in the Hellenistic Greek world, see Uhlenbrock 1990. It is uncertain whether this label would have been used by the craftspeople who created Hellenistic Babylonian figurines or the patrons who purchased them; as a result, I prefer to use more generic English terms such as "craftsperson" throughout this volume. As the gender of these artists is also unknown, I similarly employ gender-inclusive terms and pronouns.

56. The figurines discussed in this volume were likely made by craftspeople and intended for private ownership and use. Evidence for figurine workshops near marketplaces has been discovered at Seleucia-on-the-Tigris (Menegazzi 2014, 55–58); see also the discussion of workshops and the selling of figurines in Karvonen-Kannas 1995, 28. However, some figurines were made by temple personnel and intended for official cult activities. As discussed in Langin-Hooper (2013b, 458–459): "Anthropomorphic figurines were commonly used in Mesopotamian rituals to stand in for living people, whether a particular individual, such as in the *maqlû* incantations against witches (Abusch 2002), or the entire Babylonian population, as in purification of the *Esagila* temple for the *akītu* festival (Bidmead 2002, 54–59)." Note that these cultic figurines were usually consumed or destroyed during the course of the ceremony, or soon afterwards, thus it is unlikely that any surviving figurines, such as those discussed in this volume, were participants in such rituals.

57. For discussion of these life-like potentialities of ceramic, and how this vital quality of clay impacts the artistic process of contemporary ceramicists, see Richards 1989, 9–32; Shapiro 2004.

58. Walker and Dick 1999, 97, 114.

59. The power of the viewer's inability to conceptualize how an artwork was created is discussed by Gell as one of the principle attractions of art, using the term "technology of enchantment" (1992, see particularly pages 49–53). The appeal of this particular kind of enchantment can be seen in miniatures from other cultural contexts; for instance, disguising the means of manufacture as was valued in the production of ceramic figurines during the Renaissance era in Europe (Kemp 1995, 191).

60. Such balls of clay are easily produced as a waste product of trimming modifications to ceramics in a leather-hard state and can adhere to the surface of terracotta figurines when the clay has not yet been fired. For general discussion of the mechanics and techniques of ceramic production, see Rawson 1984, 23–63.

61. This is especially the case when compared with the famous Tanagra figurines; for examples of these, see Jeammet (ed) 2010a.

62. See, for instance, Karvonen-Kannas 1995, 28.

63. Chemical identification and analysis of surface treatments and colorants on figurines from Seleucia-on-the-Tigris can be found in Passmore 2014.

64. Menegazzi 2014, 53.

65. Darby 2014a, 15–16.

66. A phenomenon discussed in detail by Menegazzi 2014, 49–51.

67. For discussion of the complex relationship between artist, mold, and the authored (or author-less) creation of figurines in the Ancient Near East, including the degree to which craftspeople left behind marks of manufacture on figurines and how those marks might have been interpreted, see Assante 2002, 3–18; Petty 2006, 40–41.

68. Bailey 2005, 28–35.

69. Further discussion of deliberate manufacturing marks and their role in marking object surfaces as places of past and future sensory encounter can be found in Robertson (2003, 149) and Hay (2010, 91).

70. For discussion of the "supremely coded" social information that decorative surfaces offer, see Hay 2010, 87. Living human skin can also be viewed as a social surface; see Barthes ([1967] 1983), Wobst (1977), and Turner (1980).

71. Stewart 1984, 28.

72. See Roaf (2004, 35) for a map of natural resources in the Near East.
73. For discussion of sculptural techniques, see Stewart 1990, Chapter 2.
74. For discussion of value and loss with relationship to jewelry, see Pointon 1999, 10.
75. For discussion of the polishing of stone, see Palagia 2006, 260–261; for discussion of surface qualities, see Spivey 2013, 71.
76. Menegazzi 2014, 54–55.
77. See discussions of the wonder, pleasure, and desire of ancient Greek sculpture in Neer 2010.
78. For theoretical discussion of proximal sense experiences (such as experiencing touch through vision), see Marks 2008.
79. Instead of fingerprints, mold marks and tool marks could be left on stone or metal sculptures. On large-scale sculptures, these marks were usually erased with rasps and abrasives (Palagia 2006, 260). Even if such marks remained visible, they are significantly less personal – and thus less clearly indexical of another human body – than fingerprints in clay.
80. Temperature sensation is a different kind of touch, involving different neuroreceptors (called thermoceptors), than pressure-based touch (which utilizes mechanoreceptors) (Paterson 2007, ix). The dual activation of both pressure and temperature receptors would have been more noticeable with stone and metal miniatures than with clay miniatures (which generally feel "room temperature"), thus creating a more intensive sensory experience of these objects. For detailed discussion of the senses of touch and human experience of objects, see Paterson 2007.
81. The dynamic qualities of metal and stone are also aspects of their production, where they had been discussed in terms of liquidity, water, and fire since the Classical Greek period (see discussion in Cole 2003, 138–139).
82. As the neoclassical sculptor Antonio Canova stated, "clay is life" whereas "marble is the resurrection" (as cited by Martin 1979, 22) – marble having an "aloof smoothness" more removed from reality yet attractive to caress (Martin 1979, 22).
83. For theoretical discussion of the vitalities of such affective properties of metal, see Bennett 2010, 56, 60.
84. I thank Megan Cifarelli for pointing out the potential for disgust, as well as pleasant closeness, depending on the identity of, and one's personal connection to, the individual whose body heat and presence were being transferred in this way.
85. For the erotic properties of metal, see Bennett 2010, 61.
86. Two comparably sized female figurines at the Kelsey Museum of Archaeology serve as an excellent example of this weight disparity. A bronze female figurine (TM Unacc.15.1931/KM 2018.01.0648), similar to that pictured in Figure 1.8 and measuring a height of 6.1 cm, weighs 31.05 g. KM 16220, a terracotta figurine of similar motif and size (6.6 cm in height), weighs 19.40 g.
87. For discussion of bronze workshops, see Stewart 1990, Chapter 2.
88. Lucian, *Amores* 13–16. See discussion in Stewart 1997, 97–107.
89. Van Ingen 1939, 45–46.
90. Van Ingen 1939, 17.
91. For technical discussion of bone structure as it relates to sculptural carving in antiquity, see St. Clair 2003, 1–4.
92. For discussion of how artists could incorporate the natural properties of animal substances, such as ivory, into their carvings, see Feldman (2014, 48–50) and Gansell (2013, 402).
93. The complex relationship between animal materials and the human body are discussed with reference to skin and gloves by Stallybrass and Jones (2004).
94. Similarly, Gansell discusses the use of ivory as a sculptural material to create bodies that fit Neo-Assyrian ideals of feminine beauty, which may have included "a fair, glowing complexion" as well as "flawlessness and purity" (2013, 404).
95. For discussion of the similar properties of bone and metal as sculptural material, and the overlap of designs and motifs in Hellenistic and Roman objects made from bone and metal, see St. Clair 2003, 15–18, 31.
96. For observations of how animal materials gain a "warm human quality" through the "touches of many hands over a long period of years," see Herring 1949, 204 (quoting Cox 1946).

97. For a complete description of mold types in use in Hellenistic Babylonia, see Menegazzi 2014, 47–52.
98. For discussion of mold use, see Uhlenbrock 1990.
99. For discussion of the depiction of female breasts in Greek sculpture, see Cohen 1997.
100. For an overview of the study of dress in antiquity, including theoretical discussion of how dress provides "a 'social skin' that represents aspects of identity to a particular audience," see Cifarelli and Gawlinski 2017 (note that this discussion is without particular reference to miniaturization).
101. Cifarelli 2017, 106–107; see also Bliege-Bird and Smith 2005, 234–235.
102. For discussion of the role of dress and fashion in the creation of social norms, as well as in influencing social, political, and economic change, in the Ancient Near East, see Baadsgaard 2013.
103. A similar argument is made by McFerrin in discussing the depiction of garments on the Apadana reliefs at Persepolis (2017, 155).
104. See, for instance, the sculpted relief depictions of Nike (such as the "Sandal-binder Nike") from the parapet frieze of the Temple of Athena Nike on the Athenian Acropolis. Also see discussion of drapery as a foil to the body in Neer 2010, 140.
105. Cohen 1997.
106. Such as seen, for instance, in the Hellenistic statue of Aphrodite today known as the *Venus de Milo* (Ridgway 2000, 169).
107. For Classical Greek perspectives on the differing valences of nudity in art versus nudity in real life, see Bonfante 1989. For discussion of the existence of Hellenistic Babylonian gymnasia (at Babylon and Seleucia-on-the-Tigris), see Kirk 1935; Downey 1988, 14; Cohen 2013, 160. Note that both the unconventional architecture of the Babylon gymnasion (if it was such), as well as comparative evidence from gymnasia in Hellenistic Central Asia (such as at Ai Khanum; see Colledge 1987, 156), indicates that gymnasia membership, activities, and rules for participation, may have differed substantially from the Classical Greek gymnasion (in its most common practice), reflecting the multicultural communities in which they operated.
108. This phenomenon is also discussed with regards to marble statuary by Neer 2010, 139–140.
109. Menegazzi 2014, 71.
110. See examples at the beginning of the catalogue in Van Buren 1930.
111. It has been generally accepted that Classical Greek sculptors followed a convention of rendering the female genitalia unelaborated (as may be seen, for instance, in some copies of the Knidian Aphrodite of Praxiteles); note, however, that the pervasiveness of this sculptural practice is debated (Seaman 2004, 551–557).
112. Bonfante 1989, 558–562; Smith 1991, 79–83; Sutton Jr. 1992, 21–24.
113. For discussion of this disjunction between beauty ideals and lived bodies, see Gansell 2013, 406.
114. The linguistic idea of citational practices posits that "we constantly reproduce what we hear in order to fashion ourselves" (Goodman, Tomlinson, and Richland 2014, 450). Judith Butler adapts this concept to discuss gender as a performance in which people actively cite previous performances of their preferred/assigned gender identity (Butler 1990).

2 FASCINATION WITH THE TINY: INTERACTING WITH FIGURINES

1. Bailey 2005, 67–68.
2. The enlarged scale of the user vis-à-vis the miniature object would have been especially empowering in an Ancient Near Eastern context, as Mesopotamian culture (in particular) had a long history of equating large size with the material expression of social and political dominance (see discussion in Osborne 2014).
3. Van Ingen 1939, 27.
4. See, for instance, the red painted bridle and reins on a figurine from Nippur in the Oriental Institute (OI A28896).
5. Bailey 2005, 28–35; Langin-Hooper 2018a.
6. For one example of such an explanation, see Hopkins 1972, 37.
7. Derevenski 2000, 3–7; Lopiparo 2006, 157–162; for overview of developments in the archaeology and anthropology of childhood, see Kamp 2001; Hirschfeld 2002; Baxter 2005a.

8. Lillehammer 2000; Baxter 2005c.
9. Langley 2018; Riede, Johannsen, Högberg, Nowell, and Lombard 2018.
10. Baxter 2005b; Kamp 2005, 118; Wilson 2006, 230.
11. For discussion of children having a social life, including as social mediators for adults, see Sillar 1994, 49; Wilkie 2000, 107–110. For the vital role that children can play in economic life, including as workers, see Kamp 2002; Lancy 2018. For children, some as young as three years old, participating in Classical Athenian festivals, see Beaumont 2000, 40–42; for schooling in Classical Athens, see Beaumont 2000, 45–46.
12. For discussion of the broad range of adult and child interactions with toys (and miniatures that might sometimes have been used as toys), see Wilkie 2000; Kamp 2005, 120; Park 2005. For the role of nostalgia in adult interaction with, and production of, toys for children, see Joyce 2006, 284.
13. For the relative uniqueness of modern, Western conceptions and experiences of childhood, see Kamp 2001; Rothschild 2002; Ardren 2006.
14. Kamp, Timmerman, Lind, Graybill and Natowsky 1999.
15. Haines 1967, 71–73.
16. See Legrain 1930, Plates 47–51; Van Ingen 1939, Plates 30 and 75; Ziegler 1962, Plates 39–43; Klengel-Brandt and Cholidis 2006, Plates 125–146.
17. For discussion of the various Parthian hats, see Curtis 1998; 2007.
18. For detailed description and diagrams, see Saatsoglou-Paliadeli 1993, particularly page 130. For this hat being worn by cavalry members in the Parthenon frieze, see Stevenson 2003, 631.
19. Identified as such on figurine examples by Legrain (1930, 32) and Moorey (2000, 479; 2003, 211–212).
20. The origins of the *kausia* have been debated, with Kingsley (1981; 1991) espousing the view that the hat was adopted by the Macedonian military from clothing styles used in the eastern-most parts of Alexander's empire, while other scholars claim a Macedonian origin for the garment (see discussion of the arguments in Fredricksmeyer 1986). This debate is peripheral to my argument here, which is that this style of hat would have had a Macedonian, and particularly a military, association for Hellenistic Babylonian viewers.
21. See for instance Van Ingen 1939, No. 1448i.
22. Van Ingen 1939, 27; Van Buren 1930, 165–166.
23. Information on both graves comes from S. Yeivin's notes in the Seleucia Excavation Archives (Box 19, Season E), 1930–1936, Kelsey Museum, University of Michigan, Ann Arbor.
24. Hellenistic grave stele, such as those at Smyrna, most commonly memorialize children by referencing their future status as adults, including specific symbols of the occupations and achievements that would have been theirs had only they lived; see Zanker 1993, 221–222.
25. Bonfante and Jaunzems 1988, 1390.
26. Menegazzi 2014, 265. Note that 42 percent of the figurines discovered in the Italian excavations at Seleucia-on-the-Tigris come from one of the fifteen deposits on the southern side of the Archives Square (Menegazzi 2014, 45); thus, this particular findspot does not mark the archer figurines as especially noteworthy. What does distinguish them, however, is that they were all members of the same mold series, as well as the uniqueness of their motif to this one context and city – both of which indicate a limited audience and popularity.
27. Menegazzi (2014) catalogues over 600 such figurines from Seleucia-on-the-Tigris alone.
28. McCown 1967, 91–92; Moorey 2000, 470.
29. See discussion in Menegazzi 2014, 280.
30. For historical discussion of the many Hellenistic-era wars, see Shipley 2000, 271–325. For the Parthian army's relationship with Babylonia, see Keall 1975.
31. See Romero (2017, 31–32) for discussion of how toys can be used in periods of warfare to express both fear and admiration of military events.
32. Stewart 1984, 60.
33. Similar discussion of the allure of miniaturized battles because they allow the user a "safe, hero's-eye view, suspended in time" can be found in Kellum 2018, 200.
34. Uhlenbrock 1990.
35. As noted by Van Ingen regarding the figurines of Seleucia-on-the-Tigris, the soldier figurines "have been called Parthian,

but there is nothing distinctively Parthian about them" (1939, 27).
36. For discussion, as well as a chart detailing the specific make-up of the Seleucid army during different campaigns, see Sherwin-White and Kuhrt 1993, 53–59.
37. As critiqued by Sherwin-White and Kuhrt 1993, 53.
38. Clarysse 1985.
39. Goldsworthy 2016, 331–332.
40. Keall 1975, 632; Reade 1998, 68.
41. See Darby 2014b for extensive discussion (particularly on pages 55–58) and critique of this approach.
42. Calligaro, Bouquillon, Querré, and Poirot 1999, 220.
43. A similar point is made by Fowlkes-Childs and Seymour (2019, 233). For Mesopotamian beliefs regarding divine radiance and composite statues, see Winter 1994.
44. Fowlkes-Childs and Seymour 2019, 233.
45. Fowlkes-Childs and Seymour 2019, 234.
46. These are often labeled as "finished off" arms in specialist studies; see Karvonen-Kannas 1995, 47.
47. See Menegazzi 2014, Plates 552–553.
48. Although note that there is no evidence that such arms were permanently adhered to the body, either before firing (through scoring and slipping the wet clay) or after firing by permanent binding methods such as plaster or bitumen.
49. For instance, at Seleucia-on-the-Tigris, Menegazzi (2014) catalogues only thirty-two jointed-arm standing female figurines in contrast to the hundreds of similar figurines without such added arms.
50. Note the absence of figurines in this motif and morphology from the city of Nippur; see further discussion in Chapter 5.
51. Twenty-nine known examples from Babylon, if the unpublished examples from the Harvard Semitic Museum are taken into account (see also Karvonen-Kannas 1995; Klengel-Brandt and Cholidis 2006); compare with thirty-two from Seleucia-on-the-Tigris (see Van Ingen 1939; Menegazzi 2014).
52. Van Ingen 1939, Plates LXXXIII-LXXXVII.
53. Fowlkes-Childs and Seymour 2019, 234–235.
54. See Van Ingen 1939, Plate 82.
55. See, for instance, KM 14159 from Seleucia-on-the-Tigris, at the Kelsey Museum of Archaeology.
56. Figurines depicting female bodies with both arm and leg "stumps" (without holes for attachment) are known from Classical Greece; Reilly (1997, especially 160–161) provides an extensive list of examples, and interprets these figurines as votive dedications representing the wish for healthy, functioning female reproductive anatomy.
57. See, for instance, Merker 2000; Ammerman 2002.
58. Van Ingen 1939, 32.
59. As support for her theory that bone figurines with movable arms were used in domestic shrines, Van Ingen states that such figurines were often found in the same house rooms as terracotta and alabaster figures that may have held "religious or magical significance" (1939, 45) such as jar carriers, boys wearing three-pointed headdresses, priest-like figures carrying offerings, birds, animals, riders on horseback, and musicians. While it is possible that such figurines were dedicated in household shrines, the wide-ranging nature of this list (which encompasses a large percentage of the figurine motifs found at the site of Seleucia-on-the-Tigris) lessens the certainty that this association points to any one specific meaning, such as votive use. Most figurines with this appearance have been recovered from the domestic, workshop refuse, or secondary contexts common to most Hellenistic Babylonian figurines (Van Buren 1930, 165–166; Van Ingen 1939, 27; Menegazzi 2014, 45).
60. Ambos 2003, 243–244; Fowlkes-Childs and Seymour 2019, 233–235.
61. For instance, only forty-one figurines out of a total of nearly 11,000 figurines excavated at Seleucia-on-the-Tigris were found in tombs (Menegazzi 2014, 70–71).
62. Skeleton 2, Tomb 169 at Seleucia-on-the-Tigris (Van Ingen 1939, 342).
63. Ambos 2003, 243–244.
64. See, for instance, Van Ingen 1939, No. 316a (which she classifies as male).
65. See, for instance, Mollard-Besques 1963, Plates 9, 11; Thompson 1965, Plate 21; Merker 2000, Plates 12–13, 16.
66. Many thanks to Ilona Zsolnay for pointing out the similarity of these figurines, and their visual effect of hindered movement, to historical practices such as foot binding in East Asia.

67. In using these terms, I draw upon Gaze theory in its discussion of the sexual power of looking, and the desire of the viewer to control the object of his (or her) Gaze. For foundational literature, see Mulvey 1975; Lacan 1977; Pollock 1988; Olin 2003. The gratification provided by the figurine to the Gazing viewer could also be enhanced by the "pleasure and security that miniaturism provides," in which "the spectator is enlarged and made omnipotent" (Bailey 2005, 131) as well as made confident that he or she cannot be discovered in his or her scopophilia by the non-sentient object of his or her attentions. As with the Gaze – and perhaps even more intimately so – "the Caress" allowed by figurines (as three-dimensional representations of the human body) could also have positioned the interlocutor in a position of power over the depicted figure.
68. Havelock 1995, 77–80; note that, as extensively discussed in Havelock's work, the *pudica* type was only one of the many versions of Aphrodite popular in the Hellenistic world. Other Aphrodite types that were more forthright and less concealing of their nudity were also popular – and it was these types, such as the *Aphrodite anadyomene*, that found some measure of popularity in Babylonia; see discussion in Chapter 5.
69. Stewart 1984, 65.
70. These two groups of figurines are also compared in Langin-Hooper (2018b) with specific reference to issues of fragmentation. In that publication, I argue that fear of trauma would be too close to reality for soldiers and horse riders, and thus figurines in these motifs were deliberately made "always whole" in contrast to the more experimental, and deliberately "broken," bodies of female figurines with separately added arms.
71. Stewart 1984, 172; see also Mack 2007, 158.
72. See the single example in the Babylon corpus catalogued by Karvonen-Kannas (1995, No. 47).
73. The illusion of female enjoyment is often a crucial aspect in the appeal of modern pornography as well, which MacKinnon describes as "a whole industry in buying and selling captive smiling women, acting as if they like it" (1994, 4).
74. Adams 2017, 207.
75. DuBois 1996. For the legendary erotic appeal of one-legged prostitutes in the Roman period, see Garland 1995, 52.
76. See discussion in Bahrani 1996.
77. Foster 2005, 498–505.
78. Richon 1985, 38. For the concept of hyper-reality, see also Baudrillard [1981] 1994 and Eco 1986. Eco in particular discusses how objects that are meant to recreate a "completely real" experience actually become more fake and distant from real life in the process, producing "a reality so real that it proclaims its artificiality from the rooftops" (1986, 6).
79. Fowlkes-Childs and Seymour 2019, 233.
80. Such joint attachments were used to create figurines that more closely resemble children's toys, with visually awkward but structurally robust attachments (see, for instance, Higgins 1967, Figures 31c, 35a, 35c).
81. This topic is discussed in detail in the "Nudity and Clothing" section in Chapter 4.
82. Fowlkes-Childs and Seymour 2019, 234.
83. See discussion in Chapter 4.
84. See Van Ingen 1939, Nos. 812, 814, 815.
85. Assante 2000; Bahrani 2001; Graff 2013.
86. For similar interpretations of the influential power of modern pornographic images, see Willis 1997 (for perspective based on phenomenology) and McGlynn 2016 (for perspective based on propaganda). For foundational theoretical work on the authoritative nature of pornography and its power to influence real-life sexual behaviors, see MacKinnon 1994; Langton 2009.
87. Stewart 1984.
88. Van Ingen 1939, 25, 170. Kuttner (1999, 106) also discusses how Hellenistic images of performers were often portrayed with "anonymous" features.
89. See Van Ingen 1939, Plate 42.
90. Indeed, the idea of songs and singing implied by this figurine were among the most popular aspects of Classical drama; see Hall 2002, 4.
91. Fox 1986, 395; also Arnott 1988, 1485–1487.

92. For the theater at Babylon, see Koldewey 1925, 297–298; Wetzel, Schmidt and Mallwitz 1957, 3–22. Tell 'Umar at Seleucia-on-the-Tigris was almost certainly a theater; see Invernizzi 1993, 243; Messina 2010.
93. For the transporting effect of theater, which also has the power to reinforce local cultural communities, see discussion and further references in Inomata and Coben 2006, 21–33.
94. For instance, see Walker (2004) for the theatrical exchange and influence between the Hellenistic world and India. For the more diverse nature of Hellenistic theater generally as compared with the Classical periods, see Brown 2005, 539–540. For the involvement of noncitizens and foreigners in Athenian theatrical productions of the Classical and Hellenistic periods, see Roselli 2011, 118–157. For the Hellenistic actor as foreigner and diplomat, see Duncan 2006, 122–123. For the Hellenistic-period flourishing of theater in the western Mediterranean and Italy, see Bosher (ed) 2012.
95. For the expense of attending the theater in early Hellenistic Greece, see Roselli 2011, 115. The prices and specific availability of admission to the theater in Hellenistic Babylonia are, to my knowledge, unknown. Van der Spek (2001) discusses in detail the cuneiform documents relating to the theater in Babylon.
96. Pollitt 1986, 4–7; Bergmann 1999, 10; Kuttner 1999, 102.
97. Bergmann (1999, 15) makes a similar argument about figurines and other private art that depicted actors and the events of the theater.
98. For the popularity and theatricality of Hellenistic festivals, see Chaniotis 1997.
99. As Ristvet (2014; 2015) has argued, drama and ritual activity were closely intertwined in both Greek and Babylonian cultures, and may have provided avenues for cultural intersection in Hellenistic Babylonia. Roman elements were added by some of the later Seleucid kings as well; see Edmondson 1999.
100. Bailey (2005, 32–33) makes a similar argument about the possibilities of abstraction in figurines. For the intersection of figurines and embodied agency, see Joyce 2008, 37; Meissner, South, and Balkansky 2013, 12–13. For the performative nature of identity and personhood, with discussion of foundational literature on the topic, see Conklin and Morgan 1996.
101. Von Hesberg 1999.
102. For the behavior of audiences, see extensive discussion in Roselli 2011, 31–62; for attempts in the Hellenistic period to control that behavior, see Roselli 2011, 109–115.
103. See examples of all three groups in Menegazzi 2014, Plates 295, 303–305.
104. This idea of impersonation and substitution was also a feature of Hellenistic elite portraiture; see discussion in Kuttner 1999.
105. In this way, the user was also distanced from being identified as a professional actor, whose ability to embody multiple identities and shift between appearance and reality were sometimes considered threatening in the Classical world; see discussion in Duncan 2006, 1–24.
106. All examples come from Seleucia-on-the-Tigris, of which the figurine seen in Figure 2.14 is the best preserved. For the handful of figurines that might have operated similarly, see Van Ingen 1939, 128–136, 179–181 (note that the majority of the figurines discussed on those pages are either dwarf figurines with no indication of a puppet-like feature, or puppet-figurines that cannot be definitely identified as dwarves).
107. Khodza 1984; Roselli 2011, 112; Mitchell 2013, 280–281.
108. Discussion of the pose and its meaning can be found in Zanker 1995, 44–49; see also Chaniotis 1997, 231–232; Masséglia 2015, 96–99.
109. Aeschines, in particular, was not always taken seriously by his peers because of his role on the stage; see Duncan 2006, 58–89.
110. For comprehensive discussion of these phenomena, see Garland 1995, 73–86. See also Masséglia (2015, 266–299) for discussion of grotesque figurines as theatrical in an aspirational sense, as disabled or dwarf entertainers were a high-end luxury in the Hellenistic world.
111. Menegazzi 2014, 319.
112. Menegazzi 2014, 320.
113. Van Ingen 1939, 32.
114. See, for instance, the high percentage of such figurines that were found in the G6 dwelling block at Seleucia-on-the-Tigris (Menegazzi 2014, 334, 340).

115. Trial Trench 4, Grid A2 (Van Ingen 1939, 171).
116. Early excavations at Seleucia-on-the-Tigris by the University of Michigan team labeled this building the "Parthian Villa." In his later publication of the Seleucia-on-the-Tigris excavations, Hopkins (1972) reinterprets the building as a Seleucid Heroon, based on a dedicatory Greek inscription found at the site which names "priests of the dead Seleucid kings and of the living ruler" (see discussion in Downey 1988, 55). Both Seleucid- and Parthian-era use, repairs, and some remodeling of the building are evident.
117. Van Ingen 1939, 171, 306; Hopkins 1972.
118. Room 18 might have functioned as a main temple entrance (as suggested by Manasseh 1931, 11) or as an area adjoining the primary cultic space or *naos* (as suggested by Hopkins 1972, 22). The vast difference between these interpretations is due to the contested reconstruction of the exterior wall of Room 18.
119. Similar paved spaces inside the temple meant for ceremony spectators and foot traffic are found at temples in Dura-Europos (see discussion in Hopkins 1972; Downey 1988, 57).
120. This potential for public access to the interior temple spaces of the Seleucid Heroon is not unique in Hellenistic Babylonia. As Ristvet (2014, 260) describes, the Hellenistic-era "building plan of the Reš temple at Uruk now provided visual access to the cult image from the entrance into the main courtyard ... [which] could have accommodated gatherings of the Urukean citizenry like the ones attested in the Esagila at Babylon."
121. Ristvet 2014, 260.
122. Ristvet (2014) presents a compelling case that ritual and drama overlapped substantially in Hellenistic Babylonia; thus, almost every ritual space could also be associated with the performance of cultural negotiation via theatrical enactment of identity. In my opinion, the Seleucid Heroon (if it was, in fact, a Heroon) was particularly well-suited to such dramas, as it was founded with the specific political/cultural purpose of commemorating the Seleucid kings.
123. Note that in my *World Archaeology* article (Langin-Hooper 2015), where this figurine is also discussed, the object number of this figurine was confused with another example discussed in the same article when this contextual information was presented.
124. Hopkins 1972, 13.
125. Ristvet 2014, 261; Karvonen-Kannas 1995; for extended discussion of Greek and Mesopotamian miniature terracotta masks, see Carter 1987. Greek theater and its accoutrements were popular subjects of art in a variety of media across the Hellenistic world; see, for instance, an extensive discussion of Hellenistic mosaics featuring theater masks in Stewart and Martin 2003, 134–141. Note, however, that miniature masks were also used early in Mesopotamian art; see Dietrich, Notroff, and Dietrich 2018.
126. This miniaturization may have been even more noticeable because Classical Greek theater masks were usually larger than the face; see vase painting evidence in Wiles 2007, 15–43.
127. Menegazzi catalogues 841 masks or mask fragments from Seleucia-on-the-Tigris; of those with published images, perhaps fifteen can be securely identified as having holes in both the eyes and mouth. Only one of the masks from Babylon published by Klengel-Brandt and Cholidis has holes in both eyes and mouth (2006, No. 4149). For particularly good examples, see Menegazzi 2014, Plates 496–497; also Karvonen-Kannas 1995, No. 507. Terracotta masks – some of which had their "eyes and mouth cut out" – were also used as votive offerings at Greek sites from the sixth century BCE through the Hellenistic period (Uhlenbrock 1996, 582).
128. Such possibilities align with the Classical Greeks' own thinking about vision as providing the opportunity for "long-distance touch" (Stewart 2008, 198), in which "intimate contact between the viewer and the viewed object" was created (Stansbury-O'Donnell 2006, 61). That this remotely tactile visual process was imagined to have operated by means of objects emitting "miniature replicas of themselves" (Stansbury-O'Donnell 2006, 62) further reinforces the capacity for real miniature objects to stimulate this sense.
129. Wiles 2007, 54.
130. For a discussion of miniature terracotta masks and the issue of whether (and how) they might have been worn in both Greece and Mesopotamia, see Carter 1987. For the

interplay of gazes that masks create, as well as examples of Classical Greek vase painting showing the contemplation of masks that are not being worn, see Wiles 2007, particularly 32–33 and 41–42.

131. Indeed, this would have reinforced the already disconcerting "otherness" produced by masks, which elide the illusion of the mask façade with the reality of the actor's face beneath; see Duncan 2006, 9. As Classical Greek masks were discussed and depicted as uniting with the actor's face to become a single entity, called a *prosōpon*, the inability for a miniature mask to create this fusion would have been especially noticeable; see Wiles 2007, 15.
132. Langin-Hooper 2013a, 106–108.
133. For instance, the Babylonian tradition of using miniature terracotta masks (such as those representing the face of the monster Humbaba from the Epic of Gilgamesh) for apotropaic purposes (Van Buren 1930, Photo Nos. 270 and 271; Karvonen-Kannas 1995; Ristvet 2014, 261). For the apotropaic uses of Gorgons and their connections with masks on Greek *kylixes*, see Bundrick 2015.
134. Winter 1992; Walker and Dick 1999.
135. Mayer 1978, 458; Walker and Dick 1999, 67–68.
136. Trial Trench 4, Grid Z1 (Van Ingen 1939, 306).
137. Although it is unclear whether or not the monumental Heroon was begun in the earliest period of occupation at Seleucia-on-the-Tigris, the archaeological evidence indicates a public "open district" on this spot, as opposed to domestic occupation (Hopkins 1972, 17).
138. Plato (Lg. 653d-e) correlates the uncontrolled cries and movements of young children with the song and dance of the theater; see discussion in Huffman 2005, 304.
139. See Karvonen-Kannas 1995, No. 223.
140. Hall 1977.
141. Needham 1967. See also extensive discussion in Chapter 3.
142. See, for instance, Van Buren 1930, Plates 3–10.
143. Indeed, Legrain identifies the rattles from Nippur as depictions of women (1930, 22). Note that the presence of breasts also does not negate the possibility that the depicted figure is a child; in the few figurines of clearly female children (see, for instance, Van Ingen 1939, No. 750), small breasts are depicted. This may have been done because it would be otherwise difficult to clearly signal female sex on clothed figurines of children, or perhaps because female children were viewed in reference to the adult female role which they would soon inhabit.
144. Horn and Martens 2009, 184–185.
145. A fact that the famous Greek "clapper [or rattle] of Archytas" praised by Aristotle was meant to alleviate, with the noise and energy of the rattle replacing that of the child; see Huffman 2005, 303–305.

3 THREE'S A CROWD: SPECTATORSHIP OF FIGURINES

1. See, for instance, discussion of domestic spaces at Seleucia-on-the-Tigris by Hopkins (1972).
2. Van Buren 1930, xlv.
3. For instance, Klengel-Brandt and Cholidis 2006, Plates 19–21. See also Langin-Hooper 2015, 62–64.
4. Erlich and Kloner 2008, Plates 7–8.
5. See, for instance, Fischer 1994, Plates 88–90, 93; Barrett 2011, Figures C13, C15, and C16 (all from the Cairo Museum, not Delos).
6. Bonfante 1984; Shepherd 2012, 218. They are also found in Classical-period Italy; see Ammerman 2002, 128–134.
7. Bonfante 1997; 2000, see especially 280; Merker 2000, 70–71.
8. In her paper at the American Schools of Oriental Research annual meeting, 2017.
9. See, for instance, Ziegler 1962, Figure 350. A rare example of an inward-gazing relationship proves the rule; see Karvonen-Kannas 1995, Figure 141.
10. Stearns 2009, 67. Ancient medical texts recognized this fact; see Fildes 1988, 20.
11. A poignant example of such breastfeeding difficulty in the ancient world can be seen in the Roman author Plutarch's consolation to his wife, Timoxena, after the death of their two-year-old daughter (*Consolatio ad Uxorem*). The consolation letter mentions the prior death of their infant son, whom Timoxena had nursed. During breastfeeding, Timoxena experienced problems with her

11. breasts that were severe enough to require surgery. See discussion in Marshall 2017, 185–186.
12. Kukla 2006, 164.
13. Steele 2007, 305.
14. "If a man gives his son to a wet nurse and that child then dies while in the care of the wet nurse, and the wet nurse then contracts to care for another child without the consent of his (the dead child's) father and mother, they shall charge and convict her, and, because she contracted to care for another child without the consent of his father and mother, they shall cut off her breast" (Roth 1995, 120). Discussion of other laws and contracts concerning wet-nursing can be found in Couto-Ferreira 2016, 31.
15. Pomeroy 1984, 161–163; Stol 1995, 129.
16. Marshall 2017, 187–188, 191.
17. Pomeroy 1984, 161–163. For discussion of a free, albeit poor, woman hiring herself out as a wet nurse, see Fisher 1993, 102.
18. Zimmermann 1980, 192–194; Oakley 2000, 242–244.
19. Clairmont 1970, 95–96; Oakley 2000, 244. Of course, both of these object types were actually commissioned by the wealthy employers or owners of wet nurses, not the women themselves; for critique of scholars' presumed ability to reconstruct the opinions of wet nurses, see Joshel 1986. Nevertheless, these objects document prevailing attitudes toward the practice of wet-nursing and are therefore useful in understanding the social reception of the figurines.
20. Stol 2016, 379–380; see also discussion in Couto-Ferreira 2016, 30.
21. Higgins 1967, 103.
22. Oakley 2000, 235–236.
23. Bonfante 1997, 175.
24. Stol 2016, 376.
25. In the Hebrew Bible, there are several instances of women used to bear children on behalf of another; for instance, Hagar for Sarah, Zilpah for Leah, and Bilhah for Rachel (Genesis 16–20; 25; 29–30). The physical and emotional violence of this practice has recently been discussed by several scholars, including Joseph (2017).
26. Turp, Guler, Bozkurt, Uysal, Yilmaz, Demir and Karabacak 2018.
27. Postgate 1992, 105; Steele 2007, 310.
28. See discussion in Stol 2016, 168–171.
29. Westbrook 1988, 106; Veenhof 1989, 186; Stol 2016, 172–174.
30. For a Greek red-figure vase depicting a man, presumably the father, watching as his child is nursed, possibly by its mother, see Fildes 1988, 15. As Marshall (2017) convincingly argues, male audiences for Greek plays, as well as many of the male characters presented, were expected to have detailed knowledge of breastfeeding and childcare situations in their own households, including seeing breastfeeding firsthand. Marshall makes a similar point to the one I propose here: namely, that breastfeeding and the care of infants was at the center of a range of social and intimate relationships, not just the connection between mother and child. For discussion of nurses observed or actively inspected in the course of their childcare duties by Roman mothers, see Bradley 1986, 220; Fildes 1988, 7.
31. Stol 2016, 377–379.
32. This was particularly the case with "foster brothers" or "bosom brothers," non-relative children who had been nursed by the same woman and who often maintained a family-like connection throughout their lives. Such connections could bridge social classes, as the biological children of the nurse herself (who were often poor) could be included in such relationships (Treggiari 1976, 88–89). Social connections could thus be elevated through the practice of wet-nursing, even for the elite; in particular, some Mesopotamian kings claimed "milk brotherhood" with certain gods through the belief that maternal goddesses, particularly Ninhursaga, were wet nurses for the king (Groneberg 2007, 324). For Roman opinions on the potential for negative effects in the infant's exposure to nonfamilial social circles, see Joshel 1986, 7–8. For Roman grave epitaphs commemorating deceased children that were set up by a combined social group of the biological parents and the nurse(s), see Joshel 1986, 17–19.
33. For extensive discussion of Roman sources that echo this opinion, see Joshel 1986, 6.
34. For discussion of the connection between pre-Christian figurine traditions in Egypt, including *lactans* and *kourotrophos* figurines, and later Christian practices (including the representation of the Virgin Mary), see Corrington 1989; Frankfurter 2015.

35. For specific discussion of the role of breastmilk and nursing in the Isis-Horus relationship, see Laskaris 2008, 462.
36. Hall 1977, 55.
37. Frankfort 1948, 6; Tran Tam Tinh 1973, 43; Corrington 1989, 398–399, 411.
38. As Corrington puts it: "the divine queen-mother manifesting her child to the world" (1989, 412).
39. Tran Tam Tinh 1973, 33; Karvonen-Kannas 1995, 58.
40. Corrington (1989, 402) and Frankfurter (2015, 200) make similar points about the ambiguous identification of Egyptian figurines.
41. See also Van Ingen 1939, No. 65; Klengel-Brandt and Cholidis 2006, No. 2285.
42. See Legrain 1930, Figures 38, 39; and Ziegler 1962, Figures 184, 185, 186, 188.
43. See, for example, Legrain 1930, Figures 40–45; Ziegler 1962, Figures 259, 262, 265–274; Klengel-Brandt and Cholidis 2006, Plates 19–21.
44. Winter 1995, 2578.
45. Corrington 1989. Thanks are due to my student, Kathryn Bozentka, who spurred my thinking on this particular point.
46. This association of the female with the left side encompasses both the female's left, and the left side of the person associated with her: "The female protective deity walks at a person's left hand; before birth a girl is on the left side in her mother's belly; and women are according to a Sumerian literary stock phrase said to wear their clothes 'on the left'" (Stol 1995, 124).
47. Bradley 1986; Bonfante 1997, 183, 186.
48. Nakamichi and Takeda 1995; Scola and Vauclair 2010a; 2010b.
49. Forrester, Crawley, and Palmer 2014.
50. Vervloed, Hendriks, and van den Eijnde 2011.
51. Reissland, Hopkins, Helms, and Williams 2009.
52. Langin-Hooper 2015, 71–75.
53. Ridgway 1987, 407–409; Dean-Jones 1991; King 1998; Laskaris 2008.
54. For discussion of the Greek transition of a woman from *nymphē* (bride) to *gunē* (married mother), see Taraskiewicz 2012.
55. See discussion in Langin-Hooper and Pearce 2014. Note that Babylonian women of earlier periods could often exercise legal and social freedoms as well; see discussion in Steele 2007.
56. Smith 1991, 80.
57. For examples of female groups and age differences in the Tanagra tradition, see Becq 2010, 211; Jeammet 2010b, 182–183.
58. This ritual interpretation is among the most common explanation advanced by scholars for these figurines. For an extensive discussion and examples of such interpretations, see Moorey 2003.
59. Bahrani makes a similar point in her discussion of Ishtar and Mesopotamian figurines (1996, 12).
60. See, for instance, Van Ingen 1939, Plates LIV–LV; Karvonen-Kannas 1995, Plate 45.
61. Van Ingen 1939, Nos. 855a and 856.
62. For the manner in which art conditions the parameters and expectations for its own reception, see Jauss 1982, 21.
63. Mulvey 1975; Lacan 1977; Olin 2003, 327. See also scholarship on the appeal of particular kinds of spectatorship and voyeurism in modern pornography: MacKinnon 1994; Willis 1997; Langton 2009; McGlynn 2016.
64. Barbara Kruger, 1981. *Untitled (Your gaze hits the side of my face)*, photograph and type on paperboard.
65. Pollitt 1986, 130–135.
66. Stafford 1991–1993.
67. For detailed discussion of these sculptural types, see Smith 1991, 127–154.
68. For masterful discussion of viewing possibilities and multicultural audiences for the "Slipper-Slapper" group, see Martin 2017, 152–168.
69. Pliny (*Natural History* 36.20–22) records a particularly famous account of a man who assaulted the Knidian Aphrodite, leaving "a stain, an indication of his lust" on the statue (Stewart 2008, 260).
70. See, for instance, Van Ingen 1939, Figure 842 (incorrectly labeled in the plates as 844).
71. Stafford 1991–1993, 112.
72. Discussion of the pose and its meaning can be found in Zanker 1995, 44–49. This pose is also similar to the Large and Small Herculaneum Women poses in Roman statuary; for a discussion of those poses and their potential embodiment of the values of *sophrosyne*, modesty, and self-restraint, see Davies 2018, 180.
73. See discussion in Chapter 2 (with reference to puppets) and Chapter 4 (with reference to

figurines of individual clothed men and women).
74. Masséglia 2015, 99.
75. Smith 1991, Figure 113.
76. Dillon 2012b, 265.
77. The Hellenistic Babylonian figurine corpus lacks depictions of many adult relationships – such as between mother and teenage/adult daughter or between two brothers – despite the fact that such relationships were commonly depicted in private art elsewhere in the Hellenistic world (such as figurines [Erlich and Kloner 2008, Plate 1; Becq 2010, 211; Jeammet 2010b, 182–183] and grave stelae [Zanker 1993]) *and* sometimes shown in other Hellenistic Babylonian miniature arts, such as coins (such as with depictions of the Dioscuri [McDowell 1935a, 5]).
78. See, for instance, discussion in Karvonen-Kannas 1995, 74–75. Note that Menegazzi (2014, 95) also tentatively suggests that couple figurines in which the woman is clothed are Dionysos and Ariadne.
79. See Van Ingen 1939, No. 842 (incorrectly labeled in the plates as 844) and Karvonen-Kannas 1995, No. 257.
80. See Van Ingen 1939, No. 844.
81. See Van Ingen 1939, No. 850.
82. For images of reclining banqueters depicted on tombstones and votive stelae, or otherwise associated with funerary practices, see Thönges-Stringaris 1965; Wild 1973, 176–177; Baughan 2013. This point will be returned to in Chapter 5.
83. Stewart 2014, 238; Masséglia 2015, 278. For the erotic appeal of physical deformities in the Roman world, see Garland 1995, 52–53. A few figurines in Hellenistic Babylonia followed this Hellenistic trend (Menegazzi 2014, Plates 381–382), yet overall the corpus differed; see further discussion in Chapter 5.
84. Bonfante 1989, 552; Cohen 1997, 72.
85. Particularly for eunuchs or those forced to shave as punishment for a crime; see Assante 2017, 66.
86. Harrison 1996, 212.
87. Ridgway 2001, 114; Stewart 1993, 75.
88. Roth 1987, 737; Just 1989, 64. It should be borne in mind, however, that this was the average age at the time of the first marriage; women, especially in Classical Athens, were often widowed and subsequently remarried.
89. Stewart 2008, 179.
90. See, for instance, the Old Babylonian plaques discussed in Assante 2002. Similar plaques were also used in the Hellenistic period; see Menegazzi 2014, Plates 676–677.
91. Dillon 2012b, 265.
92. Van Buren 1930, Plates XXXIX–XL.
93. The most prominent example is that of Antiochis, the "business-minded wife" (Doty 1988, 99) of Anu-uballiṭ–Kephalōn, Seleucid-era governor of Uruk. She invested in temple allotments that she purchased from members of other Babylonian families: cook's prebend (NCBT 1961=YOS 20 58); temple-enterer's prebend (VS 15 7, BiMes 24 6; Wallenfels [1994b, 436] suggests these may be duplicate documents). Wunsch (2005) sketches the evidence for the economic status and activity of women in the Neo-Babylonian and Achaemenid periods and it is clear that the situation in Hellenistic Babylonia echoes that of the preceding periods. For further discussion, see Langin-Hooper and Pearce 2014.
94. Indeed, the space between their heads was sometimes perforated, with a hole bored through the clay increasing the sense of separation between the two figures; see Menegazzi 2014, Nos. 10.G198 and 10.G199.
95. See Barrelet 1968, Figure 591.
96. See Rashid 1984, 144.
97. Knoblich and Sebanz 2008; see particularly discussion of joint intentionality and entrainment on page 2026. For discussion of the visual effects of synchronized swimming, in which the author describes synchronization as the "art of becoming one with the other and with the music", see Sydnor 1998, 254. For the role of synchronized dancing in creating and reinforcing community solidarity, see Spalding 1994.
98. For discussion of the various ways in which musicians and dancers can, in fact, synchronize their efforts, in ways often imperceptible to the audience, see overview of recent scholarship in Keller and Rieger 2009.
99. Contemporary ballet dancers are trained to anticipate the audience perspective and "cultivate unself-consciousness" in order to make their synchronized movements appear reflex-like (Kleiner 2009, 236).
100. Wilson 2005, 184.
101. This quote is from a passage in Xenophon's *Oeconomicus*:

My dear, there is nothing so convenient or so good for human beings as order. Thus, a chorus is a combination of human beings; but when the members of it do as they choose, it becomes mere confusion, and there is no pleasure in watching it; but when they act and chant in an orderly fashion, then those same men at once seem worth seeing and worth hearing.

(8.3–8.7, trans. E. Marchant)

102. Rimmer also comments on this (1969, 42). For discussion of molds as a technology, see Uhlenbrock 1990.
103. See Legrain 1930, No. 92; Van Ingen 1939, Nos. 590, 599b, 600; Ziegler 1962, Nos. 395, 396; Karvonen-Kannas 1995, Nos. 328, 329, 330, 332.
104. There are over thirty-five photographs of pipe and drum playing musician pair figurines across the major Hellenistic Babylonian figurine catalogues; the actual number of figurines is higher. In contrast, there are only eight published photographs of musician pairs playing other instrument combinations.
105. Landels 1999, 1.
106. Many Greek visual representations of the *aulos* show the two pipes of the instrument held further outwards from the chest, and with the two pipe barrels spread apart at a greater (yet still acute) angle than what is depicted in the Hellenistic Babylonian figurines (Rashid 1984, 144; Bundrick 2005, 40–46; for technical discussion of the instrument's construction, as well as images of surviving ancient examples, see Bellia 2012, 91–109). In contrast, the figurines show the pipes held tight to the chest with the two barrels close together; in some cases, such as those seen in Figures 3.9 and 3.11, the two barrels run almost parallel and nearly touch for their entire length. The close proximity of the pipes to the chest may have been necessitated by the practicalities of mold-made figurine manufacture, but the spreading angle of the pipes was not. This has caused some scholars to opt for more generic terminology for the instrument, labeling it a "double oboe" or similar term; see, for instance, Rashid 1984, 144.
107. Rashid 1984, 94–95; Caubet 2014, 174–175.
108. Landels 1999, 7; Bundrick 2005, 36–40.
109. Bundrick 2005, 41; discussion of the *aulos* as a professional instrument continues on page 42.
110. Alexiou 2002, 60.
111. Wilson 2005, 185; see also West 1992, 105.
112. Wilson 1999, 83–85.
113. There are perhaps four known examples of musician pairs with partial nudity: Ziegler 1962, No. 398; Karvonen-Kannas 1995, No. 326; and Menegazzi 2014, Nos. 10.G211 and 10.S92.
114. Rashid 1984, 144; note that Rashid also suggests that the drum had a fur-lined top.
115. West 1992, 105.
116. West 1992, 122.
117. The *tympanon* (frame drum), the *krotala* (clappers), and the *kymbala* (metal finger cymbals); see Bundrick 2005, 46.
118. See descriptions in Shehata 2014, 112–115. However, it is only with one type of drum, the kettledrum *lilis*, that the visual depiction of the drum can be firmly linked with its name, and this drum is far too large to be equivalent to the instrument depicted in the figurines (Shehata 2014, 115–116; see also illustration in Rashid 1984, 140). For detailed discussion of the rituals associated with the kettledrum, see Linssen 2004, 92–100.
119. CT 42 Pl. 30b rev. 7, as referenced in Shehata 2014, 113; see also Kilmer 1977, 133. While this description has been equated with frame drums depicted in Old Babylonian terracotta figurines (Kilmer 1977, 133; Shehata 2014, 113), the *tympanon*-style frame drums depicted in Hellenistic Babylonian figurines are usually shown held at the shoulder rather than in front of the chest. This makes the small drum held in the musician pair figurines a more likely comparison.
120. Sachs 1940, 76.
121. In the Seleucid texts, even drums used in earlier periods for more joyful purposes were sometimes reinterpreted and utilized in more somber rituals (such as with the *tigi* drum [Volk 1989, 202; Shehata 2014, 108]), perhaps indicating a more general association between drums and mourning in this period.
122. A rare example where the figurine was made in a single mold can be found in Ziegler (1962, Figure 722).
123. These figurines were particularly popular at Babylon (see Karvonen-Kannas 1995, Plate 51; Klengel-Brandt and Cholidis 2006, Plate

97) and Nippur (Legrain 1930, Nos. 75–86; see also extensive unpublished examples in the Oriental Institute at the University of Chicago and the Semitic Museum at Harvard University).
124. See discussion in Haines 1967, 88.
125. Sachs 1940, 76; Rimmer 1969, 23–24.
126. This word derives from the Greek verb τύπτω, "to beat, strike," and is used in several figurine catalogues to refer to drum-like percussion instruments. However, these instruments may have been called by other names, such as "rhoptra," in antiquity (Mathiesen 1999, 174–175).
127. Bundrick 2005, 48.
128. Tripolitis 2002, 23.
129. Thompson 1963, Plates VIII–X; Piccioni 2016.
130. Erlich 2010, 119 and Figure 4.
131. For more technical discussion, see Rashid 1984, 140.
132. For discussion of the ways in which visual representations of musical performances serve to socialize sound, see Leppert 2014, 9.
133. Langin-Hooper 2011.

4 IMAGES OF THE SELF: IDENTIFYING WITH FIGURINES

1. As Stewart similarly argues in her discussion of Victorian-era dollhouses, such self-contained displays of everyday identities are intended to be "consumed by the eye" (Stewart 1984, 62). It is revealing that both Stewart's dollhouses and Hellenistic Babylonian figurines were diverse and widely popular with adults (not primarily as playthings for children) at a time when their respective societies were involved in broad-scale cross-cultural interaction and social redefinition – indicating that both were appealing, at least in part, because they helped their users to navigate and renegotiate a rapidly changing social world.
2. For figurines as citational precedents for real-world self-fashioning of bodies and identities, see discussion in Chapter 1; also theoretical discussion in Butler 1990; Goodman, Tomlinson, and Richland 2014.
3. For similar argument, see Nakamura and Meskell 2009.
4. Langin-Hooper 2018a.
5. As described by Stewart (1996, 143), "the idea that art could persuade the viewer to imitation was popular in antiquity." For discussion of Greek images as role models for idealized real-world behavior, see Stansbury-O'Donnell 2006, 67–88. For discussion of Mesopotamian reactions to deity and royalty images as ideally consisting of active admiration and aroused awe (with implications of attraction to, and refashioning of the self in concordance with, the image), see Winter 1996, 19–23; Winter 2000.
6. Menegazzi 2014, 237.
7. For the Hellenistic concept of *tyche* (fortune, chance, or luck) and its statue personifications, see Green 1990, 53–55; Ridgway 2001, 233–236; Stewart 2014, 166–168.
8. For Mesopotamia, see Winter 1997, 370–372; for Greece, see Lee 2015, 76.
9. Smith 1988, 46; Stewart 1993, 75.
10. For statues, see Smith 1991, 23 and Figure 12; for coins, see Lorber and Iossif 2009a.
11. Smith 1988, 46.
12. For a discussion of this and similar "campaign" beards in Hellenistic ruler portraiture, including Seleucid coins, see Lorber and Iossif 2009a.
13. Although discovered in Rome, the confident pose of the statue points to an Eastern Mediterranean origin; it perhaps depicts a member of the Seleucid royal family (see extensive discussion of the possibilities in Meyer 1996).
14. For an example where the lower body is more completely preserved, see Karvonen-Kannas 1995, No. 354.
15. See discussion in Menegazzi 2014, 247–249.
16. For similar, albeit primarily female, figurines found at Merv (in modern Turkmenistan), see Simpson and Herrmann 1995.
17. See Karvonen-Kannas 1995, No. 354.
18. See discussion in Van Ingen 1939, 35–36.
19. See discussion in Karvonen-Kannas 1995, 90.
20. This argument is also made by Menegazzi (see 2014, 247–249). For examples, see Klengel-Brandt and Cholidis 2006, Plates 22–23.
21. Most of the examples date to the Parthian period; see Menegazzi 2014, 249.
22. Menegazzi 2014, 66–68.
23. See discussion in Menegazzi 2014, 249.
24. See discussion in Karvonen-Kannas 1995, 90.

25. Van Ingen 1939, 35; Invernizzi 1967, 29. See also discussion in Karvonen-Kannas 1995, 90–91.
26. See discussion in Invernizzi 1985, 98; Connelly 1990, 98–99; Martinez-Sève 2002, 726–728.
27. See Van Ingen 1939, No. 252c.
28. See Van Ingen 1939, No. 251.
29. Langin-Hooper 2013b.
30. See nuanced discussion in Zsolnay 2017.
31. Bailey 2005, 199; Langin-Hooper 2015, 71–75.
32. This headgear is likely either the Greek sun hat called the *petasos* (see Saatsoglou-Paliadeli 1993, 130; Stevenson 2003, 631) or the Macedonian cavalry headgear known as the *kausia* (Kingsley 1981; Fredricksmeyer 1986; Kingsley 1991).
33. Note also that the vast majority of surviving fragments of male figurine heads, including many with Parthian-style headdresses, are beardless; see, for instance, Menegazzi 2014, Plate 433.
34. There are a very few Hellenistic Babylonian figurines of nude males which are not obviously divine or in action; see, for instance, Van Ingen 1939, Nos. 263 and 271; Menegazzi 2014, No. 6.S2. Other examples are too fragmentary to determine their complete pose or identification.
35. Bonfante 1989; Osborne 1997.
36. Winter 1985; Asher-Greve 1998, 20; Assante 2017, 64–74. However, for a critique of the wholesale reading of nonnormative masculine depictions in the Ancient Near East as necessarily coded negatively, see Peled 2016b, 164.
37. For coins, see extensive examples in Houghton and Lorber 2002; Houghton, Lorber and Hoover 2008. For seals, see Wallenfels 2015. For statue portraits, see Smith 1988.
38. See discussion in Smith 1988, 32–33.
39. See Iossif 2011 for detailed discussion and further bibliography.
40. Iossif 2011, 249. This association between king's face and youthful god's body continued in Parthian coinage; see Erickson and Wright 2011. However, they aptly note that the nudity of the Apollo figure might have been problematic to some Near Eastern viewers, prompting the introduction of a clothed archer on later Parthian coins that imitated the Seleucid type (Erickson and Wright 2011, 165–166).
41. In the most common version, the nude Apollo lounges on his netted omphalos stone and holds an arrow in his outstretched right hand, while his body is framed and contained on either side by the name and title of the king. Antiochus I standardized this image of Apollo *Toxotes* (offering/holding a bow or arrows) for his silver coinage and the type remained popular through several generations, especially in the eastern part of the Seleucid Empire that included Babylonia. For lists of the variations on the Apollo *Toxotes* motif introduced by different Seleucid kings, see Lorber and Iossif 2009b, 29–30. For discussion of the continued use of the archer Apollo on tetradrachm reverses in Babylonia and other eastern provinces, despite the adoption of an enthroned Zeus image by the western mints under the reign of Antiochus IV, see Erickson and Wright 2011.
42. For comprehensive catalogues of Seleucid seal impressions, see McDowell 1935b; Wallenfels 1994a; 2016; Lindström 2003; Bollati and Messina 2004a and 2004b. For discussion of Hellenistic Babylonian sealing practices, see Messina 2009; Wallenfels 2016.
43. Erickson also argues that the shift from Seleucus I's portrayals of Apollo using head/bust imagery on coin obverses, to Antiochus I's portrayals of the god's full body on coin reverses, "may have had the intended effect of replacing the divine authority represented on the coins with the regal authority of the king ... [and/or] associate the king with the gods he replaced" (2011, 52).
44. For lists of mints and discussion of minting practices in the Hellenistic Near East, which varied by king and period, see Houghton and Lorber 2002, and Houghton, Lorber, and Hoover 2008.
45. Wallenfels 2015.
46. See, for instance, the official administrative seals of the Seleucid government, such as the salt tax collector seal impressions (ἅλικης ἀτελῶν or ἅλικης ἐπιτελῶν) discovered in the main archives at Seleucia. These seals were impressed alongside private seals on bullae, presumably as a receipt or record of taxes paid. For discussion, see McDowell 1935b, 179–198; Invernizzi 2003, 306–307. Note

that inscriptions on royal and official seals were not exclusively written in Greek; for a discussion of cuneiform legends on Seleucid official royal seals, see Sherwin-White 1987, 25.
47. For an example of this figurine motif with the head still intact, see Van Ingen 1939, No. 295.
48. Some Greek sculptors (working in both marble and bronze) modeled the upper limbs as one piece with the torso for greater stability. However, many other sculptors more closely approximated living anatomy in designing their joins; thus, mid-limb joins in Hellenistic Babylonian figurines are not simply the residual effect of Greek sculptors' influence. Additionally, limb weight and stability are less problematic issues in miniature scale. The connection between Greek sculptural styles and the mid-limb fragmentations seen in the athlete figurines is discussed at greater length in Langin-Hooper 2018b.
49. Bailey 2005, 32–33.
50. Bailey 2005, 181–196.
51. Stewart 1984, 136.
52. See Winter 1996.
53. Fisher 2014.
54. Winter 1981; Collins 2013.
55. For discussion of the Hellenistic Baroque style, see Pollitt 1986, 111–126.
56. Langin-Hooper 2018a.
57. Bailey 2005; Graff 2013; Langin-Hooper 2015.
58. Stewart 1984, 66; emphasis original.
59. Van Ingen 1939, 8.
60. Downey 1988, 14.
61. Kirk 1935.
62. Downey 1988, 14.
63. Cohen 2013, 160.
64. "The Ai Khanum gymnasium was reminiscent of Greek types, but with prominent corridors recalling those of the Persian tradition and a puzzling central rotunda with two side rooms and a corridor of unknown purpose in the south court" (Colledge 1987, 156). See also Rapin 1990, 338; Martinez-Sève 2014.
65. See Menegazzi 2014, Plates 208–212, 234–241.
66. The connection between formalized athletic practice and social order may have already been familiar to some Greeks; see discussion in Christesen 2012, 208–225. Thus, the athlete's body might have been seen as a particularly appropriate social space onto which ideals and norms could be inscribed – including ideals that involved fragmenting the body to maintain social order.
67. Such as by Van Ingen (1939), Karvonen-Kannas (1995), and Menegazzi (2014).
68. The Hellenistic Babylonian corpus of female figurines is vast, even when the figurines of reclining females, females holding/nursing children, or females with separately added arms are not included in the count. Over 500 examples of the nude female figurines are known from Babylon (although note that some of these figurines might date to the Achaemenid period) and over 400 examples are known from Seleucia-on-the-Tigris. Clothed female figurines were similarly popular, with over 250 examples known from Babylon, and over 600 known from Seleucia-on-the-Tigris (although note that Menegazzi categorizes fragmented figurines, including heads only [which might not belong to clothed figurines] and sections of drapery [which might belong to male figurines] in her list). For these exemplars, see Karvonen-Kannas 1995, Klengel-Brandt and Cholidis 2006, and Menegazzi 2014. Note that additional examples of such figurines can also be found from Uruk, Nippur, Kish, and Sippar.
69. See, for instance, Van Buren 1930, Figures 35–37.
70. I have found only ten examples with clearly incised slits for the labia, out of the almost 1,000 nude female figurines published in the various catalogues of the Hellenistic Babylonian cities. See Karvonen-Kannas 1995, Nos. 1, 39–41; Klengel-Brandt and Cholidis 2006, Nos. 1068, 1189, 2275; Menegazzi 2014, Nos. 2.G33, 2.G53, 2.W127.
71. The only other examples of female labial definition in Hellenistic Babylonian terracottas are on a few depictions of seated female children; see Menegazzi 2014, No. 11.P47.
72. See, for instance, Karvonen-Kannas 1995, No. 19. However, few of these figurines echo the particularly narrow waist and wide hip ratio that are seen in many of the female figurines with separately attached arms (discussed in Chapter 2). Indeed, even those that do have similar proportions do not give the same impression of exaggerated voluptuousness, as their arms held tightly to their sides

obscure much of the visual effect of the waist-to-hip curvature (see, for instance, Menegazzi 2014, Plate 50).
73. As they are described by Van Ingen (1939, 57–72).
74. Karvonen-Kannas 1995, 43. See also Petty (2006, 34–42) for discussion of the scholarly history of interpreting nude female figurines as associated with the divine.
75. Scholarly analyses of female figurines often assume an implicit connection between the female body and maternity. For critique, see Darby 2014a and 2014b. The particular pose of the nude woman supporting her breasts has been subjected to more than the usual amount of such fertility and mother-centric interpretation. For discussion, see Karvonen-Kannas 1995, 50; although note that many scholars call instead for a more sexualized interpretation (see, for instance, Bahrani 2001, 81–89).
76. Smith 1991, 83. Note, however, that the pervasiveness of this sculptural practice is debated; see Seaman 2004, 551–557.
77. Smith 1991, 79–83.
78. Bonfante 1989; Cohen 1997.
79. Langin-Hooper 2007, see particularly 155–156.
80. Higgins 1967, 1–5; Uhlenbrock 1990.
81. The impact of this generative act is often overlooked when scholars describe nude standing figurines from Hellenistic Babylonia as continuations of older Mesopotamian types – as, for instance, Legrain did when he wrote that "the figure of the nude woman never changed attitude or meaning across the ages," appearing in the "same ever-recurring forms apparently going back to a very ancient tradition" (1930, 7, 3). Karvonen-Kannas makes a similar connection when she states that "Nude women supporting their breasts represent the oldest Mesopotamian figurine type, already appearing in prehistorical contexts. It was extremely popular during the third and second millennium B.C., and its development can be followed until the end of the Parthian period" (1995, 44). Karvonen-Kannas does note that the new Greek double-mold technique was sometimes used in these figurines' manufacture, but does not dwell on the ramifications of this technology shift for the motif's form and meaning. My point here is that while aspects of these Hellenistic-era figurines do engage with very ancient traditions, they are certainly not carbon-copies of Neo-Babylonian or earlier examples.
82. Langin-Hooper 2013b, 465.
83. See discussion in Karvonen-Kannas 1995, 46.
84. As is commonly seen in typological structuring in figurine catalogues; see, for instance, the division that Menegazzi makes between nude or seminude female figurines (catalogued in section two of her 2014 volumes, beginning on page 106) and clothed female figurines (catalogued in section three, beginning on page 135), whereas the child figurines are catalogued together (in section eleven, beginning on page 352) regardless of their clothed/nude state.
85. See discussion in Cohen 1997, 66–68.
86. Mumford 1934, 3–18; Gell 1992; 1998. For discussion of the stylistic implications of the intertwining of culture and technology, see Feldman 2018.
87. Approximately ten examples of standing clothed female figurines with attempted contrapposto poses (which are somewhat awkward in execution) show the exceptionality, and unpopularity, of this motif in Hellenistic Babylonia; see Menegazzi 2014, Plates 70–71.
88. For examples, see Mollard-Besques 1963, Plates 134–136; Becq 2010, 211; Jeammet 2010b, 182–183.
89. For discussion of nudity as a type of costume, see Bonfante 1989; Hurwit 2007.
90. See, for instance, Karvonen-Kannas 1995, No. 75.
91. For detailed discussion of the concept of *sophrosyne*, see North 1966.
92. Discussion of the pose and its meaning can be found in Zanker 1995, 44–49; see also Chaniotis 1997, 231–232.
93. See, for instance, Ziegler 1962, Abb. 464 and 465.
94. The fact that the nude figurines usually use their left hand to do so, while the clothed figurines reach across the torso with their right arm, may have more to do with the aesthetics (and potential awkwardness) of showing an ungainly reach across a nude torso, or the excessive bunching of cloth that would accompany the tight elbow bend needed to support a breast on the same side of the body (see, for instance, the raised ridges of cloth on the right arm in Figure 3.2).

95. See, for instance, Karvonen-Kannas 1995, Plates 52 and 54; Menegazzi 2014, Plates 293, 296, and 298.
96. See, for instance, Klengel-Brandt and Cholidis 2006, Plates 87 and 90.
97. For the tambour-drum players, see discussion in Chapter 3. For the harp players, see examples in Klengel-Brandt and Cholidis 2006, Plates 91–92; Menegazzi 2014, Plates 306–308.
98. Roller 1991, 136.
99. Naumann 1983, 239–257.
100. Bøgh 2012.
101. Additionally, if given the opportunity, individual women might have chosen to highlight different aspects of their personal identity than what society at large deemed their most important roles. See, for instance, Li's (2017) comparison between the traditional roles of women in Third Intermediate Egypt as emphasized in institutional sources (such as wife and mother) versus the choices made by individual women in their tombs (to emphasize their social power and professional identities).
102. Comprehensive statistics and discussion are presented in the introduction to Menegazzi 2014.
103. The sex of the child cannot always be ascertained; but, when sex is specified, the vast majority of children depicted with the mother are male. I know of only one example where a daughter is explicitly depicted: Van Ingen 1939, No. 631.
104. For social groups, see Klein 1932, Plates 19 and 30; Mollard-Besques 1963, Plates 134–137; Dillon 2012a, 234. For Demeter and Kore, see Merker 2000. For comprehensive discussion of mother-daughter relationships pictured in Greek art, see Foley 2003.
105. Note, however, there are a few examples, particularly from Seleucia-on-the-Tigris, that display a body type similar to the figurines with attached arms; see Menegazzi 2014, Plates 55, 57–59.
106. North 1966; McNiven 2000; Roisman 2005, 176–178; Lee 2015, 40.
107. Masséglia 2015, 130–132.
108. Masséglia 2015, 124–130, 155.
109. For discussion of female shame and its connection with *sophrosyne* in Classical Greece, see Lee 2015, 45.
110. Langin-Hooper 2018a.
111. Heyn similarly suggests that the portrayal of the adorned female body in Palmyrene funerary monuments functioned more as a "display case" for family wealth and elite ideals, rather than as a site for the inscription of other personal issues such as "cultural identity" (2017, 211–212); in making this argument, she draws upon the work of Swift (2009), who argues that this was the case throughout the Greek east. Osborne posits a deliberate flexibility of community membership as the reason for the lack of many age, status, citizenship, and other social markers on the body as depicted in Classical Greek statuary and vase painting (Osborne 2011; see particularly 119–123). Osborne's argument indicates that there was an important pre-Hellenistic precedent (albeit without a particular localization in female gendered imagery) for the manner in which I suggest that the deliberate cohesiveness in Hellenistic Babylonian figurine imagery served an agentive role in smoothing over community differences.
112. Langin-Hooper and Pearce 2014, 186–187; although for cases of women participating in economic transactions at a more intensive level than their husbands, see Doty 1988, 99.
113. For theoretical discussion of how different cultures conceptualize children, and how identities of children can be accessed in the archaeological record, see Lillehammer 1989; Derevenski 1994.
114. Most of the children are explicitly sexed as male through the depiction of male genitalia, although there are a few depictions of female children, also identified by their genitalia, at Seleucia-on-the-Tigris. For an example, see Menegazzi 2014, No. 11.P47. Note that the depiction of genitalia on a female child differs sharply from the less explicitly sexed portrayal of female infants and children in Classical Greece; see Lee 2015, 44.
115. Lee (2015, 38) makes a similar argument about Classical Greek depictions of male children. See also a discussion in McNiven (2000) of the "otherness" of boys, and its resolution via maturity, in Classical Greek art.
116. See, for instance, Menegazzi 2014, Plates 348–351.
117. For examples, see Menegazzi 2014, Plate 351. For a discussion of similar figurines of swaddled infants, and the relationship of swaddling to citizenship status, see Glinister 2017.

118. See also Karvonen-Kannas 1995, Nos. 237, 240, and 241.
119. Approximately 20 percent of the roughly 500 child figurines catalogued in Menegazzi 2014 show the child participating in some sort of servant-like work, such as carrying a jar or box.
120. See Klengel-Brandt and Cholidis 2006, Plate 103.
121. See Van Ingen 1939, No. 720. The vessel depicted was identified/interpreted as a *lagynos* by Van Ingen (1930, 201). The *lagynos*, with its "squat biconic body, narrow neck, high and straight handle," is one of many pottery vessel shapes popular at Seleucia-on-the-Tigris that has been linked to counterparts from the Greek world (Valtz 1993, 172).
122. See Van Ingen 1939, No. 694. The pose and activity are perhaps most famously seen on the tombstone of Hegeso; see Stewart 2008, 160–161. See also discussion of female slaves at domestic tasks in Oakley 2000. This servitude posture was also used for full-scale statues of free-born girls serving at temples; see Neils 2003, 138, 158–159, 289.
123. See Menegazzi 2014, No. 11.G197, in comparison with the famous Athenian calf-bearer statue of the Archaic period (see Boardman 2016, Figure 75).
124. Valtz 1993, 172.
125. Approximately ten out of the roughly 500 child figurines from Seleucia-on-the-Tigris catalogued by Menegazzi are in this pose; see Menegazzi 2014, Plates 317–318. I do not know of any examples from any of the other Hellenistic Babylonian cities.
126. Stewart 2008, 261.
127. For discussion of child slaves serving at the symposion, see Oakley 2000, 241; Neils and Oakley (eds) 2003, Catalogue Nos. 63–66; Beaumont 2012, 122–128. For child slaves as sexual partners, see Golden 1984; Shapiro 2003, 99; Wrenhaven 2012, 72–73; Cohen 2014; Corner 2014, 200–201; Hunt 2018, 99, 106. For discussion of the limited evidence for pederastic practices in the Hellenistic period, see Lear 2014, 116.
128. See extensive examples in Dandamaev 1984, especially Chapter 1.
129. This is not to say that such sexual encounters, including with slave boys, did not occur. See, for instance, McKeown (2007) for discussion of the disjuncture in ancient Rome between ideals of sexual practice involving child slaves and reality. However, idealizing and making tangible such erotic attraction in figurine form implies a certain level of acceptability that was alien to Mesopotamia.
130. For a helpful overview and list, including discussion of how such myths related to Greek art, see Shapiro 2003. Babies born in convoluted circumstances were also sometimes presented as "heroes" of a sort, or at least as having somewhat outsize influence on their immediate society, in Greek plays; see Heap 2002–2003.
131. Such an explanation is not necessarily at odds with my overarching argument in this section: namely, that figurines of children were made overtly supernatural in order to distance from reality any social negotiation and experimentation in which they were engaged, keeping safe the real-life identities of real-life children. Similar processes can be seen in operation in traditional European fairy tales and even contemporary literature, in which the child protagonist is often cast as both hero and orphan so that the agency of the child, as well as his or her adventures and perils, can be explored without too closely threatening the comfort and security of the more average child reader/user (and his or her family). See extensive discussion and examples in Bettelheim 1976, especially the introduction.
132. Indeed, Karvonen-Kannas uses these names interchangeably (1995, 67).
133. The list of scholars who have discussed this iconography is too extensive to include here. For an overview, see Porter 2003.
134. For the numerous figurines of Eros from around the Hellenistic world, see: Burr 1934, Plates 7–25; Mollard-Besques 1963, Plates 39–79; Thompson 1963, Plate V; Besques 1972, Plates 39–65; 1986; 1992; Török 1995, Plates XXVI–XXXIII; Ammerman 2002, 148, 155–164; Rumscheid 2006, 272–82, Plates 96–109; Becq, Jeammet, and Mathieux 2010, 146–149; Oggiano 2015, Figure 5; Erlich 2017, 43–44.
135. Pollitt 1986, 128–129, 135; Beaumont 2003, 81. Even the more somber statues of children dedicated in temples elsewhere in the Hellenistic world usually show the child's head facing somewhat away from the viewer, the hands grasping a pet, or other posture that

indicates childhood behavior. See extensive examples and discussion in Bobou 2015.
136. Pollitt 1986, 128–129; Ridgway 2001, 232–233.
137. Mollard-Besques 1963, Plates 161–163; Erlich and Kloner 2008, Figure 225; Rous 2010; Tezgör 2010, Figure 152; Bobou 2015 (see especially Figure 32); Oggiano 2015, Figure 8. For further examples and discussion, see Karvonen-Kannas 1995, 69.
138. Pollitt 1986, 128–129; Ridgway 2001, 232–233; Beaumont 2003, 79.
139. Smith 1991, Figure 221.
140. See Legrain 1930, No. 149.
141. See Legrain 1930, No. 124; Karvonen-Kannas 1995, No. 206.
142. Boardman 2016, Figure 205.
143. Masséglia 2015, 326.
144. For the specific link between Hellenistic Babylonian figurines and Harpocrates, see Legrain 1930, 22.
145. For detailed discussion of Harpocrates iconography in Hellenistic Egypt, including statistics regarding this god's immense popularity, see Boutantin 2013. For further Egyptian figurine examples, see Török 1995, Plates IX, XXXVI–LI. Note that the Hellenistic Babylonian figurines distort almost beyond recognition the Harpocrates headdress (the double crown of Egypt, with large lotus buds on either side), indicating that the particulars of this Egyptian iconography were either unknown or (unsurprisingly) irrelevant in Babylonia. For description and explanation of the Harpocrates crown, see Hall 1977; Török 1995, 57.
146. Hellenistic Babylonia may not have been the only place where such a connection was made: as discussed by Erlich (2017, 43), Chéhab (1951–1952, 139–142) argues for a connection between figurines of Eros and Harpocrates at Kharayeb.
147. See Karvonen-Kannas 1995, Figures 409 and 410. Note that this activity does not preclude identification with Harpocrates, as that god was often shown riding animals, including horses, in Hellenistic Egyptian figurines; see Boutantin 2013, 78.
148. See discussion in Beaumont (2003, particularly 78–81), in which these Hellenistic developments are situated within the earlier Greek history of depicting children. For detailed discussion of the literary and historical evidence for this phenomenon, see Golden 1997.
149. For general overview, see Uhlenbrock 1990; Muller 2010. For discussion of mold use at Seleucia-on-the-Tigris, see Menegazzi 2014, 47–51.
150. The British Museum object numbers of all ten examples are: BM 84-2-11-580, BM 84-2-11-581, BM 84-2-11-582, BM 84-2-11-583, BM 84-2-11-584, BM 84-2-11-585, BM 84-2-11-586, BM 84-2-11-587, BM 84-2-11-588, BM 84-2-11-589. For discussion, see Karvonen-Kannas 1995, Nos. 196–205.
151. See list in catalogue entry for Karvonen-Kannas 1995, Nos. 196–205.
152. A short list of examples at the Kelsey Museum of Archaeology:
TM 1931.545/KM 2018.01.0588, KM 18196, KM 35160, KM 35146, KM 35156, KM 35162, KM 35147, KM 35133. Castor (2017, 94–96) argues that the complexity of Hellenistic jewelry inspired those who could not afford to own such elaborate pieces (or be likely to know anyone who could afford them) to purchase ceramics decorated with representations of jewelry. Terracottas like that seen in Figure 4.22 might be an example of a similar practice.
153. Such an interpretation would fit within current trends in the study of jewelry and dress to see such adornments to the body as experienced, embodied, and performed. For a comprehensive discussion of the current state of the field, as well as its applicability to ancient Greek dress and jewelry, see Lee 2015, 10–32. For examples of such approaches in the study of Mesopotamian dress, see Thomason 2010 and Gansell 2013.
154. For similar discussion, as well as performative reconstruction, of how Roman ithyphallic pendants were worn, and could attract attention by moving in concert with the wearer's body, see Whitmore 2017.
155. West 1992, 54–55; Landels 1999, 48–49. Figurines of seemingly mortal *kithara*-playing musicians are also known, particularly from Babylon and Seleucia-on-the-Tigris; see, for instance, extensive examples in Menegazzi 2014, Chapter 10. The instrument also had associations with the god Apollo, as will be discussed in Chapter 5. However, these figures more commonly played the round-boxed *kithara*. The difference between the

kithara shapes may have been significant, as the round-based shape in Classical Greece generally connoted indoor, informal music making.
156. Gold and ivory inlays were most notable among these decorations in Classical Greece (Mathiesen 1999, 265), but terracotta ornaments might have been used as a less costly substitute.
157. In other parts of the Hellenistic world, figurines depicting Eros as a musician, particularly with the *kithara*, were placed in tombs and associated with the transition to the afterlife (see Karoglou 2016). While there is no definitive evidence to make that funerary connection for the Hellenistic Babylonian figurines, the possibility of such ritual and afterlife beliefs points to yet an additional kind of efficaciousness for these objects.
158. Shehata 2014, 108–116.
159. Figural incense burners (*thymiaterion*) are known from the Hellenistic world, including sites in Mesopotamia; see, for instance, Haider 2008, 200–201; Pilides 2009, 55; Shevchenko 2015. Such incense burners were sometimes constructed so that the human figure sits upon an altar or other large seat, similar to the cones discussed here; see Walsh 1988, Figures 2 and 3.
160. Heuzey 1891, 48–50.
161. See, for instance, Karvonen-Kannas 1995, Plate 80.
162. For examples, see Van Ingen 1939, Nos. 750, 777, and 814, and Menegazzi 2014, No. 11.G9.
163. Some terracotta depictions of children with separately made limbs were considerably larger than most Hellenistic Babylonian figurines, measuring up to 30–50 cm in height; see Karvonen-Kannas 1995: Nos. 242–252; Menegazzi 2014: Nos. 11.G303–11.G314. These figures are not discussed in this volume because of their substantial size, which verges in some instances on life-size representations of babies and toddlers. It is worth noting, however, that some scholars have suggested that these large terracotta figures were used for ritual or religious purposes (see Rostovtzeff 1937; Van Ingen 1939, 22); such an explanation would further link the child's body with ritual activity, as discussed earlier in this chapter.
164. Doty 1978; 1988; Langin-Hooper and Pearce 2014.
165. For sculptures of girls, see extensive examples in Bobou 2015. For figurines of girls, see examples throughout Jeammet (ed) 2010a.
166. Van Ingen 1939, Nos. 631, 694, 750, 770.
167. Nicholas Thomas describes how such identity constructions can work through physical resemblance to the depicted subject in art. When the viewer recognizes similarity between himself or herself and the depicted person – especially when the similarity is in a physical feature that defines a social identity (such as, in Thomas's case study, skin color and European clothing in colonial Australia) – the bond created is "not merely an ideological, but a performative and embodied connection" (Thomas 1999, 90). By representing a similarity with a certain group of people, the image also excludes another group of people – those who cannot plausibly self-identify (Thomas 1999, 90–92). This is not to say that these figurines' features were accessing similarly politicized identities. However, it is possible that, through their physical specificity, they created deeper bonds of recognition and self-identification with members of certain identity groups that shared similar physical characteristics on their own bodies.
168. Bailey 2005, 199.
169. Gosden 2005, 197.
170. The role of miniatures in identity formation and cognition is discussed by Clark, who describes how figurines participate "in the construction of new modes of thinking" (2010, 27). Jones similarly describes how miniatures

> are not mere vehicles for cognition, these things are not 'good to think with' in the sense described by Levi-Strauss; a process in which thoughts and meanings are arbitrarily attached to things or objects. Instead, I am suggesting that these artefacts are treated as active components of thought; thoughts are embodied in their fabric. These miniature artefacts act as devices for embodying ideas concerning scale, distance, connection and relationship.
> (2013, 370)

171. Hodder 2012, 88.
172. Langin-Hooper 2013b, 465.

5 THE GLOBAL AND THE LOCAL: MAKING CULTURAL AND SOCIAL CHOICES WITH FIGURINES

1. This was certainly not a unique feature of the Hellenistic Babylonian figurines; it is seen in figurines throughout the ancient world, as well as on other miniature objects, such as seals. The close connections between human and divine realms suggested by such imagery might have been further activated through tactile interaction and play; see Sillar 1994, 55–56. For the effect of a powerful being "cut down to size" through the conceit of miniaturization that is not done to scale, see discussion in Kellum 2018, 200.
2. See Menegazzi 2014, Plates 25, 27.
3. Other Aphrodite poses made famous by large-scale statuary and which are seen in other Hellenistic *koine* figurine corpora (see, for instance, Mollard-Besques 1963, Plates 12–31) are largely absent from this corpus, as is typical in miniature imagery of the goddess throughout the Near East (Çakmak 2009, 74–75).
4. While an Eros identification is not an absolute certainty, his wings and child-like proportions make no other divine identity likely, while interpretation of the figure as a mortal infant is ruled out both by the wings and the positioning of his body above his mother's shoulder and on her right side (in contrast with the near universal left-side placement of infants on figurines depicting less overtly divine mothers, as discussed in Chapter 3). Aphrodite commonly appears with her son Eros in Hellenistic depictions, where he often hovers mid-flight over her shoulder – a pose seen perhaps most famously in the so-called Slipper Slapper statue from Delos (see Martin 2017, Plate 23). While Greek vase painting of the mid to late Classical period often depicted Eros flitting around bejeweled brides and matrons (Sutton Jr. 1992, 24–27; 1997–1998, 34–43; Paul 1994–1995, 61), his appearances with women on Hellenistic statuary are more securely associated with his mother.
5. For an example of this hairstyle, see images of the "Capitoline Aphrodite" (Smith 1991, Figure 99).
6. Smith 1991, 83. See also Mollard-Besques (1963, Plate 35) for its expression in figurines from Myrina.
7. For description of this figurine style and its long history in Mesopotamia, see Van Buren 1930, xliii.
8. See Smith 1991, Nos. 104 and 105.
9. See Smith 1991, No. 75.
10. Bahrani 1996.
11. Martin 2017, 152–168.
12. For discussion of the possibilities and difficulties of such syncretism, especially for our understanding of how deity worship was practiced, see Nitschke 2013.
13. See Menegazzi 2014, Plates 5, 20.
14. Seen, for instance, on the parapet relief of the Temple of Athena Nike on the Athenian Acropolis (Stewart 2008, 198–199) and the Nike by Paionios set up at Olympia to commemorate a victory during the Peloponnesian War (Stewart 2008, 200–202). This sexualization of Nike was continued into the Hellenistic period, as seen in the Nike of Samothrace, the so-called Winged Victory (Smith 1991, No. 97).
15. For instance, Herbert (2008, 259–260) argues for the particular appeal of a military Athena in the Hellenistic Near East due to the constant strain of warfare.
16. Pollitt 1986, 47–48.
17. Smith 1991, No. 283.
18. Brijder 2014, 98.
19. Over one hundred examples of Hellenistic Babylonian figurines potentially identifiable as Herakles are known; see Legrain 1930, Nos. 129–130; Ziegler 1962, Plate 23; Klengel-Brandt and Cholidis 2006, Plates 79–82; Menegazzi 2014, Plates 7–13.
20. See discussion in Menegazzi 2014, 79.
21. Connelly 1989, 152–153; 1990, 98–99.
22. Van Ingen 1939, 106–109.
23. For the popularity of "Herakles type" figurines in the Hellenistic Near East, see discussion in Invernizzi 1985, 98; Connelly 1990, 98–99; Martinez-Sève 2002, 726–728.
24. Invernizzi 2007, 64–65.
25. These two divine names for the statue were given in the Greek and Parthian inscriptions, respectively, on the statue's legs (Potter 1991, 278–279).
26. Klengel-Brandt 1993, 198. Note that I have previously raised concerns over the specificity of this Nergal identification (Langin-Hooper

2013b, 471). Kaizer also raises similar concerns with the Nergal identification of Herakles imagery at Hatra and Palmyra (2000, 223).
27. For detailed discussion of the war and its aftermath, including the movement of the sculpture, see Potter 1991.
28. Similar arguments for "Herakles" imagery used in Hellenistic Levantine contexts have been made by Kaizer 2000, 225; Erlich 2009, 14–15; and Nitschke 2013.
29. A similar observation is made by Canepa 2015, 88.
30. This particular popularity of lion-hunting attributes (the club and the lion pelt), as opposed to other features usually associated with Herakles in the Greek world, is also shared in the terracotta figurines at Susa (Martinez-Sève 2002, 704).
31. As also discussed in Langin-Hooper 2013b.
32. Collon 1987, 130. Neo-Assyrian palaces may have been completely inaccessible by the Hellenistic period; however, Neo-Assyrian seals have frequently been recovered from later contexts (Collon 1987, 135–139)
33. Collon 1987, 92; Garrison 2000, 126–151; Curtis and Tallis 2005, 92–94.
34. On the importance of seals as portable media of idea exchange in first millennium BCE Mesopotamia, see Uehlinger 2000, xxv–xxvi.
35. Winter 1985; Asher-Greve 1998, 20; Assante 2017, 64–74. See also discussion in Chapter 4 of this volume. Note that even when the lion-hunting hero motif was depicted, the first millennium versions prior to the Hellenistic period were usually not shown completely nude.
36. I know of no Hellenistic Babylonian figurines securely identified as Dionysos, although Menegazzi does tentatively catalogue a few examples from Seleucia-on-the-Tigris as such (see, for instance, Menegazzi 2014, No. 1.S34). Figurines that can reasonably be identified as Apollo exist, but are rare: four are known from Babylon (Karvonen-Kannas 1995, Nos. 317–320) and perhaps eighteen from Seleucia-on-the-Tigris (Menegazzi 2014, Plates 13–14, 23, 27–28). Note that several of these examples (particularly from Seleucia-on-the-Tigris) are not unambiguously deities, while others, such as Menegazzi 2014, No. 1.P13 appear to be intersex or hermaphrodite figures. I think it is therefore likely that the actual number of "Apollos" is even lower than this number indicates. In contrast, for a discussion of the general popularity of the Greek gods, especially Dionysos, in figurines throughout the rest of the Hellenistic world, see Ammerman 1990, 40–41. For examples of Dionysos figurines, see Mollard-Besques 1963, Plates 93–95.
37. Karvonen-Kannas 1995, 84.
38. Al-Salihi 1987.
39. Iossif 2011, 252–262.
40. Stronach 1989, 264–269.
41. Root 1989, 45.
42. Erickson and Wright 2011; although they note that the nudity of the Apollo figure might have been problematic to some Near Eastern viewers, prompting the introduction of a clothed archer on later Parthian coins that imitated the Seleucid type (2011, 165–166).
43. Lerner 2017, 9, 13–14. For detailed discussion of this issue of the god's identity, and for a convincing explanation of why this ambiguity (especially between potential Nabu vs. Apollo identifications) was carefully cultivated to show deference to Babylonian temples and religious practice, see Erickson 2011. For discussion of the links between Apollo-Helios as Mithras, including the Persepolis tablets (possibly affixed to altars), see Lorber and Iossif 2009b. Additional evidence for the syncretism of Apollo-Mithras-Helios-Hermes can be found in the *nomos* inscription and the colossal statues at Nemrud Dagh (Brijder 2014, 45, 80).
44. See, for instance, Van Ingen 1939, Figures 538–540; Karvonen-Kannas 1995, Figure 320.
45. See masterful discussion throughout Çakmak 2009.
46. Smith 1991, 65.
47. The difference between "sex" (as a biological and physical distinction between bodies) and "gender" (as a socially constructed performance related to, but not always strictly correlated with, biological difference) has been well established in scholarship; for a discussion of feminist scholarship exploring the complicated relationship between sex and gender, particularly in reference to reconstructions of the past, see Wylie 1991, 33–35. While respecting (and agreeing with) this distinction for living bodies, I use "sex" and "gender" in slightly looser and murkier ways here. This is

because both the sex of the figurines (as determined by representations of anatomy) and the gender of the figurines (as determined by representations of social gender markers) were social constructs, as both were fashioned in a social environment and could be adapted to social pressures, rather than being biological or organic in origin. Thus, when I speak of "intersex" figurines, I am referring to figurines that are depicted as having intersexed anatomy, and thus present the illusion of anatomical/biological difference, but were nevertheless social and "gendered" in that their anatomy was selected within a social environment rather than being due to biological variation.

48. Precise numbers are difficult to obtain, partly due to scholarship's history of "blindness" when it comes to recognizing and labeling nontraditionally sexed bodies depicted in these figurines (see discussion in Langin-Hooper 2013b). However, a sense of the rarity of these figurines can be gained from a few examples. Of the 747 reclining terracotta figurines that Menegazzi (2014) catalogues at Seleucia-on-the-Tigris, there is only one (P111) that – like TM 1931.483+1931.461/KM 2018.01.0528 + 2018.01.0528 (seen in Figure 5.12) – shows clear markers of both male and female sex. The proportions are more substantial – but still with an overall scarcity – among the bone and alabaster figurines (materials which were, overall, used more rarely than terracotta): for instance, of the approximately 150 bone figurines that Van Ingen catalogues at Seleucia-on-the-Tigris, at least five have some indications of both male and female sex. This difference in the relative proportions of intersexed figurines in different materials may be due to the pleasurable tactile-kinetic aspects of bone and alabaster, which invite sustained caressing and handling, and may have encouraged a sexualized (or at least exploratory and experimental) engagement with these non-normative body types.

49. Bahrani 2001, 92.
50. There is substantial evidence that intersex, gender-fluid, and/or nonbinary gender individuals served as devotees of Ishtar (Asher-Greve 2002; McCaffrey 2002; Peled 2018), and that Ishtar was believed to have the power to change the gender of mortal humans (Assante 2017, 45). However, although the goddess herself was sometimes gender-ambiguous (see Budin 2004, 104) and embodied qualities that were often associated with the male gender, such as warfare and violence, her body morphology was described and depicted as essentially female – indeed, alluringly so (see Foster 2005, 673–679).

51. Invernizzi 2008, 265.
52. Nochlin 1988, 2.
53. Conkey and Gero 1997, 421; Pollock 1988, 18.
54. Asher-Greve 1998.
55. Peled 2016a; Peled 2016b; Peled 2018.
56. Although estimates indicate that 0.18–1.7 percent of the modern population is biologically intersexed, this percentage was likely far lower in Hellenistic Babylonia, as 1. many intersexed individuals today can only be identified as such through DNA analysis, and 2. many forms of hermaphrodism are associated with life-threatening diseases that would have likely caused most such individuals in Hellenistic Babylonia to die at an early age (Stökl 2013, 63–64).
57. LIMC, Volume 5, *Hermaphrodite*.
58. Miracle and Borić 2008, 103; see also that article's broader discussion of animal-human hybrids, with its compelling argumentation for dismantling assumptions that modern categories of body morphology (including a sharp division between animal bodies and human bodies) existed in the ancient world, and for developing more nuanced understandings of personhood that may have fluidly entangled both animal and human forms.
59. See, for instance, Van Ingen 1939, Nos. 1531, 1537, 1542a.
60. Caubet 2016, 39; Pruzsinszky 2016.
61. See, for instance, Karvonen-Kannas 1995, No. 304.
62. Bailey 2005, 72.
63. Pultz 1995, 162.
64. Bailey 2005, 81.
65. This "problem" is noted by Legrain in his catalogue of the Nippur figurines, however he does not discuss the implications of the issue (1930, 23).
66. Following Judith Butler's theories of gender as performance, in which actions both specify and create gender identities, whereas "sexual difference ... is never simply a function of material differences which are not in some

way both marked and formed by discursive practices" (1993, 1).
67. Bailey 2005, 83.
68. Karvonen-Kannas 1995, 96–97. Note that male figures could sometimes ride in this posture; see especially depictions of Dionysos, such as in the famous mosaics of Delos where he rides a panther or tiger (Pollitt 1986, 219). However, Dionysos in these depictions has a particularly feminine aspect, in keeping with the general feminization of his imagery in the Hellenistic period.
69. Boardman 1991, Figure 208.3.
70. Mayor 2016.
71. Masséglia 2015, 50.
72. Piggott 1992, 91; Rahbari 2017, 20. Achaemenid Persian women's clothing also included robes that allowed for sitting astride a horse (Goldman 1991, 95).
73. Cambon 2008, 196. Similar discussion of sculpture in Hellenistic Babylonia with reference to objects found at Begram can be found in Canepa 2015, 84–86.
74. Pollitt 1986, 134–144.
75. For overview, see Ballet and Jeammet 2011.
76. For examples and discussion, see: Mollard-Besques 1963, Plates 171–176; Higgins 1967, 99; Connelly 1990, 89–91; Fischer 1994, Plates 27, 32–35, 37–51; Khodza 2006; Rumscheid 2006, Plates 114–125; Laugier 2009; Süvegh 2014; Voegtle 2016, 8–9. For discussion of the Egyptian influence on the development of the Hellenistic "grotesque" genre, see Stevenson 1975, 149–152.
77. Khodza 1984; Roselli 2011, 112; Mitchell 2013, 280–281. See also the discussion in Chapter 2.
78. Garland 1995, 73–86; Halliwell 2008, 244–245; Mitchell 2013, 278–281. However, note that such bodies were not always considered comedic, even by Greek audiences, and that pity was one possible reaction; see discussions in Garland (2017) and Mitchell (2017, 193).
79. Giuliani 1987, 714–718; Erlich 2015, 165; Voegtle 2016, 6–7.
80. Voegtle 2016, 9–11.
81. Ballet and Jeammet 2011, 48; Mitchell 2013, 275; Süvegh 2014, 143; Adams 2017, 197.
82. Mitchell 2017, 184–185.
83. Vlahogiannis 1998, 23–33; Dillon 2017; Rose 2017; Samama 2017.
84. Régnault 1909; Stevenson 1975; Grmek and Gourevich 1998; Khodza 2006; Mitchell 2013; Mitchell 2017, 185–191.
85. Menegazzi 2014, Plates 375–376; for a comparative example from Priene, see Rumscheid 2006, Plate 115.
86. Mitchell 2017, 184.
87. However, these are less common, and often with less exaggerated genitalia, than seen elsewhere in the Hellenistic world. This may have been due, in part, to the general lack of Mesopotamian interest in phallic imagery and phallocentric constructs of masculinity (see discussion in Cooper 2017, particularly his conclusion on page 120).
88. See, for instance, Menegazzi 2014, Plates 381–382.
89. Although note Barrett's compelling argument that "grotesque" figurines even in Hellenistic Delos could have been taken seriously as religious objects (2011, 422).
90. This connection between Bes and the "grotesque" genre is also made with regards to Egyptian figurines in Ballet and Jeammet 2011, 67–68.
91. Dasen 1993, 53–83.
92. Dasen 1993, 78–82.
93. Abdi 2002.
94. Black and Green 1992, 106, 115–116, 147–148.
95. For examples of Bes iconography in Egyptian figurines, see Fischer 1994, Plates 53–55.
96. This may also reflect how many people in the Hellenistic world more generally thought about these figurines; as Masséglia argues, dwarf "grotesques" throughout the Hellenistic world were more linked to Egyptian gods, including both Bes and Harpocrates, than were most figurines in the "grotesque" genre (2015, 278–279).
97. For discussion, as well as additional bibliography and references to Mesopotamian omen texts (especially Šumma Izbu, "If a Birth Anomaly" and Šumma Alu, "If a City"), see Kellenberger 2017.
98. Scurlock and Anderson 2005, 332–336.
99. Dillon 2017, 167–169.
100. See the parallel "silence" of Achaemenid sources on the issue of disability and presence of disabled bodies (Coloru 2017).
101. The "idea of the 'monstrous' or non-normative human goes against ideal tropes in Babylonia and would, therefore, probably be

seen as anathema to the gods rather than something apotropaic. Such figures clearly portended ill" (Jay Crisostomo, personal communication). See also Rochberg 2016, 110–120.

102. Vlahogiannis 1998; 2005, 181; Adams 2017, 196; Draycott 2017, 90.

103. Family and hereditary issues could also be blamed (see Kellenberger 2017, 51); however, the threat to the community and possibility that the community at large was to blame was also implied in the omens. Note that Greek sources also indicate disabled individuals could represent a threat to the entire community (Vlahogiannis 1998, 19).

104. Langin-Hooper 2016 (for original erroneous attributions, see Legrain 1930, Nos. 144–146; Van Buren 1930, 60–62).

105. Langin-Hooper 2016.

106. Klengel-Brandt and Cholidis 2006, 257.

107. See, for instance, KM 16066 at the Kelsey Museum of Archaeology.

108. Images of reclining banqueters at the symposion were extensively depicted on Greek ceramic vessels (see Lissarrague 1990; Topper 2012), tombstones and votive stelae (see Thönges-Stringaris 1965; Wild 1973, 176–177), as well as terracotta figurines (see footnote 109), during the Archaic and Classical periods. A Late Classical or Hellenistic Macedonian tombstone with a similar motif can be seen in Barr-Sharrar 1982, 124.

109. Figurines depicting the human body in a reclined pose, supported by one (usually the left) arm, had been in use throughout the Greek mainland and Magna Graecia since the sixth century BCE (Stillwell 1952, 104–106; Karvonen-Kannas 1995, 62; Rumscheid 2006, 503–504; Menegazzi 2012, 160). These figurines were traditionally male; this likely reflected the reality of predominately male symposion participation, although the figurines may also have represented the god Dionysos (Higgins 1967, 91; Langin-Hooper 2007, 152; Menegazzi 2012, 160).

110. For a detailed listing of such imagery, see Kilmer 1993; for further discussion, see Neils 2000.

111. For an example in terracotta figurine form, see Stillwell 1952, No. XIV, 30. This motif can also be seen (rarely) in Greek ceramic painting, such as the depiction of Ariadne and Dionysos on an Athenian black-figure amphora (Topper 2012, Figure 38), as well as depictions of seemingly-mortal, respectably-dressed women reclining between men (Topper 2012, figure 20) or at the feet of a male partner (Topper 2012, Figures 22, 49, 53). The use of such imagery in Greek art may have had Etruscan origins (Peirce 1998). Topper argues that the motif of respectable female symposion participation may represent the Greek (especially Athenian) understanding of the symposion's pre-Classical past, functioning as a foil to the symposion's Classical-period role in situating women (vis-à-vis their exclusion) into their appropriate place in society (Topper 2012, 102–135).

112. Mollard-Besques 1963, Plate 153.

113. This gender transposition in the Hellenistic Babylonian figurines has already been noted by many other scholars; for recent discussions, see Klengel-Brandt and Cholidis 2006, 257–258; Menegazzi 2012, 160. There are a few examples of reclining male-female couples among the figurine corpora of Hellenistic Babylonia, particularly at Seleucia-on-the-Tigris (see Figure 3.8 in this volume, as well as Van Ingen 1939, Nos. 850–855), as well as what appear to be reclining male figurines, especially from late Parthian levels at Uruk (see Ziegler 1962, abb. 409–411), but also in other contexts (for Seleucia-on-the-Tigris, see Van Ingen 1939, Nos. 688–690). However, such figurines are far fewer in number than the reclining female figurines in Hellenistic Babylonia.

114. There are a few depictions of similar solitary reclining female figures in Greek art, but they are rare. For examples of ceramic painting depicting reclining women symposiasts without male accompaniment, see Rabinowitz 2002, Figure 5.15 and Topper 2012, Figures 45 and 46. However, as Topper suggests, this imagery, with women banqueting as equal or solitary symposiasts, was designed to give the impression of a mixed-up, "overturned world," different from reality, where nothing operates as it should (Topper 2012, 120; see also Rabinowitz 2002, 135–136). In contrast, the widespread popularity of the Hellenistic Babylonian figurines, and their usage in preference to or exclusion of similar male imagery, would suggest that they represent the lived, or even ideal, world.

115. This cultural preference has been extensively discussed throughout this volume; but see also Bahrani (2001, 91–94) for discussion with particular reference to reclining female figurines.

116. For examples from Babylon, see Legrain 1930, Nos. 144–146; Karvonen-Kannas 1995, Nos. 146–184; Klengel-Brandt and Cholidis 2006, Nos. 1551–1579. For Seleucia-on-the-Tigris, see Van Ingen 1939, Nos. 627–687. For Uruk, see Ziegler 1962, Nos. 729–737.
117. There is a current shift in scholarly thinking about whether or not even traditional images of the Greek symposion from Attic vase painting can, in fact, be regarded as "straightforward" depictions of symposion practice (see, for instance, Topper 2012). It is not my intention here to participate in that debate; rather, I suggest that whatever correlation Archaic and Classical Greek imagery had with lived symposion practice, the figurines of Hellenistic Babylonia, with their differing, female figures (as well as being removed in space, time, and, to some degree, culture, from sixth to fourth-century BCE Athenian society) had far less of a direct connection.
118. Berlin 2013; for such early use specifically at Seleucia-on-the-Tigris, see Valtz 1991, 56.
119. The most popular of these Hellenistic *koine* vessels used in Mesopotamia were: "the bowl with in-curving rim, the fish-plate, the bowl with angular profile and out-turned rim, the plate with thickened interior rim, the amphora, the *guttus*, the *lagynos* and the spiral bowl" (Potts 1997, 298). However, some cookware was also adopted; see discussion in Hannestad 1983, 105.
120. Keall and Ciuk (1991, 64–65) also note that the adoption of Hellenistic *koine* ceramic styles seems to have been motivated more by "fashion" and a desire for Hellenistic appearances, rather than an interest in changing the basic forms or functions of local Babylonian ceramics.
121. For examples from Seleucia-on-the-Tigris, see Van Ingen 1939, Nos. 620a, 632, 644, 652; for Babylon, see Karvonen-Kannas 1995, Nos. 142, 144, 145, 146; Klengel-Brandt and Cholidis 2006, Nos. 1580, 1581, 1582, 1584; for Uruk, see Ziegler 1962, Nos. 399, 400.
122. Karvonen-Kannas makes a similar argument, that "the type changed to satisfy the local cults: the man became a woman" (1995, 64). I would point out, however, that there is no clear evidence that these figurines served a cultic function (they are usually found in domestic contexts: see Van Ingen 1939, 21; see also further discussion later in this chapter), and so the male/female transposition should more likely be thought of as appealing to local traditions *in general*. For extensive discussion of the Mesopotamian preference for female-male attraction, in contrast to Greek practice, and the site of the female body as object of male desire, see Bahrani 2001.
123. See, for instance, examples in Stillwell 1952, Plates 18–23.
124. Assante 2000, 90–92. Such imagery persisted, even into the Hellenistic period, although in a limited way (for an example from Uruk, see Ziegler 1962, No. 416a).
125. The haunting presence/absence and fetishization of a single limb, and the masculine power to rebuff and discard the offerings of single female hands, is discussed with reference to Renaissance gloves in Stallybrass and Jones 2004.
126. See lengthy discussion in Hannestad 1983, 97–105 (see particularly the discussion on pages 101–102); also Gibson 1975; Valtz 1991; Potts 1997, 296–300; Petrie 2002.
127. Keall and Ciuk 1991, 64–65.
128. Downey 1988, 16–17; Potts 1997, 299.
129. Petrie 2002, 103–104.
130. Petrie 2002, 106.
131. Hannestad mentions "only two commonware bowls" from Nippur that can "show a clear Greek influence" (1983, 101).
132. The Nippur community may also have been rejecting a particular kind of tactile engagement with female figurines in general, which was not restricted to the reclining form or its possible banqueting associations. As noted in note 50 in Chapter 2, other terracotta figurines with separately added (and, in some cases, movable) arms, which encouraged tactile exploration of naked female bodies, are not generally found in the Nippur corpus (for discussion of the particulars of object provenance, see Langin-Hooper 2016, 72). The role of such figurines in Greek-Babylonian cross-cultural interactions, and their specific mediation of Babylonian ideas of sexuality (despite their manufacture in the Greek double-mold technique), may explain such figurines' relative popularity across Babylonia – and also makes their absence at Nippur notable.
133. Koldewey 1925, 212–213.
134. Klengel-Brandt 1979–1981, 120.
135. "*In Babylon kann aus den Fundumständen der Frauenterrakotten, die sich im gesamten Stadtgebiet befinden, kein besonderer Zusammenhang mit*

Bestattungen ersehen werden. Eine überzeugende Erklärung für den Typ der ruhenden Frau muß für Babylon offen bleiben" (Klengel-Brandt and Cholidis 2006, 257–258).
136. Van Buren 1930, 59–62.
137. Van Ingen 1939, 21.
138. Invernizzi 1970–1971, 368–372; Invernizzi 1985, 98.
139. Menegazzi 2014, 71.
140. Menegazzi 2014, 70–71.
141. This calculation is not provided by Menegazzi, but it was computed using the catalogue information in Menegazzi 2014.
142. Indeed, it seems possible that the meanings of such figurines at Seleucia-on-the-Tigris, where more firm evidence exists for a connection between them and funerary practice (Menegazzi 2014, 71–72), differed from the meanings of these figurines when they were used by members of other Babylonian communities.
143. Thönges-Stringaris 1965, 1, 63; Baughan 2013.
144. For discussion of the "middle ground" in colonial encounters, see Gosden 2004, 82–113.
145. Van Dommelen 1997, 309.
146. Keall 1975; Downey 1988, 144–147; although note that it is difficult to precisely distinguish Seleucid-period habitation at Nippur, due to its ceramic similarity with the Achaemenid period (see Gibson 1975; Hannestad 1983, 101).

CONCLUSION

1. This is also an argument made by Bailey (2005, 29) and Mack (2007, 69); however, both attempt to distinguish miniatures based on their fidelity as models of the real-scale world, rather than based on their affective properties.

BIBLIOGRAPHY

Abusch, I. Tzvi. 2002. *Mesopotamian Witchcraft: Toward a History and Understanding of Babylonian Witchcraft Beliefs and Literature.* Leiden: Brill Styx.

Adams, Ellen. 2017. "Fragmentation and the Body's Boundaries: Reassessing the Body in Parts." In *Bodies of Evidence: Ancient Anatomical Votives Past, Present and Future*, edited by Jane Draycott and Emma-Jayne Graham, 193–213. London and New York: Routledge.

Adams, William and Ernest Adams. 1991. *Archaeological Typology and Practical Reality: A Dialectical Approach to Artifact Classification and Sorting.* Cambridge: Cambridge University Press.

Abdi, Kamyar. 2002. "Notes on the Iranianization of Bes in the Achaemenid Empire," *Ars Orientalis* 32: 133–162.

Alexiou, Margaret. 2002. *The Ritual Lament in Greek Tradition*, second edition, revised by Dimitrios Yatromanolakis and Panagiotis Roilos. Lanham, MD: Rowman & Littlefield.

Al-Salihi, W.I. 1987. "The Weary Hercules of Mesene," *Mesopotamia*, 22: 159–167.

Ambos, Claus. 2003. "Nanaja – Eine ikonographische Studie zur Darstellung einer altorientalischen Göttin in hellenistisch-parthischer Zeit," *Zeitschrift für Assyriologie*, 93: 231–272.

Ammerman, Rebecca. 1990. "The Religious Context of Hellenistic Terracotta Figurines." In *The Coroplast's Art: Greek Terracottas of the Hellenistic World*, edited by Jaimee P. Uhlenbrock, 37–46. New Rochelle, NY: Aristide D. Caratzas.

Ammerman, Rebecca. 2002. *The Sanctuary of Santa Venera at Paestum II: The Votive Terracottas.* Arbor: University of Michigan Press.

Ardren, Traci. 2006. "Setting the Table: Why Children and Childhood Are Important in an Understanding of Ancient Mesoamerica." In *The Social Experience of Childhood in Ancient Mesoamerica*, edited by Traci Ardren and Scott R. Hutson, 3–22. Boulder, CO: University Press of Colorado.

Arnott, Peter D. 1988. "Drama." In *Civilizations of the Ancient Mediterranean: Greece and Rome*, Volume III, edited by Michael Grant and Rachel Kitzinger, 1477–1493. New York: Charles Scribner's Sons.

Asher-Greve, Julia. 1998. "The Essential Body: Mesopotamian Conceptions of the Gendered Body." In *Gender and the Body in the Ancient Mediterranean*, edited by Maria Wyke, 8–37. Oxford and Malden, MA: Blackwell.

Asher-Greve, Julia. 2002. "Decisive Sex, Essential Gender." In *Sex and Gender in the Ancient Near East, Proceedings of the 47th Rencontre Assyriologique Internationale*, Helsinki, July 2–6, 2001. Part I, edited by Simo Parpola and Robert M. Whiting, 11–26. Helsinki: Neo-Assyrian Text Corpus Project.

Assante, Julia. 2000. The Erotic Reliefs of Ancient Mesopotamia. Ph.D. diss. Columbia University, New York.

Assante, Julia. 2002. "Style and Replication in 'Old Babylonian' Terracotta Plaques: Strategies for Entrapping the Power of Images," *Ex Mesopotamia et Syria Lux; Festschrift für Manfried Dietrich zu seinem 65. Geburtstag*, Alter Orient und Altes Testament 281, edited by

Oswald Loretz, Kai Metzler, and Hans Peter Schaudig, 1–29. Alter Orient und Münster: Ugarit-Verlag.

Assante, Julia. 2017. "Men Looking at Men: The Homoerotics of Power in the State Arts of Assyria." In *Being a Man: Negotiating Ancient Constructs of Masculinity*, edited by Ilona Zsolnay, 42–82. London and New York: Routledge.

Baadsgaard, Aubrey. 2013. "Uniforms and Non-Conformists: Tensions and Trends in Early Dynastic Fashion." In *Critical Approaches to Ancient Near Eastern Art*, edited by Brian A. Brown and Marian H. Feldman 421–449. Berlin and Boston: De Gruyter.

Bachelard, Gaston. [1958] 1994. *The Poetics of Space: The Classic Look at How We Experience Intimate Places*. Translated by Maria Jolas. Boston: Beacon.

Bahrani, Zainab. 1996. "The Hellenization of Ishtar: Nudity, Fetishism, and the Production of Cultural Differentiation in Ancient Art," *Oxford Art Journal*, 19.2: 3–16.

Bahrani, Zainab. 2001. *Women of Babylon: Gender and Representation in Mesopotamia*. London and New York: Routledge.

Bailey, Douglass. 2005. *Prehistoric Figurines: Representation and Corporeality in the Neolithic*. London and New York: Routledge.

Ballet, Pascale and Violaine Jeammet. 2011. "Petite Plastique, Grands Maux. Les 'Grotesques' en Méditerranée aux Époques Hellénistique et Romaine." In *Corps outragés, corps ravagés de l'Antiquité au Moyen Âge*, edited by L. Bodiou, V. Mehl, and M. Soria, 39–82. Turnhout, Belgium: Brepols.

Barrelet, Marie-Therese. 1968. "Figurines et reliefs en terre cuite de la Mésopotamie antique, I." *Potiers, Termes de Métier, Procédés de Fabrication et Production*. Paris: Librairie Orientaliste Paul Geuthner.

Barthes, Roland. [1967] 1983. *The Fashion System*. Translated by Matthew Ward and Richard Howard. New York: Hill and Wang.

Barrett, Caitlín E. 2011. *Egyptianizing Figurines from Delos: A Study in Hellenistic Religion*. Leiden and Boston: Brill.

Barr-Sharrar, Beryl. 1982. "Macedonian Metal Vases in Perspective: Some Observations on Context and Tradition." In *Macedonia and Greece in Late Classical and Early Hellenistic Times* (Studies in the History of Art, Volume 10), edited by Beryl Barr-Sharrar and Eugene N. Borza, 122–139. Washington, DC: National Gallery of Art.

Baudrillard, Jean. [1981] 1994. *Simulacra and Simulation*. Translated by Sheila Faria Glaser. Ann Arbor: University of Michigan Press.

Baughan, Elizabeth P. 2013. *Couched in Death: Klinai and Identity in Anatolia and Beyond*. Madison, WI: University of Wisconsin Press.

Baxter, Jane Eva. 2005a. "Introduction: The Archaeology of Childhood in Context," *Archaeological Papers of the American Anthropological Association* (Issue: Children in Action: Perspectives on the Archaeology of Childhood, edited by Jane Eva Baxter), 15: 1–9.

Baxter, Jane Eva. 2005b. "Making Space for Children in Archaeological Interpretations," *Archaeological Papers of the American Anthropological Association* (Issue: Children in Action: Perspectives on the Archaeology of Childhood, edited by Jane Eva Baxter), 15: 77–88.

Baxter, Jane Eva. 2005c. *The Archaeology of Childhood: Children, Gender, and Material Culture*. Walnut Creek, CA: Altamira Press.

Beaumont, Lesley. 2000. "The Social Status and Artistic Presentation of 'Adolescence' in fifth century Athens." In *Children and Material Culture*, edited by Joanna Sofaer Derevenski, 39–50. London and New York: Routledge.

Beaumont, Lesley. 2003. "The Changing Face of Childhood." In *Coming of Age in*

Ancient Greece: Images of Childhood from the Classical Past, edited by Jenifer Neils and John H. Oakley, 58–83. New Haven, CT and London: Yale University Press.

Beaumont, Lesley. 2012. *Childhood in Ancient Athens: Iconography and Social History*. London and New York: Routledge.

Becq, Juliette. 2010. "Cyrenaica." In *Tanagras: Figurines for Life and Eternity*, edited by V. Jeammet, 204–211. Paris: Musée du Louvre.

Becq, Juliette, Violaine Jeammet and Néguine Mathieux. 2010. "Divinities and Figurines in Boeotia." In *Tanagras: Figurines for Life and Eternity*, edited by V. Jeammet, 142–159. Paris: Musée du Louvre.

Bellia, Angela. 2012. *Strumenti Musicali e Oggetti Sonorri nell'Italia meridionale e in Sicilia VI-III sec. A.C.: Funzioni Rituali e Contesti*. Lucca: Libreria Musicale Italiana.

Bennett, Jane. 2010. *Vibrant Matter: A Political Ecology of Things*. Durham, NC and London: Duke University Press.

Bergamini, Giovanni. 1988. "Excavations in Shu-Anna, Babylon 1987," *Mesopotamia* 23: 5–17.

Bergh, Susan E. 2012a. "Inlaid and Metal Ornaments." In *Wari: Lords of the Ancient Andes*, edited by Susan E. Bergh, 217–231. London and New York: Thames and Hudson.

Bergh, Susan E. 2012b. "Figurines." In *Wari: Lords of the Ancient Andes*, edited by Susan E. Bergh, 233–241. London and New York: Thames and Hudson.

Bergmann, Bettina. 1999. "Introduction: The Art of Ancient Spectacle," *Studies in the History of Art* (Symposium Papers XXXIV: The Art of Ancient Spectacle) 56: 8–35.

Berlin, Andrea. 2013. "The Alexander Effect in the Early Hellenistic East," conference paper given at the American Schools of Oriental Research Annual Meeting; November 22, 2013.

Besques, Simone. 1972. *Musée national du Louvre: Catalogue raisonné des figurines et reliefs en terre cuite grecs, étrusques et romains*. Vol. 3, *Époques hellénistique et romaine, Grèce et Asie Mineure*. Paris: Éditions des Musées Nationaux.

Besques, Simone. 1986. *Musée national du Louvre: Catalogue raisonné des figurines et reliefs en terre cuite grecs, étrusques et romains*. Vol. 4, pt. 1, *Époques hellénistique et romaine, Italie méridionale, Sicilie, Sardaigne*. Paris: Éditions des Musées Nationaux.

Besques, Simone. 1992. *Musée national du Louvre: Catalogue raisonné des figurines et reliefs en terre cuite grecs, étrusques et romains*. Vol. 4, pt. 2, *Époques hellénistique et romaine, cyrénaïque, Égypte ptolémaïque et romaine, Afrique du Nord et Proche- Orient*. Paris: Éditions des Musées Nationaux.

Bettelheim, Bruno. 1976. *The Uses of Enchantment: The Meaning and Importance of Fairy Tales*. New York: Vintage Books.

Bidmead, Julye. 2002. *The Akītu Festival: Religious Continuity and Royal Legitimation in Mesopotamia*. Piscataway, NJ: Gorgias Press.

Black, Jeremy and Anthony Green. 1992. *Gods, Demons and Symbols of Ancient Mesopotamia*. London: The British Museum Press.

Bliege Bird, Rebecca and Eric Alden Smith. 2005. "Signaling Theory, Strategic Interaction, and Symbolic Capital," *Current Anthropology*, 46: 221–248.

Boardman, John. 1991. *Greek Sculpture: The Archaic Period*. London and New York: Thames and Hudson.

Boardman, John. 2016. *Greek Art*, Fifth Edition. London and New York: Thames and Hudson.

Bobou, Olympia. 2015. *Children in the Hellenistic World: Statues and Representation*. Oxford: Oxford University Press.

Bøgh, Birgitte. 2012. "Mother of the Gods: Goddess of Power and Protector of Cities," *Numen* 59.1: 32–67.

Boiy, T. 2004. *Late Achaemenid and Hellenistic Babylon* (Orientalia Lovaniensia Analecta 136). Leuven, Paris, and Dudley, MA: Peeters Publishers.

Bollati, Ariela and Vito Messina. 2004a. *Seleucia al Tigri: le impronte di sigillo dagli Archivi, Vol. II: Divinità.* Alessandria: Edizioni dell'Orso.

Bollati, Ariela and Vito Messina. 2004b. *Seleucia al Tigri: le impronte di sigillo dagli Archivi, Vol. III: Figure umane, animali, vegetali, oggetti.* Alessandria: Edizioni dell'Orso.

Bonfante, Larissa. 1984. "Dedicated Mothers," *Visible Religion: Annual for Religious Iconography* 3 (Popular Religion): 1–17.

Bonfante, Larissa. 1989. "Nudity as a Costume in Classical Art," *American Journal of Archaeology*, 93.4: 543–570.

Bonfante, Larissa. 1997. "Nursing Mothers in Classical Art." In *Naked Truths: Women, Sexuality, and Gender in Classical Art and Archaeology*, edited by A.O. Koloski-Ostrow and C.L. Lyons, 174–196. London and New York: Routledge.

Bonfante, Larissa. 2000. "Classical Nudity in Italy and Greece." In *Ancient Italy in Its Mediterranean Setting: Studies in Honour of Ellen Macnamara*, edited by D. Ridgway, F. Serra Ridgway, M. Pearce, E. Herring, R.D. Whitehouse, and J.B. Wilkins, 271–293. Accordia Specialist Studies on the Mediterranean 4. London: Accordia Research Institute, University of London.

Bonfante, Larissa and Eva Jaunzems. 1988. "Clothing and Ornament." In *Civilizations of the Ancient Mediterranean: Greece and Rome*, Volume III, edited by Michael Grant and Rachel Kitzinger, 1385–1413. New York: Charles Scribner's Sons.

Bosher, Kathryn. ed. 2012. *Theater Outside Athens: Drama in Greek Sicily and South Italy.* Cambridge: Cambridge University Press.

Bourgeois, Brigitte. 2010. "Arts and Crafts of Colour on the Louvre Tanagra Figurines." In *Tanagras: Figurines for Life and Eternity*, directed by Violaine Jeammet, 238–243. Valencia: Fundación Bacaja.

Boutantin, Céline. 2013. *Terres cuites et culte domestique: Bestiaire de l'Égypte gréco-romaine.* Leiden and Boston: Brill.

Bowker, Geoffrey and Susan Star. 1999. *Sorting Things Out: Classification and Its Consequences.* Cambridge, MA and London: The MIT Press.

Bradley, Keith R. 1986. "Wet-nursing at Rome: A Study in Social Relations." In *The Family in Ancient Rome: New Perspectives*, edited by Beryl Rawson, 201–229. Ithaca: Cornell University Press.

Brijder, Herman A.G. 2014. *Nemrud Dagi.* Berlin and Boston: De Gruyter.

Brown, Bill. (ed.) 2004. *Things.* Chicago: The University of Chicago Press.

Brown, John Pairman. 2005. "The Privatization of Greek Specialties in the Hellenistic World: Drama, Athletics, Citizenship," *Revue Biblique* 112.4: 536–566.

Budin, Stephanie. 2004. "A Reconsideration of the Aphrodite-Astart Syncretism," *Numen* 51.2: 95–145.

Bundrick, Sheramy D. 2005. *Music and Image in Classical Athens.* Cambridge: Cambridge University Press.

Bundrick, Sheramy D. 2015. "Athenian Eye Cups in Context," *American Journal of Archaeology* 119.3: 295–341.

Burr, Dorothy. 1934. *Terra-cottas from Myrina in the Museum of Fine Arts, Boston.* Vienna: Adolf Holzhausens Nachfolger.

Butler, Judith. 1990. *Gender Trouble: Feminism and the Subversion of Identity.* New York: Routledge.

Butler, Judith. 1993. *Bodies that Matter: On the Discursive Limits of "Sex".* New York and London: Routledge.

Cahill, Nicholas. 2002. *Household and City Organization at Olynthus*. New Haven, CT and London: Yale University Press.

Çakmak, Lisa Ayla. 2009. Mixed Signals: Androgyny, Identity, and Iconography on the Graeco-Phoenician Sealings from Tel Kedesh, Israel. Ph.D. diss, University of Michigan, Ann Arbor.

Calligaro, Thomas, Anne Bouquillon, Guirec Querré, and Jean-Paul Poirot. 1999. "Les rubis d'Ishtar: Etude en laboratoire." In *Cornaline et pierres précieuses: La Méditerranée, de l'antiquité à d'Islam; Actes du colloque organisé au Musée du Louvre par le Service culturel les 24 at 25 novembre 1995*, edited by Annie Caubet, 211–227. Paris: Louvre Conférences et Colloques.

Cambon, Pierre. 2008. "Begram: Alexandria of the Caucasus, Capital of the Kushan Empire." In *Afghanistan: Hidden Treasures from the National Museum, Kabul*, edited by Fredrik Hiebert and Pierre Cambon, 145–209. Washington, DC: National Geographic Society.

Canepa, Matthew P. 2015. "Bronze Sculpture in the Hellenistic East." In *Power and Pathos: Bronze Sculpture of the Hellenistic World*, edited by Jens M. Daehner and Kenneth Lapatin, 82–93. Los Angeles: J. Paul Getty Museum.

Carter, Jane Burr. 1987. "The Masks of Ortheia," *American Journal of Archaeology* 91.3: 355–383.

Castor, Alexis. 2017. "Surface Tensions on Etruscan and Greek Gold Jewelry." In *What Shall I Say of Clothes? Theoretical and Methodological Approaches to the Study of Dress in Antiquity*, edited by Megan Cifarelli and Laura Gawlinski, 83–100. Boston: Archaeological Institute of America.

Caubet, Annie. 2014. "Musical Practices and Instruments in Late Bronze Age Ugarit (Syria)." In *Music in Antiquity: The Near East and Mediterranean*, edited by Joan Goodnick Westenholz, Yossi Maurey, and Edwin Seroussi, 172–184. Berlin and Boston: De Gruyter.

Caubet, Annie. 2016. "Terracotta Figurines of Musicians from Mesopotamia and Elam." In *Musicians in Ancient Coroplastic Art: Iconography, Ritual Contexts, and Functions*, edited by Angela Bellia and Clemente Marconi, 34–43. Pisa and Rome: Istituti Editoriali e Poligrafici Internazionali.

Chaniotis, Angelos. 1997. "Theatricality Beyond the Theater: Staging Public Life in the Hellenistic World," *Pallas* (De La Scène Aux Gradins: Théâtre Et Représentations Dramatiques Après Alexandre Le Grand) 47: 219–259.

Chéhab, Maurice H. 1951–1952. *Les terres cuites de Kharayeb* (Bulletin du Musée de Beyrouth X). Paris: Librairie d'Amérique et d'Orient, Adrien Maisonneuve.

Christesen, P. 2012. "Athletics and Social Order in Sparta in the Classical Period," *Classical Antiquity* 31.2: 193–255.

Cifarelli, Megan. 2017. "Costly Choices: Signaling Theory and Dress in Period IVb Hasanlu, Iran." In *What Shall I Say of Clothes? Theoretical and Methodological Approaches to the Study of Dress in Antiquity*, edited by Megan Cifarelli and Laura Gawlinski, 101–119. Boston: Archaeological Institute of America.

Cifarelli, Megan and Laura Gawlinski. 2017. "Introduction." In *What Shall I Say of Clothes? Theoretical and Methodological Approaches to the Study of Dress in Antiquity*, edited by Megan Cifarelli and Laura Gawlinski, ix-xvi. Boston: Archaeological Institute of America.

Clairmont, Christoph W. 1970. *Gravestone and Epigram: Greek Memorials from the Archaic and Classical Period*. Mainz on Rhine: Verlag Philipp von Zabern.

Clark, Andy. 2010. "Material Surrogacy and the Supernatural: Reflections on the Role of Artefacts in 'Off-line' Cognition." In *The Cognitive Life of Things: Recasting the Boundaries of the*

Mind, edited by Lambros Malafouris and Colin Renfrew, 23–28. Cambridge: McDonald Institute Monographs.

Clarysse, Willy. 1985. "Greeks and Egyptians in the Ptolemaic Army and Administration," *Aegyptus* 65: 57–66.

Cohen, Beth. 1997. "Divesting the Female Breast of Clothes in Classical Sculpture." In *Naked Truths: Women, Sexuality, and Gender in Classical Art and Archaeology*, edited by A. Koloski-Ostrow and C. Lyons, 66–92. London: Routledge.

Cohen, Edward E. 2014. "Sexual Abuse and Sexual Rights: Slaves' Erotic Experience at Athens and Rome." In *A Companion to Greek and Roman Sexualities*, edited by Thomas K. Hubbard, 185–198. Malden, MA: Wiley Blackwell.

Cohen, Getzel M. 2013. *The Hellenistic Settlements in the East from Armenia and Mesopotamia to Bactria and India*. Berkeley and London: University of California Press.

Cole, Michael. 2003. "The Medici 'Mercury' and the Breath of Bronze." In *Studies in the History of Art*, Vol. 64, Symposium Papers XLI: Large Bronzes in the Renaissance, 128–153. Washington, DC: National Gallery of Art.

Cole, Michael. 2011. "The Cult of Materials." In *Renouveau et invention, la sculpture à travers ses histoires matérielles*, edited by Martina Droth and Sébastien Clerbois, 1–15. Oxford: Peter Lang.

Colledge, Malcolm. 1987. "Greek and Non-Greek Interaction in the Art and Architecture of the Hellenistic East." In *Hellenism in the East*, edited by Amélie Kuhrt and Susan Sherwin-White, 134–162. London: Gerald Duckworth.

Collins, Paul. 2013. "Gods, Heroes, Rituals, and Violence: Warfare in Neo-Assyrian Art." In *Critical Approaches to Ancient Near Eastern Art*, edited by Brian A. Brown and Marian H. Feldman, 619–644. Boston and Berlin: De Gruyter.

Collon, Dominique. 1987. *First Impressions: Cylinder Seals in the Ancient Near East*. Chicago: The University of Chicago Press.

Coloru, Omar. 2017. "Ancient Persia and Silent Disability." In *Disability in Antiquity*, edited by Christian Laes, 61–74. London and New York: Routledge.

Conkey, Margaret and Joan Gero. 1997. "From Programme to Practice: Gender and Feminism in Archaeology," *Annual Review of Anthropology* 26: 411–437.

Conklin, Beth A. and Lynn M. Morgan. 1996. "Babies, Bodies, and the Production of Personhood in North America and a Native Amazonian Society," *Ethos* 24.4: 657–694.

Connelly, Joan B. 1989. "Votive Offerings from Hellenistic Failaka: Evidence for Herakles Cult." In *L'Arabie préislamique et son environnement historique et culturel*, edited by T. Fahd, 145–158. Leiden: Brill.

Connelly, Joan B. 1990. "Hellenistic Terracottas of Cyprus and Kuwait." In *The Coroplast's Art: Greek Terracottas of the Hellenistic World*, edited by Jaimee P. Uhlenbrock, 94–101. New Rochelle, NY: Aristide D. Caratzas.

Coombs, Katherine. 1998. *The Portrait Miniature in England*. London: V&A Publications.

Cooper, J.S. 2017. "Female Trouble and Troubled Males: Roiled Seas, Decadent Royals, and Mesopotamian Masculinities in Myth and Practice." In *Being a Man: Negotiating Ancient Constructs of Masculinity*, edited by Ilona Zsolnay, 112–124. London and New York: Routledge.

Corner, Sean. 2014. "Sumposion." In *A Companion to Greek and Roman Sexualities*, edited by Thomas K. Hubbard, 199–213. Malden, MA: Wiley Blackwell.

Corrington, Gail Paterson. 1989. "The Milk of Salvation: Redemption by the Mother in Late Antiquity and Early

Christianity," *The Harvard Theological Review* 82.4: 393–420.

Couto-Ferreira, M. Erica. 2016. "Being Mothers or Acting (Like) Mothers? Constructing Motherhood in Ancient Mesopotamia." In *Women in Antiquity: Real Women Across the Ancient World*, edited by Stephanie Lynn Budin and Jean MacIntosh Turfa, 25–34. London and New York: Routledge.

Crawford, Sally. 2009. "The Archaeology of Play Things: Theorising a Toy Stage in the 'Biography' of Objects," *Childhood in the Past* 2: 55–70.

Curtis, John E. and Nigel Tallis. 2005. *Forgotten Empire: The World of Ancient Persia*. Berkeley and Los Angeles: University of California Press.

Curtis, Vesta Sarkhosh. 1998. "The Parthian Costume and Headdress." In *Das Partherreich und seine Zeugnisse – the Arsacid Empire: sources and documentation, Beiträge des internationalen Colloquiums, Eutin (27.-30. Juni 1996)*, edited by Josef Wiesehöfer, 61–73. Stuttgart: F. Steiner.

Curtis, Vesta Sarkhosh. 2007. "The Iranian Revival in the Parthian Period." In *The Age of the Parthians: The Idea of Iran*, Volume II, edited by Vesta Sarkhosh Curtis and Sarah Stewart, 7–25. London: I.B. Taurus.

Dalley, Stephanie. 2000. *Myths from Mesopotamia: Creation, the Flood, Gilgamesh, and Others*, revised edition. Oxford: Oxford University Press.

Dandamaev, Muhammad A. 1984. *Slavery in Babylonia: From Nabopolassar to Alexander the Great (626–331 BC)*. DeKalb, IL: Northern Illinois University Press.

Danielsson, Ing-Marie Back. 2013. "Materials of Affect: Miniatures in the Scandinavian Late Iron Age (AD 550–1050)." In *Archaeology After Interpretation: Returning Materials to Archaeological Theory*, edited by Benjamin Alberti, Andrew Meirion Jones, and Joshua Pollard, 325–343. London and New York: Routledge.

Darby, Erin. 2014a. "Seeing Double: Viewing and Re-viewing Judean Pillar Figurines through Modern Eyes," *Occasional Papers in Coroplastic Studies* 1: 13–26.

Darby, Erin. 2014b. *Interpreting Judean Pillar Figurines: Gender and Empire in Judean Apotropaic Ritual*. Tübingen: Mohr Siebeck.

Dasen, Véronique. 1993. *Dwarfs in Ancient Egypt and Greece*. Oxford: Clarendon Press.

Davies, Glenys. 2018. *Gender and Body Language in Roman Art*. Cambridge: Cambridge University Press.

Dean-Jones, Lesley. 1991. "The Cultural Construct of the Female Body in Classical Greek Science." In *Women's History and Ancient History*, edited by Sarah B. Pomeroy, 11–37. Chapel Hill: University of North Carolina Press.

Derevenski, Joanna Sofaer. 1994. "Where are the Children? Accessing Children in the Past," *Archaeological Review from Cambridge* 13.2: 7–20.

Derevenski, Joanna Sofaer. 2000. "Material Culture Shock: Confronting Expectations in the Material Culture of Children." In *Children and Material Culture*, edited by Joanna Sofaer Derevenski, 3–16. London and New York: Routledge.

Dietrich, Oliver, Jens Notroff, and Laura Dietrich. 2018. "Masks and masquerade in the Early Neolithic: A View from Upper Mesopotamia," *Time and Mind* 11.1: 3–21.

Dillon, Matthew. 2017. "Legal (and Customary?) Approaches to the Disabled in Ancient Greece." In *Disability in Antiquity*, edited by Christian Laes, 167–181. London and New York: Routledge.

Dillon, Sheila. 2012a. "Hellenistic Tanagra Figurines." In *A Companion to Women in the Ancient World*, edited by Sharon L. James and Sheila Dillon, 231–234. Malden, MA: Wiley Blackwell.

Dillon, Sheila. 2012b. "Female Portraiture in the Hellenistic Period." In *A Companion to Women in the Ancient World*, edited by Sharon L. James and Sheila Dillon, 263–277. Malden, MA: Wiley Blackwell.

Doty, L. Timothy. 1978. "The Archive of the Nanâ-iddin Family from Uruk," *Journal of Cuneiform Studies*, 30: 65–90.

Doty, L. Timothy. 1988. "Nikarchos and Kephalōn." In *A Scientific Humanist. Studies in Memory of Abraham Sachs*, edited by E. Leichty, R. de Jong Ellis, and P. Gerardi, 95–118. Philadelphia: The University Museum.

Downey, Susan. 1988. *Mesopotamian Religious Architecture: Alexander through the Parthians*. Princeton: Princeton University Press.

Draycott, Jane. 2017. "Hair Today, Gone Tomorrow: The Use of Real, False and Artificial Hair as Votive Offerings." In *Bodies of Evidence: Ancient Anatomical Votives Past, Present and Future*, edited by Jane Draycott and Emma-Jayne Graham, 77–94. London and New York: Routledge.

DuBois, Page. 1996. "Archaic Bodies-in-Pieces." In *Sexuality in Ancient Art*, edited by Natalie. B. Kampen, 55–64. Cambridge: Cambridge University Press.

Duncan, Anne. 2006. *Performance and Identity in the Classical World*. Cambridge: Cambridge University Press.

Eco, Umberto. 1986. *Travels in Hyper Reality: Essays*. Translated by William Weaver. San Diego, New York, and London: Harcourt Brace.

Edmondson, Jonathan C. 1999. "The Cultural Politics of Public Spectacle in Rome and the Greek East, 167–166 BCE," *Studies in the History of Art* (Symposium Papers XXXIV: The Art of Ancient Spectacle) 56: 76–95.

Erickson, Kyle. 2011. "Apollo-Nabû: the Babylonian Policy of Antiochus I." In *Seleucid Dissolution: The Sinking of the Anchor* (Philippika 50), edited by K. Erickson and G. Ramsey, 51–66. Weisbaden: Harrassowitz Verlag.

Erickson, Kyle and Nicholas L. Wright. 2011. "The 'Royal Archer' and Apollo in the East: Greco-Persian Iconography in the Seleukid Empire." In *Proceedings of the XIVth International Numismatic Congress Glasgow 2009*, edited by Nicholas Holmes, 163–168. Glasgow: University of Glasgow; London: Spink.

Erlich, Adi. 2009. *The Art of Hellenistic Palestine*. Oxford: Archaeopress.

Erlich, Adi. 2010. "Part Two: Figurines, Sculpture and Minor Art of the Hellenistic and Roman Periods." In *Excavations at Dor: Figurines, Cult Objects and Amulets, 1980–2000 Seasons*, edited by Ephraim Stern, 115–209. Jerusalem: Israel Exploration Society and the Institute of Archaeology, The Hebrew University of Jerusalem.

Erlich, Adi. 2015. "Terracottas." In *The Oxford Handbook of Roman Sculpture*, edited by Elise A. Friedland, Melanie Grunow Sobocinski, with Elaine K. Gazda, 155–172. Oxford: Oxford University Press.

Erlich, Adi. 2017. "Happily Ever After? A Hellenistic Hoard from Tel Kedesh in Israel," *American Journal of Archaeology* 121.1: 39–59.

Erlich, Adi and Amos Kloner. 2008. *Maresha Excavations Final Report II: Hellenistic Terracotta Figurines from the 1989–1996 Seasons* (IAA Reports, No. 35). Jerusalem: Israel Antiquities Authority.

Falkenstein, Adam. 1941. *Topographie von Uruk, I. Teil: Uruk zur Seleukidenzeit, Ausgrabungen der Deutschen Forschungsgemeinschaft in Uruk-Warka, Band 3*. Leipzig: O. Harrasssowitz.

Favero, Lisa. 2010. "Body Into Clay," *Studio Potter* 38: 2, 12–15.

Feldman, Marian H. 2006. *Diplomacy by Design: Luxury Arts and an "International Style" in the Ancient Near East, 1400–1200*

BCE. Chicago: University of Chicago Press.

Feldman, Marian H. 2014. *Communities of Style: Portable Luxury Arts, Identity, and Collective Memory in the Iron Age Levant*. Chicago and London: University of Chicago Press.

Feldman, Marian H. 2018. "Style as a Fragment of the Ancient World: A View from the Iron Age Levant and Assyria." In *The Tiny and the Fragmented: Miniature, Broken, or Otherwise "Incomplete" Objects in the Ancient World*, edited by S. Rebecca Martin and Stephanie M. Langin-Hooper, 99–115. Oxford: Oxford University Press.

Fildes, Valerie. 1988. *Wet Nursing: A History from Antiquity to the Present*. Oxford: Basil Blackwell.

Finkbeiner, Uwe. 1987. "Uruk-Warka. The Late Periods," *Mesopotamia* 22: 233–250.

Finkbeiner, Uwe. 1993. "Uruk-Warka. Fundstellen der Keramik der Seleukiden- und Partherzeit." In *Materialien zur Archäologie der Seleukiden- und Partherzeit im südlichen Babylonien und im Golfgebiet : Ergebnisse der Symposien 1987 und 1989 in Blaubeuren*, edited by U. Finkbeiner, 3–16. Tübingen: Ernst Wasmuth Verlag.

Fischer, Jutta. 1994. *Griechisch-Römische Terrakotten aus Ägypten*. Tübingen: Ernst Wasmuth Verlag.

Fisher, N.R.E. 1993. *Slavery in Classical Greece*. London: Bristol Classical Press.

Fisher, Nick. 2014. "Athletics and Sexuality." In *A Companion to Greek and Roman Sexualities*, edited by Thomas K. Hubbard, 244–264. Malden, MA: Wiley Blackwell.

Foley, Helene. 2003. "Mothers and Daughters." In *Coming of Age in Ancient Greece: Images of Childhood from the Classical Past*, edited by Jenifer Neils and John H. Oakley, 112–137. New Haven, CT and London: Yale University Press.

Forrester, Gillian S., Molly Crawley, and Casey Palmer. 2014. "Social Environment Elicits Lateralized Navigational Paths in Two Populations of Typically Developing Children," *Brain and Cognition* 91: 21–27.

Foster, Benjamin. 2005. *Before the Muses: An Anthology of Akkadian Literature*. Bethesda, MD: CDL Press.

Fowlkes-Childs, Blair and Michael Seymour. 2019. *The World Between Empires: Art and Identity in the Ancient Middle East*. New York: The Metropolitan Museum of Art.

Fox, Robin Lane. 1986. "Hellenistic Culture and Literature." In *The Oxford History of Greece and the Hellenistic World*, edited by J. Boardman, J. Griffin, and O. Murray, 390–420. Oxford: Oxford University Press.

Foxhall, Lin. 2015. "Introduction: Miniaturization," *World Archaeology* 47.1: 1–5.

Fraleigh, Sondra. 2018. "Phenomenology and Lifeworld." In *Back to the Dance Itself: Phenomenologies of the Body in Performance*, edited by Sondra Fraleigh, 11–26. Champaign, IL: University of Illinois Press.

Frankfort, Henri. 1948. *Ancient Egyptian Religion: An Interpretation*. New York: Columbia University Press.

Frankfurter, David. 2015. "Female figurines in early Christian Egypt: Reconstructing lost practices and meanings," *Material Religion* 11.2: 190–223.

Fredricksmeyer, E. A. 1986. "Alexander the Great and the Macedonian Kausia," *Transactions of the American Philological Association (1974-)*, 116: 215–227.

Funck, Bernd. 1984. *Uruk zur Seleukidenzeit: eine Untersuchung zu den spätbabylonischen Pfründentexten als Quelle für die Erforschung der sozialökonomischen Entwicklung der hellenistischen Stadt*. Schriften zur Geschichte und Kultur des alten Orients, 16. Berlin: Akademie-Verlag.

Gansell, Amy Rebecca. 2013. "Images and Conceptions of Ideal Feminine

Beauty in Neo-Assyrian Royal Contexts, c. 883–627 BCE." In *Critical Approaches to Ancient Near Eastern Art*, edited by Brian A. Brown and Marian H. Feldman, 391–420. Berlin and Boston: De Gruyter.

Garland, Robert. 1995. *The Eye of the Beholder: Deformity and Disability in Graeco-Roman World*. Ithaca, NY: Cornell University Press.

Garland, Robert. 2017. "Disabilities in Tragedy and Comedy." In *Disability in Antiquity*, edited by Christian Laes, 154–166. London and New York: Routledge.

Garrison, Mark. 2000. "Achaemenid iconography as evidenced by glyptic art: subject matter, social function, audience and diffusion." In *Images as Media: Sources for the Cultural History of the Near East and the Eastern Mediterranean (1st Millennium BCE)*, edited by Christoph Uehlinger, 115–163. Fribourg: University Press Fribourg.

Geertz, Clifford. 1973. "Religion as Cultural System." In *The Interpretation of Cultures: Selected Essays*, 87–126. New York: Basic Books.

Gell, Alfred. 1992. "The Technology of Enchantment and the Enchantment of Technology." In *Anthropology, Art and Aesthetics*, edited by J. Coote and A. Shelton, 40–63. Oxford: Clarendon Press.

Gell, Alfred. 1998. *Art and Agency: An Anthropological Theory*. Oxford: Clarendon Press.

George, A.R. 1992. "TINTIR = BABYLON and the Topography of Babylon." In *Babylonian Topographical Texts*, Orientalia Lovaniensia Analecta 40. Leuven: Peeters Press and Departement Oriëntalistiek.

George, Andrew. 1999. *The Epic of Gilgamesh: The Babylonian Epic Poem and Other Texts in Akkadian and Sumerian*. London and New York: Penguin Books.

Gibson, McGuire. 1975. *Excavations at Nippur: Eleventh Season*. Chicago: The Oriental Institute.

Giuliani, Luca. 1987. "Die Seligen Krüppel: Zur Deutung von Missgestalten in der hellenistischen Kleinkunst," *Archäologischer Anzeiger*, 701–721.

Glinister, Fay. 2017. "Ritual and Meaning: Contextualising Votive Terracotta Infants in Hellenistic Italy." In *Bodies of Evidence: Ancient Anatomical Votives Past, Present and Future*, edited by Jane Draycott and Emma-Jayne Graham, 131–146. London and New York: Routledge.

Golden, Mark. 1984. "Slavery and Homosexuality at Athens," *Phoenix* 38.4: 308–324.

Golden, Mark. 1997. "Change or Continuity? Children and Childhood in Hellenistic Historiography." In *Inventing Ancient Culture: Historicism, Periodization, and the Ancient World*, edited by Mark Golden and Peter Toohey, 176–191. London: Routledge.

Goldman, Bernard. 1991. "Women's Robes: The Achaemenid Era," *Bulletin of the Asia Institute* 5: 83–103.

Goldsworthy, Adrian. 2016. *Pax Romana: War, Peace and Conquest in the Roman World*. New Haven: Yale University Press.

Goodman, Jane E., Matt Tomlinson, and Justin B. Richland. 2014. "Citational Practices: Knowledge, Personhood, and Subjectivity," *The Annual Review of Anthropology*, 43: 449–463.

Gorgias. 1982. *Encomium of Helen*. Translated and edited by D.M. MacDowell, Bristol: Bristol Classical Press.

Gosden, Chris. 2004. *Archaeology and Colonialism: Cultural Contact from 5000 BC to the Present*. Cambridge: Cambridge University Press.

Gosden, Chris. 2005. "What Do Objects Want?," *Journal of Archaeological Method and Theory* 12: 193–211.

Gosden, Chris. 2011. "Entangled Landscapes in Britain and Borneo".

Unpublished Keynote Address, Stanford Archaeology Center 2011 Graduate Student Conference "Entanglement in Archaeology: Exploring Relationships Between People, Environments, Objects and Ideologies." April 16, 2011.

Graff, Sarah. 2013. "Sexuality, Reproduction and Gender in Terracotta Plaques from the Late Third-Early Second Millennia BCE." In *Critical Approaches to Ancient Near Eastern Art*, edited by Brian A. Brown and Marian H. Feldman, 371–390. Berlin and Boston: De Gruyter.

Green, Peter. 1990. *Alexander to Actium: The Historical Evolution of the Hellenistic Age*. Berkeley and Los Angeles: University of California Press.

Grmek, Mirko and Danielle Gourevitch. 1998. *Les Maladies dans l'Art Antique*. Paris: Librairie Arthème Fayard.

Groneberg, Brigitte. 2007. "The Role and Function of Goddesses in Mesopotamia." In *The Babylonian World*, edited by Gwendolyn Leick, 319–331. New York and London: Routledge.

Grootenboer, Hanneke. 2012. *Treasuring the Gaze: Intimate Vision in Late Eighteenth-Century Eye Miniatures*. Chicago and London: University of Chicago Press.

Hadley, Robert A. 1978. "The Foundation Date of Seleucia-on-the-Tigris," *Historia* 27: 228–230.

Haider, Peter W. 2008. "Tradition and Change in the Beliefs at Assur, Nineveh and Nisibis between 300 BC and AD 300." In *The Variety of Local Religious Life in the Near East in the Hellenistic and Roman Periods*, edited by Ted Kaizer, 193–207. Leiden and Boston: Brill.

Haines, Richard C. 1967. "Private Houses in the Scribal Quarter: The Structural Remains." In *Nippur I: Temple of Enlil, Scribal Quarter, and Soundings*, by Donald E. McCown and Richard C. Haines, assisted by Donald P. Hansen, 34–73. Chicago: The University of Chicago Press.

Hall, Edith. 2002. "The Singing Actors of Antiquity." In *Greek and Roman Actors: Aspects of an Ancient Profession*, edited by Pat Easterling and Edith Hall, 3–38. Cambridge: Cambridge University Press.

Hall, Emma Swan. 1977. "Harpocrates and Other Child Deities in Ancient Egyptian Sculpture," *Journal of the American Research Center in Egypt* 14: 55–58.

Halliwell, Stephen. 2008. *Greek Laughter: A Study of Cultural Psychology from Homer to Early Christianity*. Cambridge: Cambridge University Press.

Hannestad, Lise. 1983. *The Hellenistic Pottery from Failaka, With a Survey of Hellenistic Pottery in the Near East*, Volume 2/1 (Jutland Archaeological Society Publications, XVI:2). Aarhus: Jysk Arkæologisk Selskab.

Harrison, Evelyn. 1996. "The Web of History: A Conservative Reading of the Parthenon Frieze." In *Worshipping Athena: Panathenaia and Parthenon*, edited by Jenifer Neils, 198–214. Madison, WI: The University of Wisconsin Press.

Havelock, Christine Mitchell. 1995. *The Aphrodite of Knidos and Her Successors: A Historical Review of the Female Nude in Greek Art*. Ann Arbor: University of Michigan Press.

Hay, Jonathan. 2010. *Sensuous Surfaces: The Decorative Object in Early Modern China*. Honolulu: University of Hawai'i Press.

Heap, Angela M. 2002–2003. "The Baby as Hero? The Role of the Infant in Menander," *Bulletin of the Institute of Classical Studies* 46: 77–129.

Herbert, Sharon. 2008. "The Missing Pieces: Miniature Reflections of the Hellenistic Artistic Landscape in the East." In *The Sculptural Environment of the Roman Near East: Reflections on Culture, Ideology, and Power*, edited by Yaron Z. Eliav, Elise A. Friedland, and

Sharon Herbert, 257–272. Leuven and Dudley, MA: Peeters.

Herring, Frances W. 1949. "The Neglected Sense," *The Journal of Aesthetics and Art Criticism* 7.3: 199–215.

Heuzey, Léon. 1891. *Catalogue des figurines antiques de terre cuite du Musée du Louvre*. Paris: Librairies-Imprimeries réunies.

Heyn, Maura. 2017. "Western Men, Eastern Women? Dress and Cultural Identity in Roman Palmyra." In *What Shall I Say of Clothes? Theoretical and Methodological Approaches to the Study of Dress in Antiquity*, edited by Megan Cifarelli and Laura Gawlinski, 203–219. Boston: Archaeological Institute of America.

Higgins, R.A. 1967. *Greek Terracottas*. London: Methuen.

Hill, James N. and Robert K. Evans. 1972. "A Model for Classification and Typology." In *Models in Archaeology*, edited by D.L. Clarke, 231–274. London: Methuen.

Hirschfeld, Lawrence A. 2002. "Why Don't Anthropologists Like Children?," *American Anthropologist* 104.2: 611–627.

Hodder, Ian. 2012. *Entangled: An Archaeology of the Relationships between Humans and Things*. Malden, MA: Wiley Blackwell.

Hopkins, Clark. 1972. *Topography and Architecture of Seleucia on the Tigris*. Ann Arbor: University of Michigan Press.

Horn, Cornelia B. and John W. Martens Press. 2009. *"Let the Little Children Come To Me": Childhood and Children in Early Christianity*. Washington DC: The Catholic University of America Press.

Houghton, Arthur and Catharine Lorber. 2002. *Seleucid Coins: A Comprehensive Catalogue, Part 1: Seleucus I through Antiochus III*, Volumes I and II. Lancaster, PA and London: Classical Numismatic Group; and New York: American Numismatic Society.

Houghton, Arthur, Catharine Lorber, and Oliver Hoover. 2008. *Seleucid Coins: A Comprehensive Catalogue, Part 2: Seleucus IV through Antiochus XIII*, Volumes I and II. Lancaster, PA and London: Classical Numismatic Group; and New York: American Numismatic Society.

Huffman, Carl A. 2005. *Archytas of Tarentum: Pythagorean, Philosopher and Mathematician King*. Cambridge: Cambridge University Press.

Hughes, Jessica. 2008. "Fragmentation as Metaphor in the Classical Healing Sanctuary," *Social History of Medicine*, 21.2: 217–236.

Hughes, Jessica. 2018. "Tiny and Fragmented Votive Offerings from Classical Antiquity." In *The Tiny and the Fragmented: Miniature, Broken, or Otherwise "Incomplete" Objects in the Ancient World*, edited by S. Rebecca Martin and Stephanie M. Langin-Hooper, 48–71. Oxford: Oxford University Press.

Hunt, Peter. 2018. *Ancient Greek and Roman Slavery*. Malden, MA: Wiley Blackwell.

Hurwit, Jeffrey M. 2007. "The Problem with Dexileos: Heroic and Other Nudities in Greek Art," *American Journal of Archaeology* 111.1: 35–60.

Inomata, Takeshi and Lawrence S. Coben. 2006. "Overture: An Invitation to the Archaeological Theater." In *Archaeology of Performance: Theaters of Power, Community, and Politics*, edited by Takeshi Inomata and Lawrence S. Coben, 11–44. Lanham, MD: Altamira Press.

Invernizzi, Antonio. 1967. "The Excavations at Tell 'Umar," *Mesopotamia*, 2: 9–32.

Invernizzi, Antonio. 1970–1971. "Problemi di Coroplastica Tardo-Mesopotamica," *Mesopotamia*, 5/6: 325–389.

Invernizzi, Antonio. 1985. "Seleucia on the Tigris: Terracotta Figurines." In *The Land Between Two Rivers: Twenty Years of Italian Archaeology in the Middle East: the Treasures of Mesopotamia*, edited by Antonio Invernizzi, Maria M.N. P. Mancini and Elisabetta Valtz, 97–99. Turin: Il Quadrante.

Invernizzi, Antonio. 1993. "Seleucia on the Tigris: Centre and Periphery in Seleucid Asia." In *Centre and Periphery in the Hellenistic World*, edited by Per Bilde, Troels Engberg-Pedersen, Lise Hannestad, Jan Zahle, and Klavs Randsborg, 230–250. Aarhus: Aarhus University Press.

Invernizzi, Antonio. 1994. "Hellenism in Mesopotamia. A View From Seleucia on the Tigris," *Al-Rafidan*, 15: 1–24.

Invernizzi, Antonio. 2003. "They Did Not Write on Clay: Non-Cuneiform Documents and Archives in Seleucid Mesopotamia." In *Ancient Archives and Archival Traditions: Concepts of Record-Keeping in the Ancient World*, edited by Maria Brosius, 302–322. Oxford: Oxford University Press.

Invernizzi, Antonio. 2007. "Introduzione All'Arte Dell'Asia Ellenizzata." In *Sulla Via Di Alessandro: Da Seleucia Al Gandhara*, 62–71. Milan: Silvana Editoriale.

Invernizzi, Antonio. 2008. "La petite sculpture." In *Babylone: À Babylone, d'hier et d'aujourd'hui*, edited by B. André-Salvini, 264–272. Paris: Musée du Louvre.

Iossif, Panagiotis P. 2011. "Apollo *Toxotes* and the Seleukids: *Comme Un Air De Famille*." In *More than Men, Less than Gods: Studies on Royal Cult and Imperial Worship* (Proceedings of the International Colloquium organized by the Belgian School at Athens, November 1–2, 2007; Studia Hellenistica 51), edited by P. P. Iossif, A.S. Chankowski, and C. C. Lorber, 229–291. Leuven, Paris, and Walpole, MA: Peeters.

Jackson, Heather. 2006. *Jebel Khalid on the Euphrates, Volume Two: The Terracotta Figurines*. Sydney: Meditarch.

Jauss, Hans Robert. 1982. *Toward an Aesthetic of Reception*. Translated by Timothy Bahti. Minneapolis, MN: University of Minnesota Press.

Jay, Martin. 2011. *Essays from the Edge: Parerga and Paralipomena*. Charlottesville, VA: University of Virginia Press.

Jeammet, Violaine ed. 2010a. *Tanagras: Figurines for Life and Eternity*. Paris: Musée du Louvre.

Jeammet, Violaine. 2010b. "Greece and North Greece." In *Tanagras: Figurines for Life and Eternity*, edited by V. Jeammet, 180–185. Paris: Musée du Louvre.

Jiménez, Alicia. 2011. "Pure Hybridism: Late Iron Age Sculpture in Southern Iberia," *World Archaeology*, 43:102–123.

Jimenez, Lissette M. 2014. Transfiguring the Dead: The Iconography, Commemorative Use, and Materiality of Mummy Shrouds from Roman Egypt. Ph.D. diss., University of California, Berkeley.

Jones, Andrew. 2013. "In Small Things Remembered: Scale, Materiality and Miniatures in the British Early Bronze Age." In *Counterpoint: Essays in Archaeology and Heritage Studies in Honour of Professor Kristian Kristiansen* (BAR 2508), edited by Sophie Bergerbrant and Serena Sabatii, 367–372. Oxford: Archaeopress.

Jordan, Julius, with Conrad Preusser. 1928. *Uruk-Warka nach den Ausgrabungen durch die Deutsche Orient-Gesellschaft*, Wissenschaftliche Veröffentlichungen der Deutschen Orient-Gesellschaft (WVDOG) 51. Leipzig: Hinrichs.

Joseph, Alison. 2017. "The Handmaid's Tale as a Legitimate Reading of Genesis?," *The Shiloh Project: Rape Culture, Religion, and the Bible*, http://shiloh-project.group.shef.ac.uk/?p=1571 (Accessed February 6, 2018).

Joshel, Sandra R. 1986. "Nurturing the Master's Child: Slavery and the Roman Child-Nurse," *Signs*, 12.1: 3–22.

Joyce, Rosemary A. 2006. "Where We All Begin: Archaeologies of Childhood in the Mesoamerican Past." In *The Social Experience of Childhood in Ancient Mesoamerica*, edited by Traci Ardren and Scott R. Hutson, 283–301. Boulder, CO: University Press of Colorado.

Joyce, Rosemary A. 2007. "Figurines, Meaning, and Meaning-Making in Early Mesoamerica." In *Material Beginnings: A Global Prehistory of Figurative Representation*, edited by Colin Renfrew and Iain Morley, 107–116. Cambridge: McDonald Institute for Archaeological Research.

Joyce, Rosemary A. 2008. "When the Flesh is Solid but the Person is Hollow Inside: Formal Variation in Hand-Modeled Figurines from Formative Mesoamerica." In *Past Bodies*, edited by Dusan Boric and John Robb, 37–45. Oxford: Oxbow Books.

Joyce, Rosemary A. 2018. "Breaking Bodies and Biographies: Figurines of the Playa de los Muertos Tradition." In *The Tiny and the Fragmented: Miniature, Broken, or Otherwise "Incomplete" Objects in the Ancient World*, edited by S. Rebecca Martin and Stephanie M. Langin-Hooper, 24–47. Oxford: Oxford University Press.

Just, Roger. 1989. *Women in Athenian Law and Life*. London and New York: Routledge.

Kaizer, Ted. 2000. "The 'Heracles Figure' at Hatra and Palmyra: Problems of Interpretation," *Iraq*, 62: 219–232.

Kamp, Kathryn A. 2001. "Where Have All the Children Gone?: The Archaeology of Childhood," *Journal of Archaeological Method and Theory* 8.1: 1–34.

Kamp, Kathryn A. 2002. "Working for a Living: Childhood in the Prehistoric Southwestern Pueblos." In *Children in the Prehistoric Puebloan Southwest*, edited by Kathryn A. Kamp, 71–89. Salt Lake City: The University of Utah Press.

Kamp, Kathryn A. 2005. "Dominant Discourses; Lived Experiences: Studying the Archaeology of Children and Childhood," *Archaeological Papers of the American Anthropological Association*, 15: 115–122.

Kamp, Kathryn A, Nichole Timmerman, Gregg Lind, Jules Graybill and Ian Natowsky. 1999. "Discovering Childhood: Using Fingerprints to Find Children in the Archaeological Record," *American Antiquity* 64.2: 309–315.

Karoglou, Kiki. 2016. "Eros *Mousikos*." In *Musicians in Ancient Coroplastic Art: Iconography, Ritual Contexts, and Functions*, edited by Angela Bellia and Clemente Marconi, 97–107. Pisa and Rome: Istituti Editoriali e Poligrafici Internazionali.

Karvonen-Kannas, Kerttu. 1995. *The Seleucid and Parthian Terracotta Figurines from Babylon*. Firenze: Casa Editrice Le Lettere.

Keall, E.J. 1975. "Parthian Nippur and Vologases' Southern Strategy: A Hypothesis," *Journal of the American Oriental Society* 95.4: 620–632.

Keall, E.J. and K.E. Ciuk. 1991. "Continuity of Tradition in the Pottery from Parthian Nippur." In *Golf-Archäologie: Mesopotamien, Iran, Kuwait, Bahrain, Vereinigte Arabische Emirate und Oman*, edited by K. Schippmann, A. Herling, and J.-F. Salles, 57–70. Buch am Erlbach: Verlag Marie L. Leidorf.

Kellenberger, Edgar. 2017. "Mesopotamia and Israel." In *Disability in Antiquity*, edited by Christian Laes, 47–60. London and New York: Routledge.

Keller, Peter E. and Martina Rieger. 2009. "Special Issue – Musical Movement and Synchronization," *Music Perception: An Interdisciplinary Journal* 26:5, 397–400.

Kellum, Barbara. 2018. "Beyond High and Low: The Beauty of Beasts at the House of the Citharist in Pompeii." In *Roman Artists, Patrons, and Public Consumption: Familiar Works Reconsidered*, edited by Brenda Longfellow and Ellen E. Perry, 191–212. Ann Arbor: University of Michigan Press.

Kemp, Martin. 1995. "Wrought by No Artist's Hand: The Natural, the Artificial, the Exotic, and the Scientific in Some Artefacts from the Renaissance." In *Reframing the Renaissance*, edited by C. Farago, 177–196. New Haven, CT and London: Yale University Press.

Khodza, Yelena. 1984. "On the Problem of Greek Comedy as Reflected in Terracotta Figurines," *Travaux du Musée de l'Ermitage* 24: 6–71.

Khodza, Yelena. 2006. "The Grotesque in the Hellenistic Coroplastics" (Russian with English Summary), *Vestnik drevnei istorii (Journal of Ancient History)* 3: 156–182.

Kilmer, Anne D. 1977. "Notes on Akkadian *uppu*." In *Essays on the Ancient Near East in Memory of Jacob Joel Finkelstein*, edited by Maria de Jong Ellis, 129–138. Hamden, CT: Archon Books.

Kilmer, Martin F. 1993. *Greek Erotica on Attic Red-Figure Vases*. London: Duckworth.

King, Helen. 1998. *Hippocrates' Woman: Reading the Female Body in Ancient Greece*. New York: Routledge.

Kingsley, Bonnie. 1981. "The Cap That Survived Alexander," *American Journal of Archaeology* 85.1: 39–46.

Kingsley, Bonnie. 1991. "Alexander's 'Kausia' and Macedonian Tradition," *Classical Antiquity* 10.1: 59–76.

Kirk, G. E. 1935. "Gymnasium or Khan? A Hellenistic Building at Babylon," *Iraq*, 2: 223–231.

Klein, Anita. 1932. *Child Life in Greek Art*. New York: Columbia University Press.

Kleiner, Sibyl. 2009. "Thinking with the Mind, Syncing with the Body: Ballet as Symbolic and Nonsymbolic Interaction," *Symbolic Interaction* 32.3: 236–259.

Klengel-Brandt, Evelyn. 1979–1981. "Some Remarks on the Terracotta Figurines from Babylon," *Sumer*, 41.1–2: 118–120.

Klengel-Brandt, Evelyn. 1993. "Die hellenistische Kultur in Babylon: Das Zeugnis der Terrakotten." In *Arabia Antiqua: Hellenistic Centres around Arabia*, edited by Antonio Invernizzi and Jean-François Salles, 183–199. Rome: Serie Orientale Roma.

Klengel-Brandt, Evelyn and Nadja Cholidis. 2006. *Die Terrakotten von Babylon im Vorderasiatischen Museum in Berlin, Teil 1: Die Anthropomorphen Figuren*. Saarwellingen: Saarländische Druckerei & Verlag.

Knoblich, Günther and Natalie Sebanz. 2008. "Evolving Intentions for Social Interaction: From Entrainment to Joint Action," *Philosophical Transactions: Biological Sciences* (The Sapient Mind: Archaeology Meets Neuroscience) 363.1499: 2021–2031.

Koldewey, Robert. 1918. *Das Ischtar-tor in Babylon*, Wissenschaftliche Veröffentlichungen der Deutschen Orient-Gesellschaft (WVDOG) 32. Leipzig: Hinrichs.

Koldewey, Robert. 1925. *Das wieder erstehende Babylon; die bisherigen ergebnisse der deutschen ausgrabungen*. Leipzig: Hinrichs.

Koldewey, Robert. 1931–1932. *Die Konigsburgen von Babylon*, Wissenschaftliche Veröffentlichungen der Deutschen Orient-Gesellschaft (WVDOG) 54–55. Leipzig: Hinrichs.

Kose, Arno. 1998. *Uruk Architektur IV: Von der Seleukiden- bis zur Sasanidenzeit, Ausgrabungen in Uruk-Warka Endberichte* (AUWE) 17. Mainz am Rhein: Verlag Philipp von Zabern.

Kose, Arno. 2004. "Kritische Bemerkungen zum vermeintlich gefundenen Bit Akitu von Babylon." In *Deutsches Archäologisches Institut Orient-Abteilung: Baghdader Mitteilungen*, Band 35, 39–57. Mainz am Rhein: Verlag Philipp von Zabern.

Knappett, Carl. 2012. "Meaning in Miniature: semiotic networks in material culture." In *Excavating the*

Mind: Cross-Sections Through Culture, Cognition and Materiality, edited by Niels Johannsen, Mads D. Jessen, and Helle Juel Jensen, 87–109. Aarhus: Aarhus University Press.

Krul, Julia. 2018. "'Prayers from Him Who Is Unable to Make Offerings': The Cult of Bēlet-ṣēri at Late Babylonian Uruk," *Journal of Ancient Near Eastern Religions*, 18: 48–85.

Kuhrt, Amélie and Susan Sherwin-White. eds. 1987. *Hellenism in the East*. London: Gerald Duckworth.

Kukla, Rebecca. 2006. "Ethics and Ideology in Breastfeeding Advocacy Campaigns," *Hypatia* 21.1: 157–180.

Kuttner, Ann. 1999. "Hellenistic Images of Spectacle, from Alexander to Augustus," *Studies in the History of Art* (Symposium Papers XXXIV: The Art of Ancient Spectacle) 56: 96–123.

Lacan, Jacques. 1977. *Ecrits*. Translated by A. Sheridan. London: Tavistock.

Lancy, David F. 2018. *Anthropological Perspectives on Children as Helpers, Workers, Artisans, and Laborers*. New York: Palgrave Macmillan.

Landels, John. 1999. *Music in Ancient Greece and Rome*. New York and London: Routledge.

Langin-Hooper, Stephanie M. 2007. "Social Networks and Cross-Cultural Interaction: A New Interpretation of the Female Terracotta Figurines of Hellenistic Babylon," *Oxford Journal of Archaeology* 26.2: 145–165.

Langin-Hooper, Stephanie M. 2011. Beyond Typology: Investigating Entanglements of Difference and Exploring Object-Generated Social Interactions in the Terracotta Figurines of Hellenistic Babylonia. Ph.D. diss., University of California, Berkeley.

Langin-Hooper, Stephanie M. 2013a. "Problematizing Typology and Discarding the Colonialist Legacy: Approaches to Hybridity in the Terracotta Figurines of Hellenistic Babylonia," *Archaeological Review from Cambridge* 28.1: 95–113.

Langin-Hooper, Stephanie M. 2013b. "Terracotta Figurines and Social Identities in Hellenistic Babylonia." In *Critical Approaches to Ancient Near Eastern Art*, edited by Brian A. Brown and Marian H. Feldman, 451–479. Berlin and Boston: De Gruyter.

Langin-Hooper, Stephanie M. 2015. "Fascination with the Tiny: Social Negotiation through Miniatures in Hellenistic Babylonia," *World Archaeology* 47.1: 60–79.

Langin-Hooper, Stephanie M. 2016. "Seleucid-Parthian Figurines from Babylon in the Nippur Collection: Implications of Misattribution and Re-evaluating the Corpus," *Iraq*, 78: 49–77.

Langin-Hooper, Stephanie M. 2018a. "Gender Experiments in Hellenistic Babylonian Figurines." In *Gender, Methodology, and the Ancient Near East*, edited by A. Garcia Ventura and S. Svärd, 203–231. University Park, PA: Penn State University Press.

Langin-Hooper, Stephanie M. 2018b. "Stronger at the Broken Places: Affect in Hellenistic Babylonian Miniatures with Separately-Made and Attached Limbs." In *The Tiny and the Fragmented: Miniature, Broken, or Otherwise "Incomplete" Objects in the Ancient World*, edited by S. Rebecca Martin and Stephanie M. Langin-Hooper, 116–144. Oxford: Oxford University Press.

Langin-Hooper, Stephanie M. and Laurie Pearce. 2014. "Mammonymy, Maternal-Line Names and Cultural Identification: Clues from the Onomasticon of Hellenistic Uruk," *Journal of the American Oriental Society* 134:2, 185–202.

Langley, Michelle C. 2018. "Magdalenian Children: Projectile Points, Portable Art and Playthings," *Oxford Journal of Archaeology* 37.1: 3–24.

Langton, Rae. 2009. *Sexual Solipsism: Philosophical Essays on Pornography and Objectification*. Oxford: Oxford University Press.

Laskaris, Julie. 2008. "Nursing Mothers in Greek and Roman Medicine," *American Journal of Archaeology* 112.3: 459–464.

Laugier, Ludovic. 2009. "Les grotesques de Smyrne, types pathologiques et caricatures." In *D'Izmir à Smyrne: Découverte d'une cité antique* edited by Jean-Luc Martinez, Isabelle Hasselin Rous, and Ludovic Laugier, 170–173. Paris: Musée du Louvre.

Lear, Andrew. 2014. "Ancient Pederasty: An Introduction." In *A Companion to Greek and Roman Sexualities*, edited by Thomas K. Hubbard, 102–127. Malden, MA: Wiley Blackwell.

Lee, Mireille M. 2015. *Body, Dress, and Identity in Ancient Greece*. New York and Cambridge: Cambridge University Press.

Legrain, Leon. 1930. *Terra-cottas from Nippur* (University of Pennsylvania, The University Museum, Publications of the Babylonian Section, Vol. XVI). Philadelphia: University of Pennsylvania Press.

Lenzen, Heinrich. 1956. "Zur Datierung des Tempels in Qd/Qe XIV 5. Grabung in K XVIII. Bit Akitu," *Vorläufiger Bericht über die von dem Deutschen Archäologischen Institut und der Deutschen Orient-Gesellschaft aus Mitteln der Deutschen Forschungsgemeinschaft unternommenen Ausgrabungen in Uruk-Warka, Winter 1953–54–Winter 1954–55* (UVB 12/13). Berlin: Verlag Gebr. Mann.

Lenzen, Heinrich. 1959. "Die deutschen Ausgrabungen in Uruk von 1954–1957." In *Neue deutsche Ausgrabungen im Mittelmeergebiet und im Vorderen Orient (Deutsches Archäologisches Institut)*, edited by Erich Boehringer, 12–30. Berlin: Verlag Gebr. Mann.

Leppert, Richard. 2014. "Seeing Music." In *The Routledge Companion to Music and Visual Culture*, edited by Tim Shephard and Anne Leonard, 7–12. New York: Routledge.

Lerner, Jeffery D. 2017. "Mithradates I and the Parthian Archer." In *Arsacids, Romans, and Local Elites: Cross-Cultural Interactions of the Parthian Empire*, edited by Jason M. Schlude and Benjamin B. Rubin, 1–24. Oxford and Havertown, PA: Oxbow Books.

Lesure, Richard. 2011. *Interpreting Ancient Figurines: Context, Comparison, and Prehistoric Art*. Cambridge: Cambridge University Press.

LIMC 1981–2009. *Lexicon iconographicum mythologiae classicae* (Artemis).

Li, Jean. 2017. *Women, Gender and Identity in Third Intermediate Period Egypt: The Theban Case Study*. London and New York: Routledge.

Lillehammer, Grete. 1989. "A Child is Born: The Child's World in an Archaeological Perspective," *Norwegian Archaeological Review* 22.2: 89–105.

Lillehammer, Grete. 2000. "The World of Children." In *Children and Material Culture*, edited by Joanna Sofaer Derevenski, 17–26. London and New York: Routledge.

Lindström, Gunvor. 2003. *Uruk: Siegelabdrücke auf hellenistischen Tonbullen und Tontafeln*, Ausgrabungen in Uruk-Warka Endberichte (AUWE) 20. Mainz am Rhein: Verlag Phillip von Zabern in Wissenschaftliche Buchgesellschaft.

Linssen, Marc J.H. 2004. *The Cults of Uruk and Babylon: The Temple Ritual Texts as Evidence for Hellenistic Cult Practices*. Leiden and Boston: Brill Styx.

Lissarrague, François. 1990. *The Aesthetics of the Greek Banquet: Images of Wine and Ritual*. Translated by A. Szegedy-Maszak. Princeton: Princeton University Press.

Lloyd, Stephen and Kim Sloan. 2008. *The Intimate Portrait: Drawings, Miniatures and Pastels from Ramsay to Lawrence*. Edinburgh and London: National Galleries of Scotland and the British Museum.

Lopiparo, Jeanne. 2006. "Crafting Children: Materiality, Social Memory, and the Reproduction of Terminal Classic House Societies in the Ulúa Valley, Honduras." In *The Social Experience of Childhood in Ancient Mesoamerica*, edited by Traci Ardren and Scott R. Hutson, 133–168. Boulder, CO: University Press of Colorado.

Lorber, Catharine C. and Panagiotis P. Iossif, 2009a. "Seleucid Campaign Beards," *L'Antiquité Classique* 78: 87–115.

Lorber, Catharine and Panagiotis Iossif. 2009b. "The Cult of Helios in the Seleucid East," *Topoi* 16:1, 19–42.

Mack, John. 2007. *The Art of Small Things*. Cambridge, MA: Harvard University Press.

MacKinnon, Catharine. 1994. *Only Words*. London: Harper Collins Publishers.

Manasseh, N. 1931. "Architectural Notes, Season 1927–29." In *Preliminary Report upon the Excavations at Tel Umar, Iraq, Conducted by The University of Michigan and The Toledo Museum of Art*, edited by Leroy Waterman, 9–17. Ann Arbor: University of Michigan Press.

Markman, Arthur B. and Dedre Gentner. 1993. "Structural Alignment During Similarity Comparisons," *Cognitive Psychology* 25: 431–467.

Marks, Laura. 2008. "Thinking Multisensory Culture," *Paragraph* 31(2): 123–137.

Marshall, C. W. 2017. "Breastfeeding in Greek Literature and Thought," *Illinois Classical Studies* 42.1: 185–201.

Martin, F. David. 1979. "Sculpture and 'Truth to Things'," *The Journal of Aesthetic Education* 13.2: 11–32.

Martin, S. Rebecca. 2017. *The Art of Contact: Comparative Approaches to Greek and Phoenician Art*. Philadelphia: University of Pennsylvania Press.

Martin, S. Rebecca and Stephanie M. Langin-Hooper. 2018. "In/Complete: An Introduction to the Theories of Miniaturization and Fragmentation." In *The Tiny and the Fragmented: Miniature, Broken, or Otherwise "Incomplete" Objects in the Ancient World*, edited by S. Rebecca Martin and Stephanie M. Langin-Hooper, 1–23. Oxford: Oxford University Press.

Martinez-Sève, Laurianne. 2002. *Les figurines de Suse: De l'époque néo-élamite à l'époque sassanide*. Paris: Musée du Louvre.

Martinez-Sève, Laurianne. 2014. "The Spatial Organization of Ai Khanoum, a Greek City in Afghanistan," *American Journal of Archaeology* 118.2: 267–283.

Masséglia, Jane. 2015. *Body Language in Hellenistic Art and Society*. Oxford: Oxford University Press.

Mathiesen, Thomas. 1999. *Apollo's Lyre: Greek Music and Music Theory in Antiquity and the Middle Ages*. Lincoln: University of Nebraska Press.

Mayer, W.R. 1978. "Seleukidische Rituale aus Warka mit Emesal-Gebeten," *Orientalia*, 47: 431–458.

Mayor, Adrienne. 2016. "Warrior women: the archaeology of Amazons." In *Women In Antiquity: Real Women across the Ancient World*, edited by Stephanie Lynn Budin and Jean Macintosh Turfa, 969–985. London and New York: Routledge.

McCaffrey, Kathleen. 2002. "Reconsidering Gender Ambiguity in Mesopotamia: Is a Beard Just a Beard?." In *Sex and Gender in the Ancient Near East, Proceedings of the 47th Rencontre Assyriologique Internationale, Helsinki, July 2–6, 2001*, edited by Simo Parpola and Robert M. Whiting, 379–391. Helsinki: Neo-Assyrian Text Corpus Project.

McCown, Donald E. 1967. "Private Houses in the Scribal Quarter: The Objects." In *Nippur I: Temple of Enlil, Scribal Quarter, and Soundings*, by Donald E. McCown and Richard C. Haines, assisted by Donald

P. Hansen, 77–117. Chicago: The University of Chicago Press.

McCown, Donald E. and Richard C. Haines, assisted by Donald P. Hansen. 1967. *Nippur I: Temple of Enlil, Scribal Quarter, and Soundings*. Chicago: The University of Chicago Press.

McDowell, Robert. 1935a. *Coins from Seleucia on the Tigris*. Ann Arbor: University of Michigan Press.

McDowell, Robert. 1935b. *Stamped and Inscribed Objects from Seleucia on the Tigris*. Ann Arbor: University of Michigan Press.

McEwan, Gilbert. 1981. *Priest and Temple in Hellenistic Babylonia*. Wiesbaden: Franz Steiner Verlag GMBH.

McFerrin, Neville. 2017. "Fabrics of Inclusion: Deep Wearing and the Potentials of Materiality on the Apadana Reliefs." In *What Shall I Say of Clothes? Theoretical and Methodological Approaches to the Study of Dress in Antiquity*, edited by Megan Cifarelli and Laura Gawlinski, 143–159. Boston: Archaeological Institute of America.

McGlynn, Aidan. 2016. "Propaganda and the Authority of Pornography," *Theoria: An International Journal for Theory, History and Foundations of Science* 31.3: 329–343.

McKeown, Niall. 2007. "Had They No Shame? Martial, Statius, and Roman Sexual Attitudes towards Slave Children." In *Children, Childhood and Society* (BAR International Series 1696), edited by Sally Crawford and Gillian Shepherd, 57–62. Oxford: Archaeopress.

McNiven, Timothy J. 2000. "Behaving Like an Other: Telltale Gestures in Athenian Vase Painting." In *Not the Classical Ideal: Athens and the Construction of the Other in Greek Art*, edited by Beth Cohen, 70–97. Leiden: Brill.

Meissner, Nathan J., Katherine E. South, and Andrew K. Balkansky. 2013. "Figurine Embodiment and Household Ritual in an Early Mixtec Village," *Journal de la Société des américanistes* 99.1: 7–43.

Menegazzi, Roberta. 2007. "La Coroplastica della Mesopotamia Ellenizzata." In *Sulla Via Di Alessandro: Da Seleucia Al Gandhara*, 128–133. Milan: Silvana Editoriale.

Menegazzi, Roberta. 2012. "Creating a new language: the terracotta figurines from Seleucia on the Tigris." In *Proceedings of the International Congress on the Archaeology of the Ancient Near East, Band 7: Volume 2: Ancient & Modern Issues in Cultural Heritage, Colour & Light in Architecture, Art & Material Culture, Islamic Archaeology*, edited by R. Matthews and J. Curtis, 157–167. Wiesbaden-Erbenheim: Harrassowitz Verlag.

Menegazzi, Roberta. 2014. *Seleucia al Tigri Le Terrecotte Figurate: Dagli Scavi Italiani e Americani* (Monografie di Mesopotamia XVI). Firenze: Casa Editrice Le Lettere.

Merker, Gloria. 2000. *The Sanctuary of Demeter and Kore: Terracotta Figurines of the Classical, Hellenistic, and Roman Periods* (Corinth, Volume XVIII, Part IV). Princeton: The American School of Classical Studies at Athens.

Merleau-Ponty, Maurice. 2012 [1945]. *Phenomenology of Perception*. Translated by Donald A. Landes, London and New York: Routledge.

Meskell, Lynn. 2007. "Refiguring the corpus at Çatalhöyük." In *Material Beginnings: A Global Prehistory of Figurative Representation*, edited by C. Renfrew and I. Morley, 137–150. Cambridge: McDonald Institute Monographs.

Meskell, Lynn. 2015. "A society of things: animal figurines and material scales at Neolithic Çatalhöyük," *World Archaeology* 47.1: 6–19.

Messina, Vito. 2009. "Witnesses and Sealers of Seleucid Mesopotamia: A Comparison Between the Seal Impressions from Uruk and Those from Seleucia on the Tigris." In *Witnessing in the Ancient Near East (Acta Sileni – II)*, edited by Nicoletta Bellotto and Simonetta Ponchia, 175–190. Padova: S.A.R.G.O.N. Editrice e Libreria.

Messina, Vito. 2010. *Seleucia al Tigri: il monumento Di Tell 'Umar: lo Scavo e le fasi architettoniche*. Firenze: Le lettere.

Meyer, Hugo. 1996. "The Terme Ruler: An Understudied Masterpiece and the School of Lysippos," *Bullettino della Commissione Archeologica Comunale di Roma* 97: 125–148.

Miller, Daniel. (ed). 2005. *Materiality*. Durham, NC: Duke University Press.

Miller, Margaret C. 1997. *Athens and Persia in the Fifth Century BC: A Study in Cultural Receptivity*. Cambridge: Cambridge University Press.

Miracle, Preston and Borić, Dušan. 2008. "Bodily beliefs and agricultural beginnings in Western Asia: animal-human hybridity re-examined." In *Past Bodies: Body-Centered Research in Archaeology*, edited by D. Borić and J. Robb, 101–113. Oxford: Oxbow Books.

Mitchell, Alexandre. 2013. "Disparate bodies in ancient artefacts: The function of caricature and pathological grotesques among Roman terracotta figurines." In *Disabilities in Roman Antiquity: Disparate Bodies A Capite ad Calcem*, edited by Christian Laes, C.F. Goodey, and M. Lynn Rose, 275–297. Leiden and Boston: Brill.

Mitchell, Alexandre. 2017. "The Hellenistic Turn in Bodily Representations: Venting Anxiety in Terracotta Figurines." In *Disability in Antiquity*, edited by Christian Laes, 182–196. London and New York: Routledge.

Mollard-Besques, Simone. 1963. *Musée national du Louvre: Catalogue Raisonné des Figurines et Reliefs en Terre-cuite Grecs et Romains. Vol. 2, Myrina*. Paris: Éditions des Musées Nationaux.

Moorey, P.R.S. 2000. "Iran and the West: The Case of the Terracotta 'Persian' Riders in the Achaemenid Empire." In *Variatio Delectat: Iran und der Westen, Gedenkschrift für Peter Calmeyer*, edited by R. Dittmann, B. Hrouda, U. Löw, P. Matthiae, R. Mayer-Opificius, and S. Thürwächter, 469–486. Munster: Ugarit-Verlag.

Moorey, P.R.S. 2003. *Idols of the People: Miniature Images of Clay in the Ancient Near East*. Oxford: Oxford University Press.

Moreiras, Alberto. 1999. "Hybridity and Double Conciousness," *Cultural Studies* 13.3: 373–407.

Muller, Arthur. 1996. *Les terres cuites votives du Thesmophorion: De l'Atelier au Sanctuaire, Volume 2 – Planches*. Athens: École Française d'Athènes.

Muller, Arthur. 2010. "The Technique of Tanagra Coroplasts: From Local Craft to 'Global Industry'." In *Tanagras: Figurines for Life and Eternity*, edited by V. Jeammet, 100–109. Paris: Musée du Louvre.

Mulvey, Laura. 1975. "Visual Pleasure and Narrative Cinema," *Screen* 16.3: 6–18.

Mumford, Lewis. 1934. *Technics and Civilization*. New York: Harcourt, Brace.

Nakamichi, Masayuki and Shohei Takeda. 1995. "A Child Holding Thought Experiment: Students Prefer to Imagine Holding an Infant on the Left Side of the Body," *Perceptual and Motor Skills*, 80: 687–690.

Nakamura, Carolyn and Lynn Meskell. 2009. "Articulate Bodies: Forms and Figures at Çatalhöyük," *Journal of Archaeological Method and Theory* 16.3: 205–230.

Naumann, Friederike. 1983. *Die Ikonographie der Kybele in der Phrygischen und der Griechischen Kunst*. Istanbuler Mitteilungen. Beiheft, 28. Tübingen: Verlag Ernst Wasmuth.

Needham, Rodney. 1967. "Percussion and Transition," *Man* 2.4: 606–614.

Neer, Richard. 2010. *The Emergence of the Classical Style in Greek Sculpture*. Chicago and London: University of Chicago Press.

Neils, Jenifer. 2000. "Others Within the Other: An Intimate Look at Hetairai and Maenads." In *Not the Classical Ideal: Athens and the Construction of the Other in Greek Art*, edited by Beth Cohen, 203–226. Leiden: Brill.

Neils, Jenifer. 2003. "Children and Greek Religion." In *Coming of Age in Ancient Greece: Images of Childhood from the Classical Past*, edited by Jenifer Neils and John H. Oakley, 138–161. New Haven, CT and London: Yale University Press.

Neils, Jenifer and John H. Oakley. (eds). 2003. *Coming of Age in Ancient Greece: Images of Childhood from the Classical Past*. New Haven, CT and London: Yale University Press.

Nelson, Robert. 2007. "Empathetic Vision: Looking at and With a Performative Byzantine Miniature," *Art History* 30.4: 489–502.

Ng, Diana Y. 2018. "The Salutaris Foundation: Monumentality through Periodic Rehearsal." In *Roman Artists, Patrons, and Public Consumption: Familiar Works Reconsidered*, edited by Brenda Longfellow and Ellen E. Perry, 63–87. Ann Arbor: University of Michigan Press.

Nitschke, Jessica. 2013. "Interculturality in Image and Cult in the Hellenistic East: Tyrian Melqart Revisited." In *Shifting Social Imaginaries in the Hellenistic Period*, edited by Eftychia Stavrianopoulou, 253–282. Leiden: Brill.

Nochlin, Linda. 1988. *Women, Art, and Power: And Other Essays*. New York: Harper & Row.

North, Helen. 1966. *Sophrosyne: Self-Knowledge and Self-Restraint in Greek Literature*. Ithaca, NY: Cornell University Press.

Oakley, J. 2000. "Some 'Other' Members of the Athenian Household: Maids and their Mistresses in Fifth-Century Athenian Art." In *Not the Classical Ideal: Athens and the Construction of the Other in Greek Art*, edited by Beth Cohen, 227–247. Leiden: Brill.

Oggiano, Ida. 2015. "Le sanctuaire de Kharayeb et l'évolution de l'imagerie phénicienne dans l'arrière-pays de Tyr," *Topoi (La Phénicie Hellénistique: Acts du colloque international de Toulouse [18–20 février 2013]*, edited by Julien Aliquot and Corinne Bonnet), Supplément 13: 239–266.

Olin, Margaret. 2003. "Gaze." In *Critical Terms for Art History*, Second Edition, edited by Robert S. Nelson and Richard Shiff, 318–329. Chicago and London: The University of Chicago Press.

Osborne, James F. 2014. "Monuments and Monumentality." In *Approaching Monumentality in Archaeology*, edited by James F. Osborne, 1–19. Albany: SUNY Press.

Osborne, Robin. 1997. "Men Without Clothes: Heroic Nakedness and Greek Art," *Gender & History* 9: 504–528.

Osborne, Robin. 2001. "Why Did Athenian Pots Appeal to the Etruscans?," *World Archaeology* 33.2: 277–295.

Osborne, Robin. 2011. *The History Written on the Classical Greek Body*. Cambridge: Cambridge University Press.

Palagia, Olga. "Marble Carving Techniques." In *Greek Sculpture: Function, Materials, and Techniques in the Archaic and Classical Periods*, edited by Olga Palagia, 243–279. Cambridge: Cambridge University Press.

Park, Robert W. 2005. "Growing Up North: Exploring the Archaeology of Childhood in the Thule and Dorset Cultures of Arctic Canada," *Archaeological Papers of the American Anthropological Association* 15: 53–64.

Passmore, E. 2014. "Analytical Results for Pigment Traces on Selected Seleucid

Terracotta and Plaster Figurines from the Kelsey Museum." In *Seleucia al Tigri Le Terrecotte Figurate: Dagli Scavi Italiani e Americani*, edited by R. Menegazzi, 19–21. Firenze: Le Lettere.

Paterson, Mark. 2007. *The Senses of Touch: Haptics, Affects and Technologies*. Oxford and New York: Berg.

Paul, Aaron J. 1994–1995. "A New Vase by the Dinos Painter: Eros and an Erotic Image of Women in Greek Vase Painting," *Harvard University Art Museums Bulletin* 3.2: 60–67.

Pedde, Friedhelm. 1993. "Frehat en-Nufegi: Two Seleucid Tumuli Near Uruk." In *Arabia Antiqua: Hellenistic Centres Around Arabia*, edited by A. Invernizzi and J.-F. Salles, 205–221. Rome: Serie Orientale Roma.

Peirce, Sarah. 1998. "Visual Language and Concepts of Cult on the 'Lenaia Vases'," *Classical Antiquity*, 17.1: 59–95.

Peled, Ilan. 2016a. *Masculinities and Third Gender: The Origins and Nature of an Institutionalized Gender Otherness in the Ancient Near East* (Alter Orient und Altes Testament, Band 435). Münster: Ugarit-Verlag.

Peled, Ilan. 2016b. "Visualizing Masculinities: The Gala, Hegemony, and Mesopotamian Iconography," *Near Eastern Archaeology* 79.3: 158–165.

Peled, Ilan. 2018. "Identifying Gender Ambiguity in Texts and Artifacts." In *Gender and Methodology in the Ancient Near East: Approaches from Assyriology and Beyond* (Barcino monographica orientalia 10), edited by Stephanie Lynn Budin, Megan Cifarelli, Agnès Garcia-Ventura, and Adelina Millet Albà, 55–63. Barcelona: Edicions de la Universitat de Barcelona.

Petrie, C.A. 2002. "Seleucid Uruk: An Analysis of Ceramic Distribution," *Iraq* 64: 85–123.

Petty, Alice. 2006. *Bronze Age Anthropomorphic Figurines from Umm el-Marra, Syria: Chronology, Visual Analysis and Function* (BAR International Series 1575). Oxford: Archaeopress.

Piccioni, Aura. 2016. "Cybele, the Drum, and the Role of Female Musicians." In *Musicians in Ancient Coroplastic Art: Iconography, Ritual Contexts, and Functions*, edited by Angela Bellia and Clemente Marconi, 157–162. Pisa and Rome: Istituti Editoriali e Poligrafici Internazionali.

Piggott, Stuart. 1992. *Wagon, Chariot and Carriage: Symbol and Status in the History of Transport*. New York: Thames and Hudson.

Pilides, Despo. 2009. "Evidence for the Hellenistic Period in Nicosia: The Settlement at the Hill of Agios Georgios and the Cemetery at Agii Omologites," *Cahiers du Centre d'Etudes Chypriotes* 39: 49–67.

Pointon, Marcia. 1999. "Valuing the Visual and Visualizing the Valuable: Jewellery and its Ambiguities," *Cultural Values* 3.1: 1–27.

Pollitt, J. J. 1986. *Art in the Hellenistic Age*. Cambridge: Cambridge University Press.

Pollock, Griselda. 1988. *Vision and Difference: Feminism, Femininity, and the Histories of Art*. London and New York: Routledge.

Pomeroy, Sarah B. 1984. *Women in Hellenistic Egypt: From Alexander to Cleopatra*. New York: Schocken Books.

Ponzi, Mariamaddalena. 1970–1971. "Excavations in Squares CLXXI, 54/55/63/64/74," *Mesopotamia* 5–6:31–39.

Porter, Barbara Nevling. 2003. *Trees, Kings, and Politics: Studies in Assyrian Iconography*. Fribourg: Academic Press.

Postgate, J. N. 1992. *Early Mesopotamia: Society and Economy at the Dawn of History*. New York and London: Routledge.

Potter, David S. 1991. "The Inscriptions on the Bronze Herakles from Mesene: Vologeses IV's War with Rome and the Date of Tacitus' Annales," *Zeitschrift für Papyrologie und Epigraphik* 88: 277–290.

Potts, Daniel T. 1997. *Mesopotamian Civilization: The Material Foundations*. Ithaca, NY: Cornell University Press.

Pultz, John. 1995. *Photography and the Body*. London: Weidenfeld & Nicholson.

Prier, Raymond. 1989. *Thauma Idesthai: The Phenomenology of Sight and Appearance in Archaic Greek*. Tallahassee: Florida State University Press.

Pruzsinszky, Regine. 2016. "Musicians and Monkeys: Ancient Near Eastern Clay Plaques Displaying Musicians and their Social-Cultural Role." In *Musicians in Ancient Coroplastic Art: Iconography, Ritual Contexts, and Functions*, edited by Angela Bellia and Clemente Marconi, 23–34. Pisa and Rome: Istituti Editoriali e Poligrafici Internazionali.

Rabinowitz, Nancy Sorkin. 2002. "Excavating Women's Homoeroticism in Ancient Greece: The Evidence from Attic Vase Painting." In *Among Women: From the Homosocial to the Homoerotic in the Ancient World*, edited by N.S. Rabinowitz and L. Auanger, 106–166. Austin: University of Texas Press.

Rahbari, Ladan. 2017. "Women's Agency and Corporeality in Equestrian Sports: The Case of Female Leisure Horse-Riders in Tehran." In *Equestrian Cultures in Global and Local Contexts*, edited by K. Thompson and M. Adelman, 17–34. Cham, Switzerland: Springer.

Rapin, Claude. 1990. "Greeks in Afghanistan: Ai Khanoum." In *Greek Colonists and Native Populations: Proceedings of the First Australian Congress of Classical Archaeology held in honour of Emeritus Professor A. D. Trendall*, edited by Jean-Paul Descoeudres, 329–342. Oxford: Clarendon Press.

Rashid, Subhi Anwar. 1984. *Musikgeschichte in Bildern: Mesopotamien*. Leipzig: VEB Deutscher Verlag für Musik.

Rawson, Philip. 1984. *Ceramics*. Philadelphia: University of Pennsylvania Press.

Reade, J. E. 1998. "Greco-Parthian Nineveh," *Iraq* 60: 65–83.

Régnault, Félix. 1909. "La syphilis est-elle représentée sur les terres cuites grecques de Smyrne," *Bulletin de la Société d'Anthropologie de Lyon* 18: 33–39.

Reilly, Joan. 1997. "Naked and Limbless: Learning about the feminine body in ancient Athens." In *Naked Truths: Women, Sexuality, and Gender in Classical Art and Archaeology*, edited by A. Koloski-Ostrow and C. Lyons, 154–173. London and New York: Routledge.

Reissland, Nadja, Brian Hopkins, Peter Helms, and Bob Williams. 2009. "Maternal Stress and Depression and the Lateralisation of Infant Cradling," *Journal of Child Psychology and Psychiatry* 50: 263–269.

Renfrew, Colin. 2001. "Symbol before Concept: Material Engagement and the Early Development of Society." In *Archaeological Theory Today*, edited by Ian Hodder, 122–140. Cambridge and Malden, MA: Polity Press.

Reuther, Oskar. 1926. *Die Innenstadt von Babylon (Merkes)*, Wissenschaftliche Veroffentlichungen der Deutschen Orientgesellschaft (WVDOG) 47. Leipzig: Hinrichs.

Richard, Suzanne. 2019. "Miniatures and Miniaturization in EB IV at Khirbat Iskandar, Jordan." In *Pearls of the Past: Studies on Near Eastern Art and Archaeology in Honour of Frances Pinnock*, edited by Marta D'Andrea, Maria Gabriella Micale, Davide Nadali, Sara Pizzimenti, and Agnese Vacca, 813–838. Münster: Zaphon.

Richards, M.C. 1989. *Centering*, 2nd ed. Middletown: Wesleyan University.

Richon, Olivier. 1985. "Representation, the Harem and the Despot," *Block* 10: 34–41.

Ridgway, Brunilde S. 1987. "Ancient Greek Women and Art: The Material

Evidence," *American Journal of Archaeology* 91: 3, 399–409.

Ridgway, Brunilde S. 2000. *Hellenistic Sculpture II, The Styles of ca. 200–100 B.C.* Madison, WI and London: University of Wisconsin Press.

Ridgway, Brunilde S. 2001. *Hellenistic Sculpture I: The Styles of ca. 331–200 B.C.* Madison, WI and London: University of Wisconsin Press.

Riede, Felix, Niels N. Johannsen, Anders Högberg, April Nowell, and Marlize Lombard. 2018. "The role of play objects and object play in human cognitive evolution and innovation," *Evolutionary Anthropology* 27.1: 46–59.

Rimmer, Joan. 1969. *Ancient Musical Instruments of Western Asia in the Department of Western Asiatic Antiquities, The British Museum.* London: British Museum.

Ristvet, Lauren. 2011. "Excavating the Akītu: Ritual, Politics and Society in First Millennium Babylonia". Conference paper given at the American Schools of Oriental Research Annual Meeting; November 17, 2011.

Ristvet, Lauren. 2014. "Between Ritual and Theatre: Political Performance in Seleucid Babylonia," *World Archaeology* 45.4: 256–269.

Ristvet, Lauren. 2015. *Ritual, Performance, and Politics in the Ancient Near East.* Cambridge: Cambridge University Press.

Roaf, Michael. 2004. *Cultural Atlas of Mesopotamia and the Ancient Near East.* Oxford: Facts on File.

Robb, John. 2009. "People of Stone: Stelae, Personhood, and Society in Prehistoric Europe," *Journal of Archaeological Method and Theory* 16.3: 162–183.

Robertson, Lisa. 2003. *Occasional Work and the Seven Walks from the Office for Soft Architecture.* Astoria, OR: Clear Cut Press.

Rochberg, Francesca. 2016. *Before Nature: Cuneiform Knowledge and the History of Science.* Chicago and London: The University of Chicago Press.

Roisman, Joseph. 2005. *The Rhetoric of Manhood: Masculinity in the Attic Orators.* Berkeley: University of California Press.

Roller, Lynn E. 1991. "The Great Mother at Gordion: The Hellenization of an Anatolian Cult," *The Journal of Hellenic Studies* 111: 128–143.

Romero, Margarita Sánchez. 2017. "Landscapes of Childhood: Bodies, Places and Material Culture," *Childhood In The Past* 10.1: 16–37.

Root, Margaret Cool. 1989. "The Persian Archer at Persepolis: Aspects of Chronology, Style, and Symbolism," *Revue des Études Anciennes* 91: 1–2, 33–50.

Root, Margaret Cool. 2018. "A Response: Scaling the Walls of Persepolis toward an Imaginal Social/Material Landscape." In *The Tiny and the Fragmented: Miniature, Broken, or Otherwise "Incomplete" Objects in the Ancient World*, edited by S. Rebecca Martin and Stephanie M. Langin-Hooper, 188–216. Oxford: Oxford University Press.

Rose, Martha Lynn. 2017. "Ability and Disability in Classical Athenian Oratory." In *Disability in Antiquity*, edited by Christian Laes, 139–153. London and New York: Routledge.

Roselli, David Kawalko. 2011. *Theater of the People: Spectators and Society in Ancient Athens.* Austin: University of Texas Press.

Rostovtzeff, M. 1937. "The Squatting Gods in Babylonia and at Dura," *Iraq* 4.1: 19–20.

Roth, Martha T. 1987. "Age at Marriage and the Household: A Study of Neo-Babylonian and Neo-Assyrian Forms," *Comparative Studies in Society and History* 29.4: 715–747.

Roth, Martha T. 1995. *Law Collections from Mesopotamia and Asia Minor.* Atlanta: Scholars Press.

Rothschild, Nan A. 2002. "Introduction." In *Children in the Prehistoric Puebloan*

Southwest, edited by Kathryn A. Kamp, 1–13. Salt Lake City: The University of Utah Press.

Rous, Isabelle Hasselin. 2010. "Children and Death: The Contents of an Eretrian Tomb Now in the Musée du Louvre." In *Tanagras: Figurines for Life and Eternity*, edited by V. Jeammet, 176–177. Paris: Musée du Louvre.

Rumscheid, Frank. 2006. *Die figürlichen Terrakotten von Priene: Fundkontexte, Ikonographie und Funktion in Wohnhäusern und Heiligtümern im Licht antiker Parallelbefunde*. Wiesbaden: Deutsches Archäologisches Institut.

Saatsoglou-Paliadeli, Chryssoula. 1993. "Aspects of Ancient Macedonian Culture," *The Journal of Hellenic Studies* 113: 122–147.

Sachs, Curt. 1940. *The History of Musical Instruments*. New York: W.W. Norton.

Samama, Evelyne. 2017. "The Greek Vocabulary of Disabilities." In *Disability in Antiquity*, edited by Christian Laes, 121–138. London and New York: Routledge.

Schmid, H. 1960. "Die Grabung an der NO-Einschliessung des Bit-Res," *Vorläufiger Bericht über die von dem Deutschen Archäologischen Institut und der Deutschen Orient-Gesellschaft aus Mitteln der Deutschen Forschungsgemeinschaft unternommenen Ausgrabungen in Uruk-Warka, Winter 1957–58* (UVB 16), edited by Heinrich Lenzen. Berlin: Verlag Gebr. Mann.

Schmidt, Erich. 1941. "Die Griechen in Babylon und das Weiterleben ihrer Kultur," *Archaologishcer Anzeiger* 56: 786–844.

Schmidt, J. 1970. "Uruk-Warka, Zusammenfassender Bericht über die 27. Kampagne 1969." In *Deutsches Archäologisches Institut Orient-Abteilung: Baghdader Mitteilungen*, Band 5, 51–96. Mainz am Rhein: Verlag Philipp von Zabern.

Schmidt, Jurgen. 1972. *Anu-Zikkurat, Vorläufiger Bericht über die von dem Deutschen Archaologischen Institut und der Deutschen Orient-Gesellschaft aus Mitteln der Deutschen Forschungsgemeinschaft unternommenen Ausgrabungen in Uruk-Warka, 1968 und 1969* (UVB 26/27). Berlin: Gebr. Mann.

Schmidt, Jurgen. 2002. "Das Bit Akitu von Babylon." In *Deutsches Archäologisches Institut Orient-Abteilung: Baghdader Mitteilungen*, Band 33, 281–317. Mainz am Rhein: Verlag Philipp von Zabern.

Scola, C. and J. Vauclair. 2010a. "Is Infant Holding-Side Bias Related to Motor Asymmetries in Mother and Child?," *Developmental Psychobiology* 52: 475–486.

Scola, C. and J. Vauclair. 2010b. "Infant's Holding Side Biases by Fathers in Maternity Hospitals," *Journal of Reproductive and Infant Psychology* 28: 3–10.

Scurlock, JoAnn and Burton R. Anderson. 2005. *Diagnoses in Assyrian and Babylonian Medicine: Ancient Sources, Translations and Modern Medical Analyses*. Urbana, IL and Chicago: University of Illinois Press.

Seaman, Kristen. 2004. "Retrieving the Original Aphrodite of Knidos," *Atti della Accademia Nazionale dei Lincei*, 15.3: 531–594.

Shapiro, H.A. 2003. "Fathers and Sons, Men and Boys." In *Coming of Age in Ancient Greece: Images of Childhood from the Classical Past*, edited by Jenifer Neils and John H. Oakley, 84–111. New Haven, CT and London: Yale University Press.

Shapiro, Mark. 2004. "Linda Sikora: Beneath the Surface," *Studio Potter* 32.2: 7–14.

Shehata, Dahlia. 2014. "Sounds from the Divine: Religious Musical Instruments in the Ancient Near East." In *Music in Antiquity: The Near East and Mediterranean*, edited by Joan Goodnick Westenholz, Yossi Maurey, and Edwin Seroussi, 102–128. Berlin and Boston: De Gruyter.

Shepherd, Gillian. 2012. "Women in Magna Graecia." In *A Companion to Women in the Ancient World*, edited by Sharon L. James and Sheila Dillon, 215–228. Malden, MA: Wiley-Blackwell.

Sherwin-White, Susan. 1987. "Seleucid Babylonia: A Case-Study for the Installation and Development of Greek Rule." In *Hellenism in the East*, edited by Amélie Kuhrt and Susan Sherwin-White, 1–31. London: Gerald Duckworth.

Sherwin-White, Susan and Amélie Kuhrt. 1993. *From Samarkhand to Sardis: A New Approach to the Seleucid Empire*. London: Gerald Duckworth.

Shevchenko, Tetiana M. 2015. "Bust Thymiateria from Olbia Pontike," *Les Carnets de l'ACoSt* 13: 1–22.

Shipley, Graham. 2000. *The Greek World After Alexander: 323–30 BC*. London and New York: Routledge.

Siebert, Charles. 2018. "Schleich Figurines," *New York Times Magazine* 3.25: 26–27.

Sillar, Bill. 1994. "Playing with God: Cultural Perceptions of Children, Play and Miniatures in the Andes," *Archaeological Review from Cambridge* 13.2: 47–63.

Silliman, Stephen W. 2015. "A Requiem for Hybridity? The Problem with Frankensteins, Purées, and Mules," *Journal of Social Archaeology* 15.3: 277–298.

Simpson, St John and Georgina Herrmann. 1995. "'Through the Glass Darkly': Reflections on Some Ladies from Merv," *Iranica Antiqua* 30: 141–158.

Smith, R.R.R. 1988. *Hellenistic Royal Portraits*. Oxford: Clarendon Press.

Smith, R.R.R. 1991. *Hellenistic Sculpture: A Handbook*. London and New York: Thames and Hudson.

Spalding, Susan. 1994. "Definition of Community in Old Time Dancing in Rural Southwest Virginia," *Dance Research Journal* 26.1: 1–7.

Spivey, Nigel. 2013. *Greek Sculpture*. Cambridge: Cambridge University Press.

Stafford, Emma J. 1991–1993. "Aspects of Sleep in Hellenistic Sculpture," *Bulletin of the Institute of Classical Studies* 38: 105–120.

Stallybrass, Peter and Ann Rosalind Jones. 2004. "Fetishizing the Glove in Renaissance Europe." In *Things*, edited by Bill Brown, 174–192. Chicago and London: The University of Chicago Press.

St. Clair, Archer. 2003. *Carving as Craft: Palatine East and the Greco-Roman Bone and Ivory Carving Tradition*. Baltimore and London: The Johns Hopkins University Press.

Stansbury-O'Donnell, Mark. 2006. *Vase Painting, Gender, and Social Identity in Archaic Athens*. Cambridge: Cambridge University Press.

Stansbury-O'Donnell, Mark. 2011. *Looking at Greek Art*. Cambridge: Cambridge University Press.

Stearns, Cindy A. 2009. "The Work of Breastfeeding," *Women's Studies Quarterly* 37.3/4: 63–80.

Steele, Laura D. 2007. "Women and Gender in Babylonia." In *The Babylonian World*, edited by Gwendolyn Leick, 299–316. New York and London: Routledge.

Stevens, Kathryn. 2014. "The Antiochus Cylinder, Babylonian Scholarship and Seleucid Imperial Ideology," *The Journal of Hellenic Studies* 134: 66–88.

Stevenson, Tom. 2003. "Cavalry Uniforms on the Parthenon Frieze?," *American Journal of Archaeology* 107.4: 629–654.

Stevenson, III, William Edward. 1975. The Pathological Grotesque Representation in Greek and Roman Art. Ph.D. diss., University of Pennsylvania, Philadelphia.

Stewart, Andrew. 1990. *Greek Sculpture: An Exploration, Volume 1: The Text*. New

Haven, CT and London: Yale University Press.

Stewart, Andrew. 1993. *Faces of Power: Alexander's Image and Hellenistic Politics*. Berkeley: University of California Press.

Stewart, Andrew. 1996. "Reflections." In *Sexuality in Ancient Art*, edited by N. B. Kampen, 136–154. Cambridge: Cambridge University Press.

Stewart, Andrew. 1997. *Art, Desire, and the Body in Ancient Greece*. Cambridge: Cambridge University Press.

Stewart, Andrew. 2008. *Classical Greece and the Birth of Western Art*. Cambridge: Cambridge University Press.

Stewart, Andrew. 2014. *Art in the Hellenistic World: An Introduction*. Cambridge: Cambridge University Press.

Stewart, Andrew and S. Rebecca Martin. 2003. "Hellenistic Discoveries at Tel Dor, Israel," *Hesperia: The Journal of the American School of Classical Studies at Athens* 72.2: 121–145.

Stewart, Susan. 1984. *On Longing: Narratives of the Miniature, the Gigantic, the Souvenir, the Collection*. Baltimore and London: The Johns Hopkins University Press.

Stillwell, A. 1952. *Corinth: Results of Excavations conducted by The American School of Classical Studies at Athens, Volume XV, Part II: The Potters' Quarter, The Terracottas*. Princeton: The American School of Classical Studies at Athens.

Stockhammer, Philipp W. 2012. "Entangled Pottery: Phenomena of Appropriation in the Late Bronze Age Eastern Mediterranean." In *Materiality and Social Practice: Transformative Capacities of Intercultural Encounters*, edited by Joseph Maran and Philipp W. Stockhammer, 89–103. Oxford: Oxbow Books.

Stökl, Jonathan. 2013. "Gender 'Ambiguity' in Ancient Near Eastern Prophecy? A Reassessment of the Data behind a Popular Theory." In *Prophets Male and Female: Gender and Prophecy in the Hebrew Bible, the Eastern Mediterranean, and the Ancient Near East*, edited by J. Stökl and C. Carvalho, 59–79. Atlanta, GA: Society of Biblical Literature.

Stol, Martin. 1995. "Women in Mesopotamia," *Journal of the Economic and Social History of the Orient* 38.2: 123–144.

Stol, Martin. 2016. *Women in the Ancient Near East*. Translated by Helen and Mervyn Richardson. Boston and Berlin: De Gruyter.

Stronach, David. 1989. "Early Achaemenid Coinage: Perspectives from the Homeland," *Iranica Antiqua* 24: 255–279.

Sutton, Jr., Robert F. 1992. "Pornography and Persuasion on Attic Pottery." In *Pornography and Representation in Greece and Rome*, edited by Amy Richlin, 3–35. New York and Oxford: Oxford University Press.

Sutton, Jr., Robert F. 1997–1998. "Nuptial Eros: The Visual Discourse of Marriage in Classical Athens," *The Journal of the Walters Art Gallery* 55/56: 27–48.

Süvegh, Eszter. 2014. "Hellenistic Grotesque Terracotta Figurines: Problems of Iconographical Interpretation." In *Dissertationes Archaeologicae ex Instituto Archaeologico Universitatis de Rolando Eötvös nominatae*, Ser. 3. No. 2., 143–156. Budapest: Eötvös Loránd University, Institute of Archaeological Sciences.

Swift, Ellen. 2009. *Style and Function in Roman Decoration: Living with Objects and Interiors*. Farnham, Surrey: Ashgate.

Sydnor, Synthia. 1998. "A History of Synchronized Swimming," *Journal of Sport History* 25:2: 252–267.

Taraskiewicz, Angela. 2012. "Motherhood as *Teleia*: Rituals of Incorporation at the Kourotrophic Shrine." In *Mothering and Motherhood in Ancient Greece and Rome*, edited by Lauren Hackworth Petersen and Patricia Salzman-Mitchell, 43–69. Austin: University of Texas Press.

Tezgör, D. Kassab. 2010. "Egypt and East Greece: Alexandria and Myrina." In *Tanagras: Figurines for Life and Eternity*, edited by V. Jeammet, 186–193. Paris: Musée du Louvre.

Thomas, Nicholas. 1991. *Entangled Objects: Exchange, Material Culture, and Colonialism in the Pacific*. Cambridge, MA: Harvard University Press.

Thomas, Nicholas. 1999. *Possessions: Indigenous Art/Colonial Culture*. London: Thames and Hudson.

Thomason, Allison Karmel. 2010. "Banquets, Baubles, and Bronzes: Material Comforts in the Neo-Assyrian Palaces." In *Assyrian Reliefs from the Palace of Ashurnasirpal II: A Cultural Biography*, edited by Ada Cohen and Steven E. Kangas, 198–214. Hanover, New Hampshire: Hood Museum of Art, Dartmouth College and University Press of New England.

Thompson, Dorothy Burr. 1963. *Troy: The Terracotta Figurines of the Hellenistic Period*. Supplementary Monograph 3. Princeton: Princeton University Press.

Thompson, Dorothy Burr. 1965. "Three Centuries of Hellenistic Terracottas," *Hesperia: The Journal of the American School of Classical Studies at Athens* 34.1: 34–71.

Thönges-Stringaris, R. 1965. "Das Griechische Totenmahl," *Mitteilungen des Deutschen Archäologischen Instituts, Athenische Abteilung* 80: 1–68.

Topper, Kathryn. 2012. *The Imagery of the Athenian Symposium*. Cambridge: Cambridge University Press.

Török, László. 1995. *Hellenistic and Roman Terracottas from Egypt*. Rome: "L'Erma" di Bretschneider.

Tran Tam Tinh, V. 1973. *Isis Lactans: Corpus des Monuments Greco-Romains d'Isis allaitant Harpocrate*. Leiden: Brill.

Treggiari, Susan. 1976. "Jobs for Women," *American Journal of Ancient History* 1: 76–104.

Tripolitis, Antonía. 2002. *Religions of the Hellenistic-Roman Age*. Grand Rapids, MI: William B. Eerdmans.

Turner, Terence S. 1980. "The Social Skin." In *Not Work Alone: A Cross-Cultural View of Activities Superfluous to Survival*, edited by Jeremy Cherfas and Roger Lewin, 112–140. Beverly Hills, CA: Sage Publications.

Turp, Ahmet Berkiz, Ismail Guler, Nuray Bozkurt, Aysel Uysal, Bulent Yilmaz, Mustafa Demir and Onur Karabacak. 2018. "Infertility and Surrogacy First Mentioned on a 4000-Year-Old Assyrian Clay Tablet of Marriage Contract in Turkey," *Gynecological Endocrinology* 34.1: 25–27.

Ucko, Peter. 1968. *Anthropomorphic Figurines of Predynastic Egypt and Neolithic Crete with Comparative Material from the Prehistoric Near East and Mainland Greece*. London: A. Szmidla.

Uehlinger, Christoph. 2000. "Introduction." In *Images as Media: Sources for the Cultural History of the Near East and the Eastern Mediterranean (1st Millennium BCE)*, edited by Christoph Uehlinger, xv-xxxii. Fribourg: University Press Fribourg.

Uhlenbrock, Jaimee. 1990. "The Coroplast and His Craft." In *The Coroplast's Art: Greek Terracottas of the Hellenistic World*, edited by Jaimee Uhlenbrock, 15–21. New York: Aristide D. Caratzas.

Uhlenbrock, Jaimee ed. 1990. *The Coroplast's Art: Greek Terracottas of the Hellenistic World*. New York: Aristide D. Caratzas.

Uhlenbrock, Jaimee. 1996. "Greece, Ancient, IX: Terracotta." In *The Dictionary of Art*, Volume 13, edited by J. Turner, 577–583. Oxford: Grove.

Valtz, Elisabetta. 1988. "Seleucia, 13th Season," *Mesopotamia* 23: 19–29.

Valtz, Elisabetta. 1991. "Pottery from Seleucia." In *Golf-Archäologie: Mesopotamien, Iran, Kuwait, Bahrain,*

Vereinigte Arabische Emirate und Oman, edited by K. Schippmann, A. Herling, and J.-F. Salles, 45–56. Buch am Erlbach: Verlag Marie L. Leidorf.

Valtz, Elisabetta. 1993. "Pottery and Exchanges: Imports and Local Production at Seleucia-Tigris." In *Arabia Antiqua: Hellenistic Centers Around Arabia*, edited by Antonio Invernizzi and Jean-François Salles, 167–182. Rome: Istituto Italiano per il Medio ed Estremo Oriente.

Van Buren, E. Douglas. 1930. *Clay Figurines of Babylonia and Assyria*. New Haven, CT: Yale University.

Van der Spek, R.J. 1992. "Nippur, Sippar and Larsa in the Hellenistic Period." In *Nippur at the Centennial. Papers Read at the 35e Recontre Assyriologique Internationale. Philadelphia 1988*, edited by Maria deJong-Ellis, 235–260. Philadelphia, PA: University Museum, University of Pennsylvania.

Van der Spek, R.J. 1993. "The Astronomical Diaries as a Source for Achaemenid and Seleucid History," *Bibliotheca Orientalis* 50: 91–101.

Van der Spek, R.J. 2001. "The Theatre of Babylon in Cuneiform." In *Veenhof Anniversary Volume: Studies Presented to Klaas R. Veenhof on the Occasion of his Sixty-Fifth Birthday*, edited by W.H. van Soldt, J. G. Dercksen, N.J.C. Kouwenberg, and Th.J.H. Krispijn, 445–456. Leiden: Nederlands Instituut Voor Het Nabije Oosten.

Van Dommelen, P. 1997. "Colonial Constructs: Colonialism and Archaeology in the Mediterranean." *World Archaeology* 28.3: 305–323.

Van Ingen, Wilhelmina. 1939. *Figurines from Seleucia on the Tigris: Discovered by the Expeditions Conducted by the University of Michigan with the Cooperation of the Toledo Museum of Art and the Cleveland Museum of Art 1927–1932*. Ann Arbor: University of Michigan Press.

Veenhof, K. R. 1989. "Three Old Babylonian Marriage Contracts involving Naditum and Shugitum." In *Reflets des deux flueves: Volume de mélanges offerts à André Finet*, edited by M. Lebeau and Ph. Talon, 181–189. Leuven: Peeters.

Vervloed, M. P., A. W. Hendriks, and E. van den Eijnde. 2011. "The Effects of Mothers' Past Holding Preferences on their Adult Children's Face Processing Lateralisation," *Brain and Cognition* 75: 248–254.

Vlahogiannis, Nicholas. 1998. "Disabling Bodies." In *Changing Bodies, Changing Meanings: Studies on the Human Body in Antiquity*, edited by Dominic Montserrat, 13–36. London and New York: Routledge.

Vlahogiannis, Nicholas. 2005. "'Curing' Disability." In *Health in Antiquity*, edited by Helen King, 180–191. Abingdon: Routledge.

Voegtle, Simone. 2016. "A Grotesque Terracotta Figurine of the First Century C.E. from Muralto, Ticino, Switzerland: Function, Use, and Meaning," *Les Carnets de l'ACoSt* 15: 1–19.

Voigt, Mary. 1983. *Hajji Firuz Tepe, Iran: The Neolithic Settlement*. Philadelphia: University Museum, University of Pennsylvania.

Volk, Konrad. 1989. *Die Balaĝ-Komposition úru àm-ma-ir-ra-bi: Rekonstruktion und Bearbeitung der Tafeln 18 (19'ff.), 19, 20 und 21 der späten, kanonischen Version*, Freiburger altorientalische Studien, Bd. 18. Stuttgart: F. Steiner Verlag Wiesbaden.

Von Hesberg, Henner. 1999. "The King on State," *Studies in the History of Art* (Symposium Papers XXXIV: The Art of Ancient Spectacle) 56: 64–75.

Walker, Christopher. and Michael B. Dick. 1999. "The Induction of the Cult Image in Ancient Mesopotamia: The Mesopotamian Mīs Pî Ritual." In *Born in Heaven, Made on Earth: The Making of the Cult Image in the Ancient*

Near East, edited by M.B. Dick, 55–122. Winona Lake, IN: Eisenbrauns.

Walker, Steven F. 2004. "The Invention of Theater: Recontextualizing the Vexing Question," *Comparative Literature* 56.1: 1–22.

Wallenfels, Ronald. 1994a. *Uruk: Hellenistic Seal Impressions in the Yale Babylonian Collection*, Ausgrabungen in Uruk-Warka: Endberichte (AUWE) 19. Mainz am Rhein: Verlag Philipp von Zabern.

Wallenfels, Ronald. 1994b. "A New Volume of Texts from Hellenistic Uruk (Review of *The Late Babylonian Texts of the Oriental Institute Collection*)," *Journal of the American Oriental Society* 114: 435–439.

Wallenfels, Ronald. 2015. "Seleucid Babylonian 'Official' and 'Private' Seals Reconsidered: A Seleucid Archival Tablet in the Collection of the Mackenzie Art Gallery, Regina," *Journal of Ancient Near Eastern History* 2.1: 55–89.

Wallenfels, Ronald. 2016. *Hellenistic Seal Impressions in the Yale Babylonian Collection: Ring-Bullae and other Clay Sealings*. Bethesda, MD: CDL Press.

Walsh, John. 1988. "Acquisitions/1987," *The J. Paul Getty Museum Journal* 16: 133, 135–199.

West, M. L. 1992. *Ancient Greek Music*. Oxford: Clarendon Press.

West, M. L. 1999. *Hesiod, Theogony and Works and Days, A New Translation by M.L. West*. Oxford: Oxford University Press.

Westbrook, Raymond. 1988. *Old Babylonian Marriage Law* (Archiv für Orientforschung, Beiheft 23). Horn, Austria: Berger.

Westh-Hansen, Sidsel Maria. 2011. "Cultural Interaction and the Emergence of Hybrids in the Material Culture of Hellenistic Mesopotamia: An Interpretation of Terracotta Figurines, Ceramic Ware and Seal Impressions." In *From Pella to Gandhara: Hybridisation and Identity in the Art and Architecture of the Hellenistic East*, edited by A. Kouremenos, S. Chandrasekaran, and R. Rossi, 103–116. British Archaeological Reports International Series 2221. Oxford: Archaeopress.

Wetzel, F., E. F. Schmidt, and A. Mallwitz. 1957. *Das Babylon der Spätzeit*. Berlin: Gebr. Mann.

Wetzel, F. and F.H. Weissbach. 1938. *Das Hauptheiligtum des Marduk in Babylon, Esagila and Etemenanki*, Wissenschaftliche Veröffentlichungen der Deutschen Orient-Gesellschaft (WVDOG) 59. Leipzig: Hinrichs.

Whitmore, Alissa. 2017. "Fascinating *Fascina*: Apotropaic Magic and How to Wear a Penis." In *What Shall I Say of Clothes? Theoretical and Methodological Approaches to the Study of Dress in Antiquity*, edited by Megan Cifarelli and Laura Gawlinski, 47–65. Boston: Archaeological Institute of America.

Wild, Gerlind. 1973. Seleucid and Parthian Figurines: Contribution to a Study of the Typology of Mesopotamian Terra Cotta Figurines. MA diss., American University of Beirut, Lebanon.

Wiles, David. 2007. *Mask and Performance in Greek Tragedy: From Ancient Festival to Modern Experimentation*. Cambridge: Cambridge University Press.

Wilkie, Laurie. 2000. "Not Merely Child's Play: Creating a Historical Archaeology of Children and Childhood." In *Children and Material Culture*, edited by Joanna Sofaer Derevenski, 100–113. London and New York: Routledge.

Willis, Clyde E. 1997. "The Phenomenology of Pornography: A Comment on Catharine MacKinnon's *Only Words*," *Law and Philosophy* 16.2: 177–199.

Wilson, Ian Douglas. 2012. "Judean Pillar Figurines and Ethnic Identity in the Shadow of Assyria." *Journal for the Study of the Old Testament* 36: 259–278.

Wilson, Jean. 2006. "Review of The Archaeology of Childhood: Children, Gender and Material Culture by Jane Eva Baxter," *Journal of Field Archaeology* 31.2: 229–232.

Wilson, Peter. 1999. "The *Aulos* in Athens." In *Performance Culture and Athenian Democracy*, edited by Simon Goldhill and Robin Osborne, 58–95. Cambridge: Cambridge University Press.

Wilson, Peter. 2005. "Music." In *A Companion to Greek Tragedy*, edited by Justina Gregory, 183–193. Oxford: Blackwell.

Winter, Irene. 1981. "Royal Rhetoric and the Development of Historical Narrative in Neo-Assyrian Reliefs," *Studies in Visual Communication* 7: 2–38.

Winter, Irene. 1985. "After the Battle is Over: The Stele of the Vultures and the Beginning of Historical Narrative in the Ancient Near East." In *Pictorial Narrative in Antiquity to the Middle Ages*, edited by H. Kessler and M. S. Simpson, 11–32. Washington D.C.: National Gallery.

Winter, Irene. 1989. "The Body of the Able Ruler: Towards an Understanding of the Statues of Gudea." In *DUMU-E2-DUB-BA-A: Studies in Honor of Ake W. Sjöberg*, edited by H. Behrens, D. Loding, and M. T. Roth, 573–583. Philadelphia: The University Museum, University of Pennsylvania.

Winter, Irene. 1992. "'Idols of the King': Royal Images as Recipients of Ritual Action in Ancient Mesopotamia," *Journal of Ritual Studies* 6: 13–42.

Winter, Irene. 1994. "Radiance as an Aesthetic Value in the Art of Mesopotamia (With some Indian Parallels)." In *Art, the Integral Vision: A Volume of Essay in Felicitation of Kapila Vatsyayan*, edited by B. N. Saraswati, S. C. Malik, and M. Khanna, 123–132. New Delhi: D.K. Printworld.

Winter, Irene. 1995. "Aesthetics in Ancient Mesopotamian Art." In *Civilizations of the Ancient Near East*, edited by Jack M. Sasson, 2569–2580. New York: Scribner.

Winter, Irene. 1996. "Sex, Rhetoric and the Public Monument: The Alluring Body of the Male Ruler in Mesopotamia." In *Sexuality in Ancient Art*, edited by N.B. Kampen, 11–26. Cambridge: Cambridge University Press.

Winter, Irene. 1997. "Art in Empire: The Royal Image and the Visual Dimensions of Assyrian Ideology." In *Assyria 1995: Proceeding of the 10th Anniversary Symposium of the Neo-Assyrian Text Corpus Project Helsinki, September 7–11, 1995*, edited by Simo Parpola and Robert M. Whiting, 359–381. Helsinki: Neo-Assyrian Text Corpus Project.

Winter, Irene. 2000. "The Eyes Have It: Votive Statuary, Gilgamesh's Axe, and Cathected Viewing in the Ancient Near East." In *Visuality Before and Beyond the Renaissance*, edited by R. Nelson. Cambridge: Cambridge University Press.

Wobst, H. Martin. 1977. "Stylistic Behavior and Information Exchange." In *For the Director: Research Essays in Honor of James B. Griffin*, edited by Charles E. Cleland, 317–342. Ann Arbor: Museum of Anthropology, University of Michigan.

Wrenhaven, Kelly L. 2012. *Reconstructing the Slave: The Image of the Slave in Ancient Greece*. London: Bristol Classical Press.

Wunsch, Cornelia. 2005. "Women's Property and the Law of Inheritance in the Neo-Babylonian Period." In *Women and Property in Ancient Near Eastern and Mediterranean Societies*, edited by D. Lyons and R. Westbrook. Cambridge, MA: Center for Hellenic Studies, Harvard University. Available online at http://chs.harvard.edu/CHS/article/display/1219.

Wylie, Alison. 1991. "Gender Theory and the Archaeological Record: Why Is

There No Archaeology of Gender?." In *Engendering Archaeology: Women and Prehistory*, edited by J. Gero and M. Conkey, 31–54. Oxford and Cambridge, MA: Wiley-Blackwell.

Xenophon. 2013. *Memorabilia. Oeconomicus. Symposium. Apology.* Translated by E. C. Marchant, O. J. Todd. Revised by Jeffrey Henderson. Loeb Classical Library 168. Cambridge, MA: Harvard University Press.

Zanker, Paul. 1993. "The Hellenistic Grave Stelai from Smyrna: Identity and Self-Image in the Polis." In *Images and Ideologies: Self-Definition in the Hellenistic World*, edited by Anthony W. Bulloch, Erich S. Gruen, A.A. Long, and Andrew Stewart, 212–230. Berkeley: University of California Press.

Zanker, Paul. 1995. *The Mask of Socrates: The Image of the Intellectual in Antiquity.* Translated by Alan Shapiro. Berkeley: University of California Press.

Ziegler, Charlotte. 1962. *Die Terrakotten von Warka,* Ausgrabungen der Deutschen Forschungsgemeinschaft in Uruk-Warka, Band 6. Berlin: Verlag Gebr. Mann.

Zimmermann, Konrad. 1980. "Tätowierte Thrakerinnen auf griechischen Vasenbildern," *Jahrbuch des Deutschen Archäologischen Instituts* 95: 163–196.

Zsolnay, Ilona. 2017. "Introduction." In *Being a Man: Negotiating Ancient Constructs of Masculinity*, edited by Ilona Zsolnay, 1–11. London and New York: Routledge.

INDEX

Achaemenid culture
   bearded and beardless figurines and, 149–152
   horse rider figurines and, 62–65
Aeschines, 87
agency
   in female figurines, 182–185
   figurine production and, 10
   figurines as representations of, 16, 23–24
   interactive figurines and, 52–53, 62–64
age specificity
   in Babylonian figurines, 128–132
   child figurines, 185–200
   in heterosexual couples sculptures, 128–132
   lack of, female figurines, 166–185, 197–200
   male body in figurines, 149–156
   young and beardless male figurines, 156–162
Alexander the Great, 1–2, 4, 160–161
amateurism, in musician figurines, 141–143
Ankh-nes-merira (Queen), figurine of, 109–110
anthropology, 7–11
   miniaturization theory in, 14
Antiochis, 264 n.93
ape figurines, 225–226
Aphrodite, figurines depicting, 205–212
Aphrodite anadyomene, 258 n.68
Aphrodite pudica, 78
Apollo
   coins, 160–162
   figurines of, 160–161, 217–219
   intersexuality in figurines of, 218–219, 223–224
   non-human representations of, 225–226
Apollo *Toxotes*, 218–219
apotropaism, masks and, 92–94
archaeological research
   on childhood, 53–57, 59–60
   limitations in, 7–11
arm positions
   athlete figurines, 162–166
   child figurines, 197–200
   construction of, 66–70, 72–76
   female body figurines, 167–176
   fragility of, 76–78
   pseudo-intimacy of, 78–80
   reclining female figurines, 237–246
   votive function for, 70–76
art history, 7–11

Assyrian peoples
   in Seleucia-on-the-Tigris, 4
   slave-surrogacy and, 109
Athena, figurines depicting, 210–212
athlete figurines, 162–166
Attis, 109–110
audience
   masks on figurines, 89–94
   for mother and child figurines, 102–107
   for musician figurines, collaboration with, 132–143
   puppet figurines and, 82–89
aulos (double-piped instrument), 137–140

babies, figurines of, 91
Babylon
   alleged abandonment of, 249 n.4
   Aphrodite figurines in, 205–212
   figurine production in, 3
   Hellenistic ceramics in, 243–246
   intersexed figurines in, 221–222
   moveable arms on figurines from, 68
   nude figurines in, 46–50
   reclining figurines in, 237–246
   theater in, 84–86
Bachelard, Gaston, 15–16
Bahrani, Zainab, 210
Bailey, Douglass, 14–15, 22–23
banqueting figurines, 238–240, 241–242
"Barberini Faun," 122–123
bearded and beardless figurines
   in heterosexual couples sculptures, 128–132
   mature male figurines, 149–152
   royal image and, 156–162
bent arms, female body figurines, 167–176
Bes, 233–235
bird-teasing motif, in child figurines, 190
Bit Akitu, 5
Bit Resh, 5
bodily proximity. *See corporeality*
bone figurines
   abstract forms, 35–38
   moveable arms on, 69
   naturalistic motifs in, 35–38
   schematic figurines, 35–38
Borsippa, figurine production in, 3

breastfeeding
  figurines depicting, 106–107
  wet-nurses and, 107–110
Bundrick, Sheramy, 137–140
Butler, Judith, 276–277 n.66

children, archaeology of, 53–57, 59–60
children, figurines of, 94–98, 185–200
  as deities, 189–193
  ritual and, 193–197
  as slaves or servants, 185–189
  user interaction with, 197–200
Cifarelli, Megan, 42
Clark, Andy, 22
Classical Greek sculpture
  age specificity in, 128–132
  Babylonian figurines and, 247–248
  bearded and beardless figurines and, 149–152
  homoeroticism in, 162–166
  instruments for musician figurines in, 136–140
  koine tradition and, 102
  limb modeling in, 268 n.48
  masks and, 261 n.131
  mother and child figurines in, 116–117
  nude figures in, 46–50, 159–162
  social positioning of women in, 115
  symposion imagery in, 238–240
  vision as touch in, 260 n.128
clay
  firing process for, 25–31
  in mythology, 252 n.52
  properties and availability of, 25–31
Cleopatra VII, 115
coinage, nude figures on, 160–161
Commagene sculptures, 212–217
constraints of candidacy, 201–202
coroplast, 25
corporeality
  child figurines, 185–200
  clay and, 25–31
  cross-cultural interaction and, 12, 147–148, 201–202
  female figurines, 166–185
  fully clothed figurines, 40–42
  in horse rider figurines, 227–230
  of interactive figurines, 52–53
  intimacy illusion of figurines and, 18–24
  male figurines, 148–166
  masks and, 90
  miniaturization theory and, 15–16
  naturalistic figurines, 35–38
  nude figurines, 46–50
  partially clothed figurines, 42–46
  stone and metal figurines, 31, 254 n.88
  theatricality and, 82–98
craftspersons, clay modeling process and, 25
cross-cultural interaction
  child figurines and, 197–200

double-piped instruments and, 137–140
  entanglement and, 251 n.21
  in female figurines, 167–176, 183–185
  figurine corpus and, 12, 147–148, 201–202
  figurines as expression of, 1–7, 12, 147–148, 201–202
  in heterosexual couples figurines, 128–132
  research methodology for, 8–9
  selective hybridity and, 246
cultic figurines, 25–26, 92–94, 139–140, 253 n.56, 279 n.122
cuneiform tablets, in Uruk, 5
Cybele, 109–110, 141–143, 210

defects in figurines, 26–29
deities, figurines depicting. *See also specific deities, e.g. Herakles*
  characteristics of, 141–143
  child figurines as, 189–193
  global context for, 204–219
  heterosexual couples as, 125–128
  nude figurines as, 160–161
desire, sexuality in figurines and, 118–120
Dionysian worship, 141–143
Dionysos, figurines of, 160–161, 217–219
disability
  absence in Hellenistic Babylonian figurines, 128–132
  in figurines, 230–236
double-mold technique
  in Hellenistic Babylonian figurines, 4, 6–7
  heterosexual couples figurines and, 118–120
  hybridity in use of, 10
  musician figurines and, 141–143
  in Seleucia-on-the-Tigris figurines, 4
  unfinished elements in, 26–29
drums
  double-pipes paired with, 139–140
  figurines including, 136–140, 141–143, 196–197
dwarfism, in figurines, 230–236

E-anna, 5
enchantment, Gell's theory of, 251 n.9, 253 n.59
entanglement, cross-cultural hybridities and, 251 n.21
Erlich, Adi, 102, 142–143
Eros
  Aphrodite figurines with, 205–212
  child figurines of, 189–193
  sculptures of, 127
  with Psyche, 125, 127–128
erotic subject matter. *See also homoeroticism; sexuality in figurines*
  heterosexual couples figurines, 117–132
  sexualized relationships with figurines, 65–71
  stone and metal figurines, 34–35

Etruscan art, influence on Greek sculpture of, 278 n.111
exclusion, sexuality in figurines and, 120–125
extramission, Greek concept of, 16–17

family relationships
　audience admiration for, 102–107
　in heterosexual couples figurines, 117–132
　mother-and-child figurines and, 16, 94–98, 101–103, 107–110
　slave surrogates in, 109
　social conduits and expectations in, 113–117
female body, figurines depicting. *See also women*
　children included in, 185–200
　cohesiveness in age and body types and, 166–185
　gender ambiguity in figurines and, 224–230
　nudity and clothing and, 167–176
　reclining figurines, 237–246
　sexualized relationships with, 65–71
　women in society and, 181–185
figurine assemblages, 100–101
foster children, socialization and, 262 n.32
fragility
　in heterosexual couples figurines, 124–125
　of moveable arm figurines, 76–78
fragmentation
　athlete figurines, 165–166
　bone figurines, 35–38
　child figurines, 197–200
　moveable arm figurines, 258 n.70
　reclining figurines, 243–246
frame drum, 141–143
Frehat En-Nufegi Tumuli, 5
fully clothed figurines, 40–42
　female body in, 167–176
　heterosexual couples figurines, 125–128
　male body, 150–153, 156–162
funerary deposits, 270 n.111
　bone figurines in, 72–76
　mounted horse rider figurines in, 59–60
　in Nippur, 5–6
　rarity of, in Hellenistic Babylonia, 72–76
　reclining figurines in, 245–246

Gansell, Amy Rebecca, 254 n.94
Gaze theory, miniaturization and, 258 n.67
Gell, Alfred, 251 n.9, 253 n.59
gender ambiguity, in figurines, 220–230
global trends and styles
　deity figurines, 204–219
　local styles *vs.*, 203–204
Gorgias, 16–17
Greek New Comedy
　breastfeeding in, 262 n.30
　dwarfism, disability, and grotesque in, 230–236
　puppet figurines and, 88
　wet-nurses in, 107–108
Greek peoples, migration by, 1–2
grotesque body types, 230–236
　puppet figurines and, 87
grouped figurines. *See also heterosexual couples, figurines depicting; mother and child figurines*
　audience admiration for, 102–107
　characteristics of, 100–101
　musical figurines, 132–143
　relationship and spectatorship and, 143–146
Gulliver's Travels (Swift), 13–14
gymnasia
　athlete figurines and, 165–166
　multicultural variations in, 255 n.107
　in Hellenistic Babylonia, 4

Hammurabi, Code of, 107–110
hand-modeled figurines, 141–143
Harpocrates, 94–98, 109–110
　figurines of, 192–193
Hebrew Bible, 108
Hellenistic motifs. *See also* koine *tradition*
　bearded and beardless figurines and, 149–152
　boundaries of attraction and, 80–81
　in child figurines, 189–193
　drums and, 140, 141–143
　Hellenistic *koine* vessels, 279 nn.119–120, 243–246
　in heterosexual couples figurines, 128–132
　India and, 259 n.94
　koine motifs and styles, 6–7
　in male figurines, 153–154
　nude figurines, 159–162
　puppet figurines, 97, 150–151
　Rococo style sculpture, 122–123, 124–125
　in Seleucia-on-the-Tigris, 4
　theater masks, 89–94
　in Uruk, 5
Hellenization theory, repudiation of, 9–10
Herakles, 153–154, 212–217
hermaphrodites, in figurines, 220–230
hetairai, Greek depictions of, 238–240
heteronormativity, dominance in figurines of, 128–132
heterosexual couples, figurines depicting, 117–132
　desire and imagination in, 118–120
　exclusion and voyeurism and, 120–125
　mortals and deities, 125–128
　social roles and cross-cultural interaction, 128–132
Heyn, Maura, 270 n.111
homoeroticism
　child figurines and, 187–188
　in Classical Greek sculpture, 162–166
horse rider figurines
　abstraction and play with, 53–57
　agency and interaction with, 53
　diversity in, 64–65
　fighting or battle poses for, 62–64
　mold-made construction of, 57–61
　otherness in, 227–230

Horus, 109–110. *See also Harpocrates*
human facture, miniaturization theory and role of, 29–31
hybridity
    animal-human hybrids, 225–226
    boundaries of attraction and, 80–81
    cross-cultural interaction and, 9–10, 246
    in female figurines, 167–176, 183–185
    in horse rider figurines, 64–65
    local context and, 236–246
    in mother-and-child figurines, 115–117
    multiculturalism and, 11–12
    "otherness" in figurines and, 219–236
    post-colonial theory and, 10
    puppet figurines, 82–89
    theoretical approaches to, 10
hyperreality in figurines, 78–80

iconography of service, mother-child figurines as, 107–110
identity
    figurines and, 143–146, 201–202
    self-presentation and, 147–148, 201–202
    young and beardless male figurines, 156–162
    youthful male bodies, 156–162
imagination
    abstraction and play with figurines, 53–57
    miniaturization and stimulation of, 22–23
    sexuality in figurines and, 118–120
incense burners, figurines as, 196–197
instruments in figurines, 195. *See also specific instruments*
    ape figurines, 225–226
    arm placement and, 179–181
    attachment of, 195
    audience collaboration and, 132–143
    horse riders, 227–230
    paired instruments, 137–138
    performance and, 84–86, 133–136
    professional distance *vs.* amateurish immediacy with, 141–143
    puppet figurines, 82–89
    relations and spectatorship involving, 143–146
    stringed instruments, 26–29
interactive figurines
    abstraction and play with, 53–57
    boundaries of attraction for, 80–81
    broken bodies and hyper-reality of, 78–80
    fighting or battle poses for, 61–64
    fragility and sexuality of, 76–78
    horse riders and soldiers, 53
    hybridity in, 64–65
    intimacy of, 52–53, 98–99
    masks and babies, 89–94
    mounted horse rider figurines, 57–61
    moveable arms on, 66–70
    puppets, 82–89
    rattles, 94–98
    sexualized relationships with, 65–71
    soldiers, 61–64
    theatricality and performance and, 82–98
    two-piece mounted soldiers, 57–61
    votive function for, 70–76
intersexuality, in figurines, 220–230
intimacy, figurines and illusion of, 10–11
    bone figurines, 37–38
    community motivations and, 23–24
    fully clothed figurines, 40–42
    heterosexual couples figurines and, 118–120
    interactive figurines, 52–53, 98–99
    miniaturization theory and, 14, 18–24
    mother-and-child figurines and, 102–107
    moveable-arm figurines and, 78–80
    nude figurines, 46–50
    object *vs.* representation and, 38–40
    partially clothed figurines, 42–46
    rattles and, 94–98
    stone and metal figurines and, 34–35
    theatricality and, 82–98
Irigal, 5
Ishtar, figurines of, 210–212
    gender ambiguity in, 221
Isis, 109–110

jewelry, miniaturization and, 193–197
Joyce, Rosemary, 14–15, 16

Kish, figurine production in, 3
kithara (box lyre), 195
Klengel-Brandt, Evelyn, 245–246
Knappett, Carl, 22
Knidian Aphrodite, 31, 46–50, 78
koine tradition, 6–7. *See also Hellenistic motifs*
    Aphrodite figurines in, 205–212
    Apollo figurines, 218–219
    athletic figurines in, 162–166
    Babylonian figurines and, 247–248
    child figurines in, 189–193
    deity figurines in, 204–219
    dwarfism, disability, and grotesque in, 230–236
    figurines of "otherness," 219–236
    fully clothed figurines, 40–42
    gender ambiguity in figurines and, 224–230
    global *vs.* local context for, 203–204
    Herakles in, 212–217
    heterosexual couples figurines in, 124–125, 128–132
    local nature of, 11–12
    mother and child figurines in, 101–103, 107–108, 116–117
    nude figurines in, 159–162
    partially clothed figurines, 42–46
    stone and metal figurines and, 31
    Tanagra tradition, 182
    widespread distribution of, 240

Koldewey, Robert, 245–246
kourotrophos (child-carrying) figurines, 101–103
Kruger, Barbara, 122

lagynos pottery, 185–189
left-side positioning of child, in mother-and-child figurines, 110–113
lion-hunting figurines, 212–217
local context
   hybridity within, 236–246

Macedonian peoples, migration by, 1–2
Mack, John, 252 n.38
male body, figurines depicting, 148–166
   age specificity and, 128–132, 149–156
   athlete figurines, 162–166
   child figurines, 185–200
   diversity in, 148–166
   gender ambiguity in figurines and, 224–230
   mature male figurines, 149–156
   puppet figurines, 88
   reclining figurines, 241–242
   royal image and, 156–162
   unified pose of, 152–153
   young and beardless images, 156–162
manufacturing process for figurines, 25–31
Martin, S. Rebecca, 210
masks, figurines and, 89–94
Masséglia, Jane, 127
material culture research, 7–11
materiality
   masks and, 90
   miniaturization theory and, 15–16
Menegazzi, Roberta, 7–8, 28–29, 88, 245–246
Meskell, Lynn, 17
Mesopotamia
   couples figurines from, 131–132
   drum use in, 140, 141–143
   gender ambiguity in, 224–230
   Herakles imagery in, 212–217
   left-side positioning of child in mother and child figurines from, 110–113
   non-human figurines in, 225–226
   nude figurines in, 46–50, 159–162
   scarcity of metal and stone materials in, 31, 34–35
   sexual attraction in, 80–81
   size and dominance linked in, 255 n.2
   terracotta figurines, 25
   wet-nurses in, 107–110
metal figurines, 31, 254 n.88
mid-limb joining technique, athlete figurines, 162–166
miniaturization
   affect of figurines and, 50–51
   anthropology and, 14
   bodily proximity and, 15–16
   child figurines, relative scale of, 193–197
   contextual analysis of, 17

Gaze theory and, 258 n.67
   gender ambiguity in figurines and, 224–230
   grouped figurines and, 143–146
   hybridity and, 9–10
   intimacy illusions and, 18–24
   manufacturing process and, 29–31
   mid-limb joining technique, 162–166
   mother and child figurines, scale in, 113–117
   practical rationalizations in, 17–18
   principles of, 10–11
   social cohesion and, 247–248
   theater masks and, 89–94
   theatricality and, 82–98
   theory, 7–8
mortals, heterosexual couples figurines as, 125–128
mother and child figurines
   audience admiration for, 102–107
   bent arms in, 167–176
   characteristics of, 16, 94–98, 101–103
   as iconography of service, 107–110
   left-side positioning of child in, 110–113
   slave surrogates in, 109
   social conduits and expectations in, 113–117
"mouth-opening" (pit pî) ritual, 92–94
"mouth-washing" (mīs pî) ritual, 92–94
moveable arms
   in figurine production, 76–78
multiculturalism
   boundaries of attraction and, 80–81
   horse rider figurine and, 64–65
   hybridity and, 11–12
musicians. *See also instruments in figurines*
   Apollo and, 218–219
   bent arms in, 179–181
   grouped figurines of, 132–143
   performance and repetition in, 133–136
   pipes and drum in, 136–140
   professionals *vs.* amateurs and, 141–143
   women figurines as, 133–136
Myrina site, Greek figurines from, 238–240
mythology
   child figurines from, 271 n.130
   clay as motif in, 252 n.52

Nakamura, Carolyn, 17
Neo-Babylonian era
   male figurines from, 152–153
   mother and child figurines from, 110–113, 115–117
Nike, figurines depicting, 210–212
Nippur
   absence of Hellenistic *koine* vessels in, 243–246
   absence of reclining female figurines in, 237–246
   figurine production in, 3, 5–6, 11–12, 29
   heterosexual couples figurines from, 123–124
   horse rider figurines from, 55–56
   rattles from, 261 n.143
   tactile interaction with figurines in, 279 n.132

non-human figurines, 225–226
nude figurines, 46–50
   of Apollo, 218–219
   athlete figurines, 162–166
   of children, 185–189
   female body in, 167–176
   male body in, 153–154, 159–162
   moveable arms on, 66–70
   reclining figurines, 240–243
   tactile interaction with, 46–50

Old Kingdom figurine, 109–110
On Longing: Narratives of the Miniature, the Gigantic, the Souvenir, the Collection (Stewart), 14–15
Osborne, Robin, 270 n.111
"otherness," figurines of, 219–236
   dwarfism, disability, and the grotesque, 230–236
   hermaphrodites, intersex, and gender ambiguity, 220–230

Paleolithic figurines, 13–14
Parthian period
   bone figurines during, 35–38
   horse rider figurines and, 64–65
   male figurines and, 150–153
   in Nippur, 5–6
   puppet figurines and, 88–89
   Seleucid kingdom and, 1–2
partially clothed figurines, 42–46
performance
   cross-cultural interaction and, 143
   interactive figurines and, 82–98
   miniaturization and, 82–98
   musician figurines and, 133–136
   puppet figurines, 82–89
   rattles and, 94–98
Persian culture. *See Achaemenid culture*
pipes, musician figurines including, 136–140
plaque-style figurines, 120–125
play, with interactive figurines, 53–57
Plutarch, 261–262 n.11
pornography, 80–81
power dynamics
   male figurines and, 155–156
   sexualized relationships with figurines and, 78–80
professional distance, in musician figurines, 141–143
Psyche, 127
pudicitia pose, female figurines, 183
puppet figurines, 82–89

rattles, figurines and, 94–98, 196–197
reclining figurines, 237–246
repetition, in musician figurines, 133–136
representations, objects *vs.*, 38–40
research methodology, overview of, 7–11
ritual
   child's body in, 193–197
   drums and, 139–140
   masks and, 92–94
   theatricality and, 260 n.122
Rococo style sculpture, 122–123, 124–125
   child figurines in, 189–193
royal image, 156–162

Sassanian period, 150–152
scalar displacement, 52–53
scopophilia, sexuality in figurines and, 120–125
seals, 160–161
Selective concretization, miniaturization and, 22
Seleucia-on-the-Tigris
   Aphrodite figurines in, 205–212
   child figurines from, 185–189
   dwarfism, disability, and grotesque in figurines of, 230–236
   figurine production in, 3, 4
   Hellenistic ceramics in, 243–246
   Herakles statue from, 212–217
   intersexuality in figurines from, 222
   mounted horse rider figurines in, 59–60
   moveable arms on figurines from, 68–68
   nude figurines in, 46–50, 160–162
   puppet figurines in, 88–89, 259 n.106
   reclining figurines in, 237–246
Seleucid Heroon, 88–89, 93–94
Seleucid kingdom, Parthian conquest of, 1–2
Seleucus I, 149–152
self-presentation
   identification with figurines and, 147–148, 201–202
   object agency of figurines and, 11
   royal image and, 156–162
   young and beardless male figurines, 156–162
Šem /meze drum, 140
sensory perception, miniaturization and limits of, 20
servants, children as, 185–189
sexuality in figurines
   desire and imagination in, 118–120
   exclusion and voyeurism and, 120–125
   gender ambiguity and, 220–230
   in heterosexual couples figurines, 117–132
   musical couples figurines, 133–136
   reclining figurines, 240–243
   stone and metal figurines, 76–78
sexualized relationships with figurines, 65–71
   boundaries of attraction and, 80–81
   fragility and, 76–78
   hyper-reality of, 78–80
single mold technique
   child figurines, 193–197
   fully clothed figurines, 40–42
   heterosexual couples figurines and, 118–120
Sippar, figurines from, 68

skin contact
  bone figurines, 37–38
  with figures and figurines, 38–40
  fully clothed figurines, 40–42
  nude figurines, 46–50
  object *vs.* representation and, 38–40
slaves
  child-rearing by, 109
  children as, 185–189
"Slipper Slapper" Aphrodite, 210
social structure
  child figurines and, 185–189
  family structure and, 262 n.32
  female body in figurines and, 181–185
  figurine corpus and, 11, 29–31, 201–202
  figurines as reflection of, 203–204
  gender ambiguity in, 224–230
  grouped figurines and, 143–146
  in heterosexual couples figurines, 128–132
  interactive figurines and, 52–53
  mother-and-child figurines and, 113–117
  nude figurines and, 50
  puppet figurines and, 88
  reclining figurines and, 243–246
  role of figurines in, 247–248
soldiers
  fighting or battle poses for, 61–64
  interactive figurines as, 53
  mounted soldiers, production of, 57–61
solo musicians, figurines of, 141–143
Sophocles, 87
sophrosyne (self-control), 182–185
Stewart, Susan, 14–15, 266 n.1
stone figurines, 31, 254 n.88
  intersexuality in, 221–222
  sexuality of, 76–78
  votive function for, 72–76
supernatural, child figurines and, 189–193
Swift, Jonathan, 13–14, 19
symplegmata (sexualized struggle or fighting), 122–123

tactile interaction
  abstraction and play with figurines, 53–57
  bone figurines, 37–38
  fully clothed figurines, 40–42
  interactive figurines, 52–53
  intimacy illusion and, 18–24
  miniaturization theory and, 14–18
  mother-and-child figurines and reduction of, 102–107
  nude figurines, 46–50
  partially clothed figurines, 42–46
  with reclining figurines, 240–243
  sexualized figurines and, 76–78
  skin contact with figures and figurines, 38–40
  stone and metal figurines, 31, 254 n.88

  substance of figurines and, 24–25
  visual process and, 260 n.128
Tanagra tradition, 40–42
  female figurines in, 182
  mother and child figurines in, 116–117
Tell 'Umar (Seleucia-on-Tigris), 4
temperature sensation, stone and metal figurines, 254 n.80
Terme Ruler statue, 149–152, 160–161
terracotta, production of, 25–31, 66–70, 70–76, 82–94
theatricality
  miniaturization and, 82–98
  puppet figurines, 82–89
  rattles and, 94–98
thing theory, 15–16
Thomas, Nicholas, 273 n.167
three-peaked headdress, in child figurines, 192–193
Topper, Kathryn, 278 n.111,
toys
  interactive figurines as, 53–57
  mounted horse rider figurines as, 57–61
Treasury Relief at Persepolis, 150–152

ub / uppu drum, 140
unfinished elements in figurines, 26–29
unpredictability, of miniaturization, 20–22
Uruk
  Aphrodite figurines in, 205–212
  figurine production in, 3, 5
  Hellenistic ceramics in, 243–246
  intersexed figurines from, 220–230
  moveable arms on figurines from, 68
  reclining figurines in, 237–246

Van Buren, E. Douglas, 245–246
Van Ingen, Wilhelmina, 245–246, 257 n.59
Venus of Willendorf, 13–14
votive functions
  of male figurines, 152–153
  moveable arm figurines, 70–76
voyeurism, sexuality in figurines and, 120–125

Wari culture figurines, 252 n.36
"Weary Herakles," 212–217
Weary Herakles sculpture, 153–154
wet-nurses, figurines depicting, 107–110
Winter, Irene, 111
women
  economic status and activity of, 264 n.93
  figurine representations of, 16
  fully clothed figurines, 40–42
  in horse rider figurines, 227–230
  interactive figurines of, 52–53
  in mother and child figurines, 94–98, 101–103
  in musician couples figurines, 133–136
  nude figurines of, 46–50

women (cont.)
  relationships and role of, 143–146
  service images of, 107–110
  as slave surrogates, 109
  social positioning of, in mother and child figurines, 113–117
  in society, female body in figurines and, 181–185
  stone and metal figurines of, 32–34
  workshops for figurine production, 253 n.56

ziggurats, 5

CPSIA information can be obtained
at www.ICGtesting.com
Printed in the USA
LVHW061507020423
743235LV00003B/249